TEXTS AND STUDIES

CONTRIBUTIONS TO
BIBLICAL AND PATRISTIC LITERATURE

EDITED BY

J. ARMITAGE ROBINSON, D.D.
HON. PH.D. GÖTTINGEN HON. D.D. HALLE
DEAN OF WELLS

VOL. IX

No. 1. PELAGIUS'S EXPOSITIONS OF THIRTEEN EPISTLES OF ST PAUL: INTRODUCTION

PELAGIUS'S EXPOSITIONS OF THIRTEEN EPISTLES OF ST PAUL. I

INTRODUCTION

BY

ALEXANDER SOUTER, B.A.

M.A. (OXON.) D.LITT. (ABERD.)
REGIUS PROFESSOR OF HUMANITY AND LECTURER IN MEDIAEVAL PALAEOGRAPHY IN THE UNIVERSITY OF ABERDEEN
FORMERLY SCHOLAR OF GONVILLE AND CAIUS COLLEGE, CAMBRIDGE

Wipf & Stock
PUBLISHERS
Eugene, Oregon

Wipf and Stock Publishers
199 W 8th Ave, Suite 3
Eugene, OR 97401

Pelagius's Expositions of Thirteen Epistles of St. Paul
Introduction
By Souter, Alexander
ISBN: 1-59244-829-1
Publication date 8/26/2004
Previously published by Cambridge, 1922

†

ALVREDO · HOLDER

CODICVM · AVGIENSIVM · CVSTODI
EORVNDEM · DESCRIPTORI · DILIGENTISSIMO
LINGVAE · LITTERARVM · QVE · LATINARVM
VOCABVLORVM · CELTICORVM
PERITISSIMO · COGNITORI
CAESARIS · HORATI · BAEDAE · OPERVM
EDITORI
LIBRORVM · MANV · SCRIPTORVM
VNDIQVE · CONQVISITORVM
CONLATORI · CVRIOSISSIMO
CVIVS · THENSAVRI
SEMPER · MIHI · LARGISSIME · PATEBANT
HVNC · TOMVM
CARITATE · INMORTALI
INCONSOLABILIS
OFFERO

PREFACE

A NATURAL sequel to *A Study of Ambrosiaster* in the present series (volume VII, part 4, 1905) would have been a critical edition of his commentary on the Epistles of St Paul; but the task of preparing such an edition had already been assigned by the Vienna Academy of Sciences to my friend Father Brewer, S.J. It was therefore necessary that I should turn to something else. When casting about in 1904 for an unworked field of research, I received the same suggestion independently from two scholars, the Editor of this series and Dr C. H. Turner, that I should edit the commentary of Pelagius on the Epistles of St Paul. The suggestive book of the late Professor Heinrich Zimmer of Berlin, *Pelagius in Irland*, published in 1901, had provided certain materials, and furnished some hints as to how the original commentary of Pelagius could be reconstructed, or partially reconstructed, from the works of later authors who had used it. I had not then the slightest expectation that three copies of the commentary in its original form would fall into my hands, one in 1906 and two in 1913: yet such was to be the case.

The fortunate discoveries, however, did not, I felt, exempt me from the duty of reconstructing textually the archetypes of authorities like Pseudo-Jerome, originally edited by Erasmus in 1516, and Pseudo-Primasius, first published by Gagney in 1537, who had incorporated the greater part of Pelagius's work in their own[1]. For it was obvious that these two authorities had employed other copies of the original Pelagius than those that were in my hands, and that by their aid I could control the texts I had found. Further, certain other writers, like Sedulius Scottus whose commentary was first published in 1528, and Zmaragdus whose compilation was first printed in 1536, had made considerable use of Pelagius, and had copied his work in general with accuracy. Their

[1] It gave me the intensest satisfaction to be able, in 1906, to restore the Pseudo-Primasius to Cassiodorus and his pupils.

quotations from Pelagius had in consequence to be restored to their original form, as far as it was possible for me to do so. One could also have gone on exploring the mediaeval commentaries and publishing certain of them (like most of those of Claudius of Turin, which still await an editor), but I have left such work, if it be thought necessary, to my successors. They will find in these volumes[1], I trust, a sufficiently secure basis for further enquiry.

It is obvious that the preparation of an edition like the present, in which an endeavour has been made to repair the undeserved neglect of four centuries, has cost much money, time and trouble. I cannot sufficiently express my gratitude to the Trustees or Managers of the following institutions or funds for the ungrudging confidence and lavish help extended to the researcher from 1906 to 1915: the Hort Fund at Cambridge; the Revision Surplus Fund at Oxford; the Schweich Fund of the British Academy; Magdalen College, Oxford; and the Carnegie Trust for the Universities of Scotland. The work has entailed nine journeys on the Continent, which occupied fourteen months in all. The collations were made with the utmost fullness I could attain, in order that I might learn the exact relationship between the manuscripts, and represent in my critical apparatus the readings of archetypes rather than those of individual *codices*. I was desirous also to write part of the extraordinary history of Pelagius's commentary in the Middle Ages, and to do this properly required the preparation of a critical edition of the interpolations foisted on it.

The book could never have been completed without the generous help of many scholars at home and abroad. It would not be fitting to record here the names of leading biblical, patristic and palaeographical authorities of our time, to whom I have submitted my various difficulties as they arose. I have tried to specify each obligation in its proper place in the body of the work. To the librarians and officials at the libraries of Aberdeen, Arras, Bamberg, Basle, Berlin, Cambridge (University, Corpus, St John's), Dublin (Trinity College), Einsiedeln, Florence (Laurentian), Gotha, Grenoble, The Hague (Royal Library, Museum Meermanno-

[1] The second volume, containing text, critical apparatus and indexes, should appear about a year after this. The third, containing the interpolations, is postponed till the arrival of better economic conditions.

Westreenianum), Karlsruhe, London (British Museum), Luxemburg, Manchester (John Rylands), Milan, Munich (State and University), Nürnberg (Stadtbibliothek, Germanisches Museum), Oxford (Bodleian, Balliol, Magdalen, Mansfield, Merton), Paris (Bibliothèque Nationale, Mazarine, Ste Geneviève), Rome (Vatican, Basilicana, Angelica, Casanatense, Vallicelliana, Vittorio-Emmanuele), St Gall (Stiftsbibliothek, Stadtbibliothek), Salisbury, Troyes, and Zürich (Kantonsbibliothek, Stadtbibliothek) my heartiest thanks are due. Nor must I forget the friends in various countries whose gracious hospitality cheered the exile's loneliness.

The commentary here printed for the first time in its original form happens to be the earliest extant work by a British author[1]. Theologians will perhaps be glad to see the earliest Pelagian document as it first appeared. It also contains within it, if I am right, a form of Old-Latin text of the Epistles of St Paul read by our ancestors of the British Church two centuries before Augustine ruled the Province of Canterbury. The second volume will shed some light on the history of the Vulgate of St Paul's Epistles.

I am deeply conscious of the defects of my work. The mass of material collected has proved immensely difficult to control, and the arrangement of it for press has been attended by many vexatious interruptions. Yet the book contains some new things, and my task was well worth attempting. Best thanks are due not only to the Editor of the series but to all who have taken part in the printing of the book, for the valuable help they have rendered.

A. SOUTER.

ABERDEEN,
March 6th, 1922.

1 *The Cambridge History of English Literature*, vol. I (1908), p. 65 (M. R. James).

CONTENTS

BIBLIOGRAPHY[1].

A. BRUCKNER, *Quellen zur Geschichte des Pelagianischen Streites* (Tübingen, 1906).

D. DE BRUYNE, 'Le Prologue Inédit de Pélage à la Première Lettre aux Corinthiens' (*Revue Bénédictine* XXIV [1907] pp. 257–263).

D. DE BRUYNE, 'Étude sur les Origines de notre Texte Latin de Saint Paul' (*Revue Biblique* nouv. sér. XII [1915] pp. 358–392). Cf. *Revue Bénédictine* XXXIII (1921) Bull. pp. 6–9.

J. B. BURY, 'The Origin of Pelagius' (*Hermathena* XIII [1905] pp. 26–35).

J. CHAPMAN, 'Cassiodorus and the Echternach Gospels' (*Revue Bénédictine* XXVIII [1911] pp. 283–296).

H. DENIFLE, *Die abendländischen Schriftausleger bis Luther über* Justitia Dei (Rom. 1, 17) *und* Justificatio, *Beitrag zur Geschichte der Exegese, der Literatur und des Dogmas im Mittelalter* (Mainz, 1905).

E. v. DOBSCHÜTZ, 'Ein Bücherkleinod' pp. 18 (*Jahresbericht der Schles. Gesellschaft für vaterl. Cultur* 1913).

M. ESPOSITO, 'A Seventh-Century Commentary on the Catholic Epistles' (*Journal of Theological Studies* XXI [1919–20] pp. 316–318).

J. GWYNN, *Liber Ardmachanus: The Book of Armagh*, edited with introduction and appendices (Dublin and London, 1913).

S. HELLMANN, *Sedulius Scottus* (München, 1906 [published 1905]).

P. LEHMANN, *Iohannes Sichardus und die von ihm benutzten Bibliotheken und Handschriften* (München, 1911).

P. LEHMANN, 'Cassiodorstudien, VII. Der Römerbrief Kommentar' (*Philologus* LXXIV [1917] pp. 354–356).

F. LOOFS, 'Pelagius, gest. nach 418, und der pelagianische Streit' (*Realencyklopädie für protestantische Theologie und Kirche*...Herzog...Hauck, XV [Leipzig, 1904] pp. 747–774) (with an extensive bibliography).

F. LOOFS, *Leitfaden zum Studium der Dogmengeschichte* 4te Aufl. (Halle, 1906).

F. LOOFS, 'Pelagius' (*Realencykl.*...Herzog...Hauck, XXIV [Leipzig, 1913] pp. 310–312) (with an extensive bibliography of the recent period).

E. MANGENOT, 'Saint Jérôme ou Pélage éditeur des Épîtres de Saint Paul dans la Vulgate' pp. 37 (*Revue du Clergé français*, 1916).

G. MERCATI, 'Some New Fragments of Pelagius' (*J.T.S.* VIII [1906–7] pp. 526–535).

G. MORIN, 'Jean Diacre et le Pseudo-Jérôme sur les Épîtres de S. Paul' (*Revue Bénédictine* XXVII [1910] pp. 113–117).

[1] For the older literature especially, see under 'F. Loofs' in this bibliography.

G. MORIN, 'Un Traité Inédit attribué à Saint Augustin, le *de* VIII *Quaestionibus ex Vet. Test.* du Catalogue de Lorsch' (*R.B.* XXVIII [1911] p. 3).

G. MORIN, 'A Propos du *Quicumque*: Extraits d'Homélies de S. Césaire d'Arles sous le nom de S. Athanase' (*R.B.* XXVIII [1911] pp. 420–421).

G. MORIN, *Études, Textes, Découvertes: Contributions à la Littérature et à l'Histoire des douze premiers siècles* t. I (Maredsous and Paris, 1913), pp. 23, 345 especially.

E. RIGGENBACH, *Unbeachtet gebliebene Fragmente des Pelagius-Kommentars* (Gütersloh, 1905).

E. RIGGENBACH, *Die ältesten lateinischen Kommentare zum Hebräerbrief* (Leipzig, 1907).

E. RIGGENBACH, 'Eine wichtige Entdeckung für die Pelagius-forschung' (*Theologisches Literaturblatt* XXVIII [1907] pp. 73–75).

E. RIGGENBACH, 'Neues über Pelagius' (*Theologisches Literaturblatt* XXVIII [1907] p. 425).

H. v. SCHUBERT, *Der sogenannte Praedestinatus, ein Beitrag zur Geschichte des Pelagianismus* (Leipzig, 1903).

ALFRED J. SMITH, 'The Latin Sources of the Commentary of Pelagius on the Epistle of St Paul to the Romans' (*J.T.S.* XIX [1917–18] pp. 162–230; XX [1918–19] pp. 55–65, 127–177).

A. SOUTER, 'The Commentary of Pelagius on the Epistles of St Paul' (*The Expositor* 1907 I pp. 455–467). (Written May, 1906.)

A. SOUTER, 'Prolegomena to the Commentary of Pelagius on the Epistles of St Paul (*J.T.S.* VII [1905–6] pp. 568–575).

A. SOUTER, 'The Commentary of Pelagius on the Epistles of Paul: the Problem of its Restoration' (*Proceedings of the British Academy* II [1905–6] pp. 409–439). (Read Dec. 12, 1906.)

A. SOUTER, 'The Relation of the Roman Fragments to the Commentary in the Karlsruhe MS (Augiensis CXIX)' (*J.T.S.* VIII [1906–7] pp. 535–536).

A. SOUTER, 'Contributions to the Criticism of Zmaragdus's *Expositio Libri Comitis*' (*J.T S.* IX [1907–8] pp. 584–597).

A. SOUTER, 'An unrecorded Reference to the *Rules* of Tyconius' (*J.T.S.* XI [1909–10] pp. 562–563).

A. SOUTER, 'Another New Fragment of Pelagius' (*J.T.S.* XII [1910–11] pp. 32–35).

A. SOUTER, 'An Interesting Latin Subscription' (accompanied by a note from J. Loth) (*Revue Celtique* XXXII [1911] pp. 152–153).

A. SOUTER, 'Freiburg Fragments of a MS of the Pelagian Commentary on the Epistles of St Paul' (*J.T.S.* XIII [1911–12] pp. 515–519).

A. SOUTER, 'Cassiodorus's Copy of Eucherius's *Instructiones*' (*J.T.S.* XIV [1912–13] pp. 69–72).

A. SOUTER, 'Dismembered Manuscripts' (*R.B.* XXIX [1912] pp. 367–368).

A. SOUTER, 'The Commonitorium of Fulgentius of Ruspe on the Holy Spirit' (*J.T.S.* XIV [1912–13] pp. 481–488).

A. SOUTER, 'New Manuscripts of Pelagius' (*Theologische Literaturzeitung*, XXXVIII [1913] p. 442).

A. SOUTER, 'Pelagius and the Pauline Text in the Book of Armagh' (*J.T.S.* XVI [1914–15] p. 105).

A. SOUTER, 'Pelagius' Doctrine in Relation to his early life' (*The Expositor* 1915 I pp. 180–182). See p. 3 n. 5.

A. SOUTER, 'A Theological Tractate on the Divinity of the Son, from Paris MS B.N. Lat. 653' (*J.T.S.* XVII [1915–16] pp. 129–136).

A. SOUTER, 'The Character and History of Pelagius' Commentary on the Epistles of St Paul' (*Proceedings of the British Academy* VII [1915–16] pp. 261–296). (Read March 15, 1916.)

A. SOUTER, 'Pelagius' Text of Romans v 12, with Comment' (*Expository Times* XXVIII [1916–17] pp. 42–43).

A. SOUTER, 'The Sources of Sedulius Scottus' *Collectaneum* on the Epistles of St Paul' (*J.T.S.* XVIII [1916–17] pp. 184–228).

A. SOUTER, 'The Earliest Surviving Book of a British Author' (*The Contemporary Review* CXV [1919 I] pp. 76–82).

A. SOUTER, 'Further Contributions to the Criticism of Zmaragdus's *Expositio Libri Comitis*' (*J.T.S.* XXIII [1921–22] pp. 73–76).

L. C. STERN, *Epistolae Beati Pauli glosatae glosa interlineali* (Halle, 1910).

C. H. TURNER, 'Pelagius' Commentary on the Pauline Epistles and its History' (*J.T.S.* IV [1902–3] pp. 132–141).

A. VACCARI, *Un Commento a Giobbe di Giuliano di Eclana* (Roma, 1915).

H. ZIMMER, *Pelagius in Irland: Texte und Untersuchungen zur patristischen Litteratur* (Berlin, 1901).

CHAPTER I

PELAGIUS AND HIS COMMENTARY. INTRODUCTION. A RECORD OF PREVIOUS RESEARCH

The Name 'Pelagius.' The name Pelagius is obviously Greek in ultimate origin, being derived from πέλαγος, 'the sea.' To judge, however, by the Greek *Onomasticon* and indexes to inscriptions and papyri, it appears to have been comparatively rare in that language[1]. The oldest instance of the name that I can find in Greek characters is in an inscription of Halaesa in Sicily, belonging to the period of the Roman republic[2]. The name, meaning *Seaman*, appears to have had no vogue in the Greek world until about the second or third century of our era. But already in the first century before Christ the common noun πέλαγος, along with its derivative adjective πελάγιος, had become a Latin word also. It doubtless became familiar to Westerns, at first, as a name sometimes borne by Greek slaves. As such, it was kept as a *cognomen* or an *agnomen* on manumission. And in fact there are at least three clear instances of it with this value in Latin inscriptions[3]. In other inscriptions it is found standing by itself[4]. The oldest dated Latin example of the name is in an inscription of A.D. 145[5]. Both in Greek and in Latin there are a good many instances of the feminine Πελαγία (*Pelagia*) also. The *Dictionary of Christian Biography* knows a dozen persons with the name *Pelagius*, besides one or two with the name *Pelagia*.

[1] W. Pape's *Wörterbuch der griechischen Eigennamen* 3 Aufl. bearb. v. G. E. Benseler (Braunschw. 1884) s.v. gives only three or four examples, none of which is perhaps earlier than the fourth century of our era. See also *Inscriptiones Graecae* vol. III p. 2 (Berol. 1882) 3439 (Attica and Christian); vol. XIV (Berol. 1890) 352 (Halaesa in Sicily); *Oxyrhynchus Papyri* 43 (A.D. 295).

[2] See note 1.

[3] C.I.L. VIII 9689 (Cartenna in Mauretania); IX 3941 (Alba Fucens in Italy); XIV 1119 (Ostia).

[4] E.g. C.I.L. II 5812 (Segisamo in Spain: A.D. 239); X 670 (Salernum in Italy); 2038 (Puteoli); it seems to be a *nomen* in C.I.L. XII 1815 [= Dessau, *Inscr. Lat. Sel.* 7264] (Vienne in France) Ant. Pelagius.

[5] C.I.L. III 7024 [= Dessau 8722[a]] (Docimium in Phrygia) Pela(gius).

Though it was not a frequent name, it was thus sufficiently common to negative the underlying idea of some investigations that it was specially invented to represent the native Celtic name of the most famous person who ever bore it. That he was far from being the earliest Latin bearer of the name is sufficiently proved by the fact that more than one Pope took it after his time. This clearly goes to show that the name enjoyed sufficient currency, apart from its evil association with the celebrated heresiarch, to make its survival possible among Christians. Finally, if there had been anything peculiar about the name, it is certain that Pelagius's adversaries would have made fun of it; but of this there is not a trace.

Pelagius the Briton or the Irishman. Very little is known of the life of our Pelagius. The date and place of his birth and death are alike uncertain. His contemporaries are not even unanimous on the country of his origin. For, while Augustine[1], Orosius[2], Marius Mercator[3], and Prosper[4] speak of him as British (*Britto, Britannus*), Jerome appears to refer to him as Irish[5] (*Scottus*). Professor Bury would reconcile the two statements by explaining that he was an Irishman born in Britain[6]. According to Roman usage, *Britto* or *Britannus* was applicable to any inhabitant of the Roman province or provinces named *Britannia*[7], and there is evi-

[1] *Ep.* 186 1 § 1 (C.S.E.L. LVII 45) (A.D. 417?) *Pelagium, quem credimus, ut ab alio distingueretur, qui Pelagius Terenti dicitur, Brittonem fuisse cognominatum.*

[2] *Apolog.* 12 3 (C.S.E.L. V. 620) (A.D. 415) *Britannicus noster.*

[3] *Liber Subnot. in Verba Iuliani* prol. ed. Baluze (Paris, 1684) p. 2 (Migne, *P.L.* XLVIII 111 A) (A.D. 431—2) *Pelagium gente Britannum monachum.*

[4] Chron. A.D. 413 (Mommsen, *Chronica Minora* I 467) *eodem tempore Pelagius Britto*; carm. de ingrat. l. 2 (Migne, *P.L.* LI 94 B) (ca A.D. 430) *coluber...Britannus*: so also in Gennadius, *Uir. Inlust.* 43 (ca A.D. 496) *Pelagius Britto haeresiarches*, but Richardson's edition omits *Britto*: Bed. *H.E.* I 10 (ca A.D. 731) *Pelagius Bretto.*

[5] If indeed the words in *In Hierem. proph. prol.* § 4 (C.S.E.L. LIX p. 4 l. 20) (A.D. 415) *stolidissimus et Scottorum pultibus praegrauatus*, and *In Hierem.* III 1 § 4 (C.S.E.L. LIX p. 151 ll. 15 f.) *habet enim progeniem Scotticae gentis de Brittannorum uicinia* refer to him: they are for us of irritating vagueness. We now know that *Alpinum* (not *Albinum*) *canem* is the true reading (on p. 151 l. 13 of Reiter's ed. of Hier. *in Hierem.*), but these words could hardly refer to Pelagius.

[6] *Life of St Patrick* (London, 1905) pp. 296, 43: 'It is possible that, as some claim, Pelagius was born in Ireland, but the evidence rather points to the conclusion that he belonged to an Irish family settled in western Britain': see also *Hermathena* xiii pp. 26 ff.

[7] Cf. W. M. Ramsay in *Studia Biblica* IV (Oxon. 1896) pp. 34 ff.

dence of an Irish colony in Britain at an early date[1]. But the fact that the name '*Scottus*' or 'Irish' undoubtedly conveyed a reproach in Jerome's day tells against the view that Pelagius was Irish. Claudian speaks of the Irish as cruel[2], and in several passages refers to Roman conflicts with them[3]. And Jerome himself, having learnt from historical or geographical works that the Irish had been guilty of a number of even worse crimes than that of cruelty, alluded to the Irish with contempt long before he ever heard of Pelagius[4]. Certainly the Irish of succeeding centuries, and few apart from them, treated Pelagius with the highest respect[5]. On the other hand, the literary style of Pelagius's work is so accomplished that it seems more probable that he obtained his higher education in Britain than in Ireland, which was never a part of the Roman Empire. The present writer is, however, more concerned with philological than historical problems, and does not feel called upon for a definite decision on this interesting question.

His Commentary on thirteen Epistles of St Paul. Whatever his origin, Pelagius appears to have found his way to Rome towards the end of the fourth, or very early in the fifth century. We can only guess the purpose which took him there, or the source from which he drew the necessary means for travel, and support in the great city. The suggestion has been made that he had a serious disagreement with his father, and that he in consequence left home and lived away from Britain for the rest of his days[6]. Whether that conjecture be true or not, it is perfectly clear that he had received a first-rate education[7], and it may thus be presumed that

1 See Bury, op. cit. p. 350.

2 *De Bello Gothico* 417 *Scotto...truci.*

3 See the index in Koch's edition, ss.vv. *Scotticus*, *Scottus*.

4 Zimmer, *Pelagius in Irland* p. 20, n.**, quotes them: *Epist.* 69 3 § 6 (C.S.E.L. LIV 684 ll. 17 ff.) (ca A.D. 397) *Scottorum et Aticottorum ritu...promiscuas uxores, communes liberos habeant*; *Adu. Iouin.* II 7 (Migne, *P.L.* XXIII 296 A) (ca A.D. 392) *Scottorum natio uxores proprias non habet.*

5 The thesis of Zimmer's book, so ably defended.

6 By the present writer in an article entitled, 'Pelagius' Doctrine in Relation to his early Life,' *Expositor* for 1915 vol. I pp. 180 ff. Other references bearing on the point, viz. *in* 1 *Cor.* iiii 16, xiii 4; *Eph.* vi 2, might be added to those given in that paper.

7 H. Williams, *Christianity in Early Britain* (Oxford, 1912) p. 181, is in agreement; see also pp. 199 f.

he was of wealthy family. The records show that in Rome he lived a pure life in solitude, devoted to sacred study. His deep knowledge of scripture will be sufficiently proved in subsequent parts of this book. He was also well read in the earlier Latin Christian writers as well as those of his own day. It has been generally believed that he had a first-hand acquaintance with various Greek Christian writers also. Certainly he shows on occasion the knowledge of classical Latin literature he had acquired in his youth[1].

Marius Mercator tells us that Pelagius ventured, before the devastation of the city of Rome[2], to compose commentaries on the Apostle Paul and to circulate them among those on whose friendship he could rely. He believed himself to be *explaining individual words or thoughts of the Apostle*[3]. Augustine's language with regard to this work is very similar. He tells us in 412 that he had read certain writings of Pelagius (who was reported to him to be a holy man, far advanced in Christian graces), containing *short expositions of the Epistles of Paul the Apostle*[4]. These two writers not only allude to the commentaries, but, as will be set forth in detail later[5], also make quotations from them. The book itself contains evidence that part of it at least was written not earlier than about 406[6]. Also the use of the

[1] On all these matters see chap. v.

[2] I.e. by Alaric the Goth in A.D. 410.

[3] *Commonitorium super nomine Caelestii*, ed. Baluze, p. 135 (Migne, *P.L.* XLVIII 83 A) (written in Greek A.D. 429, translated into Latin by the author, A.D. 431): *ausus est memoratus (Pelagius) ante uastationem urbis Romae in apostolum Paulum commentarios condere, et his edere, de quorum amicitia praesumebat. Explanare autem se putauit singula apostoli uerba uel sensus.* The commentary is referred to also in the *Liber Subnotationum*, ed. Baluze, p. 2 (Migne, *P.L.* XLVIII 111—112) (written A.D. 431—2).

[4] *De Peccatorum Meritis et Remissione* III 1 § 1 (C.S.E.L. LX 129 ll. 6 ff.) *legi Pelagii quaedam scripta, sancti uiri, ut audio, et non paruo prouectu Christiani, quae in Pauli apostoli epistolas expositiones breuissimas continerent.*

[5] Chap. ii pp. 35 ff.

[6] If we could tell the exact date of Jovinian's death, we could from this fact get a *terminus post quem*, for Jovinian was clearly dead at the time *in Phil.* iii 18 was written but all we can say is that Jovinian was certainly dead in 406; how much earlier than that we do not know (cf. W. Haller, *Iovinianus*...Leipzig, 1897 [= *Texte u. Untersuchungen*, N.F. II Bd. Heft 2]) p. 131. Haller is absolutely ignorant of the four references to Jovinian in our commentary.

Origen-Rufinus commentary on Romans was not possible before about A.D. 405[1].

After the research of the past few centuries, there need be little hesitation in affirming that no copy of Pelagius's commentaries, with his name at the head of it, any longer exists. It is probable that originally this brief and unassuming work was issued without an author's name, and that, while in certain circles its authorship was known, and in others, where sympathy with its author's distinctive views was felt, his name was actually attached to it, the majority of copies remained anonymous. From the time of *Praedestinatus*[2] down to the middle of the seventh century, not a single quotation from the commentary by its author's name has been produced. But between the anonymous commentary on the Catholic Epistles[3] of the latter date and the thirteenth century we find a considerable number of quotations from the commentary labelled 'Pelagius,' as Zimmer was the first to point out[4]. Some of this evidence comes from glossed copies of St Paul's Epistles in Latin, and needs considerable sifting before it can be safely used. It seems, therefore, best to start merely with the quotations in Augustine and Marius Mercator, and to try to discover a commentary, which, though lacking, as it inevitably must, the name of Pelagius, shall be proved by internal evidence to be a reliable copy of the seemingly lost production. Before proceeding, however, to this identification, it is a duty to record the appearance of certain modern publications that have a bearing on our problem.

[1] See chap. v below, pp. 188 f.

[2] I 88, a rather paraphrastic quotation from Pelagius's note on Rom. v 15 (cf. also Migne, *P.L.* LIII 618 A, 619 A, 665 B). The much discussed *Praedestinatus*, written perhaps in the fourth decade of the fifth century, is probably the work of Arnobius Iunior, cf. Dom Morin's *Études, Textes, Découvertes* t. I (Maredsous and Paris, 1913) pp. 315 ff., especially 345 n. 4; or *Revue Bénédictine*, t. XXVIII (1911) p. 158. The parallels with Sang. Aug. Merc. in this work are given by H. v. Schubert, *Der sogenannte Praedestinatus* (Leipzig, 1903) [= *Texte u. Unters.* N.F. IX (4)] pp. 33 ff.

[3] This Irish-Latin commentary is contained in *Cod. Aug.* CCXXXIII (saec. IX) at Karlsruhe, and the reference to Pilag(ius) [*in Eph.* vi 14] *sicut lurica—uirtutibus ornatur* was first discovered by me. I am glad to accept Mr Esposito's date for it as the middle of the seventh century, half a century earlier than I ventured to put it in 1906 (*Proc. Brit. Acad.* vol. II p. 431 [= 23]): see his careful and learned article in *J.T.S.* vol. XXI [1919—20] pp. 316 ff.

[4] *Pelagius in Irland* pp. 162 f., summing up the first half of his book.

History of Pseudo-Jerome Commentary in print. In the ninth and last volume of his edition of the works of St Jerome, published at Basle in 1516, Erasmus committed to the press a brief commentary on thirteen Epistles of St Paul, which he had found in a manuscript, bearing the name of Jerome as author. The words of the preface to this part of his great edition are these: '*Postremo commentarios in omnes diui Pauli epistolas, quas Hieronymo uendicabat codex quidam, obsoletae uetustatis, Gotthicis characteribus exaratus, sic sane perplexis et iam prae uetustate euanidis, ut coacti fuerimus in elementariorum ordinem rursus descendere, et quod in ludo puelli faciunt, litterariis apiculis noscitandis operam dare: sed et ii sicut proxime superiores, indigni sunt iudicandi qui Hieronymo tribuantur. Quando enim sic ineptit Hieronymus, ut hic interpres quisquis is demum fuit: quando sic balbutit, ut hic frequentissime soloecissat. Tametsi is qui glossam (ut uocant) ordinariam consarcinauit, Hieronymi titulo nonnulla citat, quae nominatim in iis commentariis comperiuntur. At hoc neutiquam satis probauerit Hieronymi Stridonensis esse, quod scilicet sint illius nomine citata. Neque enim hoc agebat glossarius iste, siue Rabanus is fuit, siue alius quispiam, ut cuius essent inquireret, sed pro tempore quod ad rem suam faciebat, id excerpebat...quaedam inuenire licet, quae doctis etiam placere possint*[1].'

No one has, I believe, ventured to dispute Erasmus' opinion, and to claim these commentaries for Jerome[2]. They have nevertheless been reprinted in successive editions of the works of Jerome down to that in Migne's Patrology, in which, according to the example of Vallarsi, they get the very last place, just before the index. Some care seems to have been exercised in the reprinting of them in the editions of Erasmus, Victorius, and Martianay, but through sheer carelessness the text in Vallarsi (at least in the later quarto edition), and hence in Migne, is far inferior in accuracy to that of the *editio princeps*. To this subject we return later[3].

[1] I have expanded the abbreviations of the original.

[2] With the exception of a rather careless correspondent of Erasmus, Hieronymus Dunghersheym, writing from Leipzig to Erasmus on 18 Mar. 1517, who quotes from Ps.-Jerome on *Phil.* ii 6 (*Opus Epistolarum Des. Erasmi Roterodami*, recogn. P. S. Allen, t. II (Oxon. 1910) no. 554 p. 507).

[3] Chap. vi pp. 281 f.

Ambrosius Catharinus Politus, Archbishop of Compsa[1], and Sixtus of Siena[2] observed that the commentaries were tainted with Pelagianism. The most important remarks of Sixtus are these: '*Annotationes in tredecim Pauli Epistolas, quanquam in fronte praeferant praefatiunculam Hieronymi ad Heliodorum scribentis, styli tamen diuersitas, et dogmatum discrimen, ipsius non esse indicant. Ambrosius, Compsae Archiepiscopus, autumat, scriptorem operis fuisse Pelagium, quia in expositione octaui et noni capitis epistolae ad Romanos, doceat praedestinationem aeternam esse ex meritis electorum diuina praescientia praeuisis. Ego uero, ut libere pronunciem quid sentiam, nihil dubito authorem, quisquis ille fuerit, Pelagiana peste laborasse, prout apertissime deprehendi potest ex annotationibus septimi capitis epistolae ad Roman. ubi edisserens illud,* Sine lege peccatum erat mortuum, *insanire*[3] *eos putat, qui credunt peccatum Adae ex traduce parentum in nos deriuasse, affirmans, idem peccatum non propagatione, sed exemplo duntaxat ad posteros transfusum. Ex quo satis liquet, Hieronymum, Pelagiani dogmatis hostem acerrimum, non fuisse huius operis authorem. Sunt et alia quaedam his commentariis asserta, haereseos suspicione non carentia, quae nos una cum praedictis erroribus sequenti uolumine annotauimus*[4]. *Non sum tamen in sententia Ambrosii praeceptoris mei, ut arbitrer hos commentarios esse Pelagii: is enim ut August. in* 3. *de baptismo paruulorum testatur, in explanationibus quas admodum breues edidit in epist. ad Roman. tanta modestia usus est, ut non sub propria, sed sub aliena persona proposuerit argumentum aduersus originale peccatum, quae August. ibidem ad uerbum transcripta recenset.*' In his own *Annotationes*[5] also Sixtus takes occasion to criticize the pronouncements of the commentary on various subjects. In *Ann.* 238 (p. 516) he attacks the note on Rom. v 12 *In quo omnes peccauerunt,* and quotes the pub-

[1] *In omnes Divi Pauli...epistolas...commentaria* (Paris, 1566): 'quidam non incuria Pelagium eius operis authorem credidere' (praef.): quoted by Sixtus and Victorius, ll.cc.

[2] *Bibliotheca Sancta* (preface, 1566) (Paris, 1610) p. 247 (1) D, quoted below: (Colon. 1626), p. 309.

[3] We shall see afterwards that the passage here objected to is an interpolation into the original commentary.

[4] References to these follow immediately.

[5] =ed. Colon. 1626, p. 661 etc.

lished notes on *In hunc mundum peccatum intrauit et per peccatum mors*: Exemplo uel forma. *Et ita in omnes* etc. (Migne 668 C) down to 'ipsa morietur': then *In quo omnes peccauerunt*, with the note on it[1]. Then follows the note on Rom vii 8, referred to above: 'Item, si cum,' etc. (Migne 676 B) to 'non est legi subiectus' (676 C). He then points out that this error and interpretation are condemned by a decree of an African Council, cap. 77, with which the Synod of Trent later agreed. In *Ann.* 240 (p. 517) there is another reference to the note on Rom. vii 8. In *Ann.* 244 (p. 518) the note on Rom. viii 3 is criticized, because it insinuates that in Christ's flesh there was an inclination to sin: the words quoted are: 'Filius Dei, suscepta carne' down to 'contagione peccati' (Migne 679 C). In *Ann.* 251 (p. 522) the commentary is quoted among those which hold the view that predestination is after merits have been foreseen: the particular passages mentioned are: Rom. viii 19 *Praedestinauit conformes fieri* etc. down to 'conformes in gloria' (Migne 685 A), 'quos praesciuit credituros'—'non inuitos' (*ibid.*), Rom. ix 15 *Miserebor, cui miserebor*. 'Hoc recto sensu' to 'sim misertus' (Migne 689 B). In *Ann.* 280[2] (p. 537) the note on Gal. iv 24, *Quae sunt per allegoriam dicta* is referred to, the words cited being: 'Dedit regulam' to 'exponamus,' 'et hoc ipsum ibi' to 'fieri uoluisse' (Migne 817 B, C). In *Ann.* 324 (p. 549) the note on 1 Tim. iii 8 is quoted, namely the words 'Quaeritur cur de' to 'episcopos ordinauit' (Migne 880 A, B).

Io. Garetius of Louvain in his *De Vera Praesentia Corporis Christi in Sacramento Eucharistiae*[3], some years before Sixtus, had headed a section with the words 'Pelagius haeresiarcha, gratiam Dei oppugnare coepit circa annum 419,' and then proceeds to quote the notes, from that on 1 Cor. xi 23 *Ego enim accepi a Domino* (Migne 751 D) down to 'existamus ingrati' (752 B), from *Itaque quicumque manducauerit* etc. to 'mundus manducabit' (752 C), from 'Unde oportet otiosum' to 'sancte percipiat,' and from *Probet autem se ipsum* to 'habere, quam nouam' (752 D). He thus has not the slightest hesitation in regarding this commentary as the work

[1] There are minor differences from the printed text. Certain of the portions he objects to will afterwards be seen to be not by Pelagius.

[2] The reference to this note in the index is false.

[3] Antv. 1561, class. viii p. 208 r.

of Pelagius, and he makes in the margin a reference to 'B. August. lib. de peccatorum meritis et remissione' in connexion with it.

Similar statements were made by the second great editor of Jerome, namely Marianus Victorius of Reate, Bishop of Ameria, who writes as follows: '*Commentarii in tredecim Pauli Apostoli epistolas, Hieronymi, ipsi etiam minime sunt: nam nec eius phrasim habent, nec eruditionem: quamuis in fronte operis epist. ad Heliodorum inscriptam, contineant: Quin potius hominis esse Pelagiana labe commaculati compertissimum est (ni ea tantum quae orthodoxa non sunt, ab haereticis potius sint adiecta). Notauit hoc ante nos Ambrosius Catharinus Politus Compsae Archiepiscopus, catholicae religionis assertor: notauit et Sixtus Senensis, quarto et sexto Bibliothecae sanctae uolumine: uterque errores Pelagianae haereseos, qui eo in opere inueniuntur, redarguentes. Si quis autem scire hoc concupiscat, liquido ex expositione quinti ad Romanos capitis inueniet: ubi Adae peccatum in humanum genus, non propagatione, et traduce, sed exemplo tantum, et imitatione diffundi asserit: ac si illud non contrahant, nisi qui aetate adulta, et ad peccandum iam apta, Adam sceleribus imitentur. Quod ipsum ex interpretatione septimi capitis liquidius apparet. Enarrans enim illud,* SINE LEGE PECCATVM ERAT MORTVVM, *ita scribit.* Item[1] si cum lex non esset, peccatum mortuum est: insaniunt qui de Adam per traducem asserunt ad nos venire peccatum. *Quae opinio quam impia, et haeretica sit, nemo catholicorum ignorat. Ego quid de operis auctore statuam, certi habeo nihil: nisi quod Hieronymi illud non esse, compertissimum est. Edi tamen curauimus eo modo, quo antea typis mandatum circumferebatur, ne quid priori editioni deesset, nulla quidem syllaba a nobis auctum, diminutum, aut immutatum: Lectorum arbitrio, quid de illo existimare uelint, penitus derelinquentes*[2].'

The position of Robert, Cardinal Bellarmine, is the same, as appears from these words: '*Commentaria in omnes Epistolas, non solum non sunt Hieronymi, sed, quod magis mirum est, Pelagii haeresiarchae sunt. Nam sanctus Augustinus, lib. 3. de peccatorum meritis, et remiss. cap. 1. dicit, se legisse Commentaria Pelagii breuia*

[1] The words *Item* to *uenire peccatum* are interpolated, as we have seen, p. 7 n. 3.

[2] *Sancti Hieronymi Stridonensis Operum* Tomus IIII (Paris, 1609) pp. 461—462; the date of the eighth volume of Victorius' earliest edition is 1572 (Schoenemann, *Biblioth....Patrum Latinorum*, t. I [Lips. 1792] p. 503).

in omnes Epistolas Pauli: et infra cap. 12. *allegat quaedam ex Commentario in caput* 7. *prioris ad Corinth. quae in his Commentariis inueniuntur. Vide auctorem horum Commentariorum, in cap.* 5. 6. 7. *et* 8. *et* 11. *ad Romanos; item* 1. *Corint.* 4. *Philip.* 1. *&* 3. *& in caput* 6. *prioris ad Timot. et inuenies sententias manifeste Pelagianas*[1].'

G. J. Voss, in one of the most learned books ever published on the Pelagian controversy[2], sums up his own and his predecessors' research thus: '*Etiam Pelagius edidit* XIV[3] *Expositionum libros in epistolas Paulinas. Meminit eorum Augustinus lib.* III. *de peccat. meritis et remiss. c.* 1. *et de gestis Palaestinis cap.* XVI. *Valde autem eo inclinat animus, ut putem eos ipsos esse, qui commentariis Hieronymi in epistolas aliquot Paulinas subjungi vulgo solent. Cui non tenui suspicioni locum magnum dedit, quod scriptor hic statuat passim, neminem per Adamum peccati reum esse, nisi quatenus eius imitetur exemplum: cumque omnes in eo peccasse dicuntur, id non ἁπλῶς intelligi debere, sed de genere improborum: quando alii praeter hos sint, qui juste vivendo secundum Adamum, hoc est Christum, sequi ament. Audiamus ipsum in cap.* V. *ad Rom. sic scribentem:* then follow "Ut qui sequentes"—"reconciliaremur Deo" (Migne 668 B). *Et mox:* "Quomodo cum non esset"—"est revocata" (ibid.). *Ibidem ad illud,* Et ita in omnes homines (Migne 668 C)—"ritu vivebant" (ibid.). *Et pauculis interjectis:* In quo omnes peccaverunt: "hoc est" (ibid.)—"exemplo Adae peccant" (668 D). *Et mox:* "Forma Christi Adam factus[4]" (Migne 669 B)—"eum volentibus[5]" (669 C). *Et post aliqua ad illa verba:* Sicut per unius delictum in omnes, etc. "Quomodo," *inquit,* "potest unius" (Migne 670 C)—"significat multitudinem" (671 A). *Et mox:* "Sicut exemplo inobedientiae" —"justificantur multi[6]" (ibid.). *Item in cap.* VI. "Qui veterem ho-

[1] *De Scriptoribus Ecclesiasticis Liber Unus* (Col. Agr. 1613) p. 165, or ed. 6 (Lovan. 1678) p. 120 = *Opera,* t. VII (Colon. 1617) p. 73 B—D. Ph. Labbe, *De Scriptoribus Ecclesiasticis* t. I (Paris, 1660) p. 441, objects to the Pelagian authorship on the ground of the absence of the Augustinian quotations from the published commentary.

[2] *Historiae de Controversiis, quas Pelagius eiusque reliquiae mouerunt, libri septem* (2nd edition) (Amstel. 1655, sm. 4to) pp. 11 ff. (original ed. 1618).

[3] An error due to carelessness, found also in other works on the subject.

[4] We shall see that this passage is an interpolation on the original Pelagius.

[5] So *Voss*: *Migne* cupientibus.

[6] Here Migne is corrupted by homoeoteleuton: see my text in vol. II: Voss is using an earlier and better edition.

minem" (Migne 672 B)—"imitando peccabant" (ibid.). *Item:* "Homo membra sua" (Migne 673 A)—"arbitrii libertatem" (ibid.). *Ubi palam est, eum naturam liberi arbitrii considerare citra ullam Spiritus S. gratiam. Quemadmodum et cum paullo post ad illud,* Humanum dico, propter etc. "Humana," *inquit,* "ratione"—"nullus abnuere" (Migne 674 A). *Sed omnium maxime scriptorem prodit, quod cap. sequenti, hoc est septimo, ait:* "Insaniunt qui"—"venire peccatum" (Migne 676 B)[1]. *Idem in epist. ad Philipp. cap.* II.[2] "Occasio fidei"—"utique crederemus" (Migne 844 B). *Paullum hic pedem figamus. Agnoscit bonitatis esse divinae, quod Christus venerit in mundum, ut nos doceret, quid credere debeamus: absque hoc esset, credenda ignorarentur, eoque nec crederentur. Quid uero aliud hîc requirit, quam ut bonitas divina nobis doctores mittat, qui extrinsecus instruant verbo? Nam opem spiritus Sancti ad fidem ingenerandam nec hîc necessariam esse dicit, nec alibi usquam. Unde cognoscimus, quomodo intelligere oporteat, quod in cap.* XI. *ad Rom. ait;* Fidem bonitate Dei conferri (Migne 698 B). *Cujusmodi a Catholicis omnibus probarentur, nisi constaret a quibus dicerentur. Atque ut haec ejus libri scriptorem Pelagianum esse clare ostendunt, ita eum non alium quam ipsum Pelagium esse verisimile faciunt, quae de Pelagii libro refert Augustinus. Nam lib.* III. *de peccatorum meritis et remissione cap.* I. *scribit in hunc modum,* Post paucissimos dies legi Pelagii quaedam scripta, quae in Pauli Apostoli epistolas expositiones brevissimas continerent. *At commentarii quos habemus, sunt brevia in omnes Pauli epistolas scholia. Subjicit mox Augustinus:* Atque ibi comperi, cum ad illum venisset locum, ubi dicit Apostolus: Per unum hominem peccatum intrasse in mundum, et per peccatum mortem, atque ita in omnes homines pertransisse: quandam eorum argumentationem, qui negant parvulos peccatum originale gestare. Argumentatio illa sic posita est; Si Adae peccatum etiam non peccantibus nocuit, ergo et Christi justitia etiam non credentibus prodest. *Atqui hunc in modum ratiocinatur, qui commentarios istos scripsit: quemadmodum videre ex iis fuit, quae supra adduximus. Quanquam illa ipsa penitius consideranti fatendum est, satis obscure hanc ex iis sententiam elici. Verba sane ipsa non legas. Sed fortasse haec inde exciderint: quod arbitratur Gretzerus defensione Bellarmini*

[1] On this passage see p. 7 n. 3.

[2] This should be I.

de verbo Dei lib. IV. *cap.* V. *Praeterea cap.* V. *ejusdem libri ait Augustinus, Pelagium non uno modo explicuisse illud Pauli ad Rom.* V. Adam forma futuri. *Atqui hoc facit commentator iste, his verbis:* "Sive ideo forma fuit" (Migne 669 B)—"Sicut enim Adam etc.[1]" (ibid.). *Denique apud Augustinum duodecimo ejusdem libri capite (ubi Paulinum illud expendit* 1. *Cor.* vii. Sanctificatus est vir infidelis in uxore, et sanctificata est mulier infidelis in fratre: alioqui filii vestri immundi essent, nunc autem sancti sunt) *magnus haec commentatur antistes:* Aut sic est accipiendum, quemadmodum et nos alibi, et Pelagius, cum eandem ad Corinthios epistolam tractaret, exposuit, quod exempla jam praecesserant et virorum, quos uxores, et feminarum, quas mariti lucrifecerant Christo, et parvulorum, ad quos faciendos Christianos voluntas Christiana etiam unius parentis evicerat. *Atque ita interpretatur scriptor horum scholiorum. Verba eius apponam:* "Exemplum refert" (Migne 736 D) —"verbo lucrifiant" (737 A). *Pelagium igitur istorum esse scholiorum scriptorem, verisimillimum videtur. Interim de hoc nolumus cum quoquam ducere contentionis funem: dummodo si non Pelagii, saltem Pelagiani alicujus credantur: quod etiam agnoscunt Sixtus Senensis lib.* IV. *Bibl. Sanct. verbo Hieronymus: Iohannes Garetius de sacrificio Missae centur.* V. *fol.* 43. *Bellarminus in catal. script. Eccles. et lib.* IV. *de verbo Dei cap.* V. *et lib.* IV. *de amiss. gratiae, atque alibi: item Pererius comm. in Gen. cap.* XIV. *n.* 8. *Marianus Victorius censurâ tom.* 8. *Hieron. Scultingius in censurâ confess. Hieron. Salmeron in epist. Pauli disp.* XVI. *Coccius Thesauri T.* 2. *artic.* 11. *ut interim de Witakero, Perkinso, Iunio, Rob. Coco, plurimisque aliis nihil dicam*[2].'

To recapitulate. Erasmus had contented himself with denying the paternity of Jerome. Succeeding scholars pointed out the Pelagianism in the commentary, and some boldly identified it with the commentary of Pelagius himself mentioned and quoted by Augustine. The difficulty that certain of Augustine's quotations are wanting to the would-be Jerome, was hardly faced by anyone. With the publication of the first printed edition of Marius Mercator

[1] This last part is an interpolation in Pelagius.

[2] Of the authorities here enumerated I have consulted such as were accessible to me: some are quoted above: the reference to Pererius appears to be wrong. On Phil. Labbe's view, published in 1660, see above, p. 10 n. 1.

in 1671, and particularly that by Jean Garnier in 1673, the problem assumed a somewhat different aspect.

Slightly prior to Garnier, however, Enrico de Noris, of Verona, had observed the bearing of the new information supplied by Mercator on the subject of the Pelagian commentary, but it did not lie within his province as a historian to work the matter out with Garnier's fullness[1]. It does not appear that either author's work was known to the other, and we have here therefore an example of that curious coincidence in research which occurs so often. Noris alleges a reference to Pelagius's commentary in cap. 16 of Augustine's *De Peccato Originali*, which, so far as I know, had not been previously observed[2], and he quotes Mercator on the date of the Pelagius commentary, direct from the Vatican codex, p. 37[3]. He then mentions Jansen's agreement with Voss that the Hieronymian commentary is undoubtedly that by Pelagius, and proceeds to confirm this view by the quotations Marius Mercator gives from the commentary[4]. An interesting suggestion which he then makes must be quoted in his own words: '*Scio S. Doctorem* [i.e. Augustine] *lib.* 3. *de pec. mer. et remis. nonnullas ex eisdem Pelagii commentariis argumentationes ad verbum recitare, quae in editis non leguntur, sed illud satis verisimillimum judico, eas ratiocinationes Celestii manu insertas, eoque pacto in S. Doctoris manus venisse, etenim familiare Celestio fuit, brevissimis syllogismis ad haeresim stabiliendam uti; Jansenius existimavit, easdem expositiones Pelagii ipsius manu fuisse subinde parumper immutatas, de quo nolo cum eodem ducere contentionis funem. Porro apertis verbis ibidem peccatum originale excluditur, nam cap.* 5. *ista leguntur:* "Quomodo potest" (Migne 670 C) —"homines iustificati sint[5]?" (671 A) *quo loco pluribus tradit, Adam nocuisse posteris exemplo tantum, ac forma, qua mors animae, non*

[1] *Historia Pelagiana et Dissertatio de Synodo V. Oecumenica*, etc. (Patav. 1673: also Amstel. 1677). The dedication is dated 23 March 1673, but the permission of the Prior General of the Augustinians is dated 20 June 1672; the book must therefore have been completed before the latter date. For the use of Mercator by De Noris cf. pp. 5, 14 f. etc. of ed. Amstel.

[2] p. 14 ed. Amstel. There is a clearer instance, however, in c. 21 § 24, which he failed to quote: unless indeed 16 be a wrong reference, for 21.

[3] p. 14 ed. Amstel.

[4] For these, see below, pp. 41 ff.

[5] *Migne* sunt.

vero corporis Adami culpam imitantibus intimatur. Et cap. 7. *totum se prodit inquiens:* "Insaniunt"—"venire peccatum" (676 B). *Vides ergo Pelagium strenuum Rufini defensorem. Praeterea in eisdem commentariis universum haeresis, quam postea fusius docuit, virus evomuit. In c.* 8 *laudatae epistolae ad Romanos ad illa verba:* Lex enim—"appellat" (Migne 679 B), *et inferius:* "Quicumque secundum doctrinam"—"Dei aguntur[1]" (Migne 681 D); *Neutrobique enim gratiam Spiritus Sancti a lege, et doctrina distinguit. In cap.* 11. *vers.* 7. Electio autem consecuta est, *haec scribit:* "Divina Scriptura" (Migne 696 A)—"dedit libertatem" (Migne 696 B). *Quibus actuale Dei auxilium prorsus negavit, admittens tantum adjutorium possibilitatis, quod idem est, ac liberum arbitrium naturae rationali insertum. Augiae[2] stabulum purgare mallem, quam illorum commentariorum errores in indicem cogere[3].*'

Garnier did not content himself with the issue of Mercator's text, but furnished it with copious notes and dissertations, which still possess interest and value[4]. He mentions that some attributed the Hieronymian commentary to Primasius, others to Sedulius[5]: but of these attributions I can find no trace. That there is, however, a close relationship both between 'Primasius' and 'Hieronymus,' and between Sedulius and 'Hieronymus' we shall afterwards see[6]. Garnier himself states that in his time no one doubted that the commentaries were not merely by a Pelagian, but by Pelagius himself. He then quotes *Praedestinatus* and the passages of Augustine, to which reference has already been made, including *De Peccat. Orig.* c. 21[7] and *Op. Imp. c. Iulian.* I c. 54, which last passage, so far as I know, had never been adduced by anyone else[8]. As has been said above, he also takes full advantage of the evidence of Mercator in support of the Pelagian authorship. But perhaps

1 An interpolated passage.

2 Sic.

3 Ed. Amstel. p. 15.

4 *Marii Mercatoris S. Augustino aequalis Opera quaecumque exstant.* Prodeunt nunc primum studio J. Garnerii: reprinted in Migne, *P.L.* XLVIII. The 'nunc primum' is not strictly correct, as Schoenemann, *Bibliotheca Patrum*, t. II (Lips. 1794) p. 550 = Migne, *P.L.* XLVIII 53 A—B, shows: an earlier edition appeared in 1671.

5 Migne XLVIII 83 B.

6 Chap. VI pp. 322 ff., 338 f.

7 See above, p. 13 n. 2.

8 Migne XLVIII 84 A—B: Labbe, p. 795, had noted Sedulius's connexion.

his greatest service in connexion with the whole matter was to call attention to a passage in Cassiodorus that had been overlooked by all the earlier investigators[1].

Cassiodorus, in the eighth chapter of his invaluable work, *Institutiones Divinarum Litterarum*, written about the middle of the sixth century, is describing Latin commentaries on the New Testament Epistles contained in the library of the monastery he had founded at Vivarium. This chapter is of the utmost importance to its subject, and must be quoted here, because of the light it sheds on the problems with which we are dealing. By the kindness of Dr C. H. Turner, I am enabled to give the text according to the Bamberg eighth century MS, the best of all[2].

§ 1. Octauus codex canonicas epistulas continet apostolorum. sed in epistolis tredecim sancti Pauli annotationes conscriptas in ipso initio meae lectionis inueni, quae in cunctorum manibus ita celebres habebantur, ut eas a sancto Gelasio papa urbis Romae doctissimi uiri studio dicerent fuisse conscriptas. quod solent facere, qui res uitiosas cupiunt gloriosi nominis auctoritate defendere: sed nobis ex praecedentibus lectionibus diligenti retractatione patuerunt subtilissimas quidem esse ac breuissimas dictiones, sed Pelagiani erroris uenena illic esse seminata. et ut procul a uobis fieret error hereticus, primam epistolam ad Romanos qua potui curiositate purgaui, reliquas in chartaceo codice conscriptas uobis emendandas reliqui: quod facile subiacebit, quando praecedenti exemplo audacior reddatur sequentis imitatio.

§ 2. Sed inter has sollicitudines grauiter aestuatus, quendam anonymum codicem subnotatum diuina reperi prouisione collatum, qui tredecim epistulas sancti Pauli non ignobili annotatione tractauit. hic diligenter excussus secundum uobis ac securum genus commentorum, domino largiente, praestabit.

§ 3. Ad Hebreos uero epistulam, quam sanctus Iohannes Constantinopolitanus episcopus triginta quatuor omeliis Attico sermone tractauit,

[1] Migne 84 c.

[2] Ed. Garet, t. II (Venet. 1729) p. 514, Migne LXX p. 1119: the Bamberg MS is HJ iv 15 (Patr. 61), saec. VIII ex.; see E. A. Lowe, *The Beneventan Script* (Oxford, 1914) passim. It appears to be a direct, or almost direct, copy of the Cassiodorian autograph. P. Corssen, *Jahrbücher für protestantische Theologie* IX (1883) pp. 619—633, made admirable use of another part of it, as also Th. Zahn, *Gesch. d. ntl. Kanons* II Bd. (1) (Erl. u. Leipz. 1890) pp. 268 ff. Another really old, but fragmentary, MS of this work is at Vercelli, Bibl. Capitolare, CLXXXIII (saec. VIII), of which one page is photographed in *Specimina Codicum Latinorum Vaticanorum* coll. F. Ehrle et P. Liebaert (Bonn, etc. 1912) no. 9. There are MSS also at Hereford, Karlsruhe, St Gall, etc.

Mucianum uirum disertissimum transferre fecimus in Latinum, ne Epistularum ordo continuus indecoro termino subito rumperetur.

[*The next four paragraphs are omitted here, because they concern only the Canonical or Catholic Epistles.*]

§ 8. Tertium uero codicem reperi epistolarum sancti Pauli, qui a nonnullis beati Hieronymi annotationes breuissimas dicitur continere, quem uobis pariter, Christo largiente, dereliqui.

§ 9. Post haec uero tria paria, quae diximus, commentorum, Petrus, abbas Tripolitanae prouinciae, sancti Pauli epistulas exemplis opusculorum beati Augustini subnotasse narratur, ut per os alienum sui cordis declararet arcanum ; quae ita locis singulis competenter aptauit, ut hoc magis studio beati Augustini credas esse perfectum. mirum est enim sic alterum ex altero dilucidasse, ut nulla uerborum suorum adiectione permixta desiderium cordis proprii complesse uideatur ; qui uobis inter alios codices, diuina gratia suffragante, de Africana parte mittendus est[1].

§ 10. Sic totus ordo epistularum canonicarum tam sancti Pauli quam diuersorum apostolorum domini fauore completus est.

§ 11. Dicitur enim et beatum Ambrosium subnotatum codicem epistularum omnium sancti Pauli reliquisse, suauissima expositione conpletum, quem tamen adhuc inuenire non potui, sed diligenti cura perquiro.

At this point we may leave the text of Cassiodorus, following the example of the men of that day. We shall see later that if they had read farther, they would have solved one problem at once.

Garnier's interpretation of Cassiodorus' statements is this. After paraphrasing § 1, he expresses doubt whether Cassiodorus's pupils ever carried out the revision he suggested, but points out that in published editions of the Hieronymian commentary the passages alleged by Augustine, Marius Mercator, and *Praedestinatus* as tainted with Pelagian error, are wanting: the probable reason for this is that our copies are descended from the copy made by Cassiodorus for his monks. Garnier feels the difficulty of the presence of the *Insaniunt* passage in Rom. vii 9 (Migne 676 B), and explains that, after it had been removed by Cassiodorus, it had been inserted again by a scribe[2]. In a later part of his book he subjects the whole question to a somewhat more elaborate examination, and sets forth the quotations from Pelagius in Mercator side by side

[1] This work has not been printed, but a MS exists in the Vatican, lat. 4950 (saec. XI), formerly S. Petri Damiani in Avellino, as Dr H. M. Bannister informed me. See also Denifle, *Luther und Luthertum* I (2), p. 22.

[2] As a matter of fact, this passage was never before Cassiodorus's eyes, cf. p. 7 n. 3.

with the corresponding Hieronymian comments. His conclusion is that the would-be Jerome is the original Pelagius as revised by Cassiodorus, who made excisions in the interests of orthodoxy[1].

The industry which Garnier displayed gained a signal reward: his opinion remained practically undisputed for two centuries. Succeeding statements are quoted here for the sake of relative completeness, but to all intents and purposes Garnier's view held the field right down to and even beyond the time of Klasen (1885).

Cave[2] obviously depends in part on Garnier. He mentions the evidence in Augustine, Marius Mercator, *Praedestinatus*, and Cassiodorus, that Pelagius wrote a commentary on 'xiv' Epistles of St Paul, and that Vossius and most scholars regard it as identical with the Hieronymian commentary in our possession. He records, however, at some length Ussher's dissent from this opinion[3]. Ussher's views show an interesting originality. He regards Pelagius as the author of the first commentary mentioned by Cassiodorus, but considers that the Hieronymian commentary is a comparatively late compilation from Pelagius, Jerome, and Primasius, a jumble of contrary opinions, heterodox from the first of these sources, orthodox from the second and third, put together by an ignorant person. He cites a contradiction between *in Rom.* xi 22 that 'faith' is conferred by God's goodness (Migne 698 B) with many other passages, on the one hand[4], and Pelagian views on the other, and holds that therefore those who attribute the whole work to Pelagius are mistaken. He then calls attention to the fact that three passages quoted by Augustine from Pelagius, are nowhere to be found in the Hieronymian commentary, and that the Pelagian prefaces and arguments to the Epistles are also absent from it[5]. He allows, however, the presence of Pelagian material in the com-

[1] Diss. VI pars ii cap. 2, 'Expositiones breves in omnes Epistolas Pauli apostoli' (Migne XLVIII 587 C—593 A).

[2] *Scriptorum Ecclesiasticorum Historia Literaria* (Lond. 1688) pp. 292 f.: (Colon. 1720) pp. 244 f.

[3] Abp Ussher p. 574 (of what work I cannot discover, prob. MS, see p. xlvi of later ed. of Cave).

[4] He quite rightly says that no other author more frequently insists on our justification by the free grace of God, and faith alone. See my chap. iii p. 70.

[5] This is the first occasion on which that element enters into the controversy; Ussher of course knew the *Book of Armagh*, where this prefatory material occurs under the name of Pelagius: see below, p. 25.

mentary, namely the already quoted note on Rom. vii (Migne 676 B)[1], the remaining quotations in Augustine, and the quotations made in the Irish Canons[2]. The best part of it, however, he thinks was taken from the very brief notes of Jerome, of which Cassiodorus speaks, as is suggested by the name of Jerome in the title, and the preface to Heliodorus. He reminds us that Walahfrid Strabus in the *Glossa Ordinaria* constantly quotes, and Sedulius[3] once (*in* 1 *Cor.* vii, Migne CIII, 144 A) appears to allude to the commentary, under the name of Jerome; 'non parentes' (Migne 740 A)—'incorruptam seruare' (740 B)[4]. Cave concludes by quoting Garnier's opinion as to the Hieronymian commentary in its present state.

Du Pin in his *Nouvelle Bibliothèque des Auteurs Ecclésiastiques*[5] says: 'Les Commentaires ou les notes sur toutes les Epîtres de Saint Paul ne sont point de Saint Jerôme, mais d'un Auteur Pelagien, qui enseigne ouvertement ses erreurs en plusieurs endroits, et principalement sur le chapitre 7. de l'Epître aux Romains. Il est certain que Pelage avoit fait un Commentaire sur les Epîtres de Saint Paul, que Saint Augustin cite en quelques endroits du troisiéme livre des merites et de la remission des pechez. Ce même Commentaire de Pelage est encore cité par Marius Mercator, et l'on trouve dans celui-cy la pluspart des passages rapportez par ces deux Auteurs. Il y en a neanmoins un ou deux qui ne s'y trouvent pas; ce qui donneroit lieu de douter si c'est entierement le même, si Cassiodore ne nous avertissoit qu'il en a retranché quelques passages.' In a later note[6] he adds: 'Quelques-uns doutent si ce Commentaire est celui que Saint Augustin cite sous le nom de Pelage: 1. parce qu'on trouve aussi parmi les Œuvres de Saint Ambroise un Commentaire Pelagien sur les Epîtres de Saint Paul: 2. parce que l'on ne trouve pas tous les passages que Saint Augustin rapporte, comme étant du Commentaire de Pelage, ou du moins ne les y trouve-t-on pas dans les mêmes termes. La

[1] pp. 7 ff. [2] The reference to the Irish Canons first appears in Ussher.

[3] The Bamberg MS of Sedulius here assigns to H., but the reference may be to some passage of the genuine Jerome, perhaps *Adu. Iouin.* I 13 (cf. *J.T.S.* vol. XVIII p. 228).

[4] This passage is an interpolation on the original Pelagius.

[5] T. III (Paris, 1689) p. 426.

[6] Op. cit. p. 492 note c.

premiere de ces deux raisons est tres-foible, puisqu'il est fort possible qu'un Auteur Pelagien ait fait des Commentaires sur Saint Paul, differens de ceux de Pelage. La seconde seroit de quelque poids, si l'on ne trouvoit pas dans ce Commentaire attribué à Saint Jerôme la pluspart des passages citez par Saint Augustin. Car 1. Saint Augustin dans le ch. 16 du livre des Actes de Pelage dit, que cét Heretique a expliqué ces paroles du chapitre 9. de l'Epître aux Romains, *Neque volentis, neque currentis est Dei* (sic!), en disant que Saint Paul avoit ainsi parlé par interrogation, *Voce interrogantis et redarguentis*. Cette même explication, ces mêmes mots se trouvent dans le Commentaire dont nous parlons. 2. Saint Augustin au livre 3. des Merites des pechez chapitre 12. dit, que Pelage expliquant ce passage du chapitre 7. de l'Epître aux Corinthiens, *Sanctificatus est vir infidelis*, remarque qu'il y avoit eu des exemples de femmes Fideles qui avoient converti leurs maris Infideles. Cette même remarque est dans ce Commentaire. 3. Saint Augustin dans le même livre chapitre 4. dit, que Pelage a dit sur ces paroles *Rom.* 5. *Quae est forma futuri*, qu'elles se peuvent entendre de plusieurs manieres. La même chose est remarquée dans ce Commentaire; mais ce qui met la chose hors de doute, c'est que Marius Mercator dans son Memoire instructif cite un long passage tiré des Commentaires de Pelage, qui se trouve tout entier dans celui-ci. Il est vrai que S. Augustin au livre 3. des Merites des pechez (*sic!*) chapitre 2. rapporte un argument contre le peché originel, qui ne se trouve point dans ce Commentaire, et qu'il cite dans le chapitre 3. un endroit qui est aussi rapporté par Marius Mercator, qui n'est point non plus dans ce Commentaire attribué à Saint Jerôme. Mais il y a apparence que ces endroits ont été effacez et raiez par quelques Catholiques.'

Richard Simon, the greatest of all students of ancient commentaries on the New Testament, records the opinions of Sixtus of Siena, Catarinus, Bellarmine and Labbe[1]. Without naming Garnier, he adopts the same opinion as his, that the Hieronymian commentary is the work of Pelagius, as revised by Cassiodorus. He makes a curious mistake, in stating that Cassiodorus reports that some assigned the commentary with the Pelagian poison to

[1] *Histoire Critique des principaux Commentateurs du Nouveau Testament...* (Rotterdam, 1693) c. 16 pp. 236 ff.

Primasius[1]. Cassiodorus, as a matter of fact, never mentions Primasius in this connexion. But in spite of such a mistake as this, Simon's chapter on the Pelagian commentary is, as might be expected, one of the most valuable ever written. We shall return later to his work, but at this stage it may be well to quote some of his further remarks. 'Pelage fait paroître dans tout cet ouvrage, qui ressemble plus à des Scolies qu'à un Commentaire, qu'il étoit exercé dans le stile des Livres Sacrez. Si l'on excepte quelques endroits de S. Paul, qu'il a interpretez selon ses faux préjugez, il peut être mis au rang des habiles Commentateurs du N. Testament. Il paroît même que Sedulius, Primasius, Haimo, et quelques autres en ont copié la meilleure partie dans leurs Commentaires. Bien qu'il n'ait point expliqué l'Epître aux Ebreux, il la cite souvent sous le nom de Saint Paul. Il a eu apparemment égard à l'usage de quelques Eglises Latines, qui ne la lisoient point alors dans les assemblées publiques....Si l'on ôte ce qui regarde la grace, et quelques autres points qui sont connus de tout le monde, Pelage a suivi la creance commune de l'Eglise, qu'il a même defenduë avec vigueur contre les Heretiques. Son Commentaire sur S. Paul merite d'être lu, mettant à part ses erreurs....le nom de Pelage qui est devenu odieux, ne nous doit point detourner de la lecture de son Commentaire, où il donne des preuves de son habileté....L'on prendra même garde, que pour ne pas s'accorder avec la doctrine, qui a été la plus commune après S. Augustin parmi les Latins, il n'est pas pour cela Heretique, dans tous les endroits où il ne convient point avec ce Pere: autrement il faudroit accuser d'heresie la plûpart des anciens Docteurs de l'Eglise. Je croy même que Pelage avoit composé son Commentaire sur les Epîtres de Saint Paul, avant qu'il eût été declaré novateur. Comme l'on est obligé de rendre justice à tout le monde, l'on distinguera ce qu'il a de commun avec les anciens Ecrivains Ecclesiastiques, d'avec ce qu'il a avancé de luy-même, sans être fondé sur la Tradition. Car c'est en cela seulement qu'on peut l'accuser d'avoir été novateur.' The justice of these remarks is evident, and it is regrettable that they required to be made. One is also impressed by the fact that Simon

[1] It looks as if Simon here had unwittingly taken Garnier's note on Marius Mercator for a quotation from Cassiodorus himself. On p. 238 he also quotes Cassiodorus inexactly.

had read through the published commentary with care. I take leave to doubt whether many of the others who have written about it, have done the same. Otherwise, it is strange that for four centuries the text should have been suffered to remain so ridiculously corrupt[1].

The great Tillemont's contribution to this question is in these terms: 'Nous avons parmi ses œuvres (i.e. those of Jerome) un commentaire sur toutes les epistres de S. Paul, hormis sur celle aux hebreux. Mais quoiqu'il porte le nom de ce Saint, et qu'on y trouve à la teste une lettre à Heliodore, neanmoins et les Catholiques et les Calvinistes conviennent qu'il n'est point de Saint Jerome, mais de quelque Pelagien, et apparemment de Pelage mesme, [ce que nous n'examinerons pas ici. C'est peutestre celui] dont on avoit parlé à Cassiodore; car il ne dit point que l'epistre aux Hebreux y fust. Mais il ne le dit point non plus de celle aux Romains, que Saint Jerome n'avoit point encore expliquée, lorsqu'il écrivit à Algasie [en l'an 407; et il ne paroist point qu'il l'ait jamais fait]. Cassiodore parle encore de quelques notes fort courtes sur les epistres de Saint Paul, que quelques uns disoient estre de S. Jerome. [Je n'en ay point d'autre connoissance.][2]'

Le Clerc reprinted the Hieronymian commentary in the twelfth volume of the Antwerp (Benedictine) edition of St Augustine's works in 1703[3], but without any attempt, so far as tests have been able to show, to improve the text. His standpoint with regard to it was probably that of Garnier.

In the fifth volume of the Martianay edition, published in 1706[4], there is a note pointing out that the preface beginning *Litteris tuis cursim* is not to be found 'in veteri codice[5],' and that the commentary, though attributed in MSS to Jerome, is really to be ascribed to a

[1] Take such passages as 2 *Cor.* xi 9, 10; 1 *Tim.* iiii 8; 2 *Tim.* ii 24, and compare them with the text in my second volume.

[2] *Memoires pour servir à l'Histoire Ecclésiastique des six Premiers Siècles*, t. XII (Paris, 1707) pp. 115 f. He cites Lab. *scr.* t. I pp. 441, 794. In the latter passage L. quotes Aubertinus, p. 596, with approval.

[3] pp. 315—458.

[4] *Sancti Eusebii Hieronymi Stridonensis Presbyteri Operum* Tomus Quintus... Parisiis, 1706, pp. 925—6.

[5] The reference would seem to be to Paris B.N. 1853 (saec. VIII—IX), my M: the other old Paris MS, B.N. 9525 (saec. VIII ex.), my E, was not in Paris till a century after this time.

Pelagian, or to Pelagius himself. The editor had also noticed a reference to a copy of Pelagius on *XIII* epistles of St Paul in the catalogue of the library of St Riquier[1], unobserved by any previous scholar. What follows must be quoted in Martianay's own words: '*Propterea in quibusdam veteribus codicibus praefixa est his Commentariis concordia Epistolarum Beati Pauli, quam omnes veteres codices Pelagio tribuunt.*' The reference here is, I think, to the 'concordia' which occurs in Paris MS B.N. 1853 (saec. VIII—IX), but neither in that MS nor in any other known to me, is it attributed to Pelagius. The use of our commentary by Primasius and Sedulius is then referred to, and he ends his note by explaining that when the name of Pelagius became unpopular, all the Pelagians in Gaul read the commentary under the name of Jerome.

The erudite Jo. Albert Fabricius in his great *Bibliotheca Graeca* lib. iv (Hamburgi, 1708) p. 204, quoting Cotelier and others, gives 'Pelagius sive potius Pelagianus quidam' as the author.

Ceillier contented himself with a very brief résumé of Garnier's researches in the following words: 'On croit avec beaucoup de vraisemblance que ce commentaire est celui-la même que nous avons parmi les œuvres de saint Jérôme, puisqu'on y trouve la plupart des endroits qu'en ont cités saint Augustin et Marius Mercator, et qu'ils sont remplis d'erreurs pélagiennes. Il est vrai qu'un des principaux passages cités par saint Augustin ne s'y voit plus: mais il est aisé ou que Pélage l'ait supprimé lui-même, ou qu'il en ait été ôté par Cassiodore qui, croyant que le pape Gélase était auteur de ce commentaire, en avait purgé l'Epître aux Romains avec tout le soin possible, afin que d'autres corrigeassent à son exemple ce qu'il y avait d'erroné dans ce *Commentaire sur les autres Epîtres de saint Paul*[2].'

Vallarsi, at the end of his edition of the works of St Jerome, prefixes an 'admonitio' to his careless reprint of our commentaries, based almost entirely on Garnier's work and accepting its con-

[1] The exact words are: '*In codice Bibliothecae S. Richarii recensentur Commentarii Pelagii in XIII Epistolas Pauli.*' Zimmer learned this reference from Becker (see *Pelagius in Irland* p. 158): the mention of it in Martianay has escaped notice. On the library of S. Riquier, cf. L. Traube in *Abh. d. bayer. Akad.* XIX (1892) pp. 326, 329, 331.

[2] *Histoire Générale des Auteurs Sacrés et Ecclésiastiques*...nouv. éd. t. VII (Paris, 1861) p. 543 (original date, about 1750).

clusions. He adds, however, two new facts on his own account, one when he points out that in the thirteenth century the commentary was known to a certain John of Verona as the work of Pelagius. The identity of this John is uncertain, Panvinius being of opinion that he is a certain John a Deacon, Pastrengicus that he was a 'Presbyter Mansionarius' of the same name. It appears that he wrote a history, unprinted in Vallarsi's time, and perhaps still so, in which these words occur: '*Vidi ego ipse Ioannes Commentarium Pelagii praedicti, super Epistolas Pauli, in quo licet multa bene et eleganter exponat, tamen subtiliter infundit uenenum haeresis suae.*' The second new fact is contained in the statement that the better manuscripts of the Hieronymian commentary are without the preface (to Heliodorus)[1]. As we shall see later, this is quite true.

Jean-Baptiste Morel, priest of Auxerre, one of the acutest and most learned patristic scholars that ever lived, did not edit the commentary, but in his *Éléments de Critique,* issued in 1766[2], he proves that he had read it with great care: for he furnishes a number of emendations of the text, most of which are absolutely correct[3], but have been taken no notice of either by Vallarsi in his later edition, or by Migne in his reprint, or in fact by anybody at all.

C. T. G. Schoenemann in his admirable *Bibliotheca Historico-Literaria Patrum Latinorum* gives an account of the editions of the Hieronymian commentary[4]. Towards the end of his account of Erasmus's edition, he makes a very pertinent suggestion, which, however, fell on deaf ears: '*Interim...optandum duxerim, ne doctum aliquem virum in hac sacrarum literarum parte habitantem pigeat denuo eadem excutere et imprimis inuestigare, annon fortasse assumenta aliquot vilioris panni insint, quibus ineptus aliquis glossator vel compilator ad totius operis contemtum Erasmum provocaverit*[5].' How much truth lies behind this suspicion will be apparent from a later part of the present volume[6].

[1] This fact had, however, been already observed by Martianay: see above, p. 21.

[2] More accessible in Migne's reprint, *Première Encyclopédie Théologique,* t. XLVII (Paris, 1866) pp. 969—1116.

[3] For example, *in* 1 *Thess.* iiii 13, *fleri* for *fieri* (Migne reprint, p. 1025).

[4] Vol. II (Lips. 1794) cap. 5 sect. 7 pp. 436 ff.

[5] p. 439.

[6] pp. 35 f. etc.

If editors and historians of Latin literature have given but scanty attention to the Hieronymian commentary, commentators on St Paul have made abundant use of it. It was a primary authority for a number of commentaries from the sixth century onwards, and modern expositors have not neglected it. Among those of the nineteenth century, Bornemann, commentator on the Epistles to the Thessalonians, Bp Lightfoot[1], and Sanday and Headlam on the Epistle to the Romans may be mentioned. Their attitude to the commentary is naturally that of Garnier.

Garnier's view was disputed in a long paper by Klasen in the *Theologische Quartalschrift* for 1885[2]. He compares the notes on Rom. v, as they appear in Augustine, Mercator, and the Hieronymian commentary, and acutely observes that, though there are many differences in form, the contents exactly harmonize[3]. He subjects the theology of the commentary to a thorough examination, and defends at great length the thesis that the work as we have it is all by one hand, and that hand is not Pelagius, but a Pelagian of the latest period, when Pelagianism was becoming Semi-Pelagianism. As most of the argument is theological, and the present writer is not a theologian, he cannot form an estimate of its value. Nor does he know any examination of the paper by a competent theologian, and he can only conclude either that the paper has been overlooked, or that the theologians regard it as negligible. Loofs in the earlier editions of his *Leitfaden zum Studium der Dogmengeschichte* is not sure whether the Hieronymian commentary has been worked over, or not, and avoids using it as an authority for Pelagius' theological views[4]. Gregory in his *Textkritik des Neuen Testamentes*[5] holds that the Hieronymian commentary is 'sehr mutilirt.'

It will be the lasting merit of the late Professor Heinrich Zimmer of Berlin that he drew the whole subject out of the state of

[1] Cf. especially his commentary on the Epistle to the Galatians (Cambr. and London, 1865), pp. 222 f.

[2] Vol. LXVII, pp. 244—317, 531—577.

[3] pp. 267—270.

[4] In his article on 'Pelagius,' however, in the Herzog-Hauck *Realencykl.* (1904), and in the latest edition of the *Leitfaden* (1906), considerable use is made of it.

[5] Leipz. 1909 (this part 1902) p. 810: supplemented by later bibliography on p. 1353.

stagnation into which it had fallen. His proper field was Keltic studies, and the book *Pelagius in Irland*, published in 1901[1], was what he might have called a 'Seitenstück.' He was a man of virile and suggestive mind, interested in problems both of history and philology. In the course of philological study, he came in contact with certain documents which shed light on the history of the Pelagius commentary, and with characteristic enthusiasm he turned to this subject, and worked it out in his own way. If it has fallen to me to correct some errors of his, and to introduce new elements into the problem, I wish nevertheless to record here with the utmost gratitude the stimulus I have received from his work. In fact, when I took up the subject, it was with the intention simply of working out certain lines of investigation which he had suggested. Nor is it only to myself that stimulus has come from his work. A number of scholars have been led to interest themselves in the problem, such as Turner, Loofs[2], Riggenbach, Hellmann, Morin and De Bruyne.

Zimmer[3] points out that the *Book of Armagh*, the well known MS in the library of Trinity College, Dublin, written in 808, contains a prologue to the Epistles of St Paul, a prologue to the Epistle to the Romans, and separate arguments for each of the epistles, nearly all of which are specifically assigned to Pelagius[4]. He draws attention also to a MS of the early part of the eighth century in Würzburg[5]. This is a MS of the Epistles of Paul in Latin, which is heavily glossed. Most of the glosses, actually 949[6], are stamped *pl*, and one of them coincides with a comment quoted by Marius

[1] Berlin, Weidmann, pp. viii + 450.

[2] See his article in Herzog-Hauck's *Realencykl.*[3] XV (Leipz. 1904) pp. 747—774; also the supplementary and corrective article in Bd. XXIV (Leipz. 1913) pp. 310—312.

[3] In this and following paragraphs I follow very closely the wording of my lecture, published in the *Proceedings of the British Academy* vol. II (1905—1906) pp. 409—439, which in its separate form has been for some time out of print.

[4] But see page 17, above, for the proof that Ussher had noticed this fact much earlier, as also S. Berger, *Histoire de la Vulgate* (Paris, 1893) pp. 32 f.; *Les Préfaces jointes aux livres de la Bible* (Paris, 1902) p. 26.

[5] Since published in photographic facsimile by L. C. Stern (Halle a. S. 1910). The date I take from W. M. Lindsay, *Notae Latinae* (Cambr. 1915) p. 493, who says: 'glosses most of them patently much later than the text.'

[6] Zimmer, p. 112, for statistics.

Mercator[1]. The majority of these, actually 840, are to be found in our Pseudo-Jerome commentary, but the remainder are not to be found there. There are also, however, 348 glosses, with no author's name attached, that are to be found in the Pseudo-Jerome. The total reaches altogether 1311[2]. Zimmer has published a list of the glosses that are connected with the Pelagian commentary, and has added convenient symbols, first, to show when the gloss, though denominated *pl*, is not to be found in our Pseudo-Jerome, and second, when, though anonymous, it is to be found there. He has also discovered on examination that some of the glosses, labelled *pl*, are not really by Pelagius, but are derived from the commentary which was first printed in 1537 as a work of Primasius[3]. The original compiler of these glosses appears to have possessed an unmutilated Pelagius, since many passages which we cannot find in Pseudo-Jerome, are to be found either in Pseudo-Primasius or in Sedulius Scottus, both of whom made extensive use of Pelagius[4]. Some of those passages are to be found in both of these compilers.

From his study of the anonymous glosses in this MS, Zimmer found that the so-called Primasius commentary was sometimes used by the compiler, though not cited by any name. This commentary Haussleiter had proved to have no connexion with Primasius[5], and Zimmer claimed to be the first to point out that the principal source used in it is the Pelagius commentary, in an unmutilated state[6]; but here he overlooked the work of some seventeenth century scholars[7], though the Primasian authorship was then hardly doubted[8]. Zimmer, however, deserves all credit for

[1] On Rom. v 15; Zimmer, p. 40: see the next chapter.

[2] Zimmer, p. 132.

[3] pp. 45, 68, 129.

[4] Aubertin ap. Labbe, t. I p. 796, and Simon, pp. 336 ff., 380, had pointed this out long before. Before Simon the Benedictines of St Maur had observed it, as regards Primasius; see their *Augustine*, t. x (Paris, 1690) praef.: *Primasium ex hoc commentario* (i.e. Ps.-Hier.) *non pauca desumsisse, fonte interim, unde illa duceret, non indicato, ab eruditis obseruatum est.* See also H. B. Swete, *Theodori Episcopi Mopsuesteni in epist. B. Pauli Commentarii* vol. I (Cambr. 1880) p. xlv n. 1.

[5] Zahn's *Forschungen z. Gesch. des neutestamentl. Kanons* IV (Erl. & Leipz. 1891) pp. 24—35.

[6] His words are 'was bisher noch nirgends erkannt wurde' (p. 122).

[7] See the above note.

[8] Yet it was noticed that the comm. on Hebr. was identical with that of Haymo (Migne, *P.L.* CXVII) and Remigius (not in Migne): see Tho. Gataker, *Adv. Misc.* II 20 ('si is est'); Simon, p. 368; Westcott's ed. of *Hebrews* (Lond. 1889) p. vii.

the detailed manner in which he has dealt with the question. He shows, for example, that the borrowing is much easier to detect in the later epistles than in the Epistle to the Romans, and that the whole commentary[1] is an anonymous anti-Pelagian revision of the Pelagius commentary[2]. He also allows that in the Würzburg codex a portion of the anonymous glosses, which ultimately belongs to Pelagius, may have come to it through pseudo-Primasius, shows that sometimes there are errors in the citations[3], and, further, proves that the compiler of the glosses sometimes abridged his sources[4].

As to the date and place of origin of the pseudo-Primasius commentary, Zimmer argues that Pelagianism on the Continent ended with the decrees of the Synods of Orange and Valence in 529, and that this date provides a *terminus ante quem* for a commentary containing polemics against the Pelagians. He seeks further to draw from the allusion 'fuerunt Hunni usque ad Attilam[5]' an argument that the compiler could not have lived long after the death of Attila (454), and that the last third of the fifth century is the latest possible date for the commentary. He thinks it came into being in South Gaul or North Italy in connexion with the semi-Pelagian controversies, and proposes to identify it with the commentary which Cassiodorus knew as attributed by some to Pope Gelasius and which he himself afterwards revised. This reasoning is able and learned, but fallacious, as we shall see. There is, however, no need to disagree with Zimmer as to the date when the pseudo-Primasius commentary came to Ireland, namely in 641[6]. He further mentions that this commentary is used in the Haymo-Remigius commentary of the ninth century[7].

Besides the Würzburg codex, Zimmer drew attention to two other MSS of the Epistles in Latin, which provide similar material, though much inferior in bulk. They are Vienna MS 1247, written

1 Excepting, of course, Hebr.

2 pp. 121 ff.

3 pp. 127 ff., 133.

4 p. 133.

5 Migne, *P.L.* LXVIII, 441 B; Zimmer, p. 135.

6 Zimmer, p. 137.

7 pp. 135, 162. It is much to be desired that the extent of this indebtedness should be made the subject of a special monograph. In the course of the slight study I have been able to give to the question, I have not noticed that the indebtedness extends far. Also Haymo worked up his sources, and did not transfer them unaltered.

in 1079, and Berne MS A 73, of the thirteenth century. The former contains 203 direct citations from Pelagius: of these 167 are to be found in pseudo-Jerome, while 36 are there lacking. In 57 places also where no name is attached, words are given which appear in our pseudo-Jerome. Both MSS give the same prologue to the Epistles as is given by the *Book of Armagh,* and under Pelagius's name. The total number of independent glosses in the Würzburg and Vienna MSS together reaches 1535[1]. Zimmer also refers to citations of Pelagius in the Irish Canons of the end of the seventh or the beginning of the eighth century[2].

He next points out that there is evidence for the existence in the ninth and tenth centuries of MSS of Pelagius's commentary in three[3] libraries, all of them connected with the Irish mission to the Continent, at St Riquier, Lorsch, and St Gall[4]. Of these the St Gall MS appears to have survived in the anonymous 73, which will be further described immediately.

He then shows quite clearly, in opposition to the ruling view of Garnier and Simon, that the pseudo-Jerome commentary shows no prevailing anti-Pelagian tendency[5], and that it cannot therefore be the revision by Cassiodorus. In this respect pseudo-Jerome is to be contrasted with pseudo-Primasius, Sedulius, the Würzburg and Vienna glosses, to mention the other commentaries which employ Pelagius throughout. He proceeds to show by copious illustrations that frequently all other authorities have preserved the true text against pseudo-Jerome, and suggests—quite rightly, as will afterwards be proved—that many of the errors of that form will vanish when MSS of it are collated[6]. One of the best parts of Zimmer's book is his proof that Pelagius wrote no commentary on the Epistle to the Hebrews, though he regarded it as Pauline[7]. Fresh arguments will be adduced to confirm his conclusion[8].

[1] Zimmer, p. 155. [2] p. 162, etc.

[3] Prof. S. Hellmann adds a fourth, that at Murbach: the entry in the catalogue (dated about 840) (ed. Bloch, p. 271) is:—210, *Exposicio Pelagii in epistolas Pauli.*

[4] Zimmer, pp. 156 ff. [5] pp. 164 ff.

[6] Zimmer, pp. 169—175.

[7] pp. 178 ff. In this connexion he gives Haussleiter the credit of observing that the commentary on Hebrews in ps.-Primasius is identical with that in Haymo-Remigius; but this had been observed long before: see p. 26 n. 8 above.

[8] ch. vi. Cf. also De Bruyne in *Revue Biblique*, nouv. sér. XII (1915) p. 372.

Zimmer identifies the pseudo-Jerome commentary with that mentioned by Cassiodorus as containing short notes which were ascribed by some to Jerome. The second commentary mentioned by Cassiodorus he identifies with 'Ambrosiaster.' The first of the three anonymous commentaries mentioned by Cassiodorus, which Garnier and others have, in my opinion rightly, believed to be the unmutilated commentary of Pelagius, Zimmer considers to have been identical with our pseudo-Primasius. With regard to the revision by Cassiodorus and his pupils, he is of opinion that it has perished.

His view as to the manner of production of the pseudo-Jerome commentary must be mentioned. He considers that some one in the first half of the fifth century, before the suppression of Pelagianism, wrote out notes from the Pelagius commentary in a copy of the Epistles of Paul in Latin, that these notes fell into the hands of a man who knew nothing of Pelagius and was no heretic hunter, about the end of the fifth or the beginning of the sixth century, and that this man ascribed them to Jerome and edited them as his[1].

Zimmer's researches[2], of which we have here given a rather incomplete account, were crowned by the discovery of what appears to be the St Gall MS above referred to. Manuscript no. 73 in the Stifts-Bibliothek contains an anonymous commentary on fourteen Epistles of St Paul[3]. Its special characteristics are illustrated in great detail, by its discoverer, who compares it with pseudo-Jerome. It has some distinct differences from the published form attributed to Jerome. For example, it gives a long quotation in its proper place, which was already known from Augustine and Mercator[4], but is wanting in pseudo-Jerome, and in text it agrees with Augustine against Mercator. In the commentary on First Corinthians it frequently lacks one of the two explanations which pseudo-Jerome offers for one verse, and this Zimmer attributes to the editing of some Irish scholar. But the St Gall MS is not a pure

[1] pp. 200 ff.

[2] Some of them were anticipated in his article, 'Keltische Kirche in Britannien und Irland' in Bd. x (1901) (especially p. 211) of Herzog-Hauck's *Realencyklopädie*: the article was afterwards published as a book in an English translation, *Celtic Church in Britain and Ireland*, by A. Meyer (London, 1902).

[3] Zimmer, pp. 219—279.

[4] See below, pp. 36 f., 45 f.

Pelagius. It is heavily interpolated from known sources, especially in the commentaries on Ephesians, Titus, and Philemon, where passages from the genuine commentaries of Jerome on these epistles are interwoven with the Pelagian original, without acknowledgment. There are also citations from Augustine and Gregory the Great. These additions Zimmer regards not as specialities of the Irish recension of Pelagius, but as peculiar to the St Gall MS or its original[1]. The Irish appear from early times to have added notes to their copies of Pelagius, and thus in Irish circles passages came to rank as Pelagius which were not really by him. Zimmer suggests that Sedulius[2] and the Würzburg and Vienna MSS[3] are thus interpolated. After sketching the only plan by which an edition of Pelagius could then be made, Zimmer presents his readers with a collation of the St Gall MS made with the text of pseudo-Jerome[4]. The collation is fairly exact as far as it goes, but is defective to an incredible degree[5]. In spite of the care he exercised[6], Zimmer appears to have been physically incapable of making a really exact and full collation of a manuscript. Yet by this publication he did a great service to the study both of pseudo-Jerome and of Pelagius, as he at once removed a large number of the corruptions of the printed text of the former.

The next step in investigation was taken by Dr C. H. Turner in a most valuable review in the *Journal of Theological Studies*[7]. He joined issue with Zimmer on one point only, namely his view as to the pseudo-Primasius commentary. This commentary, as we have seen, Zimmer seeks to identify with the first commentary mentioned by Cassiodorus, from which Cassiodorus says he afterwards removed the Pelagian characteristics. Turner rightly objects that the pseudo-Primasius is 'definitely and consciously anti-Pelagian throughout,' and that it is in the commentary on Romans that Pelagius has been specially re-written. He proceeds: 'Pseudo-Primasius is based on Pelagius: if Garnier and the scholars who

[1] My own researches confirm this conclusion; see below, pp. 239 ff.

[2] I should not agree here, except perhaps in a very limited sense.

[3] Zimmer, pp. 268—271.

[4] Except that Rom. i and v 12—21 and Hebr. are copied *in extenso*.

[5] Hardly less than 2000 omissions have been noted.

[6] He tells us that he revised the collation with the original (pp. 449 f.).

[7] Vol. IV (1902—1903) pp. 132—141.

have followed him are right, Cassiodorus revised Pelagius. Pseudo-Primasius is an anti-Pelagian edition of Pelagius: so was that of Cassiodorus. Pseudo-Primasius has revised his original more on the doctrinal than on the linguistic side, more in the Epistle to the Romans than in the other epistles[1]; Cassiodorus, "in order to remove far the error of heresy," purged the Epistle to the Romans with all the *curiositas* that he could, leaving the rest of the revision to his pupils, whose work will doubtless have been much more perfunctory than their master's. Pseudo-Primasius adds to the genuine Pelagius on the thirteen epistles a commentary on the Hebrews, which depends on Chrysostom's Homilies[2]: but it was Cassiodorus who, in order to provide a commentary on an epistle which both Ambrosiaster and Pelagius had neglected, caused a certain Mutianus to translate these Homilies of Chrysostom into Latin[3]. The correspondence appears to be exact: pseudo-Primasius is surely nothing else than the new and standard commentary on the completed Pauline epistles evolved out of Pelagius and Chrysostom by Cassiodorus and his monks of Vivarium[4].'

Though Zimmer had very fully reviewed the mediaeval authorities which made use of Pelagius, there was one at least which escaped him. Zmaragdus, abbot of St Mihiel at the end of the eighth century and the beginning of the ninth, had compiled out of the writings of some twenty authors, whom he names in his preface, a commentary on the lessons read in church, and indicated his borrowings by symbols in the margins. This commentary was published at Strasbourg in 1536, and reprinted in Migne's Latin Patrology, vol. CII, in 1851. In this reprint Dom Pitra had called attention to the fact that Pelagius was one of the authors used and named by Zmaragdus, and Primasius another, and had brought into clear relief some instances of disagreement between his quotations and the pseudo-Jerome. Pitra's work had been overlooked by Zimmer, and the connexion of Zmaragdus with Pelagius was rediscovered about the same time by Riggenbach, Hellmann, Morin, and myself.

[1] Zimmer, p. 122. [2] Zimmer, pp. 183—195. [3] Zimmer, p. 202.

[4] The suggestion with regard to pseudo-Primasius on Hebr., here made by Turner, is mistaken. Pseudo-Primasius on Hebr. is really the work of Haymo of Auxerre, and quotes Cassiodorus by name. Its union, therefore, with the pseudo-Primasius on the other epistles cannot have begun before the ninth century. See below, pp. 321 ff.

Riggenbach, in 1905, published an article pointing out the value of Zmaragdus in this respect[1]. He was able to identify the original editor of Zmaragdus as Caspar Hedio[2]. He very acutely observed, from Pitra's collation of the symbols in a Boulogne MS of Zmaragdus, that the symbol $\overline{\mathrm{P}}$ in the manuscript was used by Zmaragdus only in commenting on the Epistles of Paul, and $\overline{\mathrm{PRI}}$ or $\overline{\mathrm{PR}}$ only in comments on the Apocalypse, and that $\overline{\mathrm{P}}$ therefore means Pelagius, $\overline{\mathrm{PRI}}$ or $\overline{\mathrm{PR}}$ Primasius. He rightly concludes that Zmaragdus knew no Primasius on the Epistles, and that the first editor had resolved the symbol $\overline{\mathrm{P}}$ wrongly, when he took it everywhere to mean Primasius. Riggenbach's paper, though brief, is also in other respects extremely suggestive. He shows that Zmaragdus and pseudo-Primasius agree on occasion in providing a text of Pelagius, which is different from, and obviously better than that provided by either pseudo-Jerome or the St Gall MS[3], and he conjectures that the two last authorities represent a definite recension of the original commentary. He also draws up a very useful list of the quotations in Zmaragdus labelled $\overline{\mathrm{P}}$, as far as he could learn them from Pitra's reports. He has examined some attributions to 'Primas.' in the printed text, and has rejected them on internal evidence. On the whole he was disposed to regard pseudo-Jerome as an abridged form of the original Pelagius. He adds a new glossed MS to the list provided by Zimmer, namely Berlin Codex Phillippicus 1650 (saec. XI ex., formerly of St Vincent at Metz), which introduces some glosses with the letters 'Pel': this MS I also had noted.

Hellmann in his *Sedulius Scottus*, published early in 1906, took occasion to include a careful study of the use of Pelagius made by Sedulius in his own commentary. The value of his work was heightened by the fact that he examined the MSS of Sedulius's work as well as the printed text. He overthrows Zimmer's conten-

[1] 'Unbeachtet gebliebene Fragmente des Pelagius-Kommentars zu den Paulinischen Briefen' (*Beiträge zur Förderung christlicher Theologie* IX 1. Gütersloh). I owe my first knowledge of this paper to the late Rev. Prof. John E. B. Mayor.

[2] One of the lesser Reformers, and Münsterprediger at Strasbourg: see *Corpus Reformatorum* XCIV (1911) p. 213 n.; P. Kalkoff, *W. Capito im Dienste Erzbischof Albrechts von Mainz* (Berlin, 1907) pp. 38 f. etc.

[3] Of course, as reported by Zimmer, from whom *ex silentio* inferences are never safe. Pseudo-Jerome as printed, also, is a very different thing from pseudo-Jerome as textually restored.

tion that the St Gall MS with Sedulius and the Würzburg and Vienna MSS represents the Irish tradition of Pelagius, as against the Continental tradition represented by pseudo-Jerome and pseudo-Primasius, and shows on the contrary that there is a real relationship between the St Gall MS and pseudo-Jerome over against all other authorities for Pelagius[1]. This relationship shows itself in community of corruption, in cases where the true text can be elicited from pseudo-Primasius, Zmaragdus, and Sedulius Scottus. Hellmann handles much material of varying quality with great skill, and makes many suggestive remarks on this difficult subject. He also shows that Isidore of Seville used Pelagius in one form or another[2], that several glossed MSS of St Paul's Epistles contain Pelagian matter (Clm. 9545 [saec. X][3], 18530 [saec. XI—XII], Berlin. theol. fol. 481, Einsiedeln 16, Karlsruhe Augiensis LXXXIII [saec. XI][4]), and that the so-called Pelagian prologues occur—though without his name—in the oldest Vulgate MSS we possess.

I think I have now given some account of every important publication on this subject prior to the appearance of my own earliest article on it (July, 1906). Since about 1904 I had been taking an active interest in the matter, had collated portions of the Bodleian MS of Zmaragdus and certain Pelagian prologues, and had also in 1905 and 1906 put together a tentative list of MSS with some bearing on the problem of the Pelagian commentary[5]. As research proceeded I published a number of articles on special points, as well as two summaries of progress in the *Proceedings of the British Academy*, volumes II (1907) and VII (1916). If I do not at this point chronicle the valuable articles published by other scholars since the summer of 1906, I hope my attitude will not be misunderstood. As these articles have in great part grown out of my own, it seems more suitable to the scheme of the present work to incorporate their results at the proper points in the succeeding chapters.

1 Here again the qualifications stated in the above note, p. 32 n. 3, must be kept in mind.

2 pp. 152, 184.

3 pp. 186—190.

4 p. XV.

5 Published in *Journal of Theological Studies* vol. VII (1905—1906) pp. 568—575.

CHAPTER II

HOW TO IDENTIFY THE PELAGIUS COMMENTARY

FROM the previous chapter it will have been gathered that the Pelagius commentary encountered some strange experiences in the course of its history. To identify it among existing commentaries is a work requiring caution. The method adopted here is to confront the claimants in succession with the quotations made by Augustine and Mercator, these being contemporary or almost contemporary witnesses to its text. Augustine indeed became acquainted with it at least as early as 412, some three years after its completion. The Mercator quotations have a value all their own, though they show some verbal differences from those of Augustine.

The claimants are four in number, Pseudo-Jerome; the text in St Gall MS 73; the text in Paris MS 653; and the text in Karlsruhe, cod. Augiensis, CXIX, and Balliol College, Oxford, MS 157. These authorities will be described in full later. It will be sufficient at this stage to note that Pseudo-Jerome is, as here printed, critically reconstructed from a number of MSS, and not merely copied from a printed edition; that the text of St Gall MS 73 is given according to Zimmer's collation, revised by me with the original; that the Paris MS 653 is an anonymous MS, written in the Veronese district late in the eighth century, containing a long commentary on fourteen Epistles of St Paul; that the Karlsruhe MS was written at Reichenau about the same date and contains a short anonymous commentary on thirteen Epistles of St Paul, while the Balliol MS, an Italian product of the mid-fifteenth century, though it bears the name of Jerome in its title, contains substantially the same commentary as the Karlsruhe MS.

AUGUSTINE

(*De Pecc. Mer. et Rem.* III ii 2 to 'perierunt': iii 5 to 'aliena.' (C.S.E.L. LX pp. 129, 132): cf. viii 15, 16 (p. 141), x 18 (p. 144), *De Pecc. Orig.* XXI 24 (C.S.E.L. XXXXII p. 183), *Epist.* 190, 22 (C.S.E.L. LVII p. 158), *Op. imperf. c. Iulian.* I 56, *c. Iul. Pelag.* VI vii 18)

hi autem qui contra traducem peccati sunt, ita illam impugnare nituntur: 'si Adae,' inquiunt, 'peccatum etiam non peccantibus nocuit, ergo et Christi iustitia etiam non credentibus prodest, quia similiter, immo et magis, dicit per unum saluari, quam per unum ante perierunt.' deinde aiunt: 'si baptismus mundat antiquum illud delictum, qui de duobus baptizatis nati fuerint debent hoc carere peccato; non enim potuerunt ad posteros transmittere quod ipsi minime habuerunt. illud quoque accedit (*most MSS* accidit), quia, si anima non est ex traduce, sed sola caro, ipsa tantum habet traducem peccati, et ipsa sola poenam meretur.' iniustum esse dicentes, ut hodie nata anima non ex massa Adae tam antiquum peccatum portet alienum, dicunt etiam nulla ratione concedi, ut deus, qui propria peccata remittit, imputet aliena.

remittit] dimittit *Epist.* 190.
imp. aliena] unum inp. alienum *Epist.* 190.

PSEUDO-JEROME

in Rom. v 15

hic manifeste docet quia non generaliter de omni homine dicit, dicens: unius delicto multi mortui sunt, quia communi et naturali morte non solum peccantes, sed et iusti moriuntur.

AUGUSTINE

(*De Gestis Pelagii* XVI 39 (C.S.E.L. XXXXII p. 94)) (paraphrastic)

hoc quod scriptum est [Rom. viiii 16], non ex persona Pauli adserit dictum, sed eum uoce interrogantis et redarguentis usum fuisse, cum hoc diceret, tamquam hoc dici utique non deberet.

PSEUDO-JEROME

in Rom. viiii 16

unde intellegitur quia hic interrogantis uoce utitur et redarguentis potius quam negantis.

(*De Pecc. Mer.* III xii 21 (C.S.E.L. LX p. 148)) (paraphrastic)

exempla iam praecesserant et uirorum quos uxores et feminarum quas mariti lucri fecerant Christo et paruulorum ad quos faciendos Christianos uoluntas christiana etiam unius parentis euicerat.

in 1 *Cor.* vii 14

exemplum refert quia saepe contigerit ut lucri fieret uir per mulierem ....saepe enim sic contigerat ut filii illum parentem qui crediderat sequerentur.

While from the second and third (paraphrastic) quotations one might very well conclude that Pseudo-Jerome was the original Pelagius, the first long and exact quotation clearly proves that Pseudo-Jerome cannot be the original Pelagius, for here the two authorities differ entirely. Let us next compare Augustine with St Gall MS 73.

AUGUSTINE

hi autem qui contra traducem peccati sunt, ita illam impugnare nituntur: 'si Adae,' inquiunt, 'peccatum etiam non peccantibus nocuit, ergo et Christi iustitia etiam non credentibus prodest, quia similiter, immo et magis, dicit per unum saluari, quam per unum ante perierunt.' deinde aiunt: 'si baptismus mundat antiquum illud delictum, qui de duobus baptizatis nati fuerint debent hoc carere peccato; non enim potuerunt ad posteros transmittere quod ipsi minime habuerunt. illud quoque accedit (*most MSS* accidit), quia, si anima non est ex traduce, sed sola caro, ipsa tantum habet traducem peccati, et ipsa sola poenam meretur. iniustum esse dicentes, ut hodie nata anima non ex massa Adae tam antiquum peccatum portet alienum, dicunt etiam nulla ratione

ST GALL MS 73

Plus praeualuit iustitia uiuificando quam peccatum in occidendo, quia Adam tantum se et suos posteros interfecit, Christus autem et qui erant tunc in corpore et posteros liberauit. hi autem qui contra traducem peccati sunt, ita illum inpugnari nituntur: 'si Adae,' inquiunt, 'peccatum etiam non peccantibus nocuit, ergo et Christi iustitia etiam non credentibus prodest, quia similiter, immo et magis, dicit per unum saluari quam per unum ante perierunt.' deinde aiunt: 'si baptismum mundat antiquum illud delictum, qui de duobus baptizatis nati fuerint debent hoc carere peccato; non enim potuerunt ad filios transmittere quod ipsi minime habuerunt. illud quoque accidit,

quia, si anima non est ex traduce, sed sola caro, ipsa tantum habet traducem peccati, et ipsa sola poenam meretur. iniustum esse dicentes, ut hodie nata anima non ex massa Adae tam antiquum peccatum portet quam alienum, dicunt etiam nulla ratione concedi, ut deus, qui propria peccata remittit, imputet aliena.

concedi, ut deus, qui propria peccata remittit, inputet aliena. hic manifeste docet quia non generaliter de omni homine dicit dicens: unius delicto multi mortui sunt, quia communi et naturali morti non solum peccantes sed et iusti moriuntur.

(paraphrastic)
(as above, p. 35)

in Rom. viiii 16
(no difference from Ps.-Hier. p. 35)

(paraphrastic)
exempla iam praecesserant et uirorum quos uxores et feminarum quas mariti lucri fecerant Christo et paruulorum ad quos faciendos Christianos uoluntas christiana etiam unius parentis euicerat.

in 1 *Cor.* vii 14
exemplum refert quia saepe contigerit ut lucri fieret (*corr.* lucrificaretur) uir per mulierem.... saepe enim si (*corr.* sic) contigerat ut filii illum parentem qui crediderat sequerentur.

The case here is different from the last. While it is true that there are some slight textual differences between the two columns of text, these are easily explicable: *illum* for *illam* is a palaeographical error; *inpugnari* for *inpugnare* is due to carelessness; *baptismus* would seem to be a correction by Augustine or his scribes of the less pure form *baptismum,* which Pelagius doubtless wrote[1]; *posteros* and the insertion of *quam* are conscious alterations on the part of revisers. But when all these facts are admitted, the St Gall MS still contains the whole passage quoted by Augustine. It also contains the passage which Pseudo-Jerome substitutes or seems to substitute for the original Pelagius, but at this stage, whatever our suspicions may be, we cannot, on the evidence submitted, deny that the St Gall MS may represent the original Pelagius.

AUGUSTINE

PARIS MS 653

Hic manifeste docet quia non generaliter de omne (*sic*) homine dicit, dicens: unius delicto multi mortui sunt, quia communi et naturali morte non solum peccantes, sed et

[1] See below Chap. iii (e) p. 95.

Hi autem, qui contra traducem peccati sunt, ita illam impugnare nituntur: 'si Adae,' inquiunt, 'peccatum etiam non peccantibus nocuit, ergo et Christi iustitia etiam non credentibus prodest, quia similiter, immo et magis, dicit per unum saluari, quam per unum ante perierunt.' deinde aiunt: 'si baptismus mundat antiquum illud delictum, qui de duobus baptizatis nati fuerint debent hoc carere peccato; non enim potuerunt ad posteros transmittere quod ipsi minime habuerunt. illud quoque accedit (*most MSS* accidit), quia, si anima non est ex traduce, sed sola caro, ipsa tantum habet traducem peccati, et ipsa sola poenam meretur.' iniustum esse dicentes, ut hodie nata anima non ex massa Adae tam antiquum peccatum portet alienum, dicunt etiam nulla ratione concedi, ut deus, qui propria peccata remittit, imputet aliena.

iusti moriuntur. [This portion comes after m u l t i m o r t u i s u n t (670 A 3), and is in turn followed by the rest of *Rom.* v 15] then :—

marginal note with reference to *plures* =quia plures inuenit quos seduceret: then *Rom.* v 16 as far as *donum* followed by :—

Plus praeualuit[1] iustitia in uiuificando quam peccatum in occidendo, quia Adam tantum se et suos posteros interfecit, Christus autem et se et qui erant tunc ⟨in⟩ corpore et posteros liberauit. Hii autem, qui contra traducem peccati sunt, ita illam inpugnare nituntur: 'si Adae,' inquiunt, 'peccatum etiam non peccantibus nocuit, ergo et Christi iustitia etiam non credentibus prodest, quia similiter, immo et magis, dicit per unum saluari quam per unum ante perierant.' deinde aiunt: 'si baptismum mundat antiquum illud delictum, qui de duobus baptizatis nati fuerint debent hoc carere peccato; non enim potuerunt ad filios transmittere quod ipsi minime habuerunt. illud quoque accidit,
quia, si anima non est ex traduce, sed sola caro, ipsa tantum habet traducem peccati, et ipsa sola poenam meretur. iniustum esse dicentes, ut hodie nata anima non ex massa Adae tam antiqua peccata portet aliena, asserunt etiam nulla ratione concedi, ut deus, qui propria peccata dimittit, inputet aliena.

Aliter: Adam solam formam fecit delicti, Christus uero et gratis peccata remisit et iustitiae dedit exemplum uiuendi. Aliter: Ostendit maiorem uim esse gratiae quo (*sic*) in se homines trahat, quam peccati, id est, diabuli:

[1] Really p̄∗ualuit.

	nam diabulus Aeuam decepit et per exemplum illius ad alios cucurrit; gratia uero et multos inuenit quos credentes iustificauit, et permultos (*or* per multos) facile in se alios inuitabit.
(paraphrastic)	*in Rom.* viiii 16
(see above, p. 35)	(no difference from Ps.-Hier. p. 35)
(paraphrastic)	*in* 1 *Cor.* vii 14
exempla iam praecesserant et uirorum quos uxores et feminarum quas mariti lucri fecerant Christo et paruulorum ad quos faciendos Christianos uoluntas christiana etiam unius parentis euicerat.	exemplum refert quia saepe contigerit ut lucri fieret uir per mulierem...... sic contigerat ut filii illum parentem qui crediderant sequerentur.

The situation here is not very unlike that in the last case. The long extract quoted by Augustine is found also in this MS, Paris 653. There are a few trifling differences in text; the frequent error *hii* for *hi*, *perierant* for *perierunt*, *baptismum* for *baptismus*, *filios* for *posteros*, *antiqua peccata portet aliena* for *antiquum peccatum portet alienum*, *asserunt* for *dicunt* and *dimittit* for *remittit*[1]. The situation *in Rom.* viiii 16 is identical with what we have found in the documents previously adduced. *In* 1 *Cor.* vii 14 it is also identical, except for the absence of *saepe enim* before *sic contigerat*, and the corruption *crediderant* for *crediderat*. All things considered, we cannot as yet refuse to this document the title to be called Pelagius, though we may well doubt the primary character of a form of the commentary that furnishes in all five notes on this passage, three of which are absent from the two authorities already examined. Moreover, one of these notes, namely that beginning *Adam solam formam fecit*, appears in Pseudo-Jerome at a somewhat later point in the commentary, where also Paris MS 653 has it a second time, namely after the last clause of *Rom.* v 16 (Migne 670 B). We shall now compare our quotations with the anonymous Reichenau MS CXIX and the Balliol College MS 157 together.

[1] Compare the variant in Aug. *Epist.* 190 recorded above, p. 35.

Augustine

hi autem qui contra traducem peccati sunt, ita illam impugnare nituntur: 'si Adae,' inquiunt, 'peccatum etiam non peccantibus nocuit, ergo et Christi iustitia etiam non credentibus prodest, quia similiter, immo et magis, dicit per unum saluari, quam per unum ante perierunt.' deinde aiunt: 'si baptismus mundat antiquum illud delictum, qui de duobus baptizatis nati fuerint debent hoc carere peccato; non enim potuerunt ad posteros transmittere quod ipsi minime habuerunt. illud quoque accedit (*most MSS* accidit), quia, si anima non est ex traduce, sed sola caro, ipsa tantum habet traducem peccati, et ipsa sola poenam meretur.' iniustum esse dicentes, ut hodie nata anima non ex massa Adae tam antiquum peccatum portet alienum, dicunt etiam nulla ratione concedi, ut deus, qui propria peccata remittit, imputet aliena.

(paraphrastic)

Cod. Aug. cxix and Cod. Ball. 157

Plus praeualuit iustitia in uiuificando quam peccatum in occidendo, quia Adam tantum se et suos posteros interfecit, Christus autem et qui erant tunc in corpore et posteros liberauit. hi[1] autem qui contra traducem peccati sunt, ita illam impugnare nituntur: 'si Adae,' inquiunt, 'peccatum etiam non peccantibus nocuit, ergo et Christi iustitia etiam non credentibus prodest, quia similiter, immo et magis, dicit[2] per unum saluari, quam[3] per unum ante perierunt[4].' deinde aiunt: 'si baptismum mundat antiquum illut[5] delictum, qui de duobus baptizatis nati fuerint debent hoc carere peccato; non enim potuerunt ad filios transmittere[6] quod ipsi minime habuerunt. illut quoque accidit, quia, si[7] anima non est ex traduce, sed sola caro, ipsa tantum habet traducem peccati, et ipsa sola paenam[8] meretur.' iniustum esse dicentes, ut hodie nata anima non ex massa Adae tam antiquum peccatum portet alienum, dicunt etiam[9] nulla ratione concedi, ut deus qui propria homini[10] peccata remittit imputet aliena[11].

in Rom. viiii 16

(no difference from Ps.-Hier. p. 35, except that *Ball. om.* et redarguentis)[12].

[1] hii *Ball.* [2] decet *Ball.* [3] qua *Ball.* [4] perierant *Ball.*
[5] Such forms are a specialty of Aug. among my MSS, see p. 208.
[6] trasmittere *Ball.* [7] quia si] quasi *Ball.* [8] poenam *Ball.*
[9] etiam *om. Ball.* [10] homini *om. Ball.*
[11] imputet aliena] aliena imputat *Ball.*
[12] *Aug.* has, after *negantis*, another explanation introduced by the usual *Siue*: see the text ad loc.

(paraphrastic)	*in* 1 *Cor.* vii 14
exempla iam praecesserant et uirorum quos uxores et feminarum quas mariti lucri fecerant Christo et paruulorum ad quos faciendos Christianos uoluntas christiana etiam unius parentis euicerat.	exemplum refert quia saepe contigerit ut lucri fieret uir[1] per mulierem.... saepe enim si[2] contigerat ut filii illorum[3] parentem qui crediderat sequerentur.

Once again we have the important Augustinian quotation completely present, as well as the requisite parallels to the two paraphrastic passages. The Reichenau and Balliol MSS also have therefore a claim to be regarded as Pelagius. A marked difference, however, between this case and that of the rivals, St Gall 73 and Paris 653, lies in the fact that, while the latter two give all that Augustine gives, they give a good deal more than that. The Reichenau and Balliol MSS would therefore, on general grounds of probability, have a better claim than their rivals to represent the original, uninterpolated Pelagius. But, meantime, if this were all our evidence, we could not be absolutely certain as between the different claimants, and it is left to the evidence of Mercator to decide the case between these[4].

A somewhat different method may be adopted on this occasion to save space. Having established a probability that the Reichenau and Balliol MSS represent the original form of the commentary, let us first set out in parallel columns the evidence of Mercator and of these MSS.

MARIUS MERCATOR[5] (References to *cod.* come from a collation kindly made by Dr C. H. Turner.)	REICHENAU AND BALLIOL MSS (*in Rom.* v 12)
per unum hominem peccatum intrauit in mundum, et per peccatum mors.	*propterea sicut per unum hominem*[6] *in hunc mundum peccatum introiit*[7], *et per peccatum mors.*

[1] *sic Aug. m* 2 *ex* tur *Aug. m* 1. [2] *sic etiam Ball.* [3] illum *recte Ball.*

[4] The importance of Mercator's evidence in this connexion first became clear to me on reading an unprinted paper by Dr Armitage Robinson, written about 1890, which he has kindly permitted me to use.

[5] Ed. Baluze, pp. 135 ff., Migne, *P.L.* XLVIII pp. 85—87; see also Garnier's comparison between Mercator and Pseudo-Jerome, pp. 589—593.

[6] These five words are given by the Balliol MS at an earlier point.

[7] intrauit *cod. Aug.*

Exemplo seu imagine usus est; quia sicut, cum non esset peccatum, per Adam subintrauit, sic et, cum non remansisset iustitia apud aliquem, uita per Christum reparata est.

et in omnes homines mors pertransiit.

Cum sic qui peccant, similiter et moriuntur: neque enim aut in Abraham aut[4] Isaac aut[4] Iacob mors pertransiit, de quibus dominus ait: 'hi[6] omnes uiuunt.' hic autem propterea dicit omnes mortuos, quoniam multitudine peccatorum non excipiuntur pauci iusti, sicut et ibi inquit: 'non est qui faciat bonitatem, non est usque ad unum'; et iterum illud inquit: 'omnis homo mendax.' Aut certe in illos omnes pertransiit, qui humano ritu, non caelesti, sunt conuersati.

ET POST PAUCA

1. Exemplo uel forma; quo modo, cum non esset peccatum, per Adam aduenit, ita etiam, cum paene apud nullum iustitia remansisset, per Christum est reuocata.
Et quo modo per illius peccatum mors intrauit, ita et per huius iustitiam uita est reparata[1].

et ita in omnes homines pertransiit[2], *in quo omnes peccauerunt.*

2. Dum ita peccantes[3] similiter moriuntur: non enim in Abraham et Isaac et Iacob[5] pertransiit, de quibus dicit dominus: 'omnes enim illi uiuunt[7].' hic autem ideo dicit omnes mortuos, quia in multitudine[8] peccatorum non excipiuntur[9] pauci iusti, sicut ibi: 'non est qui faciat bonum, non est usque ad unum'; et:
'omnis[10] homo mendax.' Siue: In eos omnes pertransiit, qui humano, non[11] caelesti, ritu[12] uiuebant.

usque ad legem enim peccatum[13] *in hoc*[14] *mundo.*

3. Lex[15] peccati uindex aduenit, ante cuius aduentum peccatores liberius uel praesentis uitae longitudine fruebantur. erat quidem ante legem peccatum, sed non ita putabatur esse peccatum, quia iam paene oblitteratum[16] fuerat in[17] natura. *peccatum autem non imputatur cum lex non est.*

4. Quo modo mors regnauit, si non inputabatur[18] peccatum, nisi subaudias: 'in praesenti,' non inputabatur.

1 ∽ praeparata est *Ball.*
2 mors pertransiit *cod. Aug.*
3 peccant et *cod. Aug.*
4 *add.* in *Garn.*
5 et Iacob *om. Ball.*
6 huic *Garn.*
7 de—uiuunt *om. Ball.*
8 multitudinem *Ball.*
9 non excipiuntur] nuncupantur *Ball.*
10 et omnis *om. Ball.*
11 non] et non *cod. Aug.*
12 more *Aug.*
13 peccatum] *add* erat *cod. Aug.*
14 hoc *om. cod. Aug.*
15 Lex *om. Ball.*
16 paene obliterata *cod. Aug.* poenę oblitterarum *Ball.*
17 in] scientia *cod. Aug.*
18 inputatur *cod. Aug.*

sed regnauit mors ab Adam usque ad Moysem, etiam in eos qui non peccauerunt[3] *in similitudinem praeuaricationis Adae.*

Siue: Cum non esset qui inter iustum et iniustum discerneret, putabat mors se omnium dominari. Siue: In eos qui mandatum tamquam Adam praeuaricati sunt: hoc est, de filiis Noe, quibus praeceptum est ut animam in sanguine non manducarent; et de filiis Abraham, quibus circumcisio mandata est: sed et in eos qui praeter mandatum legem contempserant naturalem.

qui est forma futuri.

Quoniam sicut Adam praeter coitum a deo formatus est, sic et Christus ex[6] uirgine, fabricante spiritu sancto, processit. Siue: Sicut quidam dicunt, forma a contrario; hoc est, ut[8] sicut ille caput peccati, sic[9] iste caput iustitiae est (sit *cod.*).

sed non sicut delictum, ita et donum.

Ne in forma aequalitas putaretur.

si enim in unius praeuaricatione multi mortui sunt, multo magis dono[11] *et gratia dei per unum hominem Christum in multos abundauit.*

Plus ualuit gratia in uiuificando quam peccatum in occidendo, quia Adam se[12] solum et[13] suos posteros interfecit, Christus uero et eos qui tunc erant in corpore, et eos (hos *cod.*) qui postea futuri erant, liberauit.

Hi autem, qui contra traducem peccati sentiunt, aliter[14] eos qui defendunt traducem impugnare conantur:

sed regnauit mors ab Adam usque ad Mosen, et[1] *in eos qui*[2] *peccauerunt in similitudine*[4] *praeuaricationis Adae.*

5. Siue: Dum non esset qui inter iustum et iniustum ante distingueret, putabat se omnibus dominari. Siue: Non solum in eos qui praeceptum sicut Adam transgressi sunt: hoc est, de filiis Noe, quibus iussum est ne animam in sanguine[5] manducarent; et de filiis Habrahae, quibus circumcisio mandata est: sed etiam in eos qui sine praecepto legem contempsere naturae.

qui est forma futuri.

6. Siue: Ideo forma fuit Christi, quia sicut Adam sine coitu a deo factus est, ita ille ex uirgine, spiritu sancto operante, processit[7]. Siue: Ut quidam dicunt forma a contrario; hoc est, sicut ille peccati caput, ita et iste iustitiae.

sed non sicut delictum, ita et gratia[10].

7. Ne in forma aequalitas putaretur.

si enim unius delicto multi mortui sunt, multo magis gratia dei et donum in gratia unius hominis Iesu Christi in plures abundauit.

8. Plus praeualuit iustitia in uiuificando quam peccatum in occidendo, quia Adam tantum se et suos posteros interfecit, Christus autem et qui erant tunc in corpore et posteros liberauit.

Hi autem, qui contra traducem peccati sunt, ita illam impugnare nituntur:

[1] etiam *cod. Aug.* [2] qui non *cod. Aug.*
[3] praeuaricauerunt *Garn. fort. recte.* [4] similitudinem *cod. Aug.*
[5] sanguinem *Ball.* [6] a *Garn.* [7] processit operante *Ball.*
[8] ut *om. Garn.* [9] sic] sic etiam *Garn.* [10] donum *cod. Aug.*
[11] donum *Garn.* [12] se] non se *Garn.* [13] et] sed et *Garn.*
[14] acriter *Garn.*

'si peccatum,' inquit[1], 'Adae etiam non peccantibus nocuit, ergo et Christi iustitia non credentibus prodest, quoniam similiter, immo plus, dicit apostolus per unum liberari quam per unum ante perierunt[4].' deinde dicunt: 'si baptismus mundat antiquum illud ueternosumque peccatum, qui de duobus baptizatis nati fuerint, debent hoc carere peccato; non enim potuerunt[6] ad posteros transmittere quod ipsi minime habuerunt[7].' in hoc addunt quoniam, 'si anima non est ex[8] traduce (*sicut nec est*), sed sola caro habet traducem peccati, sola et poenam meretur.' iniustum est enim ut hodie nata anima non ex massa Adae tam antiquum peccatum portet alienum, quia nec[10] rationabile est ut deus, qui propria peccata dimittit, unum[12] imputet alienum.

'si Adae,' inquiunt, 'peccatum etiam non peccantibus nocuit, ergo et Christi iustitia etiam non credentibus prodest, quia similiter, immo et magis, dicit[2] per unum saluari quam[3] per unum ante perierant[5].' deinde aiunt: 'si baptismum mundat antiquum illud delictum, qui de duobus baptizatis nati fuerint, debent hoc carere peccato; non enim potuerunt ad filios transmittere quod ipsi minime habuerunt.' illud quoque accidit quia, 'si[9] anima non est ex traduce, sed sola caro, ipsa tantum habet traducem peccati, et ipsa sola poenam meretur.' iniustum esse dicentes ut hodie nata anima non ex massa Adae tam antiquum peccatum portet alienum, dicunt etiam[11] nulla ratione concedi ut deus, qui propria[13] peccata remittit, imputet aliena[14].

A study of the contents of these parallel columns is instructive in various ways. The evidence of Mercator is more important in regard to matter than text. It must be remembered that the *Commonitorium super nomine Caelestii*, from which these quotations are taken, was composed by its author in Greek, and afterwards translated by the author himself into Latin[15]. He need not have turned up afresh the places in his copy of Pelagius's commentary, in order to give the *ipsissima uerba*, and he does not appear to have done so. The differences from Pelagius's exact words are just such as might readily have emerged in such a process.

There is only one difficulty about these quotations, and that is the short passage in the first note, from 'Et quo modo' down to 'est reparata.' Either Mercator or his scribes have, intentionally

[1] inquiunt, *Garn. recte.* [2] decet *Ball.* [3] qua *Ball.*
[4] perierat *Garn.* [5] perierunt *cod. Aug.* [6] poterunt *Garn.*
[7] habuerint *Garn.* [8] ex est *Baluze, a misprint.*
[9] quia si] quasi *Ball.* [10] quia nec] quin et *Garn.* [11] etiam *om. Ball.*
[12] unum] non *Garn.* [13] propria] *add.* homini *Aug.* [14] aliena imputat *Ball.*
[15] Cf. Teuffel, *Gesch. der röm. Lit.*[6] III (Leipz. 1913) § 456 (1); Zimmer, pp. 254 f., see above, p. 4 n. 3; Schanz, *Gesch. d. röm. Litt.* IV (2) München (1920) p. 481.

or accidentally, omitted these words. They are certainly not of material importance, being somewhat of a repetition of the preceding sentence: but on the whole it seems more probable that we have here to do with a scribal error at some stage or other.

If the rest of the columns be compared, the result is strongly in favour of the Reichenau and Balliol MSS, as representing the original form of the commentary. For it will be observed that the comments proceed in the identical order in both columns, and that in one place where 'pauca' are indeed omitted, Mercator is careful to put the words 'et post pauca,' showing that there, and there alone, he has omitted something that was not germane to his purpose. It is here that the rival MSS St Gall 73 and Paris 653 fail us, because, if Mercator's citations be compared with the commentary given in either of these, it will be found that 'pauca' are omitted by Mercator in more than one place. The same is true of the Pseudo-Jerome form, as can be readily seen from Garnier's parallel columns[1]; but it is not necessary for us to take any further account of Pseudo-Jerome's claims to be the original Pelagius, because these have already been disallowed as the result of our examination of the Augustinian quotations.

In St Gall MS 73 the following parts are found which are absent alike from Mercator and from the Reichenau and Balliol MSS.

At the end of § 1 (reparata):—

futura, non praesens.

At the end of § 2 (uiuebant):—

Item: Nunc apostolus mortem animae significat, quia Adam preuaricans mortuus est[2], sicut et propheta dicit: anima quae peccat ipsa morietur: transiuit enim et in omnes homines, qui per naturalem legem preuaricati sunt.

In quo omnes peccauerunt. Hoc est: in eo quod omnes peccauerunt, exemplo Adae peccant.

At the end of § 3 (in natura):—

Item: Dicens 'usque ad legem,' Moysi significat legem: inferens autem 'peccatum non inputatur cum lex non est,' naturalem iterum ostendit legem, per quam preuaricatus est Cain, et post ipsum qui naturalem legem preuaricati sunt.

At the end of § 5 (contempsere naturae):—

[1] Migne, *P.L.* XLVIII pp. 589—593.

[2] est (*or* et) *above the line.*

Etiam in eos qui non peccauerunt in similitudinem praeuaricationis Adae. Hii sunt qui non in similitudine preuaricationis Adae peccauerunt, qui per naturalem legem transgressi sunt, et non sicut Adam per mandatum.

At the end of § 6 (iste iustitiae):—

Item: Forma Christi Adam factus est: sicut enim Adam primus mandatum dei preuaricans exemplum est legem dei preuaricari uolentibus, sic et Christus uoluntatem patris conplens exemplum est imitari cupientibus eum.

At the end of § 8 (imputet aliena):—

Hic manifeste docet quia non generaliter de omni homine dicit dicens: 'unius delicto multi mortui sunt,' quia communi et naturali morti non solum peccantes sed et iusti moriuntur.

Thus, leaving out of account the extract last given, there are five more instances of 'pauca' in this MS than there are in the Reichenau and Balliol MSS, but of these five passages there is not a word in Mercator.

Let us next take the case of Paris MS 653. In it the following notes are found, which are present neither in Mercator nor in the Reichenau-Balliol group.

At the end of § 1 (reparata):—

Aliter: Nunc apostolus animae mortem significat, quia Eua praeuaricans mortua est, sicut et propheta Ezechiel dicit: 'anima, quae peccat, ipsa morietur': transiuit enim et in omnes homines, qui naturalem legem praeuaricati sunt. (Then follows § 2[1], preceded by its scripture text.)

At the end of § 2 (uiuebant):—

exemplo inoboedientiae.

In quo omnes peccauerunt. In quo, inobedientiae peccato. Siue: In Adam omnium peccantium paena est praemonstrata: hoc est, in eo quod omnes peccauerunt.

After 'fruebantur' in § 3:—

Aliter: Dicens 'usque ad legem,' Mosi significat legem: inferens autem 'peccatum non imputatur cum lex non est,' naturalem iterum ostendit legem, per quam praeuaricatus est Cain, et post ipsum qui naturalem legem praeuaricati sunt.

[1] Certain interesting differences of text which separate this form from all other authorities, need not be mentioned here, but see pp. 37 ff.

After *Adam* in the lemma of § 5:—

'Adam': id est, homo; hominis autem nomen tam uiro quam etiam feminae conuenit; scriptum est enim 'et benedixit illis, et uocauit nomen eorum Adam in die qua creati sunt[1].'

After *Moysen* in the lemma of § 5:—

Quidam dicunt: 'usque ad finem Moysi; id est, legis.'

After the end of the lemma of § 5 :—

Hi sunt, qui non in similitudine praeuaricationis Adae peccauerunt, qui per naturalem legem transgressi sunt, et non, sicut Adam, per mandatum.

Aliter: 'Hic est liber generationis Adam. in die qua creauit deus hominem, ad similitudinem dei fecit illum: masculum et feminam creauit eos, et benedixit eos. et uocauit nomen eorum Adam in die qua creati sunt[2].'

Item aliter: De superiore sententia.

At the end of § 6 (iustitiae):—

Aliter: Forma Christi Adam factus est: sicut enim Adam, mandatum dei per Euam praeuaricans, exemplum est legem dei praeuaricare uolentibus, sic et Christus, uoluntatem patris conplens, exemplum est imitari eum desiderantibus.

At the end of § 7 (putaretur):—

Aliter: Omnis apostoli sensus hic est, ut dicat plus egisse gratiam per Christum quam per diabulum Aeue subreptum fuisse.

With reference to *multi* in the lemma of § 8,
a marginal note says: non ergo omnes.

After *mortui sunt* in the lemma of § 8:—

Hic manifeste docet quia non generaliter de omne homine dicit, dicens: 'unius delicto multi mortui sunt,' quia communi et naturali morte non solum peccantes, sed et iusti moriuntur.

With reference to *plures* in the lemma of § 8,
a marginal note says: quia plures inuenit quos seduceret.

At the end of the lemma of § 8 :—

et non, sicut per unum peccantem, ita et donum.

At the end of § 8 (imputet aliena):—

Aliter: Adam solam formam fecit delicti, Christus uero et gratis peccata remisit et iustitiae dedit exemplum uiuendi.

Aliter: Ostendit maiorem uim esse gratiae quo in se homines

[1] Gen. v 2. [2] Gen. v 1—2.

trahat, quam peccati, id est, diabuli: nam diabulus Aeuam decepit, et per exemplum illius ad alios cucurrit, gratia uero et multos inuenit, quos credentes iustificauit, et permultos facile in se alios inuitabit.

In the case of Paris MS 653, the differences are even more glaring than in St Gall MS 73. There are in this MS, leaving out of account the extra lemma given above, and the notes at the end of § 8, eleven portions, not one of which is present either in Mercator or in the Reichenau and Balliol MSS. However interesting and even venerable the extra notes in Pseudo-Jerome, St Gall MS 73 and Paris MS 653 may be, it is now clear that they are no part of *the original form of Pelagius's commentary, which exists untouched in no known documents save the Reichenau and Balliol MSS*[1]. Of this discovery further confirmation will be adduced in the sequel.

THE VATICAN FRAGMENTS

Mgr Giovanni Mercati discovered in the Vatican Library about 1905 or 1906 two leaves of a sixth century MS in half-uncial writing[2]. This MS had become mutilated, and was further broken up to be used as guard-leaves at least as early as the eleventh or twelfth century. 'The leaves are mutilated, scribbled over and cut down, and part of the blame must rest on the nineteenth-century binder who separated them unskilfully from some unknown MS or printed book, with damage to some letters.'

'The two leaves are conjugate, but not consecutive[3], and contain (with *lacunae*) part of the Pelagian commentary on Rom. vii 9—15, viii 3—8, in a much briefer recension than that published in Migne, *P.L.* xxx (ed. 1846) 676 D—677 D, 680 A—D (=702 C—703 D, 706 B—707 A of the edition of 1865).' The conclusion to which Mercati came as to the length of the gap between the two leaves is con-

[1] The Merton MS 26 is left out of account, as it is a copy of the Balliol MS: see pp. 223 ff.

[2] See his article in the *Journal of Theological Studies* vol. VIII (1906—1907) pp. 529—535, with a supplementary note by the present writer, pp. 535 f. The words in inverted commas are quoted from this article. I have to thank him for rotographs of the pages.

[3] In fact, the third and sixth of a quaternion, Mercati on p. 531.

firmed by the Reichenau and Balliol MSS. The 'recension' is, in fact, identical with that in the Reichenau and Balliol MSS, while the scriptural lemmata approximate more to those in the latter. 'It is remarkable that the passages omitted are, as it were, so many alternative interpretations introduced by *item*, all of which can well be detached; and when they are detached the residue forms a well connected whole, noteworthy alike in style and doctrine. And the doctrine is Pelagian at Rom. vii 8.'

The MS in fact, when complete, must have been closely related to a contemporary ancestor of the Balliol MS. For proof of this readers are referred to my critical apparatus.

The arrangement of text and commentary in these venerable fragments is a matter of some consequence, and hence one page is reproduced here. The reader is referred to Dr Mercati's article for the evidence that this arrangement is maintained throughout. Letters with a dot under them survive only in part: lost letters are in italics.

(I *a*)

(*P.L.* XXX 702 C fin.) (Rom. vii. 9—13)

per scientiam naturalẹ*m et*
mortuum fuerat per oblị*uionem*
ideo dicitur reuixisse per l*egem*
(*v.* 10) ego autem mortuus sum qui ṣ*ci*
ens praeuaricaui.
et inuentum est mihi mandạ*tum*
quod erat in uita hoc esse in ṃ*orte*
quod custoditum proficieḅ*at ad*
uitam neglectum duxit a*d mortem*
(*v.* 11) nam peccatum occasione a*ccepta*
per mandatum seduxit me[1] e*t per*
(*v.* 12) illud occidit me · itaque lex q*uidem*
s̅c̅a̅ · et mandatum s̅c̅m̅ · et iuṣ*tum*
et bonum · contra inpugnaṭ*ores*
legis · et contra eos qui iustit*iam*
a bonitate secernunt · lex · *et s̅c̅a̅*

[1] me *cancelled.*

et bona dicitur · et gratia ius*ta*
nisi enim abundauerit iustị*tia*
uestra · sed et ds̄ · non numqu*am*
in ueteri bonus · et in nouo di*citur*
iustus · pater iuste ait dn̄s · h*ç *con*
tra marcioniṭ*as******

(*v.* 13) quọḍ ẹṛgọ ḅ*onum****.

The meaning of this arrangement is that scripture lemmata were always begun a little to the left of the vertical line bounding the left edge of the comments, and as a rule the comments throughout were bounded by a vertical line a little to the right of that bounding the lemmata. In this way one could more readily turn to a particular passage, the difference between text and comment being graphically represented. But still more important for our purpose is the knowledge that the arrangement was that a short extract of scripture should be followed by a short note underneath it, by a *subnotatio* in fact. Pelagius himself at *in Col.* iii 19, *sicut ad Ephesios plenius* subnotatum *est,* shows what his arrangement was. It is confirmed by the Reichenau MS, the Balliol MS for the most part, one family of Pseudo-Jerome MSS, Cassiodorus, etc., and though it is quite true that some MSS suggest a 'packing' of scripture text, for example in Philippians, that is clearly at variance with the general practice, and therefore secondary. Whatever others may have done after him, Pelagius did not insert his comments between the lines in a manuscript of the Apostle, bût copied out almost the whole of the Epistles, clause by clause, comment by comment, clause and comment alternating throughout.

The page we have copied from the Roman MS can be used also to prove in some detail that the MS when complete, was of the same content as the Reichenau and Balliol[1] MSS. Following our previous method, and taking each claimant in turn, we have the following result. On this occasion we can include Pseudo-Jerome, lest any lingering doubts as to its character should remain.

St Gall MS 73 and Ps.-Hier. add the following:—

At the end of l. 9 (ad mortem):—

Item: Poenae mortem dicit, quam nobis peccatum per decep-

[1] With the slight qualification mentioned in chap. vi p. 212.

tionem suam adquisiuit, ostendens temporalia et terrena, quae putantur esse bona, et legem praeuaricare(-i) suadens [illud peccatum], quae [et] uitam aeternam facientibus [re]promittit.

Paris MS 653 adds the following:—

At the end of l. 5 (praeuaricaui):—

Et iam nunc multi sunt Christiani, qui crimina sola putant esse peccata: si ea non fecerint uiuere se arbitrantur. sed cum eis ostensum fuerit et illa grauia esse quae faciunt, statim mortuos se esse cognoscunt.

Aliter: (then follows the explanation concluded in ll. 1—3 of the page of the Roman MS).

At the end of l. 9 (ad mortem):—

Aliter: Poene mortem dicit, qua nobis peccatum per deceptionem suam adquisiuit, ostendens temporalia et terrena, quae putantur esse bona, et legem praeuaricari suadens, quae uitam aeternam facientibus promittit.

After 'occidit' in l. 12, the MS being without 'me':—

Dum non solum peccato delector, sed etiam mandatum contemno.

For ll. 14—16 (contra—lex et) has:—

Contra Manicheos, qui uetus testamentum inpugnant. Et lex

After 'Marcionitas' in l. 22:—

et ceteros (and then ll. 14—16, as in Roman text).

It is hardly necessary to remark that not one of the additions in these authorities is to be found either in the Reichenau or in the Balliol MS.

Interpolation in Certain MSS of Ambrosiaster on First and Second Corinthians

Probably few manuscripts of Ambrosiaster have the genuine conclusion to the commentary on First Corinthians and the genuine beginning to that on Second Corinthians, but among these are the manuscripts of Troyes (432, saec. IX—X), Cologne (XXXIV, saec. X)[1], Cheltenham (518, saec. XV in. written in the Low Countries), and Petrograd (F. v. I No. 17, saec. XI, formerly of St Benignus, Dijon)[2].

[1] For these MSS see *Journ. Theol. Stud.* IV (1902—1903) p. 90.

[2] Father Brewer, S.J., the future editor, has found some others, not here given. Claudius of Turin's copy of Ambrosiaster also was of this kind.

The bulk of the manuscripts have an interpolation at this point. Even the oldest, that of Monte Cassino, 150, written in a semi-uncial hand before the year 569, contains the interpolation in place of the original text[1]. In fact the Benedictine editor was the first to publish the true text, though he strangely omitted to publish the true prologue to Second Corinthians[2]. What had happened was that, at least as early as the middle of the sixth century, an anonymous MS of the Ambrosiaster had been accidentally or intentionally mutilated at that point. When it became necessary to copy that mutilated manuscript, the loss was observed, and was made good from another commentary. The resulting composite manuscript had a large progeny. What I will proceed to show is that the commentary used was an *uninterpolated* Pelagius[3].

Without attempting to examine all the MSS of Ambrosiaster containing the interpolation, I have yet endeavoured to construct a critical text of it by the aid of some of the MSS, particularly the Monte Cassino MS, and certain MSS at Paris[4]. The Paris MSS in the order of quality are:—1759 (saec. IX in.), 1761 (saec. IX—X, of North-Italian provenance), 13,339 (saec. IX). The second MS is the earlier Colbertinus of the Benedictines[5]. The result of the critical process is to give us practically a fragment of another sixth century MS of the original form of Pelagius.

In place of *in* 1 *Cor*. XV 44—*in* 2 *Cor*. i 6, Migne *P.L.* XVII

[1] On this MS, see the literature in *Study of Ambrosiaster* pp. 14 f., and add facss. 53 and 60 in Zangemeister-Wattenbach's *Exempla*; 23 c in Steffens' *Lateinische Paläographie*[2]; *Spicilegium Casinense* vol. III (2) (1901), complete text; E. A. Lowe, *Beneventan Script* (Oxford, 1914) p. 264.

[2] Published by the present writer from collations of two MSS, lent by Father Brewer, in *Journ. Theol. Stud.* IV (1902—1903) pp. 89—92.

[3] The Benedictine editor had of course observed the connexion with Pseudo-Jerome (cf. Migne, XVII 283 D, 284 B, a note on 1 Cor. XV 44): cf. also Vallarsi (and Migne) on Ps.-Hier. ad loc.

[4] The earlier acquired Paris MSS of Ambrosiaster's commentary are accidentally omitted from the index to the old catalogue (Paris, 1744), and are thus absent from my list in *Study of Ambst.* pp. 14 ff. I ought, however, to have remembered P. Corssen's *Epistula ad Galatas* (Berol. 1885) p. 36. See the next note.

[5] See ed. Venet. IV (1751) 779 for a list of the MSS used by them. MS 1759 contains Rom., 1, 2 Cor.; 1760 (saec. X) contains Rom.; 1761 contains Rom. (last part), 1, 2 Cor., Gal., Eph., Phil., 1, 2 Thess., Col., Tit., 1, 2 Tim., Philem.; 1762 (saec. XII) contains Rom.; 1763 (saec. XIII) contains all: *ed. Rom.* below means the Cologne reprint of the Roman edition of Ambrose (t. III [1616] pp. 193 G ff.).

269 B (284 B of reprint)—277 A (292 B of reprint) these MSS and older editions have the following:—

Non enim corpus animale semper hic habere potest spiritum sanctum. tunc uero, id est in resurrectione, semper manebit in sanctis. *Surget corpus spiritale.* Quod possit ire obuiam Christo. *Sicut scriptum est: Factus est primus homo Adam in animam uiuentem; nouissimus Adam in spiritum uiuificantem.* Notandum est quod, cum duos Adam dicit, eiusdem naturae utrosque demonstrat: quod contra Manicheos et Apollinaristas facit, qui negant a dei uerbo perfectum hominem esse susceptum. *Sed non prius quod spiritale est, sed quod animale; deinde quod spiritale. primus homo de terra terrenus, secundus homo de caelo caelestis. qualis terrenus, tales et terreni.* Caelestis dicitur, quia non humanae fragilitatis ritu, sed diuinae maiestatis nutu et conceptus est et enixus: nam usque adeo naturam nostri habuit, ut secundus Adam dicatur et homo. *Et qualis caelestis, tales et caelestes.* Si ideo, ut heretici uolunt, nostri generis adsumptus homo non fuit qui caelestis dicitur, ergo nec isti naturae nostrae sunt qui caelestes appellantur: si uero de his nemo dubitat, nec de illo est ambigendum. *Igitur, sicut portauimus imaginem illius terreni, portemus et imaginem huius caelestis.* Peccator imaginem Adae portat; iustus uero imaginem Christi: ergo, sicut portauimus ueterem hominem ante baptismum, ita et post baptismum portemus nouum. *Hoc autem dico, fratres, quoniam caro et sanguis regnum dei non possidebunt, neque corruptio incorruptelam possidebit.* Frequenter scriptura carnem pro operibus nominat carnis, ut ibi: uos autem in carne non estis, sed in spiritu. Aliter: Caro, sicut est, regnum dei non possidebit nisi inmortalitate uestita. *Ecce mysterium dico.* Obscuritatem significat nominando mysterium. *Omnes quidem resurgemus, non omnes inmutabimur.* Omnes autem homines resurgent, sed soli, qui regnaturi sunt, in gloriam mutabuntur. Siue: Ita omnes resurgemus, qui in aduentu Christi mortui inueniemur. non omnes inmutabuntur qui in corpore sint reperti, quia sancti soli beati-

3. surgit *Cas.* 7. a *om. Cas.* 11. quia] qui *ed. Rom.* 15. dicatur *Cas.* 18. portabimus *Cas.* 26. inmortaliter *Cas.* mysterium] *add.* uobis *ed. Rom.* (=vg.). 28. omnes (*pr.*)] *add.* autem *ed. Rom.* autem] enim *ed. Rom.* resurgimus *Cas.* + sed *Cas.* 29. resurgimus *Cas.* 30. inuenimur *Cas.* 31. ∽ soli sancti *ed. Rom.* (*c. nostro cod. Spinal. Ps.-Hier.*).

tudinis gloriam consequentur. *In momento, in ictu oculi.* Per ictum oculi nimiam breuitatem uult significare momenti, ut quanta sit dei potentia, ex resurrectionis celeritate cognoscas. *In nouissima tuba et mortui resurgent incorrupti et nos inmutabimur.* Nouissimus aduentus intellegitur Christi; mortui autem uel peccatores intellegendi sunt, qui etiam uiuentes mortui esse dicuntur, ut ad poenam aut inmortales aut absque aliqua membrorum diminutione resurgant. uel certe simpliciter omnes mortuos resurgere dicit, et solos sanctos cum his, qui uiui iusti inuenti fuerint, in gloriam inmutari. *Oportet enim corruptibile hoc.* Necesse est fieri quod promissum est. *Induere incorruptionem et mortale hoc induere inmortalitatem.* Est quod induit, et est similiter indumentum. *Cum autem mortale hoc induerit inmortalitatem, tunc fiet sermo, qui scriptus est: Absorta est mors in uictoria.* Ut euacuatis causis mortis per diuinam uictoriam ac si absorta non pereat. *Ubi est, mors, stimulus tuus? ubi est, mors, uictoria tua?* Propheta ex persona iustorum loquitur insultantium morti. *Stimulus autem mortis est peccatum.* Sagitta mortis peccatum, per quod animae iugulantur. *Uirtus uero peccati lex.* Dum fortius et maius fit per scientiam peccatum. *Deo autem gratias, qui dedit nobis uictoriam per dominum nostrum Iesum Christum.* Uictoriam illius peccati, in quo lex per carnalem nostram uoluntatem fuerat infirmata, quam Christus cruce et exemplo destruxit. *Itaque, fratres mei.* Reddita resurrectionis ratione, de qua haesitabant, hortatur eos in dei opere permanere, iam certos de retributione futura. *Stabiles estote et inmobiles, abundantes in opere domini semper, scientes quod labor uester non est inanis in domino.* Nemo uos de gradu spei futurae ultra permoueat. *Nam de collectis quae fiunt in sanctos, sicut ordinaui ecclesiae(-is) Galatiae, ita et uos facite.* De sumptibus dicit, qui per singulas ecclesias collecti Hierosolymam sanctis pauperibus mittebantur. *Per unam sabbati.* Una sabbati

35. tuba] *add.* canet enim tuba *ed. Rom.* (=vg. Clem.) 37. etiam] iam *Cas.* ut ad poenam aut] aut quia *ed. Rom.* 38. aut (*alt.*)] aut quia *ed. Rom.* resurgant] resurgent ad poenam, dicuntur resurgere incorrupti *ed. Rom.* 40. his] iis *ed. Rom.* 42. incorruptelam *Cas. ed. Rom.* (=vg.). Est] Et *ed. Rom.* 43 et] *add.* quod induitur *ed. Rom.* 46. pereat *cod. un. ed. Rom.* pareat *codd. cet.* stimulus] aculeus *ed. Rom.* (*sic* 44). 47. insultantium *Cas.* insultando *cett.* 48 ∽ peccatum est *ed. Rom.* (=vg.). 52. nostra *ed. Rom.* 53. cruce] crucis *ed. Rom.* et *om. codd. plerique* (*add. unus cum Cas.*) *ed. Rom.* 59. ecclesiae *Cas. al.* 61. Una] Unam *Cas.*

dominica dies est, sicut in euangelio dicit[ur] dominum una sabbati resurrexisse. *Unus quisque uestrum apud se recondens quod ei bene placuerit, ut non cum uenero, tunc collectae fiant.* Ut paulatim reseruantes non una hora grauari se putent, ut hilares datores diligantur a deo. *Cum autem fuero praesens, quoscumque probaueritis per epistulam, hos mittam perferre gratiam uestram Hierusalem: quod si dignum fuerit ut et ego eam, mecum ibunt.* Per se clarum est quia utrumque in eorum arbitrio derelinquit, ut et quod dederint portetur, et per quos direxerint ipsi eant. *Ueniam autem ad uos, cum Macedoniam pertransiero: nam Macedoniam pertransibo nisi uos me duxeritis quocumque iero. nolo enim uos nunc in transitu uidere: spero enim me aliquantum temporis mansurum apud uos, si dominus permiserit.* Quia ita se agunt Macedones, ut non sit necesse mihi apud eos diutius remorari: apud uos autem necesse est ut maneam uel hiemem; multa enim sunt quae corrigantur a uobis, sicut medicus ibi moram habet ubi plures aegrotant. *Manebo autem Ephesi usque ad pentecosten: ostium autem mihi apertum est magnum et euidens, sed aduersarii multi.* Ideo ibi permanebo, quia cum mihi euidens datus sit aditus praedicandi, sunt plurimi qui resistant. *Si autem uenerit Timotheus, uidete ut sine timore sit apud uos, quia opus domini operatur, sicut et ego: nequis illum spernat.* Sine tribulationis formidine uel etiam uestri contemptus. *Deducite autem illum in pace, ut ueniat ad me: exspecto enim illum cum fratribus.* Nihil admittentes quod ad animi eius proficiat laesionem. *De Apollo autem fratre notum uobis facio, quia multum illum rogaui uenire ad uos cum fratribus, et utique non fuit uoluntas ut nunc ueniret: ueniet autem cum oportunum fuerit. uigilate, state in fide, uiriliter agite et confortamini: omnia uestra in caritate fiant.* Uigilate mentis oculis ad diaboli astutias praecauendas: state, quia stantibus difficile somnus obrepit: uiriliter

62. dicit *Cas. ed. Rom.* 63. surrexisse *Cas. ed. Rom.* 65. diliguntur *ed. Rom.* 67. Hier.] *praem.* in *ed. Rom.* (=vg.). 68. et *Cas. om. cett.* ibunt] uenient *ed. Rom.* 71. Macedoniam *alt.*] machedonia *Cas.* nisi—duxeritis] Apud uos autem forte manebo, aut etiam hiemabo: ut uos me deducatis *ed. Rom.* (*ad* vg *prope accedit*). 72. dux.] dedux. *Cas.* 75. remorari *Cas.* remanere *cett.* autem *Cas. om. cett.* 77. uobis] nobis *ed. Rom.* 78. autem] *om. unus cod.*; enim *ed. Rom.* (=vg.). 79. quia] qui *ed. Rom.* 81. resistunt *ed. Rom.* 82. apud] inter *un. cod. ed. Rom. fort. recte.* 87. uoluntas] *add.* eius *ed. Rom.* 89. et *om. Cas.* in] cum *Cas. et alius, un. cod. ed. Rom.* 91. obrepit *Cas. ed. Rom.*, obripit *cett.*

agite; muliebris enim omnis inconstantia et uarietas iudicatur: confortamini; ut sit in uestra uirtute profectus, omnia non inanis gloriae causa, sed caritatis gratia facere festinate. *Obsecro autem uos, fratres, nostis domum Stefanae et Fortunati et Achaici, quoniam sunt primitiae Achaiae, et in ministerium sanctorum se ordinauerunt, ut et uos subiecti sitis talibus et omni cooperanti et laboranti in uobis. gaudeo autem in praesentia Stefanae et Fortunati et Achaici, quoniam id quod uobis deerat, ipsi adimpleuerunt.* Quia praesentes sunt apud uos et in illis magnum potestis habere profectum. Siue: Quia mihi uenerunt pro uobis ministrare officium caritatis. *Refecerunt autem et meum spiritum et uestrum.* Meum spiritum caritate pro uobis, uestrum pro mea laetitia [meum] refecerunt. *Cognoscite ergo huius modi.* Unde et alibi ait: cognoscite eos, qui ita ambulant, ut habetis formam nostram. hic 'cognoscite' honorate cognoscentes eorum studium uel laborem. *Salutant uos ecclesiae Asiae. salutant uos in domino Aquila multum et Priscilla cum ea quae in domo eorum est ecclesia, apud quos etiam hospitor.* Domesticam congregationem fraternitatis ecclesiam nominauit. *Salutant uos fratres omnes; salutate inuicem in osculo sancto. salutatio mea manu Pauli. siquis non amat dominum nostrum Iesum Christum, sit anathema.* Sicut illis, qui eum amant, redemptio uenturus est Christus, ita qui eum non amant anathemabit; id est, ut illos abominetur et perdat. *Marana tha.* Magis Syrum est quam Hebreum, tam etsi ex confinio utrarumque linguarum aliquid Hebreum sonat, et interpretatur 'dominus noster uenit.' *Gratia domini nostri uobiscum.* Propriae manus consueta subscriptio. *Caritas mea cum omnibus uobis.* Ut quo modo uos ego diligo, ita et in Christo inuicem diligatis. *In Christo Iesu.* Non secundum saeculi caritatem. *Amen.* Confirmatio est benedictionis hic sermo, sicut superius ipse demonstrat quomodo, inquiens, dicit *Amen* super tuam benedictionem?

92. muliebris *Cas. ed. Rom.*, mulieris *cett.* 102. autem] enim *ed. Rom.* (=vg.). Meum—meum] Pro charitate uestrum, pro laetitia meum spiritum *ed. Rom.* Meum spiritum *om. un. cod.* meume *alt. om. Cas. et alii codd.* 104. huius modi] qui huius modi sunt *ed. Rom.* (cf. vg.). et *om. Cas. ed. Rom.* 105. cognoscite] *add.* id est *ed. Rom.* 111. nostrum *om. ed. Rom.* (=vg.). 113. anathemabit] anathema sit *Cas. ed. Rom.* 115. tam etsi ex confinio] tamen (=*Cas.*) ex sermone *ed. Rom.* utrumque *Cas.* 118. ego diligo *Cas. et al. cod. ed. Rom.* diligo ego *cett.* 121. dicet *ed. Rom.* (=vg).

Explicit ad Corinthios prima incipit ad eosdem secunda,

Cuius haec principalis est causa: quoniam in prima pro quorundam peccatis doctores eorum praecipue corripuerat, et multum fuerant contristati, nunc eos consolatur, suum eis proponens exemplum, et docens non debere aegre ferre quod pro aliorum sunt salute correpti, cum ipse pro aliena salute periculis cottidie et morti subiaceat.

Paulus apostolus Christi Iesu. Quaeritur cur in omnibus epistulis contra usum epistularum primo suum nomen ponat quam eorum ad quos litterae destinantur. sed hoc auctoritatis est apostolici ordinis, qua minoribus scribit, sicut etiam iudices saeculi solent ad eos quos regunt scripta dirigere. *Per uoluntatem dei.* Dei, non hominum uoluntate: simul ut ostendat non sine patris uoluntate se missum a Christo. *Et Timotheus frater, ecclesiae dei, quae est Corinthi.* Non dixit: 'Paulus et Timotheus,' quia non ambo apostoli: ad Filippenses uero, ubi non erat tanta auctoritas necessaria, 'serui' ambo ponuntur. *Cum sanctis omnibus.* Hic 'sancti' possunt accipi sacerdotes, qui in prima ponuntur dominum inuocantes, et ad Philippenses cum episcopis et diaconis. ideo autem postea nominantur, ne parum intellegentes eos praetermissos esse putarent, cum iam sint in ecclesia conprehensi. *Qui sunt in uniuersa Achaia.* Cuius est metropolis Corinthus. *Gratia uobis et pax a deo.* Gratias agunt deo, gaudentes se ideo consolari, ut ipsi alios consolentur. *Benedictus deus et pater domini nostri Iesu Christi, pater misericordiarum.* Quia ex ipso est omnis misericordia. *Et deus totius consolationis.* Id est, perfectae consolationis, quia non est minus tribulatione solacium. *Qui consolatur nos in pressura nostra.* Non

123 *sic Cas. qui add.* argumentum. Explicit in Epistolam [primam] ad Corinthios eiusdem Ambrosii I incipit epistola secunda ad corinthios *Paris*, 1759, 1761 *quorum om. primam* 1759: explicit tractus in epla · I · ad corit Incipit tractat' sci Ambrosii inepla · II · adeos, *Paris* 13339. 124. *praem.* Secundam Epistolam Apostolus scribit Corinthiis *ed. Rom.* 125. et] unde *ed. Rom.* 129. subiacet *ed. Rom.* 130. Iesu Christi *ed. Rom.* (=vg.). 131. ponat] *add.* Apostolus *ed. Rom.* 132. haec *ed. Rom.* auctoritatis *Cas.* auctoritas *cett.* 133. qua *Cas.* quia *cett.* etiam] *add.* et *Cas. ed. Rom.* 136. dei *om. ed. Rom.* 138. necessaria *om. ed. Rom.* 139. ∽ omnibus sanctis *Cas. ed. Rom.* (=vg.). 141. diacones *Cas.* 144. et *om. Cas.* Gratias—consolentur *om. ed. Rom.* 145 se] esse *Cas.* 146. domini nostri Iesu Christi *om. Cas.* 147. totius] omnis *ed. Rom.* consolationis (*alt.*)] *add.* ut significaret *ed. Rom.* 149. pressura] *praem.* omni *ed. Rom.* (cf. vg.).

in aliquibus, sed in omnibus. *Ut possimus et ipsi consolari eos qui sunt in omni angustia, per exhortationem qua exhortamur et ipsi a deo.* Propter ea liberamur, ut et nos alios consolari et de tristitia liberare possimus. Aut: Ita formam nobis dat alios consolandi, ut per exhortationem qua ipsi a deo consolamur, agnoscamus quod deus timentium se neminem derelinquat, et multo magis in futuro remuneret quos etiam in praesenti non deserit. *Quoniam, sicut abundant passiones Christi in nobis.* Id est, pro nomine Christi. *Ita et per Christum abundat etiam consolatio nostra.* Ut et Petrus est de carcere liberatus, et ipse Paulus uisione domini et uoce confirmatus in templo. *Siue autem angustiam patimur, pro uestra exhortatione et salute.* Quia uos ad salutem hortamur. Siue: Ut uobis exemplum tolerantiae praebeamus.

I have said above that this is practically a fragment of a sixth-century MS of the original form of Pelagius, but it is necessary to admit that, if our two authorities, the Reichenau and Balliol manuscripts, contain between them the whole of the original Pelagius, then this portion contains a little more than that in the section it provides. The following words or clauses are absent from the Reichenau or the Balliol MS or both: *id est in resurrectione* (l. 2), *Adam* (l. 13), *ut non cum—ipsi eant* (ll. 64—70) (the most significant of all), *nisi uos me—permiserit* (ll. 71—74), *cum fratribus* (l. 85), *de Apollo—oportunum fuerit* (ll. 86—88), *obsecro autem—in uobis* (ll. 94—98), *Salutant—Asiae* (ll. 106—107), *apud—hospitor* (l. 108), *salutatio—Pauli* (ll. 110—111). The majority of these passages are portions of scripture text, which there is some reason to believe Pelagius passed over in the course of his commentary[1]. The others must have their claims examined with the rest of the authorities. Minor variations between this text and our leading authorities need not here be referred to, especially as there are many such between

150. in aliquibus] in aliqua *ed. Rom.*; aliquid *duo codd.* omnibus] omni *ed. Rom.* 151. exhortationem qua exhortamur] consolationem qua consolamur *ed. Rom.* 152. ∽ nos et *Cas. ed. Rom.* 154. consolationem *ed. Rom.* agnoscamus *Cas. ed. Rom.* agnoscimus *cett.* 160. sive] si *ed. Rom.* angustiam patimur] angustiamur *Cas.** (*corr. m* 1). uestri *ed. Rom.* 161. Quia] *praem.* Id est *ed. Rom.* exhortamur *ed. Rom.*

[1] See the evidence ad locos.

the Reichenau and Balliol MSS themselves, and the Freiburg fragments differ at times from both.

Of greater significance is the absence from this section of passages found in all but the Reichenau and Balliol MSS.[1] They are these:—

Paris MS 653

(After 'sanctis' l. 3):—

Aliter: Animale corpus dicit, quod conditum terrae corrumpitur, spiritale uero, quod incorruptum resurgit, ut possit aerem penetrare, festinans ad caelos.

Aliter: Primus Adam ad hoc factus est tantum ut uiueret.

Aliter: Nouissimus Adam, id est Christus, ideo suscepit hominem, ut uiuificaret. (These three notes are not exactly contiguous.)

Aliter: Hic primum et secundum hominem iuxta operam terrestrem et caelestem dicit: nam et Christus secundum carnem ex nostra massa fuit.

(After 'possedebit' [*sic*] l. 22) in margin: non dixit 'non resurget.'

(After 'absorta' l. 44) in margin: in osee propheta.

(After 'peccatum' l. 48) in margin: in icto (*sic*) faciens quasi gladius.

(After 'domino' l. 57): Hoc est: non inaniter laboratis.

(Before l. 58) in margin: incipit de collectis.

(After 'per' l. 67) in margin: quasi cum epistulis meis illos mittam.

(After 'signum' [for 'si dignum'] l. 68) in margin: si non fuerit aliqua maior quae me detineat causa.

(After 'aegrotant' l. 77): Aliter: Tam diu aput uos ero quam diu uestrae placuerit uoluntati.

(After 'ostium' l. 78) in margin: ad profectum multorum.

(After 'resistant' l. 81): Aliter: Quia et ipse uirtutes faciebat et signa et in uirtutibus et in doctrina.

(After 'fuerit' l. 88): tunc ei non fuit oportunum.

(After 'eius modi' [='talibus'] l. 97): Vel fide primitiae uel honore.

[1] The St Gall MS 73 must be added to these here, because in First Corinthians, and there only, it is for the most part free of interpolation.

(After 'laboranti' l. 97): qui uel nobis cooperatur uel illis.
(After 'enim' [='autem'] l. 102): circa meum obsequium.
(After 'Christum' l. 112): non ficto ut iudas.
(After 'dei' l. 136) in margin: erat ibi et non dei.
(After 'deo' l. 144): *Patre nostro et dno ihu xpo* (=vg.): quod nos solemus ille illi salutem.

Pseudo-Jerome, but not Paris MS 653

(After 'gloriam consequentur' l. 32): Aliter: In quibusdam Grecis codicibus habet: omnes enim dormiemus, non omnes mutabimur: in aliis autem: omnes enim non dormiemus, omnes autem mutabimur, quod aptat magis ad sensum apostoli, quia hic sermo non de omnibus generaliter dicitur nisi de solis sanctis.

We have thus evidence of another practically uninterpolated copy of the original Pelagius, not later than the sixth century.

The Cassiodorian Commentary (Pseudo-Primasius)

The evidence of this commentary and of those that follow is not of the same positive character as that furnished by the preceding, but it is nevertheless not without significance. The Cassiodorian commentary employs Pelagius so largely (in some Epistles being little else than a copy of Pelagius), that it is hard to see why not a single interpolated passage of the kind we have been making acquaintance with, is found in it, unless it be the case that only the uninterpolated form was used by the author. I have gone through the whole Cassiodorian commentary, and underlined every borrowing from Pelagius. There is not a trace of a single interpolation. It is true that Cassiodorus shows knowledge of one or two passages which are absent from the Reichenau MS, but these are present in the Balliol MS, which contains a few passages absent both from the Reichenau and Roman MSS.

Cassiodorus thus furnishes additional evidence of the existence of a form of the commentary such as Augustine, Mercator, the Reichenau, Balliol, Roman and Ambrosiaster MSS prove to have existed, namely one free of interpolation.

THE EXTRACTS FROM JOHN THE DEACON

One of the numerous discoveries to the credit of Dom Germain Morin, O.S.B., introduces us to the name 'John the Deacon' in connexion with this commentary[1]. In two manuscripts, Codex latinus monacensis 14,500 (formerly of St Emmeram in Ratisbon) (saec. IX—X), and British Museum Harleianus 659 (saec. XIII), he found extracts with this name attached to them, which are really by Pelagius. As his examination of the British Museum MS was confessedly hurried, and the manuscript contains other matters of interest than this, it was possible for me to find three other passages in it[2]. The long extract from the Munich MS, which I copied in 1913, stretches from Rom. vi 3 *an ignoratis* to Rom. vi 14 *paruoli sed perfecti*. Unfortunately for our purpose, this is a section where no interpolations are to be found in Pseudo-Jerome, where in fact Pseudo-Jerome differs very slightly from Pelagius. It is not therefore possible to assert that it was the original form of Pelagius which passed under the name of Iohannes Diaconus, or was used by him. Yet there is nothing at all inconsistent with the view that it was the pure form he used.

The Harley MS has the following extracts:—

(f. 13 rb) Humanum quippe iudicium multis modis corrumpitur, amore, odio, timore: sepe iudicium integritate uiolatur et contra iusticie regulam interdum misericordia inclinatur. (Iuditium uero dei est *secundum ueritatem* quia (begins Amb].)

This is from *in Rom.* ii 2—3, and it is evident that the text has incurred some corruption in the course of transmission.

(f. 19 vb) Notandum uero quia recte dicitur redemisse nos, non emisse. Ipsius enim per naturam fueramus sed nostris delictis alienati fuimus[3]. Si igitur ad peccata non redeamus, fructuosa erit nobis redemptio Christi quem Christum deus pater proposuit.

This is from *in Rom.* iii 24, and there has been some freedom of handling.

[1] *Revue Bénédictine* XXVII (1910) pp. 113—17; *Études, Textes, Découvertes* I (Maredsous & Paris, 1913) p. 23.

[2] 23 March, 1912.

[3] This is the extract published by Morin, viz. from *Notandum* to *fuimus* (or *sumus*, as he gives).

(f. 24 va) corde · etiam in tribulationibus gloriantur magnitudinem premii cognoscentes · de tribulatione finienda infinitum premium acquisituri.

This is from *in Rom.* v 3—4, and there has again been freedom of handling.

(f. 27 vb) (Vel) forma Christi dicitur quia, sicut ille sine coitu a deo factus est, ita Christus ex uirgine spiritu sancto operante processit. Uel Adam dicitur forma Christi, quia, sicut ille est pater omnium secundum fidem et sicut (begins Aug.).

This is from *in Rom.* v 14, and again there has been some freedom of handling.

All these four extracts are quite consistent with use of the uninterpolated Pelagius. There can be little doubt that they come from the *Breuiarium de Sancto Paulo* of Iohannes Diaconus, of which a copy existed in the Benedictine Monastery of Blaubeuren in South Germany at the end of the eleventh century, as is proved by the catalogue of that library[1]. It is not so easy, however, to say which among the many persons with the name 'John the Deacon' really composed this work, as also the *Expositum* on the Heptateuch[2], and the *Breuiatio in Psalmos,* which Dom Morin has suggested, with great probability, should be identified with the well-known Pseudo-Jerome[3]. It is possible that other works should also be attributed to the same John[4], and we may assign all to the sixth century[5].

It is significant that certain even of the interpolated forms witness to the originality of the uninterpolated. Both the St Gall

[1] See G. Becker, *Catalogi Bibliothecarum Antiqui* (Bonn, 1885) p. 175: my attention was called to the fact in 1914 by Dom G. Morin, who had read the entry in a proofsheet of Dr P. Lehmann's volume of catalogues of Old German libraries: see now *Mittelalterliche Bibliothekskataloge Deutschlands und der Schweiz* I Bd. bearb. v. P. L. (München, 1918) p. 19 l. 22: 'Breuiarium Ioannis de S. Paulo.'

[2] Of which there was a copy in the Corbie library (see Becker, *Catal.* no. 136 item 245). The MS is still extant, being Paris, B.N. 12309 (saec. XI): see also *Spicilegium Solesmense* I (1852) 265 f., 278 ff.

[3] Cf. *Revue Bénédictine* XXV (1908) pp. 88—94, *Études, Textes, Découvertes,* t. I pp. 59 f.

[4] See Dom Morin, *R.B.* XXVII (1910) p. 116 for suggestions.

[5] Cf. the article 'Ioannes Diaconus' in Pauly-Wissowa, *Real-Encycl.* Bd. IX (1916) pp. 1806 f.; Manitius, *Gesch. lat. Litt. d. Mittelalters* I p. 693; Schanz, *Gesch. d. röm. Litt.* § 1241.

MS and Paris MS 653 are heavily interpolated, but the first is free from interpolation in the commentary on First Corinthians[1], while the second is free from interpolation in the commentaries on First Timothy, Second Timothy, Titus and Philemon.

LATER COMPILATIONS

Zmaragdus of St Mihiel, as we have seen, makes many quotations both from a pure Pelagius, and also from the Cassiodorian revision, both under the symbol P̄ = Pelagius. Nowhere have I found an interpolated passage. The evidence suggests that Zmaragdus possessed an uninterpolated MS which he knew to be Pelagius, in addition to the Cassiodorian revision, which also he knew to be a form of Pelagius. Doubtless both his copies were anonymous[2].

Sedulius Scottus of Liége used as his leading authority Pelagius in its original, uninterpolated form, which was doubtless accessible to him as an anonymous work[3]. It is doubtful whether he really cites a commentary on Hebrews under that name. There is no trace of interpolation in him, and he is an exact quoter. Of all compilers later than Cassiodorus he is the most satisfactory authority for the parts he employs. It is quite uncertain whether the H at p. 144 A (=1 Cor. vii 36) really refers to the interpolation in Pseudo-Jerome at that point; it may refer to some passage of genuine Jerome[4].

This part of the subject need not be pursued farther. The evidence is sufficient to show that a number of copies of the original, uninterpolated Pelagius continued to exist, even after interpolation had begun its work.

[1] Cf. Zimmer, *Pelagius in Irland* pp. 246 ff.

[2] The sources of Zmaragdus are indicated at some length in *Journ. Theol. Stud.* vol. IX (1907—1908) pp. 584—597, supplemented by vol. XXIII (1921—1922) pp. 73—76.

[3] The sources of Sedulius are fully set out in *Journ. Theol. Stud.* vol. XVIII (1916—1917) pp. 184—228.

[4] I have suggested hesitatingly *Adv. Iouin.* I 13 in the last quoted article, p. 228.

CHAPTER III

THE WHOLE COMMENTARY THE WORK OF ONE AUTHOR

It will be recollected that contemporaries quote only the expositions of Romans and First Corinthians, and, though no one has disputed the unity of the thirteen expositions, a proof that all are the production of one author will not be out of place in a work like the present. There is no hint anywhere that any one exposition circulated by itself, and all the manuscripts, uninterpolated and interpolated alike, give expositions of thirteen Epistles, some even of fourteen. Our method of proof will be not unlike that which found general acceptance in the case of Ambrosiaster[1]. We shall divide our chapter into five sections: (*a*) cross references from one part of the commentary to another; (*b*) illustrations of method of exegesis in general; (*c*) community of ideas throughout; (*d*) favourite verses of scripture; (*e*) community of style and language.

(*a*) Cross References from one part of the Commentary to another

In Rom. ii 8 iam *superius* dictum est contentiosum hunc esse specialiter, qui aliquid contra suam conscientiam nititur defensare.

This is a reference to:—

In Rom. i 29 contentio est, ubi non ratione aliquid, sed animi pertinacia defenditur, et ubi non tam ueritas quaeritur, sed intentio fatigatur.

In Gal. v 22 omnium uirtutum prima est caritas, quam in quattuor partes diuisibilem *adnotauimus.*

This is a reference to:—

In Gal. v 14 dilectio uel caritas quattuor modis constat: hoc est, *etc.*

In 1 *Thess.* v 15: in the latter part of the note a phrase is quoted from the earlier part and preceded by the words *ut superius dictum est.*

[1] *Study of Ambrosiaster* (vol. vii part 4 in this series) (1905).

In Col. iii 19 numquam rem naturalem hortaretur, nisi continentes esse coepissent, sicut ad Ephesios plenius subnotatum est.

This is a reference to:—

In Eph. v 22 quia non eos sicut incontinentes Corinthios lacte alebat, sed perfecto continentiae cibo nutriebat. timet enim ne, cessante in plerisque carnis officio, aut in mulieribus subiectio aut in uiris cessaret caritatis affectus, et non tam continentiam quam diuortium docuisse uideretur. ceterum quale est, ut nouae uitae praedicator, nulla exsistente causa, hoc doceret, quod naturaliter possidebant!

(*b*) Illustrations of Method of Exegesis in General

One of the most common features, remarked upon by St Augustine[1], is the provision of alternative explanations. These alternative explanations are introduced almost invariably by the word *Siue*. The following list of references ought to be approximately complete:—

Rom. i 8, 11, 17; ii 25, 26, 27; iii 11, 15, 20, 21; iiii 11 *bis*, 13, 15; v 6, 14 *quater*; vi 6, 9, 14, 19; vii 9, 15; viii 2, 3, 19 *bis*; viiii 16, 17 *bis*; x 8, 19; xi 15 *bis*, 29, 34; xii 8, 18; xiii 5, 6, 13; xiiii 16; xv 5, 7, 15, 24, 26, 29, 31 *bis*; xvi 1.

1 Cor. i 23; ii 6, 7, 15; iii 12, 13, 16, 17; iiii 9; v 2, 4, 5 *bis*; vi 2; vii 17, 18, 28; viiii 21; x 12; xi 4, 10, 16, 18, 19, 26; xiiii 33 *bis*, 36; xv 3, 7, 51; xvi 17.

2 Cor. i 6, 7, 11, 16; ii 3 *bis*, 5, 14; iii 2, 3, 18; iiii 6, 17; v 8; vi 10, 13, 15; vii 2, 3, 4 *bis*, 5, 10; viii 22 *bis*, (24); viiii 5 *ter*, 8 *bis*, 9 *bis*, 10, 13; x 7; xi 5; xii 4 *bis*; xiii 4.

Gal. ii 16, 19; iii 19; vi 6 *bis*.

Eph. i 4; iii 1, 6, 7, 9; iiii 5, 10 *bis*, 12, 14; vi 4 *bis*, 24 *bis*.

Phil. i 5, 6, 7, 8 *bis*, 25, 27; ii 5, 6, 17 *bis*, 18; iii 13, 21; iiii 5, 15.

1 Thess. i 5 *bis*; ii 13 *bis*, 16; iiii 6; v 17, 18, 19, 22 *bis*.

2 Thess. ii 16.

Col. ii 18; iii 5, 17, 25 *bis*; iiii 10, 18.

1 Tim. ii 2, 7; iii 3 *bis*, 9; iiii 10; v 8, 24 *quater*; vi 4, 6, 9, 12, 20.

[1] *De pecc. mer. et rem.* III 4 § 9 (C.S.E.L. LX p. 135 l. 7).

2 Tim. i 1, 12, 14; ii 1—2 *bis*, 14, 18; iii 6, 10, 13, 15 *bis*; iiii 8.

Tit. i 6, 9; ii 5, 7, 10; iii 3, 5 *bis*, 15.

Philem. 6, 14.

Occasionally an alternative explanation is introduced by *Aliter*. The following instances occur: Rom. iii 4; iiii 2, 4; vi 22; xiii 1; xv 17; 1 Cor. iii 18; vii 28; viiii 22; xv 50; 2 Cor. v 16; (viii 24); viiii 12, 13; xii 5; Phil. ii 2; Col. ii 23. The employment of *Item* to introduce an additional note, is the exclusive peculiarity of Pseudo-Jerome MSS, and it comes before interpolated notes only.

A favourite type of note is that which attempts to make the meaning of St Paul's words clearer, by pointing out what the Apostle is *not* referring to; this might be called the negative method of exegesis. An illustration or two will show what is meant:—

Rom. v 9 In sanguine ipsius.... Non animalium sanguine, sicut in lege.

2 Tim. i 1 per uoluntatem dei. Non meis meritis.

Tit. i 1 Paulus seruus dei. Non peccati.

Other instances of this type of note are:—

Rom. i 4, 8; iiii 17; v 10; vi 17, 23; vii 7, 18; viii 32; xi 1, 30; xii 6, 11; xiiii 15; xv 15.

1 Cor. iii 1, 9, 10; iiii i.

2 Cor. i 4; v 21; vi 4 *bis*; vii 1, 9, 11 *quater*; viii 5; x 12 *bis*; xi 6; xii 10 *quater*; xiii 12.

Gal. i 1, 4, 14, 15; ii 2 *bis*, 20 *bis*; iii 8, 18; vi 14.

Eph. i 1 *bis*, 3 *bis*, 4, 5 *bis*, 11; ii 8; iii 3, 4 *bis*, 7, 12; iiii 11 *bis*, 29; v 19, 21; vi 3, 7, 13, 14.

Phil. i 4, 16, 25; ii 12; iii 1, 5, 15; iiii 3, 6.

1 Thess. ii 2; iii 3, 13.

2 Thess. iii 12, 13.

Col. i 6; iii 15 *bis*.

1 Tim. i 1, 2; iii 1, 12; v 17; vi 11, 17.

2 Tim. i 1, 12; ii 9; iii 2.

Tit. i 1, 4; ii 5; iii 1, 2 *bis*, 7.

Philem. 23.

No extra-canonical writers are referred to by name, unless they happen to be also heretics. Others, whose views the author considers and usually ends in rejecting, are indicated by the vague word *quidam* (plural). An attempt will be made in a later chapter to discover some of the writers thus intended, but at this stage it will be enough to give a list of the references to *quidam*. (In one or two cases other writers are referred to as *multi* or *diuersi*.)

Rom. ii 21; iii 28; iiii 8 (*quidam*, then *alii*); v 14; viii 3, 19 (*diuersi*, *quidam*); viiii 16, 17 (*diuersi*), 20 *bis*, (21 (*eos, qui*)), (26 (*eos, qui*)); x 5; xi 20, 26; xiiii 2, 15.

1 Cor. ii 9; viii 1; viiii 22; xi 21, 27; xiiii 19; xv 28 (*multi, quidam, alii, multi*). 35 (*multi*).

2 Cor. ii 15; iii 6[1]; v 13; vii 11; viii 22; viiii 2 (*quidam, alii*); xii 7.

Gal. iii 19; v 12.

Eph. i 10 (*multi, quidam, alii, alii*); ii 2 (*multi*); iii 18; v 31; vi 5.

Phil. ii 5 (*multi*).

Col. ii 14.

2 Tim. ii 20.

Another practice followed throughout is the refutation of particular heresies from the passages under consideration. Sometimes heretics in general are referred to, but far oftener the individual heretic is attacked by name. The references to passages will be found in the index of proper names; here it may suffice to give the names, and the number of occurrences of each: Marcion, or the Marcionites, appears twice; the Manicheans eleven times; the Arians fourteen times; the Photinians five times; the Novatians four times; the Jovinianists[2] four times; Apollinaris twice; the Macedonians once. Heretics in general are referred to twenty times in all. The allusions are spread equally over the whole work, and the method of allusion is very uniform throughout, as reference to a later section of this chapter will show[3].

It is this commentator's practice to pay regard to the different sections of the Epistles, and to call attention, for instance, to the point at which the discussion of a particular topic ceases. For instance, after the note on Rom. i 7 occur the words: *huc usque praefatio*[4]; at Rom. x 17 occur the words *Hinc responsio apostoli*;

[1] v 9 in Ps.-Hier. addition has *quidam*.

[2] On the bearing these references have on the date of the commentary see chap. i p. 4 n. 6.

[3] Under **calumnior, contra** (p. 86).

[4] Probably genuine, though lacking in the Reichenau MS.

at 1 Cor. vii 1 occur the words *Incipit de coniugiis*; at vii 38 *concludit uirginum causam*; at Eph. iii 21 *huc usque de mysterio incarnationis Christi...hinc incipit moralia omni ecclesiae tradere instituta*; at 1 Tim. i 18 *Huc usque de statu suo...hinc dat.* There are many more instances of the kind, of which the commentary on First Corinthians furnishes a goodly number[1].

Perhaps in the interests of brevity, the author habitually brings his short notes into grammatical connexion with the verses or clauses commented on. In fact he carries the process so far as sometimes to bring the 'argumentum' into subordination to the title, e.g. *incipit ad Galatas argumentum, quos pseudo-apostoli*, etc.; *incipit ad Colossenses, quorum auditam fidem*, etc.; *incipit ad Titum argumentum, discipulum suum episcopum, quem commonet*, etc.; *incipit ad Philemonem, cui apostolus a Roma scribit.* Examples from the commentaries proper are: Rom. iiii 5 secundum propositum [gratiae] dei, *quo proposuit gratis...dimittere*; 1 Cor. vi 19 quem habetis a deo, *cui grauissimam iniuriam facitis fornicando*; 2 Cor. i 23 in animam meam, *cuius secreta solus agnoscit*; Gal. ii 10 ut pauperum memores essemus, *qui omnia sua distrahentes...uel: quorum bona fuerant a Iudaeis inuasa*; Eph. iii 7 secundum operationem uirtutis eius, *cuius uirtus me confirmauit, siue: cuius uirtutes*, etc.; Phil. ii 30 tradens animam suam: *in manus inimicorum*; 1 Thess. iii 11 ipse autem deus...dirigat uiam nostram ad uos, *remotis diabolicis scandalis, quibus noster impeditur aduentus*; 2 Thess. i 7 cum angelis uirtutis eius, *qui uenient uindicare*; Col. i 6 et crescit, *in numero uel uirtute*; 1 Tim. ii 9 similiter et mulieres, *in omnibus quae dixi de uiris*; 2 Tim. iii 14 et credita sunt tibi, *a deo per nos*; Tit. i 14 auersantium se a ueritate, *noui scilicet testamenti*; Philem. 5 fidem tuam et caritatem, *quae operibus innotescit.* These examples have been chosen at random, one from each commentary, out of hundreds which might have been adduced.

The separation between the various parts of this chapter is to some extent artificial, and thus some of the later arguments might very well have come in at this point.

[1] This specialty of the commentary has been noticed by De Bruyne, *Revue Bénédictine* xxiv (1907) p. 261: see also below, under **Incipio** and **causa**.

(c) Community of Ideas throughout

On this subject a whole book might easily be written, and doubtless will be written, but it must come from a theologian. I will not seek in any way to forestall his task by a treatment which must necessarily be defective. I will merely select a few themes which have struck me in the course of reading. Readers who seek a larger treatment will find it in the works of Klasen[1] and Loofs[2], from which they will eliminate such conclusions as depend on an interpolated and faulty text.

No subject occurs with more persistence than the influence of example on conduct. The author is never weary of referring especially to the force of the Apostle's good example in the lives of his converts. The word used is *exemplum*, but sometimes *forma*[3]. The following list of instances must be fairly complete: arg. omn. epist. *bis*; Rom. i 1, 10; iii 21; iiii 4, 24; v 1, 12, 16, 19; vi 11, 14, 18; viii 3, 4, 32; xii 3, 13, 15; xiii 13; xiiii 6, 13, 15, 22; xv 2, 16 *bis*, 27; xvi 5, 15, 25; 1 Cor. i 26, 28; ii 1; iii 15 *bis*, 17; iiii 6, 17 *bis*; v 6; vi 2; vii 3, 14, 25; viii 1, 11; viiii 1, 6, 7, 13; x 1, 22, 24, 32, 33; xiii 11; xiiii 6; xv 13, 32, 36, 57; 2 Cor. i 6; iiii 5; v 16 *bis*, 18; vi 3, 13 *bis*, 14; vii 2; viii 1, 10, 15; Gal. iiii 16; Eph. ii 7; v 27; Phil. i 11, 14, 24; (ii 7), 8, 12, 16, 19, 21; iiii 7, 9; 1 Thess. arg. i 5, 7 *bis*, 8, 10; ii 1, 14; iii 9; iiii 7; v 12; 2 Thess. iii 1; Col. i 23; ii 6; iii 13, 21; 1 Tim. i 16; ii 6, 15; iii 2 (also *forma*), 3; iiii 12 *bis* (also *forma*), 15, 16; v 1, 9, 11, 13, 22, 23; 2 Tim. i 4, 10, 16; ii 1—2, 15; Tit. ii 3; iii 3; Philem. arg. One or two of the examples may be quoted in full to show their character: 1 Cor. viii 11 *potest et illis dici qui destruunt* exemplo *quod aedificant uerbo*; 1 Cor. xiiii 6 *suum illis proponit* exemplum; 2 Cor. v 16 *nullius ueterum imitamur* exemplum... *quia eis* exempla *ueterum proponebant*; 2 Cor. vi 14 *ostendit neminem posse et iustum esse pariter et iniustum, ualde contraria* exempla *proponens*.

The author frequently states that we are saved gratuitously (*gratis*), e.g. Rom. i 7; iii 21, 24; iiii 4, 5, (6); viii 29; xi 6; 2 Cor. i 12;

[1] *Theologische Quartalschrift* Bd. LXVII (1885) pp. 244—317, especially the latter part.

[2] Article 'Pelagius' in Herzog-Hauck's *Real-encyklopädie*.

[3] Further examples of *forma* later in this chapter, p. 100.

Gal. v 4; Eph. i 9; 1 Tim. i 2; 2 Tim. i 9: similarly that we are saved by the grace of God, not by our own merits; arg. omn. epist. *dei se gratia, non suis meritis, esse saluatos*; cf. Rom. v 1 *nemo suo merito, sed omnes aequaliter dei gratia sunt saluati.*

He reiterates St Paul's teaching that we are justified by faith alone (*sola fides*): Rom. i 17; iii 28 *bis*; iiii 3, 5, 11; v 1; viii 29; xi 25; 1 Cor. vi 10; viiii 21; 2 Cor. v 19; Gal. i 3, 12; ii 2, 14, 17, 20; iii 5, 6, 10, 11, 12, 14, 22, 26; v 11, 24; vi 16; Eph. ii 8, 16; iii 11; v 5: cf. Phil. iii 3, 9; iiii 1.

Foreknowing and predestinating are identified (Rom. viii 29), and God called those, who he had foreknown (*praescierat*) would believe. This latter view the author may have got from Ambrosiaster: in any case the teaching occurs frequently in Rom., and also later. Examples are Rom. viii 29, 30; viiii 10, 15, 27; xi 2; Gal. i 15; Tit. i 3.

The author is intensely interested in moral progress (*proficio, profectus*[1]), and constantly refers to it. He speaks often of the apostle encouraging (*prouocare*) his converts to show it. A few instances are Rom. i 8; xv 14; 1 Cor. i 4; xi 2; 2 Cor. vi 11; vii 13, 14; Gal. iiii 21; Phil. iiii 18; 1 Thess. arg.; ii 20; iiii 1; 2 Thess. iii 1; 1 Tim. iii 2; 2 Tim. i 16. Gal. iiii 21 may be quoted in illustration: *detrimentum discipulorum confusio est magistri, sicut* profectus *eorum est gloria praeceptoris.* This last is a very favourite theme, the joy that the progress of the pupil gives to the master.

A few minor illustrations of the unity of the commentary in this matter may be added; others may be divined from the index of scripture passages or of proper names, such as the references to Ananias and Sapphira, Simon Magus, the call of Barnabas and Saul[2].

The connexion between 1 Thess. ii 14 and Hebr. x 34 is twice stated: arg. omn. epist., *De Hebraeis uero quid dicendum est, quorum Thessalonicenses, qui plurimum laudati sunt,* imitatores facti esse *dicuntur, sicut ipse ait*: et uos fratres imitatores facti estis ecclesiarum dei, quae sunt in Iudaea; eadem enim passi estis uos a contribulibus uestris, quae et illi a Iudaeis? *aput ipsos quoque*

[1] See examples of these words under section (*e*).

[2] See below, (*d*) p. 77.

Hebraeos eadem commemorat dicens: nam et uinctis conpassi estis et rapinam bonorum uestrorum cum gaudio suscepistis, cognoscentes uos habere meliorem et manentem substantiam (Hebr. x 34); which ought to be compared with the note on 1 Thess. ii 14 uos autem, fratres, imitatores facti estis ecclesiarum dei, quae sunt in Iudaea in Christo Iesu. *Quibus dicitur*: nam et uinctis conpassi estis et rapinam bonorum uestrorum cum gaudio suscepistis (Hebr. x 34). Quoniam eadem passi estis et uos a contribulibus uestris, sicut et ipsi a Iudaeis. I know no other independent commentator who brings these two passages together.

The relationship between the Acts of the Apostles and the Epistles is stated in similar language in two passages: 1 Cor. xv 32 *multa dicuntur in Epistulis, quae in Actibus non tenentur, et multa in Actibus, quae in Epistulis non scribuntur*; 2 Cor. xi 24 *haec in Actibus non omnia repperiuntur, quia nec in Epistulis omnia quae ibi scripta sunt, continentur.*

The change in the Apostle Matthew's career is stated in almost the same words in two passages: Col. iiii 14 (Lucas) *ex medico erat, sicut Matheus iam apostolus adhuc dicitur publicanus*; 1 Tim. i 15 *hic* 'sum' *pro* 'fui' *ponitur, sicut Mattheus dicitur publicanus, cum iam Christi esset apostolus.*

'Teaching,' etc. are often described as being that of the New Testament, or of the Old and New Testament together. Thus, compare the following passages: Rom. vii 12 *deus non numquam in Vetere* 'bonus' *et in Nouo dicitur* 'iustus'; Rom. x 8 uerbum fidei...*Noui scilicet Testamenti*; Rom. xv 14 repleti omni scientia. *Hoc est, et Noui et Veteris Testamenti*; 1 Cor. i 5 in omni uerbo et in omni scientia. *Id est, tam Noui quam Veteris Testamenti*; 1 Cor. vii 5; Gal. iiii 24 duo testamenta. *Vetus et Nouum singulos populos generantia*; Gal. v 23 *qui Nouum implet, non est sub Vetere Testamento*; Col. iiii 6 sermo uester in gratia. *In Nouo scilicet Testamento*; Col. iiii 11 hi soli sunt adiutores in regno dei, qui mihi fuerunt in solacio. *In Nouo Testamento, per quod intratur ad* regnum; 1 Tim. vi 3 doctrinae. *Noui Testamenti; Veteris enim erat seuera* doctrina; Tit. i 14 a ueritate. *Noui scilicet Testamenti;* Tit. iii 6 quem effudit in nos abunde...*Abundantius quam in Vetere Testamento.*

Twice he reminds his readers that there can be only one

episcopus in each *ciuitas*: Phil. i 2 *hic* episcopos *presbyteros intellegimus*: non enim in una ciuitate plures episcopi esse potuissent, sed hoc etiam in Apostolorum Actibus inuenitur; 1 Tim. iii 8 *quaeritur cur de presbyteris nullam fecerit mentionem, sed etiam ipsos in* episcoporum *nomine conprehendit, quia secundus, immo paene unus est gradus, sicut ad Philippenses* episcopis *et diaconis* scribit, cum una ciuitas plures episcopos habere non possit, et in Actibus presbyteros ecclesiae *iturus Hierosolymis congregauit, quibus inter cetera ait*: (follows Act. xx 28)...episcopos....

There are several references to the Laity in the commentary, perhaps not unconnected with the fact that the writer himself was a layman: 2 Cor. viiii 2 *quidam dicunt eum superius de* laicis *sanctis dixisse, hic uero de sacerdotibus sanctis*; 2 Cor. xiii 11 laicos *iubet se inuicem exhortari*; 1 Thess. iiii 18 consolamini inuicem in uerbis istis.] *Notandum quod* laicis *hoc praecepit, ut alterutrum se doctrinis suis instituant*; 1 Thess. v 11 consolamini inuicem et aedificate alterutrum....] *Notandum quia hoc* laicis *praecepit, quos etiam monet praepositis exhibere officia caritatis*; Col. iii 16 *Et hic ostenditur uerbum Christi non sufficienter, sed abundanter etiam* laicos *habere debere et docere se inuicem* etc.; 1 Tim. iii 1 fidelis sermo: siquis episcopatum desiderat.] *Prius* laicos *instituit, de quibus optimi quique in sacerdotium alleguntur, et sic dicit quales debeant ordinari;* 1 Tim. iii 2 unius uxoris uirum.] *Si illi nec hoc licet, quod uel* laico *conceditur, multo magis illa quae etiam in* laico *prohibentur*; 1 Tim. v 19 *iniustum est etiam aduersus* laicum *accusationem recipere, cum hoc nec saeculares iudices faciant: quanto magis aduersus domini sacerdotem!*

The Apostles had the gift of knowing what was taking place at a distance: 1 Cor. i 11 hanc gratiam habebat (apostolus), ut nosset absens quid in singulis ecclesiis ageretur, sicut dicit ad Colossensis (ii 5) *etc.*; Col. ii 5 habebant hanc gratiam apostoli, ut alibi positi, quid alibi ageretur agnoscerent, sicut Helisaei spiritus cum Giezi fuit in uia (cf. 4 Regn. v 26).

Note the identical definitions of *ecclesia*, with reference to a 'house church': Rom. xvi 5 *ostendit* congregationem *fidelium* ecclesiam nominari; 1 Cor. xvi 19 *domesticam* congregationem *fraternitatis* ecclesiam nominauit.

This section may be concluded by reference to the illustrations from medicine, employed by the commentator. Our writer is not, of course, unique in this respect[1], but they are sufficiently characteristic to deserve collection: Rom. v 4 *cum etiam multi propter spem paruae salutis et curam corporis maximos sustinuerint cruciatus, nec tamen perfectam potuerint consequi sanitatem, quae etiam si prouenerit, paulo post morte intercedente soluetur*; Rom. v 6 *peccatorum et scelerum languoribus premeremur*; Rom. viiii 17 *tale est hoc quod in Pharaone gestum est, quale si medicus de cruciatu iam damnati rei multis inueniat sanitatem, causas inquirendo morborum*; Rom. xii 15 *non dolemus de uno membro praeciso*; 1 Cor. i 21 *alia illis medicina succurritur*; 1 Cor. vii 3 *concedatur remedium...in languore incontinentiae reclamanti non denegetur remedium nuptiarum, quo modo si peritus medicus inquieto aegro et neganti se posse a pomis omnibus abstinere, saltem minus perniciosa concedat*; 1 Cor. xi 31 *huic causae humana potest succurrere medicina*; 1 Cor. xvi 6 *multa sunt quae corrigantur in uobis; sicut medicus ibi moram habet, ubi plures aegrotant*; 2 Cor. i 9 *omne humanum auxilium defecisse et ab illo solo sperandum esse remedium, cui etiam mortuos suscitare possibile est*; 2 Cor. ii 2 *si contristatur, intellegit se peccasse; sic aeger qui dolorem sentit, potest percipere sanitatem et ad medici laetitiam pertinere*; 2 Cor. iiii 4 *dari permittet, quia credere noluerunt; quia et medicus, si inoboedientem aegrum deserat, ipse ei aegritudinem dicitur prolongasse, cum tota illius culpa sit, qui audire contempsit: tamen, si rursum roget et obtemperet, potest recipere sanitatem*; 2 Cor. iiii 7 *fragili corpore..., in quo etiam cum alios sanemus, ipsi aliquotiens infirmamur*; 2 Cor. vii 9 *quasi si dicat medicus: 'etiam si doluerit mihi tam ardenti me usum esse cauterio, sed* nunc gaudeo, non quia

[1] Long ago my brother, W. Clark Souter, M.D., remarked to me that Livy was fond of medical metaphors. Philo 'reveals a quite definite interest in medicine' (H. A. A. Kennedy, *Philo's Contribution to Religion* (London, 1919) p. 13). See also A. v. Harnack, *Medicinisches aus der ältesten Kirchengeschichte* (Leipzig, 1892). Of Seneca the Younger, Mr J. D. Duff says: 'Metaphors and similes from medicine abound in his writings' (note on *ad Helu.* 19 §2). On Tertullian and medicine, see T. R. Glover, *Conflict of Religions in the Early Roman Empire* (London, 1909) p. 309, n. 3; Hoppe, *Syntax u. Stil des Tertullian* (Leipzig, 1903) pp. 217 ff. Recently Prof. A. S. Pease has published an admirable paper, 'Medical Allusions in the Works of St Jerome' (Harvard Studies in Classical Philology vol. xxv [1914] pp. 73—86). On Fulgentius, see O. Friebel *F. d. Mythograph u. Bischof* (Paderb. 1911) pp. 127 ff.

doluistis, sed quia *dolor ille uobis profuit* ad *salutem*'; 2 Cor. vii 14 *quasi peritus medicus agit, qui uulnus iam prope sanatum blandis unctionibus fouet, ut facilius cauterii ustura sanetur*; Phil. i 10 *nemo aeger ante sanatur quam quo modo sanari possit agnoscat*; 1 Thess. ii 5 *sicut qui hominibus placent, tamquam aegris desiderata omnia concedentes et mortem eorum neglegentes*; 1 Thess. v 14 *pro diuersitate morborum diuersitas adhibenda est medicinae*; 2 Thess. iii 15 *aeger curandus est, non necandus*; 1 Tim. v 23 *simul ostendit posse quasdam infirmitates creaturarum medicina sanari*; 1 Tim. vi 4 *nec enim recusando fidem penitus moritur, nec* ad ueritatis scientiam *conualescit*, sed *diuersis accessionibus*[1] languet; 1 Tim. vi 17 *principalem eorum tetigit morbum*; 2 Tim. ii 17 'cancer' *esse dicitur uulnus quod in mammillis nascitur feminarum, quibus nisi cito subuentum fuerit, cum uirus ad cor serpendo peruenerit, nullum ultra remedium est. ita et haereticorum sunt uitanda conloquia, ne per aures inremediabiliter uulnerent mentes*; Tit. i 9 'doctrina sana' *quae sanat audientes*; Tit. ii 8 *nullius adulationis accessione*[1] languentem.

(*d*) Favourite Verses of Scripture

In this section are included all cases where a verse or portion of scripture is quoted or alluded to three times or oftener.

One verse is quoted or alluded to ten times:—

Act. v 41 *apostoli ibant gaudentes quia pro nomine domini digni habiti sunt contumeliam pati* (in Phil. i 28): cf. in Rom. v 4; viii 17; in 2 Cor. i 5; viii 2; in Phil. iiii 6; in 1 Thess. i 6; in 2 Thess. i 6; iii 5; in Col. i 11.

One verse is quoted or alluded to eight times:—

Phil. ii 7 *exinaniuit se ipsum formam serui accipiens* etc. (in Rom. i 1): cf. in Rom. viii 33—4; in 1 Cor. iii 23; xi 3; in 2 Cor. iiii 5; in Eph. i 21; iiii 9; in Phil. ii 5.

Two verses are quoted or alluded to seven times:—

1 Cor. viii 10 *in idolio recumbentem...aedificabitur ad manducandum idolothyta* (in Rom. xv 2): cf. in 1 Cor. viii 1; x 7, 13, 25; in 2 Cor. vi 14; in 1 Tim. iii 3.

1 Tim. i 9 *lex...est data...peccatoribus*, etc.: cf. in Rom. iiii 15; viii 2; in 1 Cor. viiii 20; in Gal. i 4; ii 19; iii 27; v 18.

[1] See *Thes. Ling. Lat.* s.v. *accessio III.*

Five verses are quoted or alluded to six times:—

Math. v 44 *diligite inimicos uestros*, etc.: cf. in Rom. viii 9; in 1 Cor. vi 8; in Gal. v 14; in Col. iii 13, 15; in 1 Tim. ii 1.

Math. xiii 22 *sollicitudo saeculi istius et uoluntas diuitiarum*, etc.: cf. in 1 Cor. vii 26, 28, 33, 34; in Eph. iiii 18; in 1 Tim. vi 9.

2 Cor. xii 2 *in corpore*, etc.: cf. in Rom. v 15; in 1 Cor. xv 51; in Gal. ii 11; in 1 Thess. iiii 15; v 10; in 2 Tim. iiii 5.

1 Ioh. iii 2 *nondum apparuit quid erimus: scimus quoniam cum apparuerit, similes ei (illi) erimus*: in Rom. v 11; viii 17, 18; in 2 Cor. iiii 11; in 2 Thess. ii 14; in Col. iii 4[1].

1 Ioh. iiii 18 *perfecta caritas foras mittit timorem*: cf. in Rom. v 5; viii 31; xiii 7; in 2 Cor. xii 15; in Gal. v 6; in 1 Thess. i 3.

Three verses are quoted or alluded to five times:—

Esai. vii 9 *nisi credideritis, nec intellegetis*: in Rom. xi 8; cf. in 1 Cor. i 24; in 2 Cor. iii 14; in 1 Thess. ii 16; in 1 Tim. i 13.

Phil. ii 3 *nihil per contentionem neque per inanem gloriam, sed in humilitate alter alterutrum maiorem aestimantes*: cf. in Rom. xii 10; in 1 Cor. xiiii 40; xvi 14; in Gal. v 15; in 1 Thess. ii 6.

2 Tim. ii 11 *si conmortui sumus, et conuiuemus*: in 1 Cor. i 9; cf. in Rom. vii 4; in 2 Cor. iiii 10; in Phil. iii 11; in Col. iii 1.

Twelve verses are quoted or alluded to four times:—

Gen. i 26 *faciamus hominem ad imaginem et similitudinem nostram*, etc.: cf. in Rom. viii 21; in Eph. iiii 24; in Phil. ii 6; in 1 Tim. ii 9.

Math. v 39 *siquis te percusserit in dextera maxilla tua, praebe illi et alteram (aliam)*: cf. in Rom. xii 17; in 1 Cor. ii 14; iii 18; vi 8.

Math. xxiiii 13 *qui perseuerauerit usque in finem, hic saluus erit*: in Rom. ii 7; in Gal. vi 9; in Phil. ii 13; in 1 Tim. vi 14 (cf. also in 1 Thess. ii 12).

Act. xiii 2 *segregate mihi Barnaban et Saulum ad opus quod elegi eos*: in Rom. i 1; cf. in Rom. i 5; in 1 Cor. vi 2; in Tit. i 3.

Act. xx 28 *uidete gregem in quo uos spiritus sanctus episcopos ordinauit, regere ecclesiam dei, quam adquisiuit sanguine suo*: cf. in Eph. i 14; in Phil. i 2; in 2 Thess. i 3; in 1 Tim. iii 8.

Rom. iii 20 *ex operibus legis non iustificatur omnis caro coram illo: per legem enim cognitio peccati*: cf. in Rom. iii 21; x 2, 3; in Gal. ii 14.

[1] Also quoted in c. 19 of Pelagius's *Epistula ad Demetriadem*.

Rom. vi 13 *sed neque exhibeatis membra uestra arma iniquitatis peccato, sed exhibete uos deo, tamquam ex mortuis uiuentes, et membra uestra arma iustitiae deo*: cf. Rom. xii 1[1]; xv 24, 29; in 1 Cor. x 33.

1 Cor. v 1 *omnino auditur inter uos fornicatio, et talis fornicatio qualis nec inter gentes, ita ut uxorem patris aliquis habeat*: arg. omn. epist.; in 2 Cor. ii 6; vii 12; xii 21.

1 Cor. xii 11 *haec autem omnia operatur unus atque idem spiritus, diuidens singulis prout uult*: in 1 Cor. xii 6; cf. in Rom. xii 3; in 2 Cor. iii 18; viiii 14.

1 Cor. xiii 7 (*caritas*) *omnia suffert, omnia credit, omnia sperat, omnia sustinet*: cf. in 1 Cor. iiii 10; in Phil. i 7; in 1 Thess. i 3; in Col. iii 14.

Eph. v 30 *membra sumus corporis eius, de carne eius et de ossibus eius*: in Rom. vi 6; in 1 Cor. xii 27; cf. in 1 Cor. vi 15; in Gal. iii 27.

Phil. ii 8 *humiliauit semet ipsum, factus oboediens usque ad mortem, mortem autem crucis*: in Rom. i 1; cf. in Phil. ii 5, 12, 22.

About fifty verses are quoted or alluded to three times:—

Gen. iii 4, 5 *dixit autem serpens ad mulierem: Nequaquam morte moriemini: scit enim deus quod in quocumque die comederitis ex eo, aperientur oculi uestri et eritis sicut dii scientes bonum et malum*: cf. in 2 Cor. xi 3; in Gal. vi 7; in 1 Tim. vi 21.

Ps. xiii 1 *dixit insipiens in corde suo: Non est deus...non est qui faciat bonum, non est usque ad unum*: in Rom. iii 10; v 12; cf. Eph. iiii 18.

Iob i 21 *nudus egressus sum de utero matris meae et nudus reuertar illuc...sit nomen domini benedictum*: in Eph. v 20; cf. in 1 Thess. v 18; 1 Tim. vi 7.

Esai. liii 4 *ipse peccata nostra portauit*: in Rom. vi 10; in 1 Cor. xv 3; in Col. iii 13.

Math. vii 23 *numquam noui uos; discedite a me, operarii iniquitatis*: cf. in 1 Cor. xiii 2; xiiii 38; in Gal. iiii 9.

Math. x 10 *dignus est enim operarius cibo suo*: in 2 Cor. viii 15; cf. in 1 Cor. viiii 4; in 2 Cor. xi 7.

Math. xiii 43 *tunc iusti sicut sol fulgebunt*: in 1 Cor. ii 9; cf. in Rom. ii 7; in 2 Thess. i 10.

[1] This passage may however be taken to refer to a later part of the same verse.

Math. xiii 52 *omnis scriba doctus in regno caelorum similis est homini patri familias qui profert de thesauro suo noua et uetera*: in 1 Cor. i 6; cf. in 2 Cor. v 18; in 1 Tim. vi 17.

Math. xviiii 21 *uade uende omnia quae habes et da pauperibus, et habebis thesaurum in caelo, et ueni sequere me*: in 1 Cor. xiii 3; in 1 Tim. vi 19; cf. in 1 Tim. vi 17.

Math. xxv 41 *discedite a me, maledicti, in ignem aeternum, qui praeparatus est diabolo et angelis eius*: in 2 Cor. v 10; in Gal. iii 10; cf. in Eph. v 5.

Marc. vii 8 *traditionem hominum*: cf. in Gal. i 11; in Tit. i 10, 14.

Luc. x 7 *dignus est operarius mercede sua*: in 1 Cor. viiii 14; in 2 Thess. iii 9; cf. 1 Cor. viiii 4 (cf. Math. x 10 above).

Luc. xi 46 *uobis legis peritis uae: quia oneratis homines oneribus*, etc.: cf. in Gal. iii 5; v 7; in Eph. ii 14.

Luc. xxiii 34 *pater, dimitte illis: non enim sciunt quid faciunt*: cf. in Rom. viii 9; in Phil. iiii 7; in Col. iii 15.

Ioh. i 3 *omnia per ipsum facta sunt*: cf. in Rom. xi 36; in 1 Cor. i 9; viii 6.

Ioh. iii 5 *nisi quis renatus fuerit ex aqua et spiritu, non potest introire in regnum dei*: cf. in Gal. iiii 19; vi 15; Eph. ii 10.

Ioh. vi 56 *qui manducat corpus meum et bibit meum sanguinem, in me manet et ego in eo*: in 1 Cor. xi 25; cf. in Rom. viiii 2.

Act. iiii 32 *multitudinis credentium erat cor unum et anima una, nec quisquam suum dicebat, sed erant illis omnia communia*: in Eph. iiii 3; in Phil. i 27; cf. in 2 Cor. viii 15.

Act. v 5 *audiens Ananias haec uerba cecidit et expirauit*: cf. in Rom. xiii 4; in 1 Cor. iiii 21; in 2 Cor. xiii 9.

Act. xiii 11 *eris caecus*, etc.... *confestim in eum cecidit caligo*, etc.: cf. in Rom. xiii 4; in 1 Cor. iiii 21; in 2 Cor. x 4.

Act. xv 10 *nunc ergo quid temptatis deum, inponere iugum super ceruicem discipulorum, quod neque patres nostri neque nos portare potuimus?* cf. in Gal. ii 4; v 1; in Tit. i 15.

Rom. vi 6 *uetus homo*: cf. in Rom. vi 4; xiii 14; in Gal. ii 20.

Rom. vii 12 *lex quidem sancta et mandatum iustum et sanctum et bonum*: in Rom. v 7; cf. in 2 Cor. iii 7; cf. 1 Tim. i 8.

Rom. viii 24 *spe salui facti sumus: spes autem quae uidetur, non est spes*: in Rom. xii 12; in 2 Cor. iii 12; cf. in Phil. iii 12.

Rom. viiii 1 *testimonium mihi perhibente conscientia mea in spiritu sancto*: cf. in 2 Cor. iiii 2; xii 17; in 1 Tim. i 5.

Rom. xiii 10 *dilectio proximi malum non operatur: plenitudo ergo legis est caritas* (*dilectio*): in Rom. iii 28; in 1 Cor. xiii 2; cf. 1 Cor. xiii 2.

1 Cor. vi 19 *membra uestra templum est spiritus sancti*: cf. in Rom. viii 11; 1 Cor. iii 16; 2 Cor. v 5.

1 Cor. x 33 *sicut et ego omnibus per omnia placeo, non quaerens quod mihi utile est, sed quod multis, ut salui fiant*: in Rom. xv 2; in 1 Cor. viiii 22; cf. in 1 Cor. xiii 5.

1 Cor. xii 28 *et quosdam quidem constituit deus in ecclesia... deinde uirtutes, exin gratias curationum*: cf. in Rom. xii 3; in 1 Cor. iii 5; in Eph. iiii 11.

1 Cor. xiii 5 (*caritas*) *non quaerit quae sua sunt*: in 1 Cor. viii 1; cf. in 1 Cor. ii 14; in 2 Cor. iiii 5.

1 Cor. xiiii 25 *occulta etiam cordis eius manifesta fiunt, et tunc cadens in faciem adorabit deum, pronuntians quod deus uere est in uobis*: in Eph. v 13; cf. in 2 Cor. i 23; in 1 Thess. ii 4.

Gal. i 12 *neque enim ego ab homine accepi illud neque didici, sed per reuelationem Iesu Christi*: cf. in 1 Cor. xi 23; xv 3; in Gal. i 13.

Gal. iiii 7 *itaque iam non est seruus, sed filius: quod si filius, et heres per deum*: cf. in Gal. iiii 21, 24, 29.

Eph. iiii 22 *deponere uos secundum pristinam conuersationem ueterem hominem, qui corrumpitur secundum desideria erroris*: cf. in 1 Cor. v 7; xv 49; in Gal. ii 20.

Eph. v 22 *mulieres uiris suis subditae sint, sicut domino*: cf. in 1 Cor. xi 3, 4; in 1 Tim. v 13.

Eph. v 27 *ut exhiberet ipse sibi gloriosam ecclesiam, non habentem maculam aut rugam aut aliquid eiusmodi, sed ut sit sancta et inmaculata*: cf. in 1 Cor. i 2; in 1 Tim. iii 2; in 2 Tim. ii 20.

Phil. i 1 *Paulus et Timotheus, serui...omnibus sanctis...cum episcopis et diaconis*: in 2 Cor. i 1; cf. in 2 Cor. i 1; in 1 Tim. iii 8.

Col. i 24 *corpore eius quod est ecclesia*: cf. in 1 Cor. xv 28; in Eph. ii 21; iiii 12.

Col. ii 5 *et si corpore absens sum, sed spiritu uobiscum sum, gaudens et uidens ordinem uestrum*: arg. omn. epist.; in 1 Cor. i 11; in 1 Thess. ii 17.

1 Tim. v 23 *noli adhuc aquam bibere, sed uino modico utere propter stomachum tuum et frequentes tuas infirmitates*: cf. in 1 Cor. xi 31; in 1 Tim. iii 8; in Tit. ii 3.

2 Tim. iiii 7 *bonum certamen certaui, cursum consummaui, fidem seruaui*: in Rom. viiii 16; cf. in Gal. v 7; arg. in 2 Tim.

Tit. i 5 *ut...constituas per ciuitates presbyteros*: cf. in 1 Cor. iii 5; arg. in Tit.; in Tit. i 7.

Hebr. i 3 *imago expressa substantiae eius*: in 2 Cor. iiii 4; cf. in Phil. ii 6; in Col. i 15.

Hebr. x 34 *nam et uinctis conpassi estis et rapinam bonorum uestrorum cum gaudio suscepistis, cognoscentes uos habere meliorem et manentem substantiam*: arg. omn. epist.; in 1 Thess. ii 14; cf. in Gal. ii 10 (cf. pp. 70 f.).

1 Ioh. iii 6 *omnis qui in eo manet, non peccat; et omnis qui peccat, non uidit eum nec cognouit eum*: in Rom. iii 11; in Eph. iiii 13; cf. in Eph. i 17.

Apoc. vi 8 *qui sedebat desuper, nomen illi peccatum*[1] *et mors, et inferus sequebatur eum*: cf. in Rom. vii 8; in 1 Cor. xv 26; in Col. iiii 11.

I venture to think that this is a considerable body of evidence in favour of common authorship for all the expositions. The list may have at the same time some interest as a collection of the author's favourite verses of scripture, shedding further light on his personality and point of view.

(e) Community of Style and Language

The present section has not the slightest claim to be considered a complete account of the style and language of the commentaries, or even a complete account of the most characteristic elements in these. I doubt not that another student might select many other instances of equal cogency with those adduced below. It happens that Pelagius is a very correct writer, with little of the extraordinary about his vocabulary or idiom, in this respect differing very greatly from his predecessor, Ambrosiaster.

[1] On this reading see below, chap. iv p. 173.

The collection of characteristic expressions has, therefore, cost much more trouble.

The evidence in this case consists rather of many examples of a few simple phrases than of few instances of an unusual type. The portion concerned with Grammar is particularly brief.

I. *Grammar*

1. Accidence

The ablative of *uetus* is generally, perhaps always, *uetere*: Rom. vii 12; 1 Cor. vii 5; viiii 20; Gal. v 23; Eph. iiii 24; Tit. iii 6. (Ambst always, Hier. usually *ueteri*.) In abl. sing. of compar. adj. we sometimes find *-e*, e.g. *meliore* (1 Cor. iii 12), and perhaps this form should always be read.

The genitive plural of present participles ends in *-um* probably more frequently than *-ium*: examples of *-um* are 1 Thess. ii 18; 2 Tim. ii 4; 2 Tim. iiii 5.

In the matter of word formation, several instances where the preposition *ex* is concerned, may be mentioned. Just as *pro consule* is an earlier stage than the inflected substantive *proconsul*, so *ex praefecto* precedes *expraefectus* in time. At what date the latter type begins, it is not perhaps possible to state exactly, but Pelagius knows nothing of it, for in him we find only the earlier stage: Rom. xvi 23 *hic arcarium* ex arcario *dicit, sicut gentes credentes* ex gentibus *saepe nominauit*; Eph. arg. *Ephesii* ex Iudaeis *et* gentibus; Phil. iiii 3 *Clemens* ex philosopho, *magnae doctrinae uir, qui Romae episcopus fuit*; Col. iiii 14 (*Lucas*) ex medico *erat, sicut Matheus iam apostolus adhuc dicitur publicanus*; 1 Tim. arg. *rationem reddens quod non sit mirum, si ipse* ex persecutore *saluatus sit.*

2. Syntax

The author shows an extreme fondness for the ablative of the gerund, not as a mere substitute for the present participle, but with the earlier, instrumental force. The following list of examples is fairly complete:—

Rom. ii 4 *bonus est* expectando, *iustus est* puniendo; 12, 15, 27; iii 4, 28; iiii 15; v 10; vii 13; viii 3, 6; viiii 17, 22; xi 4 *bis*; xii 5, 19 *bis*, 21; xiiii 8 *bis*, 17, 23 *bis*; xvi 4.

1 Cor. i 19 elegendo *piscatores, artem rhetoricam et philosophicam reprobauit...ut...paulatim* meditando *proficiat*; 28; vi 19, 20; vii 3, 34 *bis*; viii 8 *bis*; viiii 13, 27; x 5; xv 51.

2 Cor. ii 11 *ut peccatores pereant* desperando, *quo modo in nimia remissione minime* corrigendo; iii 1, 9; vii 3; viii 14; x 14; xii 7.

Gal. iiii 24 reprehendendo *atque* uindicando *ostendit illa non se propter sua mysteria fieri uoluisse*; v 14, 15.

Eph. ii 3 *in quibus et nos omnes conuersati sumus aliquando*]. *Non solum uos gentes non* credendo, *sed et nos Iudaei* peccando; 5, 13; iii 8; iiii 8, 16; v 3, 6; vi 4.

Phil. i 5 *quod ab initio communicatis* praedicando; 6, 16, 20; ii 2, 5 *ter*, 7, 13 *ter*, 27; iii 13.

1 Thess. arg. laudando *illos apostolus ad maiora prouocat*; i 10; iiii 4.

2 Thess. iii 5 *dirigat*]. Reuelando *quanta sint quae...repromisit.*

Col. i 10 *quo modo deus det uelle et adiuuet uel confirmet*, docendo *scilicet sapientiam et intellectus gratiam* tribuendo, *non libertatem arbitrii* auferendo; ii 13, 15 *quinquiens.*

1 Tim. i 19 *habens bonam conscientiam*]. Implendo *quod doces...male* uiuendo *ipsam quoque fidem perdiderunt*; ii 8; v 3 *bis*; vi 2, 4 *bis*, 13, 17.

2 Tim. ii 10 *cum has passiones potuerim iam* moriendo *finire*; iii 12.

Tit. i 7 *turpe lucrum* adulando *sectari*; ii 6.

Another favourite construction is that of the present participle with a noun, particularly an abstract noun in the singular, in the ablative absolute. Examples are:—

Rom. ii 25 *carnis* circumcisione cessante; v 4, 14; vi 15; vii 9; viii 4; viiii 17; xi 24; xiii 7, 11, 13.

1 Cor. vii 5 uno *se* retrahente; viiii 10; xiii 3; xiiii 14, 22.

2 Cor. iii 3 confirmante *per uirtutem* spiritu sancto; 13, 18; v 1, 4, 19; vii 4.

Gal. iiii 24 manente *historiae* ueritate; v 16 *bis.*

Eph. arg. Paulo apostolo praedicante; ii 1, 5; v 22.

Phil. arg. ipso praedicante.

Col. ii 16 (*umbra*) *cessauit* corpore ueniente, *quia imagine opus non est,* ueritate praesente; 23.

2 Tim. ii 19 deo *illos suos esse* optime cognoscente.

Tit. ii 12 *perfecte,* domino ipso dicente....

Philem. 8 caritate faciente *obsecrare malumus quam iubere*[1].

It may be here noted that Pelagius is throughout very strict in regard to the sequence of tenses. Examples need not be adduced[2].

Object sentences in the later authors are especially interesting. In addition to the accusative and infinitive construction, we frequently find examples of a native Latin colloquial construction with *quod*, and also, on the analogy of ὅτι with its double sense, a Biblical Grecism, with *quia* and *quoniam.* Even *ut* is found. The later authors can be classified according to their practice in this matter. The few severe purists show the accusative and infinitive only; the somewhat less strict show also the use of *quod*; the still less strict add *quia*, and the really lax indulge also in *quoniam*: *ut* in this use is absent from most writers. I have printed statistics on this matter elsewhere[3] and will not repeat them here. *Quoniam* and perhaps *ut* are entirely absent from Pelagius, and *quod* is commoner in him than *quia.* These facts at once place him in the better class of writers. If my numeration is correct, the proportion of cases is about 98 of *quod* to 72 of *quia.* A possible example of *ut* occurs at Rom. v 15. To avoid repetition, only some of the examples of the *quod* and *quia* constructions will be given at this stage: others will be found later in the chapter[4]. *Quod* and *quia* are followed sometimes by the indicative, sometimes by the subjunctive, but while the subjunctive is much more frequent with *quod,* the indicative predominates with *quia.*

quod: (indic.) Rom. arg. *unde probatur* quod *seruiuimus*; viiii 11; x 3, 5; 2 Cor. viii 3.

(subj.) Rom. i 2 *dicit* quod...sit promissum...*et* quod...sit creatus; 19 *bis*; iii 2 *bis*; v 1; vii 8; viii 13, 31, 33–4; viiii 4, (14), 33; x 5, 14; xiiii 18; 1 Cor. i 19; vii 3; viiii 20, 21; xii 6; xv 28; 2 Cor. iii 6 *bis*; v 11; viii 15; xi 16, 33 *bis*; xii 6, 9; Gal. i 12; ii 11; iii 11; iiii 28; v 9; Eph. i 1; ii 2; iii 1, 18; Phil. ii 5; 1 Tim. iii 11.

[1] See also under **existo** below.

[2] *In Phil.* i 7 is an exception.

[3] In my linguistic introduction to Sanday's *Novum Testamentum S. Irenaei* (Old-Latin Biblical Texts, no. vii).

[4] Under **notare, adtendere, considerare** etc. on pp. 85, 89 f. etc.

quia: (indic.) Rom. iii 4 *bis*; v 6, 15; viiii 16, 30 *bis*, 33; x 2 *bis*; xi 10, 18; xv 16; 1 Cor. i 4, 23, 26; v 6; xi 4 *bis*, 26 *bis*; xv 6, 11, 28; 2 Cor. v 5; vi 11; xi 12; Gal. iiii 29; Phil. i 27; iii 13; iiii 15; Col. iiii 18; 2 Tim. i 18; iii 1; iiii 20.

(subj.) Rom. i 19; v 1; vii 25; viii 8; xi 6; xiiii 2, 11; 1 Cor. vii 14; viii 7; xi 27; 2 Cor. ii 3; viii 22; Gal. iiii 29; Philem. 22.

At least two points in regard to the arrangement of words call for remark[1]. First, Pelagius is very fond of separating a noun, usually the object, from its adjunct by interposing the governing verb. The adjunct may be an adjective or participle in agreement with the noun, or it may be another noun or pronoun in the genitive case governed by the noun. Sometimes the adjunct consists of both adjective and dependent genitive. Examples occur in abundance in the *Argumentum Omnium Epistularum* and right through to the end of the work. It is not necessary to mention more than a few:—

Arg. omn. epist.	*praesentia atque orientia resecaret uitia.*
" " "	*futuras excluderet quaestiones.*
" " "	*rediuiua semper populi conpressere peccata.*
Rom. i 8	*idolorum nimia fuerant cultura possessi.*
iiii 24	*eius quasi patris imitemur exemplum.*
1 Cor. iii 19	*suam non reseruat iniuriam.*
vii 3	*proprias in matrimonium acceperunt sorores.*
2 Cor. ii 6	*paternum polluit torum.*
v 16	*nullius ueterum imitamur exemplum.*
Gal. iiii 16	*omnem continentiam suo illis monstrabat exemplo.*
Eph. ii 12	*unum amiserunt uerum.*
Phil. iiii 9	*illa explanant superiora.*
1 Thess. i 5	*iustitiae commendatur exemplo.*
2 Thess. ii 12	*homini crediderunt diabolica arte fallenti.*
Col. iii 2–3	*caelestem sectamini sapientiam.*
1 Tim. i 9	*occasiones fugere delictorum.*
2 Tim. i 16	*ad exemplum prouocet bonum.*
Tit. ii 1	*ad uitam pertinent Christi.*
Philem. 8	*ad rem pietatis pertinet Christianae.*

The second point is the matter of rhythm. There can be no

[1] Dr Alfred J. Smith first called my attention to these points.

doubt that Pelagius, in common with other careful writers of the imperial period, paid attention to the rhythm of his sentences. It was not necessary for my purpose to make a list of the different types of *clausula* employed by him, or to calculate the number of times each occurs. It is enough to call attention to the frequency with which a sentence ends with four long syllables[1]. This ending is found in probably about a third of the total number of endings in the treatise. Another ending found frequently is the type – ⏑ – – –. From the Argumentum Omn. Epist. we take sentences ending with *trānsmīsērūnt, sūnt pōrrēctāe, ādquīsītōs, cōnflīctārēnt, sēruāuērūnt, cōnstāntēs īnuēntī*: the following occur later, to which many might be added:—Rom. i 3 *nōn ēst fāctŭs*; i 8 *dēmōnstrātŭr*; i 12 *cōnsōlēmŭr*; 1 Cor. i 5 *tēstāmēntī*; i 25 *sūnt sāluātī*; 2 Cor. ii 5 *prōfēcīstĭs; cōntrīstāuĭt*; Gal. ii 17 *īndūlgērĕ*; Eph. i 3 *īnfrā scrīptă*; Phil. arg. *Phĭlīppēnsēs īn Chrīstō*; 1 Thess. iiii 7 *nōn pērmīttĭt*; 2 Thess. iii 1 *ēxōrēmŭs*; Col. iiii 3 *īn dōctrīnā*; 1 Tim. vi 2 *praemium ōstēndēndō*; 2 Tim. ii 2 *cōnfīrmāuī*; Tit. i 16 *quāe quāerūntŭr*; Philem. arg. *cōrrēctūrŭm*. The ending – ⏑ – – –, being one of Cicero's favourites, usually numbered 1 by the students of metrical prose[2], need not be illustrated.

The only figure to which I shall call attention is that of ellipsis. The instances are not numerous, but are sufficiently interesting to have a value as evidence: Rom. xi 2 *in* Regnorum, *ubi scriptum est de Helia*; 1 Cor. vii 5 *unde et in* Regnorum *panem sacerdotalem non nisi continentes accipiunt*; the omission of *libris* in such phrases is quite in line with the practice of St Cyprian, who wrote *In Basilion* simply[3]. Another example of ellipsis occurs at Rom. vii 12 *deus non numquam in* Vetere *'bonus' et in* Nouo *dicitur 'iustus,'* where *testamento* is understood, and at Rom. viiii 4 Veteris *latio et* Noui *promissio*.

Occasionally we find what may be called philological notes: in 1 Cor. xv 25 'donec' *non semper finem significat, sicut est illud*:

[1] The spondaic cadence is rare in Cicero, but frequent in Livy: see A. C. Clark, *The Cursus in Mediaeval and Vulgar Latin* (Oxford, 1910) pp. 7 f.

[2] Cf. Clark, p. 7.

[3] Cf. C. H. Turner in *Journal of Theological Studies* vol. VI (1904—5) pp. 249, 259 f., 268. Max.-Taur. *c. Iud.* ch. 9 l. 8 (ed. C. H. Turner, *J.T.S.* vol. XX (1918—19) p. 306) also has *in Regnorum*: so also Ps.-Aug. *Speculum*.

ego deus uester donec senescatis, et cetera talia[1]; in 1 Cor. xv 31 'per' *non semper significatio iuramenti est: nam si dicam 'per' puerum misi, non statim per puerum iurasse recte putabor*; in Gal. iii 4 *hic* 'si tamen' *non dubitantis sermo sit, sed potius confirmantis, secundum illud*: si tamen iustum est aput deum retribuere his qui uos tribulant, tribulationem.

II. *Lexicography.*

Details of Phraseology and Vocabulary

(*a*) *Favourite Openings of Notes.*

One of the most constant features of the commentary is the phraseology at the beginning of the notes. Without attempting to exhaust the formulae employed for this purpose, we can easily adduce a sufficient number of examples of each to show unity of authorship throughout the commentary. A comparison with the methods of Ambrosiaster shows at once the difference of authorship here[2].

Notandum quod[3]: (*a*) c. indic. 1 Cor. vii 9; xv 45; 2 Cor. viii 7; xiii 11; Gal. v 21; Phil. iiii 18; 1 Thess. iiii 18; Tit. i 6.

(*b*) c. subjunct. Rom. v 8; xii 3; 1 Cor. x 8; xii 12; xiii 3; 2 Cor. vi 6; Eph. ii 2; 1 Thess. i 5; Col. i 29; 1 Tim. ii 15; Philem. 14.

Notandum quia: c. indic. Rom. viii 2; 2 Cor. xi 23; Gal. i 22; Eph. i 17; iiii 18; Phil. i 10; 1 Thess. v 11: no examples c. subjunct.

Notandum c. acc. et inf. Rom. xv 23; 2 Cor. vi 5; 1 Tim. v 7.

Totus: Rom. xii 9, Tota *puritas debet esse in Christiano*; 1 Cor. xv 2 Tota *ratio praedicationis nostrae haec est*; 1 Cor. xv 41 Tota *comparationis huius diuersitas ad hoc facit*; 2 Cor. viiii 2 Tota *prouincia, cuius caput estis....*

Recapitulo[4]: Rom. vii 25 Recapitulat, *ut concludat*; Rom. xiii 9 Recapitulatur *omnis iustitia in proximi dilectione.*

[1] This note was borrowed from Jerome, see chap. v p. 184.

[2] Cf. *Study of Ambrosiaster* pp. 64 f.

[3] Cf. **Simul notandum quod**, p. 90, etc.

[4] The word also Rom. viiii 30.

Quaeritur[1] etc. Argum. omn. epist. *primum* quaeritur *qua re*; Rom. i 1 Quaerimus *qua re*; 2 Cor. i 1 Quaeritur *cur*; 1 Cor. i 11, 1 Thess. iii 2 Quaeritur *quo modo*.

Vult ostendere[2] Rom. iii 26; xi 13; 2 Cor. iii 5[3]; Phil. ii 5 (followed by acc. et inf.); Rom. v 6 (followed by *quia* c. indic.), viii 31 (followed by *quod* c. subjunct.); cf. Rom. v 11 *Hic* ostendere uult (followed by acc. et inf.); 2 Cor. vii 5 ostendere...uult (*quantam* c. subjunct.). *Vult* is the first word of Rom. vi 2; x 18; 1 Cor. iii 4; Gal. i 11; 1 Tim. v 18: cf. 1 Cor. xii 31.

Hic ostendit[4] Rom. i 10, 11; viiii 9; x 1; 1 Cor. iiii 20 (ostenditur); xiiii 22 (ostenditur); 2 Cor. xii 6 (*uidetur* ostendere); Philem. 22 (ostenditur).

Ostendit Rom. i 2; ii 14; vi 4; xv 14, 21; xvi 5; 1 Cor. i 2; v 1; viiii 20; xv 34; 2 Cor. viii 10; xi 6; Gal. i 1 (ostenditur); i 4, 18; iiii 15; Phil. i 4; 1 Thess. iii 10; 1 Tim. iii 13; cf. 1 Tim. v 23.

Contra and **Hoc contra**[5] etc.: Rom. xi 22 Contra *eos qui...et* contra *eos qui...*; 2 Cor. iiii 6 Hoc contra *omnes inimicos...*; Gal. i 19 Contra *eos, qui...*; Col. i 16 Contra *Manicheos*; Gal. v 24; Hoc contra *illos qui*; 2 Tim. ii 8 Hoc contra *illos, qui*; Rom. viiii 2 Contra *Iudaeos acturus*; xv 25 hoc contra *illos facit*; 1 Cor. i 26 Hoc contra *illos agit*; viiii 21 Contra *Arrianos et Fotinianos*; xiii 3 contra *eos qui...*; xv 45 quod contra *Manicheos* et *Apollinaristas facit*; Eph. v 5 Contra *illos agit* qui; Col. ii 8 Contra *philosophos agit*. Compare also the passages with *Hic locus*, etc.; Rom. i 2 totus hic locus contra *Manicheos facit*; xi 36 *simul etiam* contra *Arrianos facit* hic locus; 1 Cor. i 9 hic locus contra *Arrianos facit*; cf. Gal. i 8 *facit autem sententia haec* contra *omnes haereticos*.

Ne frequently introduces a note, e.g. 1 Cor. vii 35 Ne *necessi-*

[1] Similarly in body of notes; with *quare* Rom. ii 26, 2 Cor. viiii 11; with *cur*, 1 Tim. iii 8; with *quo modo* Rom. iii 19; iiii 18; 1 Cor. vii 16; xiii 3; xiiii 34; with *si* Gal. iii 10; with *unde* 1 Cor. i 19; with *ut* Rom. viii 10; with *quid* 1 Cor. vii 3 *bis*.

[2] In Origen-Rufinus *in Rom.* (see Dr Smith in *Journ. Theol. Studies* vol. xx (1918—19) p. 142 n.).

[3] Also 2 Cor. v 10; Gal. i 10, 13; though not the first words.

[4] This word predominates over *monstro*: examples in the body of the notes are Rom. iii 19, 29; viii 3; xv 25; 1 Cor. i 26; ii 1; xi 4; 2 Cor. xi 1, 33; Gal. ii 11; iiii 19; v 9; Eph. ii 10.

[5] Also in body of note, 2 Thess. i 8.

tatem...; 1 Cor. x 1 *Nequis*; Gal. i 19 Ne...*uideretur* (cf. Rom. x 3; xiii 6); but is found in especial frequency with parts of **dico** and **puto**: **ne dicerent** Rom. iii 19; iiii 11; v 20; vi 2, 15; xi 6; 1 Cor. xv 33; 1 Tim. i 11; **nequis diceret** Rom. i 32[1]; Ne*quis forte* diceret Rom. ii 14; Gal. v 9; Ne*quis* dicat 2 Cor. viii 20; Ne diceret 2 Tim. ii 6; cf. *Ne...adsererent* Rom. xv 12. **Nequis putet**[2] 1 Cor. x 1, 29; Phil. iii 4; (1 Tim. iii 6). Non putet 1 Cor. vii 18. **Ne putetis**[3] 1 Cor. ii 6; xiiii 18; 2 Cor. vii 12; viii 12; xi 5; Eph. iii 13; cf. ut putetis Gal. iiii 12. Ne putaret[4] 1 Tim. v 23. Ne...putaremus Rom. xii 14[5]. **Ne putarent** 1 Cor. xv 8; Gal. ii 2[6]. **Ne putaretur**[7] Rom. v 15; Gal. i 2.

Expono[8]: Rom. ii 23 Exposuit *quid sacrilegium dixerit*; Rom. iiii 4 Exponit *exemplum*; Rom. xiiii 21 Exponit *quid sit per quod*...; Rom. xv 22 Exposuit *illud quod in capite dixerat*; 1 Cor. xi 15 Exposuit *quod dixerat*; 1 Cor. xiii 11 Exposuit *qualiter euacuentur illa*...; 1 Cor. xiiii 3 Exposuit *quot modis intellegenda sit prophetia*; 2 Cor. iii 9 Exposuit *quod superius dixerat*; Eph. iiii 9 Exponit *cur dicatur ascendisse*; Eph. iiii 22 Exposuit *quid sit uetus homo*; Eph. iiii 24 Exposuit *quid sit hominem ad imaginem dei esse creatum*; Eph. v 18 Exponit *continentiae utilitatem*; Col. iii 10 Exposuit *imaginem in actu consistere.*

Repeto[9]: Rom. xi 15 Repetit *quod dixerat superius*; Rom. xiiii 20 Repetit *quod superius dixerat*; 1 Cor. viii 4 Repetit *quod superius...dixerat*; 2 Cor. xii 4 *Quod iterum* repetit, *ostendit*...; Gal. i 9 Repetitum *fortius commendatur*; Phil. iiii 4 Repetit *ut magis ac magis gaudium confirmetur*: cf. Tit. iii 14 *Id ipsum* repetit, *quod superius dixerat.*

Incipio[10]: Rom. i 18 Incipit *ad partem gentium loqui*; 1 Cor.

[1] Also in body of note, 1 Cor. xi 16; cf. ne *de nobis* dicatur, Col. iii 4.

[2] Also in subordinate clauses, Rom. viiii 14; 2 Cor. x 10; cf. 1 Cor. xii 28.

[3] Also in subordinate clauses, 1 Cor. xiiii 33; 2 Thess. iii 13; cf. 1 Cor. iii 1; 2 Cor. i 1; 2 Cor. viii 1; Gal. iii 20.

[4] Also in subordinate clause, 1 Cor. i 16.

[5] *ne putemus* 1 Cor. xii 28.

[6] Also in subordinate clause, 2 Cor. i 1.

[7] Also in subordinate clauses, Rom. v 2; 1 Cor. v 3; xv 6; 2 Cor. i 17; xi 33; Gal. i 14; Tit. i 8.

[8] Also in body of notes, Rom. vi 12; viii 13, 19; 1 Cor. i 9; xiiii 17; Gal. vi 17; Eph. arg.; Col. i 10; 1 Tim. iii 5.

[9] Also in body of notes, Phil. iii 1.

[10] See also under **hinc** (p. 88), **causa** (pp. 95 f.); and cf. 1 Thess. iiii 1.

vii 1 Incipit *de coniugiis*; 1 Cor. vii 8 Incipit *aliam causam, de innuptis*; 1 Cor. viii 1 Incipit *de idolothytis*; 1 Cor. xi 2 Incipit *de uelamentis*; 1 Cor. xi 18 Incipit *de sacramentis*; Eph. ii 1 Incipit *collata beneficia replicare*; Eph. v 13 Incipit *lumen esse cum crediderit*; cf. also 1 Thess. iiii 1 *Post laudem et consolationem* incipit *exhortatio.*

Hinc[1]; **Iam hinc**: Rom. ii 17 Hinc *conuertitur*, etc.; Rom. vii 1 Hinc *incipit difficultatem legis ostendere*; Rom. vii 7 Hinc *in persona eius hominis loquitur*; Rom. viii 8 Hinc *probatur quia superius*; Rom. viii 18 Hinc *uult futuram gloriam commendare*; Rom. x 17 Hinc *responsio apostoli*; Rom. xiiii 1 Hinc *oblique illos increpare incipit*; Rom. xiiii 2 Hinc *probatur quia non*; Rom. xiiii 13 Hinc *subtiliter ingreditur*; 1 Cor. i 10 Hinc *iam causam contra dissensionem adgreditur*; 1 Cor. iiii 7 Hinc *ad ipsos inflatos per eloquentiam uerba conuertit*; 1 Cor. iiii 18 Hinc *incipit causam fornicationis arguere*; 1 Cor. vi 1 Hinc *probatur Christianos tunc...*; 1 Cor. vii 39 Hinc *incipit de digamis et uiduis*; 2 Cor. iii 3 Hinc *uere cognoscimini*; 2 Cor. iii 3 Hinc *iam differentiam inducit*; 2 Cor. iiii 7 Iam hinc *incipit ostendere*; 2 Cor. xii 9 Hinc *intellegimus etiam sanctos*; Eph. iiii 25 Hinc *describit ipsas species sanctitatis*; Phil. i 12 Hinc *consolatur eos*; 1 Tim. ii 4 Hinc *probatur deum nemini...*; 2 Tim. iiii 20 Hinc *probatur quia....*

Hic (pron.), in various parts of the word, very frequently, but especially in the phrase *Hoc est*, e.g. Rom. i 9 Hoc est: *in toto corde*, etc.; Rom. i 15 Hoc est *paratum*; Rom. iii 8 Hoc *fortassis ideo putabant*; Rom. viii 12 Hoc *totum agit ut...*; Rom. viiii 4 Hoc est *ministerium angelorum uel prophetarum*; Rom. xi 16 Hoc est, *et primi et nouissimi*, etc.; Rom. xiii 12; xv 4, 14, etc.; 1 Cor. iii 12 Huius *artis est qui...*; 1 Cor. v 12 Hoc est *de infidelibus*; 1 Cor. vii 26 Hic '*existimo*' *non pro dubio posuit*; 1 Cor. vii 29; viiii 12; 2 Cor. vi 9 Hoc est, *usque ad mortem peruenientes*; Gal. ii 10 Hoc est, *quod in omni...*; Eph. iiii 29 Hoc est *quod alibi dicit*; Phil. ii 11 Hoc est, *in natura et gloria deitatis*; 1 Thess. iiii 10 Hoc est, *etiam ignotos*; 2 Thess. iii 10 Haec sit *inquietudinis...emendatio*; 1 Tim. ii 9 Haec *sunt ornamenta feminae Christianae*; 2 Tim. ii 8

[1] In body of note, 1 Cor. vii 5 hinc *probatur quid possit perpetua continentia*; 2 Cor. i 2 hinc *iam gratias agunt deo*; Eph. iii 21 hinc *incipit moralia omni ecclesiae tradere instituta*; 1 Tim. i 18 hinc *dat auctoritatem ordinandi.*

Hoc *contra illos, qui*...; Tit. iii 8 Haec, *non illa quae sequuntur*; Philem. 2 Hic *diaconus erat*[1], etc.

Hic locus[2]: 1 Cor. ii 8 Hoc loco...*duae haereses abutuntur*; 1 Cor. xiiii 14 *Oratio* hoc loco *oris ratio*.

Hic (adv.)[3]: Rom. iii 4 Hic *omnes pro maxima parte dicit*; Rom. v 11 Hic *ostendere uult*; 1 Cor. viiii 24 Hic *stadii cursum iustitiae uel fidei comparauit*; 1 Cor. xii 6 Hic *uult ostendere*; 1 Cor. iiii 20; xiiii 22 Hic *ostenditur*; Col. ii 11 Hic *iam pseudo-apostolos taxat*; Col. iii 16 *Et* hic *ostenditur*; Tit. ii 2 Hic *senes... possunt intellegi*.

Reddit causam (causas): Rom. viiii 32 Reddit causas *qua re non inuenerint iustitiam*; 2 Cor. i 23 Reddit causam *non impleti promissi*; 2 Cor. xi 12 *Hic* reddit causam *qua re non acciperet*; Gal. ii 4 Reddit causas *qua re circumciderit Titum*; Eph. v 24 Reddit *iustam* causam *subiectionis*; 2 Thess. iii 11 Reddit *superioris sententiae* causas; 1 Tim. ii 14 Reddit causas *cur eas uelit esse subiectas*; 1 Tim. v 15 Reddit causas *qua re eas nubere uelle praedixerat*.

Reddit rationem (*Reddita ratione*) with **quare** or **quod** is rarer: Rom. ii 13; iii 2; 1 Cor. xv 58[4].

Talis[5]: Rom. i 7 talis *est ubique salutatio eius*; Rom. x 4 Talis *est qui Christum credidit*...; Rom. xii 1 Talis *ei placet hostia*; Eph. v 9 Talem *habet scientia fructum*; 1 Thess. i 10 Tales *estis ut*...; Col. iiii 13 Tales *erant primi temporis discipuli*; 1 Tim. v 9 Tales *uoluit eligi diaconissas*; 2 Tim. i 2 Talis *est salutatio Pauli ut*; 2 Tim. iiii 3 Tales *sibi magistros inquirent*; Tit. i 9 Talis *est eligendus qui*...; Tit. iii 1 Talem *te exhibe, ut*....

(*b*) *Similar Phrases in the Body of the Notes, and Phrases introducing Biblical Quotations.*

adtendo: Rom. iiii 5 *simul* adtendendum *quia...asseruit*; 1 Cor.

[1] In body of note, cf. 1 Cor. iii 11 hoc *solum agitur ne*; Gal. ii 11 hoc *autem totum agit ut*.

[2] Also in the body of the notes, e.g. Rom. iii 28; xi 3, 8; 1 Cor. xiiii 23; xv 24 hoc loco; 1 Cor. iii 3 *in* hoc loco; Rom. i 2; viiii 17; xi 36; 1 Cor. i 9; xii 6; 2 Cor. viiii 6 hic locus; Phil. ii 9 locus hic. See also under **Contra** above.

[3] Cf. above under **Vult ostendere, Hic ostendit**. In body of note, Rom. i 23 hic... *appellat*; Rom. iii 28 hic...*dicit*; 2 Cor. ii 11 hic *euidentissime ostenditur*.

[4] It is commoner in the middle of a note: e.g. Arg. omn. epist.; 1 Cor. xii 31; 2 Cor. xi 16; Gal. ii 14; 1 Tim. arg.

[5] So in body of note, Eph. vi 4.

vii 35 *simul* adtendendum *quia...erat*; 1 Cor. xv 38 adtende *quia ...dixerit*; 2 Cor. vi 10 *simul* adtendendum *quod...dicit*; Gal. vi 18 *simul et* adtendendum *quia...dixerit*; Col. i 28 *simul* adtende *quod...doceat*; Philem. arg. *nihil magis est in hac epistula* adtendendum *nisi quanta....*

simul notandum, or **notandum**: (*a*) **quod** c. indic.: Eph. vi 13; Tit. iii 15. c. subjunct.: Rom. vi 13; xii 8; xiiii 17; 1 Cor. vi 1; viii 12; viiii 21; xiii 2; 2 Cor. xi 16; Gal. v 24; vi 2; Eph. iii 8. (*b*) **quia** c. indic.: Rom. iii 24; Eph. iiii 29; 1 Tim. iiii 12. (*c*) c. acc. et infin.: Rom. viii 13; 1 Thess. iii 5; 1 Tim. v 8. (*d*) c. indir. interrog.: *in quibus* 2 Thess. iii 1; *quo modo* Col. i 23.

caueo: Rom. i 31 caueamus *ergo et nos ne...*; Rom. v 9 caueamus *ergo ne...*; (Rom. xii 17 *Tantum* caue *ne ideo facias...*;) Rom. xiiii 8 cauendum *ergo ne nos...*; Tit. ii 14 caueamus *ergo ne....*

considero; considerandum est: 1 Cor. xi 17 *unde* considerandum est *quid...*; Eph. ii 4 *unde* considerandum est *quantum*; 1 Thess. iiii 4 *simul* considerandum *quia*...scribit.

ne...uideatur (uideretur): Rom. xiii 6 ne uideretur *Christus superbiam docuisse*; Rom. xiiii 20 ne *creaturam damnare* uideatur; 1 Cor. xv 27 ne *deum...subiecisse* uideretur; 2 Cor. v 5 ne *cui inpossibile* uideretur; 2 Cor. vi 18 ne *cui inpossibile* uideatur. But also at beginning of note, e.g. 1 Cor. xiiii 35 Ne uideretur *eas etiam discere uetuisse*; 1 Cor. xv 1 Ne *illi hoc non credidisse* uiderentur.

potest et ita (c. infin. pass.): Rom. vii 16 potest *autem* et ita *intellegi*; 1 Cor. viiii 20 potest et ita *intellegi quod...dixerit*; 1 Cor. xi 12 potest et ita *dici* (cf. 1 Cor. i 13 Potest ita *dici*; xi 14 potest *dici*); 2 Cor. vii 12 potest et ita *dici*; cf. Tit. ii 2 *senes et aetate et ordine* possunt *intellegi.*

quid (direct interrog.), in apodosis to **si** clause: 1 Cor. iii 2 Si *ergo...illi...sunt...*, quid *de illis censendum est...?* 1 Cor. iii 15 *quod* si *ille...erit...*, quid *de illis fiet...?* 2 Cor. xi 17 si *hic... negat...*, quid *de illis sentiendum est...?*

quibus respondendum est: Argum. omn. epist.; Rom. viii 33–4; xi 26; 1 Cor. iii 17; viii 6; xv 28, 35; cf. Rom. vii 7 respondendum est.

simul (introducing a further consideration in a note): add to the examples given under *adtendo, noto,* etc. above, the following: Rom. i 16 simul *et illos haereticos tangit*; 1 Cor. xiiii 20 simul *ostendit neminem...esse perfectum*; 2 Cor. vi 14 simul *ostendit neminem posse...iustum esse...*; 2 Cor. viii 15 simul *et ostenditur... omnia aequalia esse debere*; 2 Tim. iii 8 simul*que ostendit Mosen ueritatis fuisse doctorem.*

Allusions to other passages in St Paul's Epistles are generally introduced by phrases containing the word **alibi** or the word **superius**:

sicut alibi ait: Rom. viii 26; xii 10; xv 29; 1 Cor. vii 23; viiii 27; 2 Cor. iiii 10; v 8; 1 Thess. ii 17.

sicut alibi dicit: 1 Cor. xii 28; 2 Cor. iii 2, 18; viiii 7.

et **alibi** *ait* Rom. xiii 13; *sicut ipse* alibi *ait* Rom. xi 28; *et* alibi Rom. viii 27; Eph. iii 18; *sicut* alibi 2 Cor. vi 2; 1 Thess. ii 3; *sicut ait* alibi 1 Cor. vi 20; *sicut* alibi *idem dicit* Rom. xiii 11; *sicut* alibi...*dicitur* 1 Cor. iii 23; *sicut ipse ait* Rom. viii 39; Eph. ii 6; *sicut ipse* alibi *dicit* 1 Cor. xi 23; *unde et* alibi *ait* Phil. ii 14; *ipse apostolus* alibi *dixit* 2 Cor. iiii 4; *unde et* alibi *dicit* Gal. ii 11; *unde* alibi *ait* 1 Cor. xvi 18; Col. ii 14; *unde ait* alibi 2 Cor. vi 4; *sicut et* alibi *suum nobis proponit exemplum dicens* Rom. xv 2; *suum quoque* alibi *proponit exemplum dicens* 1 Cor. viii 1; alibi *appellauit* 2 Cor. iii 7; 2 Thess. ii 3; *unde et* alibi...*est appellata* 1 Tim. i 8; *ut ibi* 1 Cor. x 13; xv 50; *sicut ibi* Rom. v 12; 1 Cor. viiii 7; *ut* alibi *dicit* 2 Tim. i 7; *sicut ibi dicit* Rom. viii 27; *ipse* alibi *dicit* Rom. ii 13; viii 6; *de quo* alibi *dicit* Tit. ii 3; *quo modo* alibi *dicat* 1 Cor. xiiii 34; cf. 2 Cor. iii 6; *quo modo scriptum est* alibi Rom. xiii 7 (cf. Rom. i 30); *dicente* alibi *apostolo* 2 Cor. v 19; *Paulum quoque ipsum* alibi *docere* Gal. arg.; *iustitia, quam loricae* alibi *comparauit* 1 Thess. v 8; *quam idem apostolus* alibi *sine macula definiuit*; *dicit enim* alibi Rom. v 7.

Rom. ii 8 *iam* **superius** *dictum est contentiosum...*; Rom. viii 8 superius *non carnem,* sed *opera accusauerit carnis*; Rom. viiii 6 *quia* superius *dixerat dolere se quod...*; Rom. viiii 29 superius *scriptum est*; 1 Cor. i 31 *in* superius *conprehensis*; 1 Cor. viiii 22 *in his quae* superius *memorauimus*; 1 Cor. x 15 *omnia quae* superius *conprehendi*; 1 Cor. xii 30; xiiii 17; xv 10; 1 Tim. vi 8 *quod* superius *dixerat*; 1 Cor. xiii 11 *illa quae* superius *memorauit*; 1 Cor. xvi 24 *sicut* superius *ipse demonstrat*; 2 Cor.

v 12 *quia* superius *dixerat*; 2 Cor. vii 3 *ut* superius *memoraui*; 2 Cor. viiii 3 superius *memoratos, qui*...; 2 Cor. viiii 9 *sicut* superius *ait*; 2 Cor. xi 16 *iam enim* superius *dixerat*; 2 Cor. xii 19 *sicut* superius *dixi*; Eph. iii 1 *huius (gratiae), quam* superius *memoraui*; Eph. iiii 17 *quos* superius *obsecrauerat, hic*...; 1 Thess. ii 8 *conuersationem*..., *quam* superius *memorauimus*; Tit. i 7 *episcopum, quem* superius *presbyterum nominauit*: cf. *supra* Rom. ii 10; viii 2[1].

The introductions to scripture passages in general are, as is natural in the case of notes so brief, themselves also brief. For example, it is rarely, if ever, that an individual Gospel is named. Of course the author is not in this respect by any means unique, as the fourfold Gospel had long been an entity[2]. Again, the author speaks of *propheta* rather than the individual prophet, sometimes *scriptura* (*sicut scriptum est*) is all that is mentioned, and occasionally a scripture quotation is introduced without any warning at all. Illustrations of these facts can be obtained by consulting the index of scripture passages, and especially those that are cited *diserte*. The point need not be elaborated here.

When a scripture passage is not quoted in full, it is customary to add *et reliqua* or *et cetera* to the quoted words: *et reliqua*[3] occurs: Rom. i 24; v 4; viii 23, 26; xii 12; xv 12; 1 Cor. i 11; xii 30; 2 Cor. vi 6; 2 Tim. i 12; Tit. ii 3: but *et cetera* is employed: Rom. viii 9, 10, 36; xiii 1, 13 *bis*; xv 3; 1 Cor. i 11; vi 1; vii 23, 31; viiii 27; x 6, 13; xiii 3; 2 Cor. iii 3; v 15; Eph. iiii 19; v 1; Phil. ii 14; Col. iii 13; iiii 6; 2 Tim. ii 20.

(c) *Characteristic Words and Phrases, alphabetically arranged.*

Words or phrases that are rarely found in the surviving literature, constitute by their presence an argument for common authorship, even if the examples adduced be few. If, however, the words are ordinary, they must occur a considerable number of times, or be used in a special way, must in fact be a sort of idiosyncrasy, to form any such argument. Examples of the latter sort bulk more largely here than those of the former, because, as has been already

[1] Cf. *inferius* Rom. ii 12; iii 12; 2 Tim. iii 9.

[2] Cf., for instance, the writer's *Text and Canon of the New Testament* (London, 1913) p. 161.

[3] On the adverbial *reliqua* see *Archiv f. lat. Lex.* II (1885) 95.

hinted, the author employs a very simple and correct style, and offers very little to the searcher after curiosities of expression. A further argument may be found in the use of ordinary words, if that use be conjoined with the absence or avoidance of equivalent words equally ordinary.

a (ab) after the comparative: 1 Cor. xv 2; 2 Cor. iii 5; xi 5, 21[1].

accessio (in the medical sense): 1 Tim. vi 4 *diuersis* accessionibus *languet*; Tit. ii 8 *nullius adulationis* accessione *languentem.*

adiutorium (excessively rare in this author, though one of the commonest words in the late period[2]): 2 Thess. i 11; 2 Tim. i 14.

adsumo (in connexion with the Incarnation): Rom. viii 33—4 *secundum* adsumpti hominis *loquitur formam*; 1 Cor. ii 8 *perfectam* adsumpti hominis *naturam*...adsumptum hominem; 1 Cor. iii 23 *hic de* adsumpti hominis *forma tractatur*; 1 Cor. xi 3; Col. i 15 *secundum* adsumpti hominis *formam*; 1 Cor. xv 48 *nostri generis* adsumptus homo; Eph. i 21 *unum est iam cum deo* adsumptus homo; Phil. ii 9 adsumptus homo; Phil. ii 10 hominem...adsumptum.

aemulor, etc.: Rom. xi 14 aemuler] *Ut omni modo talem me exhibeam, ut me desiderent* imitari; 2 Cor. vii 7 *triplex est* aemulatio: *aut* imitationis *aut inuidiae aut de qua agitur in praesenti*; 2 Cor. viiii 2 *hic* aemulatio *pro* imitatione *ponitur*; Gal. iiii 17 aemulus *et* imitator *potest et inimicus intellegi.* Once or twice 'aemulari' is defined as 'sectari[3].'

aliquanti (generally in contrast with *omnes*): Rom. viii 32; viiii 7 *bis*, 26; xi 5, 14; 2 Cor. vi 4; xiii 13; Eph. i 3; vi 13; 1 Thess. ii 2.

aliquis (in negative or quasi-negative clauses): Rom. vi 4, 22; viii 36; xii 10; xiii 5; 1 Cor. ii 2; vii 10; viiii 12; x 20; xiiii 33; 2 Cor. i 4; vii 9, 12; viii 12, 21; xi 14, 21; xii 9; Gal. ii 20; vi 10; Eph. v 15; vi 5, 18, 21; Phil. i 4, 13; ii 3; iii 1; 1 Thess. iii 3; Col. iii 16; 1 Tim. ii 5, 8; 2 Tim. i 8; Tit. ii 5; iii 1; Philem. 14, 23 (cf. *aliquando*, 2 Cor. i 18; xi 6).

alius = *alter*[4]: Rom. xi 22; 1 Cor. ii 8; vi 2; vii 5, 11; xv 2, 18; 2 Cor. xii 6.

[1] Also in the scripture of 2 Cor. xi 5, xii 11.

[2] Pel. has *auxilium, suffragium.* On *adiutorium* see J. E. B. Mayor in *Journ. Philol.* XXII (1894) pp. 187 f.

[3] The Latin rendering of ζηλωτής in Tit. ii 14 is *sectator*.

[4] See the index to J. E. B. Mayor's *Latin Heptateuch* (Camb. 1889).

alterutrum (as an adverbial phrase, = *inuicem*[1]): prol. Rom.; Rom. i 19; xii 5; xv 14; 1 Cor. xii 25; xiiii 26, 33; Gal. v 26; Eph. iiii 16, 25[2]; 1 Thess. iiii 18.

anathema: 1 Cor. xvi 22 anathema sit] *qui eum non amant,* anathematizabit, *id est, ut illos* abominetur *et perdat*; Gal. i 8 anathema sit] *Hoc est,* abominabilis *uobis sit.*

ante (adv.) is used more frequently than **antea**. *Ante* occurs: Rom. i 30; iii 24; iiii 18; v 2; vi 13, 19; vii 8; viii 3; x 18; xi 32, 34; xv 2, 4, 21; xvi 26, 27; 1 Cor. i 24; viiii 15; xv 24; 2 Cor. ii 3; xi 33; Gal. i 10; iii 28; iiii 9; Eph. ii 7; iii 21; Phil. ii 9; 1 Thess. iii 4; 2 Thess. ii 2, 10; 1 Tim. i 14; iii 15; 2 Tim. i 10. *Antea* occurs: Rom. i 1; ii 29; viii 18; viiii 30; Gal. iiii 9; Eph. i 4; v 32; Phil. ii 5; Col. i 24. When the MSS vary between them, it is not easy to decide which is the true reading[3].

arefacio: Phil. iiii 10 *iterum flore boni operis florere coepistis, qui mei inmemores occupatione, non uoluntate,* arefacti *fueratis effecti*; 1 Tim. vi 13 *omnia quae uiuunt, etiam* arefacta, *per eius potentiam reuiuescunt.*

arguo (with a simple, usually personal, object): Rom. xi 7; xiiii 12; 1 Cor. viii 1; xi 31; xv 1; Gal. iiii 9, (20); 1 Tim. (iii 13); v 22; Tit. i 14, etc.

aruspex: Rom. x 20 *daemonia interrogabant per augures et astrologos atque* aruspices idolorum; 1 Cor. xii 2 ducebamini] *A magis uel ab* aruspicibus idolorum.

auctoritas (usually with reference to St Paul's apostolic authority): Rom. xiiii 4, 10; xvi 25; 1 Cor. i 1; v 4; 2 Cor. i 1 *bis*; viii 10, 15; Gal. arg.; 1 Tim. arg.: i 1, etc.

audenter: 1 Tim. v 22 *ut possit* audenter *arguere* delinquentes; Tit. i 6 *ne non possit* audenter corripere delinquentes; Tit. ii 7 *ut* audenter corripias delinquentes.

baiulo: 2 Cor. iiii 7 thesaurum gratiae *spiritalis* in *fragili corpore* baiulamus; Gal. iiii 13 thesaurum gratiae in *uasis fictilibus* baiulabat.

[1] Cf. E. Löfstedt, *Philologischer Kommentar zur Peregrinatio Aetheriae* (Uppsala and Leipzig, 1911) p. 337.

[2] Also in the biblical text at this point (vg. *inuicem*) as in the Tertullian quotation (*resurr.* 45).

[3] Löfstedt, *Philol. Komm. z. Peregr. Aetheriae*, pp. 74 f. shows that the more popular language always preferred *ante* to *antea*.

baptismum. There must often be doubt (in oblique cases) whether an author used *baptismus* or *baptismum* in the nominative singular. In Pelagius there is no certain proof of *baptismus* in the nom. sing., whereas there is clear evidence of *baptismum* for that case. There are two examples only of *baptisma*, namely Rom. vi 3[1]; Eph. v 6. The forms of the *o* stem found are:—

nom. baptismum, Rom. v 15; vi 3.

acc. baptismum, Rom. v 17; vi 22; 1 Cor. xv 49 *bis*; 2 Cor. viiii 2; Gal. iii 27; Eph. i 1; ii 5; 1 Tim. ii 15 (*neut.*, as followed by quod); 1 Tim. ii 15 (again).

abl. baptismo, Eph. ii 9; 1 Tim. vi 12.

blasphemia (never *blasphemium*): Rom. i 18; v 2; 2 Cor. ii 7.

breuiter: Gal. i 8 Breuiter *omni uoluit praeiudicare personae*; Eph. v 3 *omnia crimina* breuiter con*prehendit*; Phil. iiii 8 *ut omnia* breuiter con*prehendam*; Col. ii 4 breuiter *omnem sapientiam in ipso esse* com*plexus sum*; 1 Tim. v 10 Breuiter *uniuersa* con*clusit*; 2 Tim. i 13 *formam...quam a me* breuiter *accepisti*.

caducus: Rom. v 4 *aeternis* caduca *mutantur*; 1 Cor. vii 38 *saecularibus et* caducis.

caerimonia: 1 Cor. vii 18 *sine* legis caerimoniis *uiuat*; 2 Cor. v 16 *carnaliter circumcisum et carnales* caerimonias *obseruantem*; Phil. iii 6 *iustificationum et* caerimoniarum *purificationumque*; Phil. iii 18 *spem...in* legis caerimoniis *collocabant*; 2 Thess. ii 4 *omnes* legis caerimonias *restaurare*; Col. arg. *ne per*...legis caerimonias *seducantur*[2]; Tit. i 11 caerimonias *Iudaeorum*.

calumnia, calumnior, used exclusively, or almost exclusively, of the views or statements of heretics: the substantive, Rom. viii 33—4; 1 Cor. viii 6, *mouere* and *commouere calumniam*; also 1 Cor. xv 27; 2 Cor. iiii 4; v 15; Phil. ii 5, sometimes in the phrase *propter calumniam*: the verb, Rom. ii 4; viiii 20; 1 Cor. xii 6; xv 24, 28.

causa (in the sense 'subject,' 'matter,' 'case'[3]): Rom. iii 12 *hoc...pertinet...ad apostoli* causam; Rom. iii 19 *talia dixerat in*

[1] Possibly the requirement of the *clausula* has to do with this example: if we substitute *baptismi* for *baptismatis*, we get a sentence ending with nine long syllables!

[2] This phrase *legis caerimoniae* occurs twice in Hieron. *in Hierem.*: see C.S.E.L. LIX 496.

[3] In the sense 'disease,' it occurs 1 Cor. xi 31.

propria causa; Rom. iii 30 *in isdem* causis; Rom. iiii 17 *ut praesenti conueniat* causae; Rom. v 1 *pertractata* causa; Rom. xi 20 *nec adtendentes* causam *uel personas*; Rom. xiii 1 *haec* causa...*prolata est*; Rom. xiiii 5 *in tali* causa; Rom. xiiii 14 *in talibus* causis; 1 Cor. i 10 *Hinc iam* causam *contra dissensionem adgreditur*; 1 Cor. iiii 18 *Hinc incipit* causam *fornicationis arguere*; 1 Cor. vi 18 *grauare uult fornicationis* causam; 1 Cor. vii 8 *Incipit aliam* causam *de innuptis*; 1 Cor. vii 15 *ligatus in eiusmodi* causa; 1 Cor. vii 38 *Ita concludit uirginum* causam; 1 Cor. xi 2 *in hac* causa; 1 Cor. xi 4 *Venit ad* causam, *quia et uiri etc.*; 1 Cor. xii 1 Causa *incipit de spiritalibus donis*; 2 Cor. viii 1 Causam *inchoat de collectis*; 2 Cor. viiii 2 *usque ad finem* causae; 1 Thess. iii 2 *In hac* causa *dumtaxat*; 1 Thess. iiii 11 *quam* causam *in secunda ad eosdem plenius exsequitur*; 2 Thess. iii 1 *notandum in quibus* causis... *poscat*; 1 Tim. ii 8 *de hac* causa...*motam fuisse quaestionem*; 1 Tim. v 23 *ut...doctrinae* causam...*curet*; Tit. i 8 *in* causa *luxuriae.*

cautela: 2 Cor. i 9 *in nostra prudentia* uel cautela; Eph. v 16 *uestra sapientia* uel cautela.

censeo: Rom. xiii 8 *omnis homo proximus* esse censendus est; 1 Cor. iii 2 *quid de illis* censendum est, *quibus...*[1]? 1 Cor. xiiii 3 *quicumque ergo haec habet, propheta* esse censendus est; Eph. v 27 *maculati ab ea alieni* esse censentur.

cohortor with personal object and **ad** followed by a noun indicating a good moral quality: Rom. arg. eos ad *pacem et* ad *concordiam* cohortatur; Rom. xii 4 eos ad *concordiam*[2] cohortatur; 1 Cor. vii 29 habentes *uxores* ad *continentiam* cohortatur; Eph. v 29 (eos) ad *continentiam* cohortatur. (So **hortor ad** Rom. xv 8; 2 Cor. i 6; Eph. vi 13; 1 Tim. iiii 2.)

commemoro, with accusative of person and sometimes of thing also, or with object clause, in the sense, 'I remind': Rom. vii 8; xv 15; 1 Cor. xi 23, 26; xv 11; Eph. ii 11; 1 Thess. ii 1. (Also in ordinary sense and construction, Rom. i 7; iii 2; xvi 24; 2 Cor. ii 4.)

commoneo Rom. i 7; viii 33—4; 1 Cor. iiii 17; vii 35; xi 26; 2 Cor. viiii 2, 3; Phil. iiii 2; 2 Thess. iii 6, 12; 1 Tim. v 1; 2 Tim. arg.; i 6, 15; iiii 5; Tit. arg.

[1] Cf. 2 Cor. xi 17 *quid de illis sentiendum est qui...?*
[2] Cf. Rom. xv 33.

concludo: Rom. iii 18 *in timore dei* conclusit; Rom. v 1 *qua ratione* conclusa; Rom. vii 25 *recapitulat, ut* concludat; Rom. viiii 19 *uestra propositio* concludetur; Rom. xi 36 *in ipso omnia* concluduntur; 1 Cor. vii 38 concludit *uirginum causam*; 2 Cor. vi 2 (*dies*) concluditur *nocte iudicii*; Gal. v 14 *legis...moralia...uno possunt sermone* concludi; Eph. vi 10 *generali epistulam exhortatione* concludit; 1 Tim. v 10 *breuiter universa* conclusit.

conparatio, in various phrases: **ad conparationem** Rom. viiii 20; 1 Cor. viii 12; 2 Cor. i 8; iiii 17; vi 10; xii 20; Eph. ii 21; Phil. iii 7; 2 Tim. i 11 *bis*: in conparatione (Augustine's favourite form) 2 Cor. iii 10; in conparationem 2 Cor. vi 2; iuxta conparationem Rom. vii 4; **per conparationem** Rom. vii 2; xii 4; 1 Cor. viiii 7; xii 12.

conprehendo ('I include') (see under **breuiter**) 1 Cor. i 31; x 15; xv 4; 2 Cor. i 1; Eph. iiii 19; v 3; Phil. iiii 1, 3; 1 Tim. iii 8, 16, etc.

conprobo (=probo, 'I prove') Rom. iii 9; 1 Cor. x 22; xi 14; 2 Cor. viii 23; Eph. i 15; 1 Thess. i 3; iii 12; 1 Tim. iii 5; v 20; 2 Tim. i 6.

consisto in c. abl. Rom. iiii 1; vii 23; viii 39; xv 13; 1 Cor. xi 22; Phil. iiii 18; 1 Thess. iii 8; 1 Tim. ii 2; Tit. ii 15.

consuetudo, in various phrases: Rom. vii 3 secundum *prioris sui uiri* consuetudinem; Rom. xvi 23 secundum consuetudinem *legis*; 1 Cor. i 22 ex consuetudine *prophetarum*; 1 Cor. iii 13 iuxta consuetudinem scripturarum; 1 Cor. v 5 *habet* consuetudinem scriptura; 1 Cor. vi 18 *illis* per consuetudinem leuissima uidebatur; 2 Cor. xi 28 *illa quae* per consuetudinem leuiora esse uidentur; 1 Cor. vii 10 secundum consuetudinem *Iudaeorum*; 1 Cor. viiii 6 *aput Iudaeos antiqua haec erat* consuetudo, *ut*...; 1 Cor. viiii 13 *aput Iudaeos* secundum consuetudinem *ueteris testamenti*; 1 Cor. xi 31 *putamus* consuetudinis *esse quod culpae est*; Gal. iiii 4 per *malam* consuetudinem; Gal. v 17 *carnalis* consuetudo *aduersus spiritale desiderium*; Eph. ii 3 *paternae traditionis* consuetudo; 2 Thess. iii 13 *boni operis* consuetudinem; Tit. i 8 secundum consuetudinem scripturarum.

contemno c. infin. Rom. ii 5; 2 Cor. iiii 4 (cf. *Thesaurus* s.v. col. 637).

contingo (3 sing. perf. tense, generally of misfortune): Rom. v 20; viiii 33; 1 Cor. i 16; vii 14.

contrarietas Col. i 20; 1 Tim. i 4.

contrarius (in adverbial phrases): **e contrario** prol. epist. Rom.; Rom. viii 14; xiiii 8; 1 Cor. iii 12; vi 8; viii 8; xiiii 19; xv 33; 2 Cor. iiii 13; viiii 6, 13; xiii 11; Gal. iii 3: **a contrario** Rom. v 14.

conuertor (depon.[1], in various senses): Rom. ii 17; iii 29; iiii 5; viii 22; viiii 4, 12, 17; x 19; xi 8, 10, 11; xii 20; 1 Cor. vi 11; 2 Cor. i 11; iii 6; Eph. arg.; Phil. iiii 22; 1 Thess. i 5, 8; 1 Tim. i 16; 2 Tim. iiii 13.

corrigo (intr.[2], of moral improvement): Rom. iii 26; 1 Cor. v 2; xiii 7; 2 Cor. ii 11, 13; vii 7; x 1; xiii 10; Gal. iii 4; Tit. iii 11; Philem. arg.

credo (in the passive, with personal subject and infinitive, in the true classical manner: often **credendus**): Arg. omn. epist. *ipsius magis esse* credenda *est*; Rom. i 1 *quod...fecisse* credendus *est*; Rom. i 8 *simpliciter eam fidem laudasse* credendus *est*; Rom. iii 28 *per fidem dixisse* credendus *est*; Rom. xii 15 *nec...flesse* credendus *est*; 1 Cor. vii 16 *semper ambigua in melius euenire* credenda *sunt*; 1 Cor. xiii 3 *magnis eam procul dubio rebus praetulisse* credendus *est*; 1 Cor. xv 35 *qui*...creditur *totum reddere*; Phil. iiii 21 *procul dubio uerum dixisse* credendus *est*; Philem. 2 *Appia uel soror* creditur *eius fuisse uel coniunx*.

denoto (with personal object): 1 Cor. xi 22; 1 Thess. iiii 12.

deputo (always[3] with accusative and dative): Rom. prol.; 2 Cor. i 23; Eph. i 2; 1 Thess. iiii 7; Col. ii 4; 1 Tim. v 6; vi 8.

deseruio (generally with **idolis** and such like[4]): Rom. prol. idola,...*quibus*...deseruistis; i 8 *ut omnium gentium* diis...deseruirent; Rom. viii 19 *corruptioni*...deseruire; Rom. viiii 21 *Istrahel ibi* idolis deseruierat; Col. iii 5 idolis...deseruire.

diaconissa: Rom. xvi 1 *etiam nunc* in orientalibus locis diaconissae mulieres *in suo sexu ministrare uidentur in baptismo*; 1 Tim. iii 11 *de his dicat, quas adhuc hodie* in oriente diaconissas *appellant*; 1 Tim. v 9 *tales*...diaconissas.

[1] Also reflexive Gal. iiii 9. See Linderbauer on Bened. *reg.* 2, 38.

[2] Also active, e.g. 2 Cor. vii 12 (in passive); Gal. vi 1; Phil. ii 12 (passive); 1 Thess. v 14; 2 Thess. ii 4; 1 Tim. arg.

[3] Except Rom. prol. where *in* c. abl. for the dative.

[4] In good sense, Rom. i 9; 1 Cor. xii 25; xv 2.

dialecticus: 1 Cor. i 22, 1 Tim. vi 21 *artis* dialecticae; 1 Cor. ii 4 dialectici *erant Corinthii*; 2 Thess. ii 2 *nec sermo* dialecticae *fallaciae seducat.*

digamus[1]: 1 Cor. vii 39; 1 Tim. iii 12[2].

dimico: Rom. xii 15; 2 Cor. vi 7; 2 Tim. ii 3; iiii 8.

distraho ('I sell'): Rom. xv 25 omnibus suis distractis *et ante* apostolorum pedes depositis; 2 Cor. i 12 *sapientia carnalis, quae mercede* distrahitur; Gal. ii 10 omnia sua distrahentes *ad* apostolorum pedes *pretia* deponebant. (Possibly *distraho* was in Pelagius's copy of Acts at iiii 34; but Wordsworth and White give no authority for this synonym of *uendo*, for which see Mayor, *Latin Hept.* p. 67.)

diuersitas: Rom. xi 5; 1 Cor. xv 39, 41, 42 *bis*; 2 Cor. v 18; Gal. iii 28; iiii 25; Eph. i 23; iiii 30; 1 Thess. v 14 *bis*; Col. iii 11; 1 Tim. vi 4. In the first, eighth(?) and ninth examples, **meritorum** is the dependent genitive.

diuersus: Rom. viiii 10, 17; xii 4; 1 Cor. xii 12; xv 2, 28 *bis*, 39, 42; Eph. i 10; ii 2; iii 6; iiii 7; Phil. ii 2; 1 Thess. iiii 11; 1 Tim. iii 5, etc.

doctor (a [Christian] teacher, sometimes probably the bishop[3]): Rom. xii 3; xv 27, 29; 1 Cor. i 2, 20; iii 10, 11, 12; iiii 6; vii 8; viiii 6; x 6; xi 19; 2 Cor. i 14; viiii 7; x 4; Eph. iiii 13; Phil. ii 2, 29; 2 Tim. ii 21; iii 3.

dono: Rom. xii 6 *donum* non *ex* nostro, sed *ex* donantis *pendet arbitrio*; 1 Cor. xii 11 *cum hoc* non *in* nostra, sed *in* donantis *sit positum potestate.*

duplex, dupliciter: adj. Rom. vii 25; 1 Cor. vi 6; vii 26; 2 Cor. i 17; viiii 12; Gal. v 16: adv. Rom. xi 28; 1 Cor. xi 29; Phil. iii 17; 1 Thess. v 13; Col. ii 13.

efficio, used in the passive, as a mere synonym of *fio*: e.g. Rom. vi 6, 13, 19; vii 15; viii 17; xii 11; xv 8, 16; 1 Cor. i 2; xi 25, 29; xii 13, 17; 2 Cor. iii 2; Gal. iii 27, 29; iiii 7; Eph. ii 4, 15; iiii 10, 16; v 14; vi 5; Phil. i 14; iiii 10; Col. ii 13; Tit. ii 5.

emendo (intransitive, of moral improvement, cf. *corrigo* above): 2 Cor. ii 3, 5; xiii 10; 2 Thess. iii 6, 14, 15; 1 Tim. i 20. (The

[1] See C. H. Turner's *Monumenta Iuris Antiquissima* t. II pp. 16 f.

[2] Here also *trigamus*.

[3] Cf. Rom. xii 3; 1 Cor. x 6.

active sense is frequently found, e.g. 1 Cor. vii 31 (in passive); 2 Cor. ii 3 (in passive); vii 12 (in passive).)

euidenter: e.g. 2 Cor. ii 11; Col. i 22; Philem. 6.

exhibeo, in reflexive construction (**me, se** cf. the Scripture of 2 Cor. vii 11, etc.): Rom. v 8; xi 14; xii 1; xv 24, 29; 1 Cor. vi 13; x 33; 2 Cor. viii 23; 1 Tim. iiii 12, etc.

existo, in combination with **causa**: Arg. omn. epist. *nouis* causis existentibus; Rom. vii 13 causa...existit; 2 Cor. i 17 *nulla maiore* causa existente; Eph. v 15 *incipiatis ei* causa *perditionis* existere; Eph. v 22 *nulla* existente causa. (Similarly with *occasio*: Gal. v 15 *dum alter alteri* occasio *perditionis* exsistit.)

exoro, not in the classical sense, 'I prevail on[1],' but as a mere synonym of *oro*: Rom. xv 30; Phil. i 4; iiii 7; 1 Thess. v 17; 2 Thess. iii 1; Philem. 3[2].

fiducialiter: 1 Thess. i 10; 1 Tim. iii 3; 2 Tim. ii 9; Tit. ii 13.

finio: Rom. xv 33; xvi 1; 1 Cor. vii 29; xiii 8; 2 Cor. iiii 18.

firmus, firmiter, firmo, used habitually of belief, faith: Rom. iiii 22 *tam perfecte et* firmiter credidit; 1 Cor. iii 11 *Iesum, cui* fide firmissima credidistis; 1 Cor. x 22 *hinc* fidem firmissimam *conprobari*; 1 Cor. xii 7 utilitatem] credentium, *ut* firmentur; 2 Cor. iiii 14 firmiter tenentes *hanc* fidem; Gal. i 13 *quam* firmiter tenuerit *Iudaismum*; Eph. arg. *Ephesii* crediderunt, *quibus* firmiter *stantibus*...; Eph. i 15 *quam* firmiter teneatis fidem *Iesu*; Eph. iii 2 firmiter retinetis *me...accepisse*...; Eph. iii 17 *ut in eius amore* firmiter *stetis*; 1 Thess. iii 6 firmiter *Christo* credentes tenetis fidem; Col. i 23 firmiter *futura* credatis.

forma ('pattern,' 'example' in conduct): Rom. v 12, 16; viii 33—4; 1 Cor. xv 22; 2 Cor. i 4; viii 8; Gal. iiii 3; v 14; (Phil. ii 5); 1 Tim. v 23, etc. (A few other examples have been given earlier in the chapter[3].)

genero (metaphorically, like *pario*): Rom. xiiii 17; 1 Cor. x 13, 23; 2 Cor. vi 6; Eph. iiii 18; Phil. ii 28; 1 Tim. v 11; vi 4; 2 Tim. i 10.

[1] Cf. R. Ogilvie, *Horae Latinae* (London, 1901) pp. 98, 226. On the opposite use, *oro* for *exoro*, see E. Löfstedt, *Philolog. Kommentar z. Peregr. Aetheriae* (Uppsala & Leipzig, 1911) p. 41.

[2] Cf. Tert. *resurr.* 63 p. 124 l. 22 Kr.

[3] p. 69.

gratias referre[1] (particularly in passive construction): Rom. xiiii 6 *bis*; 2 Cor. i 11; viiii 8; Phil. iiii 6, 18; 1 Thess. v 18; Col. ii 7; iii 17 *bis*, 23.

grauo (metaphorically), very often: e.g. 1 Cor. viiii 11; xi 11; xvi 2; 2 Cor. ii 10; Phil. i 17 (in Scripture 2 Cor. xii 13, etc.).

habeo. Besides the ordinary use of *habeo* with the infinitive (Rom. ii 26 *adferre*, Rom. v 7 *mori*, Phil. i 29 *uinci*), this author has instances of a vastly rarer use: Rom. iii 19 habent *unde* gloriari; Rom. xiii 1 habeant *quod* timere; 1 Cor. xi 2 *auctoritatem legis non* habet *quam* proferre; 2 Cor. viii 14 *non* habet *cui* dare. (Contrast the classical, Rom. v 4 habemus *ergo unde...gloriemur*; Rom. x 13 habet *unde...largiatur*; Rom. xiii 3 *bonus non* habet *quod* timeat, etc.) Colloquial in origin, the use is found in certain Old-Latin texts of Scripture and in authors later than these[2]. One or two examples from outside may be cited: Ps.-Aug. (Ambrosiaster) *Quaest. uet. et nou. test.* 112 §16 (p. 293 l. 9 ed. S.) *non* habet *unde reus* constitui; Hieron. *Tractatus De Psalmis* (Anecd. Mareds. III (2)) 61 1—2 *non* habebamus *ubi* requiescere[3]: Arnob.-Iun. *Comm. in Ps.* (Migne, *P.L.* LIII 526 A) habes *unde* uincere[4]. Further instances are quoted by Löfstedt[5].

hic. Adverbial phrases with *hic* are rather characteristic:—

ad hoc ('for this purpose') 1 Cor. i 21;
„ „ followed by **ut** Rom. i 1; iii 26; iiii 6; 1 Cor. x 27; xv 41; 2 Cor. v 2; Eph. ii 17; 2 Thess. ii 14; 1 Tim. ii 2.

ex hoc...quia Rom. v 5;
„ „ ...quo Gal. iiii 6;
„ „ ...ut Rom. xv 25;
„ „ (simply) Phil. i 17.

in hoc...quo 1 Cor. i 9; 2 Cor. vi 10;
„ „ ...quod 2 Cor. vii 13;
„ „ ...si Phil. iii 19;
„ „ ...ut 1 Cor. xi 3; (simply) Eph. i 14.

per hoc ipsum...quod 1 Cor. x 12;
„ „ (simply) 1 Cor. xi 26.

1 Phrase also in Hier. *epist.* 22, 37 §1, Max.-Taur.

2 See Ph. Thielmann in *Archiv f. lat. Lexikogr.* II (1885) pp. 63 f., III (1886) p. 532.

3 A. S. Pease in *Journal of Biblical Literature* XXVI (1908) p. 118.

4 G. Morin in *Revue Bénédictine* XXVI (1909) p. 427; *Études, Textes, Découvertes*, t. I (Maredsous et Paris, 1913) p. 378.

5 *Philolog. Komm. z. Peregr. Aetheriae* p. 251.

idcirco—quia: Rom. iiii 18; viiii 33; xvi 20; 1 Cor. i 2; 2 Cor. iiii 13; 2 Tim. i 15, 18; iii 10. The reverse order: 1 Thess. iiii 14.

idcirco—ut: Rom. vii 8; viiii 17; 1 Cor. viiii 15; xv 11; 2 Cor. xi 33.

idcirco—ne: Gal. iiii 9.

ideo—quia: Rom. i 18; iii 4, 8; v 10, 12, 14; vi 19; x 19; xi 7; xiii 6, 8; xv 15, 24 *bis*; xvi 3; 1 Cor. viii 6; xi 21; xv 24, 48; xvi 9; 2 Cor. i 12; ii 14; iii 5; iiii 13, 15; vi 2; xi 11; xiii 13; Gal. i 10; ii 12; iii 13 *bis*; v 11; Eph. iiii 18; Phil. iii 4; 2 Thess. ii 16; 1 Tim. ii 15; 2 Tim. i 18; ii 3; Tit. i 1. [The reverse order of clauses is much rarer: Rom. vii 9; xvi 13; 1 Cor. viii 8; Col. iii 12]: ideo—quo Rom. xiiii 14.

ideo—ut: Rom. iiii 24; xii 17, 20; xvi 20; 1 Cor. x 16, 30; xi 26; xii 21; 2 Cor. i 2, 7, 24; ii 4, 5; Gal. iii 13; iiii 14; Phil. iii 10; Col. ii 4; 1 Tim. vi 17; 2 Tim. ii 10; iii 17; ideo—ne Rom. iii 13; 1 Cor. vi 10; x 11; 2 Cor. i 1; x 10; Gal. iii 20; 1 Tim. v 14.

imago contrasted with **ueritas**: Rom. ii 26 *uisibilia* imago *sint inuisibilium, et inuisibilia* ueritas *sint uisibilium*...imagine *non indiget* ueritas, imago *autem indiget* ueritate; 1 Cor. vii 31 *si talis est* imago, *ipsa* ueritas *qualis est!* Eph. ii 21 *ut multo maiorem munditiam et sanctitatem habeat* ueritas *quam* imago; Col. ii 16 imagine *opus non est* ueritate *praesente*. [*Figura* is similarly contrasted with *ueritas*; 1 Cor. v 8; vii 31; x 6.]

impedio with the dative, a rare construction, is found Rom. vii 2, and possibly 1 Thess. ii 16. (The ordinary accusative occurs at Rom. viii 31[1].)

impugno: Rom. v 15; xv 25; Eph. vi 13; Phil. arg. (cf. *impugnator* Rom. vii 12).

incautus: the acc. pl. *incautos* thrice ends a sentence; 2 Cor. ii 11 *ut sub specie iustitiae* fallat incautos; 2 Cor. xi 14 *ne forte... decipiat ac* fallat incautos; Eph. iiii 14 *a recto fidei cursu detorquet* incautos.

incorruptibilitas: Rom. i 4; Col. i 18.

indebitus, indebite: Rom. iii 24 *morti se ille* indebite *tradidit*; Rom. v 6 indebite *pro nobis mortuus est*; Rom. v 8 indebite *aliquid praestatur...quid tam* indebitum *quam ut sine peccato dominus*

[1] See also Rom. xv 32; 1 Cor. viiii 25.

pro seruis impiis moreretur? Rom. xii 20 *tuam* indebitam *misericordiam*; Gal. iii 13 indebito *maledicto eius nostrum debitum conpensatum est.*

indigeo is his favourite verb[1] to express the idea, 'I need,' and is used in various constructions: (c. gen.) 1 Cor. iiii 8; 2 Cor. vi 10: (c. abl.) Rom. ii 26 *bis*; xi 33, 34; xii 13; 1 Cor. xii 25; Gal. iii 25; vi 1: (c. infin.) Rom. xv 24; 1 Cor. v 10; Gal. i 18; 1 Thess. iiii 9; 2 Tim. i 6: (absol.) Rom. xii 8; 2 Cor. xii 10; Gal. vi 10; Eph. iiii 28; 1 Thess. iii 12: (c. acc.) Rom. i 11.

inebrio (metaphorically, perhaps under the influence of Hierem. xxxi (xxxviii) 24 (25)): Rom. vii 15 *quasi* inebriatus *consuetudine peccatorum ignoro quid facio*; 2 Cor. ii 17 *adulationis mollia uerba, quibus homines non tam* inebriati *ferueant quam delectati tepescant*; Eph. iiii 26 ira *non* inebriet mentem; 1 Thess. v 6 *et curae* inebriant mentem; Col. iii 8 ira *est quae* inebriat mentem. (In the literal sense, 1 Cor. xi 19.)

ingratus c. dat.[2]: Prol. epist. Rom. *semper* his omnibus (beneficiis) extitistis ingrati; 1 Cor. xi 26 *ut* beneficiis *eius non* exsistamus ingrati; Gal. i 4 *ostendit* beneficia *Christi*, quibus existebant ingrati; Gal. ii 21 *non debeo esse* illi ingratus, *qui me tantum dilexit, ut*, etc.; Eph. arg. *ut* tantis beneficiis *non sint* ingrati; Eph. i 2 *si* ei (gratiae) *non sitis* ingrati; Eph. ii 11 *ut non sint* ingrati beneficiis *largitoris*; Tit. ii 9 *ne* homini existatis ingrati. So in Fulgentius, etc. cf. Friebel, *Fulgentius* [Paderborn, 1911] pp. 19 f.

inpossibilitas (in the active sense, 'impotence'): Rom. iiii 20; Gal. iiii 24.

inremediabiliter: Rom. xi 11 *non penitus et* inremediabiliter *ceciderunt*; 2 Tim. ii 17 *ne per aures* inremediabiliter *uulnerent mentes.*

inrogo: Rom. viiii 2 *quidquid ei* inlatum[3] iniuriae *fuerit, Christo similiter* inrogari; 1 Cor. vi 8 *cum* inlatam (iniuriam)...

[1] *Egeo* also occurs, e.g. Rom. xii 4; 1 Cor. xii 24; 2 Cor. vi 10 *bis*; viii 8, etc.

[2] Pelagius appears rather to affect adjectives followed by the dative, e.g. Rom. xi 8 *incredulus uerbis*; 1 Cor. xv 36 *infidelis promissionibus*; 2 Cor. iv 1 *idoneus officio*. Tert. (after Verg.) uses *ingratus* with the genit., cf. Mayor on Tert. *Apol.* 40 p. 118 l. 22, Löfstedt, *Krit. Bemerkungen zu Tert. Apol.* (Lund, 1918) pp. 92 ff.

[3] The classical phrase *inferre iniuriam* occurs in Rom. xii 10 and elsewhere, as well as in the above three passages.

patienter sustinere *deberetis, uos e contrario non solum non suffertis, sed etiam non facientibus* inrogatis; Gal. v 22 inlatas iniurias sustinere patienter...*nulli* iniuriam inrogare.

insensibilis: Rom. i 16 insensibile *aurum* (as used for images of gods); 1 Cor. x 20 idolum insensibile; Eph. ii 12 idola insensibilia.

is in various adverbial expressions[1]: **eo quod** Arg. omn. epist. Rom. (i 3); ii 26; iii 11; iiii 13; viii 31; viiii 2, 20; 1 Cor. ii 1; vi 5; x 27; 2 Cor. i 12; vii 9; xi 30; Eph. i 3; Phil. ii 26: **pro eo quod** Rom. i 21; 2 Cor. i 11; 1 Tim. ii 1: **ex eo quod** Rom. i 32; iiii 2; Eph. i 1: **in eo quo** Rom. viiii 10; 1 Cor. x 1; in eo quod Phil. i 9: ad id quod 1 Cor. xii 18; 2 Thess. i 11; (ad quod 1 Cor. xii 14): ab eo quod 1 Cor. xv 24[2].

iubeo c. dat. Rom. v 14; 1 Cor. i 13.

laesio: 1 Cor. xvi 11 *animi* laesionem; 2 Cor. vi 4 *omnis* laesio *tribulatio est.*

legalis: Rom. viii 33—4 *mandata*; 1 Cor. vii 18 *opera*; 1 Cor. viiii 21 *doctrinæ.*

libertas arbitrii, the two words being separated; Rom. xi 8 *ne* libertas *scilicet tollatur* arbitrii; 1 Cor. iii 23 *ad* libertatem *referre* arbitrii. Cf. 1 Cor. xv 10 *ut* liberum *seruaret* arbitrium.

ligo, participle **ligatus**, metaphorically, of persons: 1 Cor. vii 15, 27 (*bis*); Eph. iii 1; (iiii 5).

littera, in the expression **lex litterae**, meaning the written Law as contained in the Old Testament[3]: Rom. iii 20, 21; vii 6, 8; 1 Cor. viiii 21; Gal. ii 19.

locus, in abl., contrasted with some other relation[4]: 2 Cor. vi 17 exite...separamini]. *Actu uel conuersatione uel familiaritate,* non loco; Eph. v 31 relinquet homo patrem et matrem suam]. *Amore, et si* non loco.

[1] It may be noted that Pelagius uses *hic*, *ille* and *is* alike, as antecedents to *qui*.

[2] In scripture passages we find *eo quod* (2 Cor. v 4), *ex eo quod* (2 Cor. viii 11). On this type of phrase see *Year's Work in Classical Studies for 1916* pp. 44 f.

[3] The only instance of this phrase known to me, outside Pelag., was Hieron. *in Hierem.* vi 26 § 4 (C.S.E.L. LIX p. 404 ll. 25 f.) legem litterae *lege spiritus commutatam*: Dr Alfred J. Smith observes it also in Orig.-Ruf. *in Rom.*, as his list of examples in *Journ. Theol. Stud.* vol. xx (1918—19) pp. 133 f. shows; and J. P. Naish in Gaudentius.

[4] Cf. **tempore** (below), similarly used.

maculo (metaph.): Rom. xv 17; 1 Cor. iiii 4; viiii 12; Eph. v 27; 1 Tim. vi 14.

mensura: Rom. i 30 *qui effertur super* mensuram *suam*; 2 Cor. x 12 (cf. scripture text of v. 13) *non excedimus* mensurae *nostrae terminos*; 1 Tim. iii 3 *qui omnia faciat cum* mensura.

merces (much commoner than *praemium*[1], and in most passages used of the future, heavenly reward): Rom. ii 7; iiii 4; viii 28; xii 1; xiii 4; xiiii 5; 1 Cor. iii 8, 19; vii 7; xv 31; 2 Cor. i 12; viii 17; viiii 12; x 15; Gal. v 5; vi 9; Eph. vi 7, 8; Phil. i 20, 28; ii 14; iiii 14; 1 Thess. ii 2; 1 Tim. iiii 8; 2 Tim. ii 6; Tit. ii 9; Philem. 14.

mereor c. infin.[2] Rom. viii 14, 17 *bis*; x 19; xii 1; 1 Cor. vi 14; vii 5; viiii 23; xv 22; 2 Cor. v 2, 4; Gal. iiii 20; 1 Thess. iiii 3 (but *mereo*, 1 Cor. ii 10; Gal. i 10; 1 Tim. vi 2, etc.).

monstruosus: 2 Cor. xii 21 *inpudicitia*...quasi monstruosa *turpitudo*; 1 Tim. iiii 5 monstruosa nescio qua *praedicatio.*

moralis: 1 Cor. xiiii 6 *uos* moralibus *doceam* institutis; Gal. iiii 24 moralia *praecepta*...moralibus *monitis*; Gal. v 5 moralis *iustitiae*: Gal. v 7 moralibus *disciplinis*; Gal. v 14 *legis ipsa* moralia; Eph. arg. moralia...instituta; Eph. ii 15 moralia *sola decernens*; Eph. iii 21 moralia...*tradere* instituta.

munio beginning the sentence: 2 Cor. x 4 Muniunt *et circumdant doctrinam suam falsi doctores astutia argumentisque, quae aries apostolicus destruit...*; Eph. vi 14 Munit *non solum pectoris conscientiam,...*.

nec non et is much rarer in this author than in some other late prose authors. I have noted only the following examples: 1 Cor. viii 1; Eph. vi 14; 1 Tim. vi 17.

necesse est seems always to take **ut** with the subjunctive, e.g. Gal. v 3.

nitor c. infin. Rom. v 15; 1 Cor. vii 34; xiii 3; Gal. i 7; iiii 29; 1 Thess. iiii 6; Col. iii 10; 1 Tim. i 10; (c. abl. 1 Cor. viii 1).

nobilitas in certain phrases: 1 Cor. iiii 10 *uos uobis etiam* nobilitatem terreni[3] generis *uindicatis*; 2 Cor. xi 18 *in* nobilitate

[1] Which occurs, e.g. 1 Cor. vii 26, 29, 40; 2 Cor. vi 10; Phil. ii 14, 18; iii 15; 1 Tim. iii 13.

[2] See *Study of Ambrosiaster* p. 118, and add Tert. *Apol.* 33, *Orat.* 16, etc. Aug.

[3] Cf. under **terrenus** below.

terreni generis *gloriari carnale est*; 2 Cor. xi 21 *si filii dei de* terrena nobilitate *se iactent*; Eph. iiii 5 *nolite uobis de* terrena nobilitate *aliquid adrogare, ne ueram gloriam amittatis.*

nomino greatly predominates over *nuncupo*[1], *uoco*[2]: Rom. i 8, 9, 13; ii 10; vii 8; viii 27, 39; xvi 5, 23; 1 Cor. i 2; iii 10; x 16; xi 10; xii 6, 28; xv 50, 51; xvi 19; 2 Cor. i 1; vi 15; xi 3; xiii 13; Gal. i 10; Eph. ii 14; iii 1; v 3; 2 Thess. ii 16 *bis*; Col. i 23; iii 5 *bis*, 12; 1 Tim. ii 5; Tit. i 7, 8.

noui = scio[3]: Rom. i 18, 27; ii 1; iiii 19; v 5; viii 25; xv 15, 30; 1 Cor. i 11; vi 5; vii 7, 38; viii 8; x 27; xiii 2; 2 Cor. i 13; iii 4; v 11; viiii 5; xi 11; Gal. ii 14; Eph. i 17; iii 18; Phil. i 25; ii 22, 28; iiii 5, 8; 1 Tim. iii 7; 2 Tim. i 8; ii 18; iii 9; iiii 8.

nullus in the phrase **in nullo** = nulla in re[4]: Rom. vi 20; 1 Cor. iiii 8; xi 27; 2 Cor. ii 9; Gal. ii 8; 1 Tim. iii 11.

obiectio: Rom. viiii 14 *quibus exemplis per breues* obiectiones *respondens ostendit ita intellegi non debere*; Rom. x 14 *de gentibus* obiectio *Iudaeorum*; Eph. v 31 obiectio *carnaliter amare uolentium*; 1 Tim. ii 4 *illud hoc loco soluitur de induratione Pharaonis et cetera huiusce modi* obiectio *quaestionum.*

obliuio, in the phrase **in obliuionem ire**: Rom. iii 20 in obliuionem ierat lex naturae; Rom. vii 8 *paene* lex in obliuionem ierat naturalis; 1 Cor. x 6 *ut*...in obliuionem *nobis* eant *Aegypti uoluptates.*

occasio, generally of the opportunity to do evil[5]: Rom. vi 18 *non solum peccata, sed etiam* occasiones *auferri docuit* delictorum; 1 Cor. vi 12 *cum peccata non sint,* occasiones *possunt capere* delictorum; 1 Cor. viiii 12 *aduersariis* occasione *accepta deuorantibus*; 1 Cor. x 23 *per se non habent peccatum, sed non semper expediunt, quia* occasionem *non numquam generant* delinquendi; 1 Cor. x 30 *ut*...occasionem *demus infidelibus blasphemandi*; 2 Cor. xi 12 *ideo tollit* occasionem *apostolus, ut*...; Gal. v 15 *alter alteri* occasio

[1] Nowhere found, I believe; but *appello* occurs: Rom. i 14, 29; ii 10; iii 12, 19; vii 8; viii 2, 5, 6; xi 6; xiii 6, 7; xvi 3; 1 Cor. iii 3; viiii 21; xv 26, 48; 2 Cor. iii 7; vi 8; Gal. iiii 3, 29; Eph. arg.; vi 12; Col. iii 5; iiii 1; 1 Tim. i 4, 8; iii 11; 2 Tim. ii 8.

[2] Rom. viii 3 *nomine uoco.*

[3] *Scio*, e.g. 1 Cor. xii 28. On *scio*=*noui*, see Mayor on Tert. *Apol.* c. 5 p. 175 ll. 24 ff.

[4] Mayor in *Journ. Philol.* XXII (1894) p. 195.

[5] To do good, 2 Cor. ii 13.

perditionis exsistit; 2 Thess. iii 9 *necui* occasionem *auaritiae uel otii...praeberemus*; 1 Tim. i 9 *qui didicerunt etiam* occasiones *fugere* delictorum; 1 Tim. ii 9 *non debent* occasionem *dare concupiscentiae*; 1 Tim. v 4 *ne eis ipsa* occasionem *det saeculo seruiendi.*

opto (in present tense[1]): Rom. i 7 *ut ea* optet *in nobis integra permanere*; Rom. vii 19 *etiam cum non* optat, *incurrit*; Rom. xii 18 optantes...*conuersionem eorum...*; Rom. xv 25 *quibus oblationem suam esse* optat *acceptam*; Gal. vi 18 optat ut *gratia cum eis domini, non legis opera comitentur*; Eph. i 17 optat ut *agnoscant deum*; 1 Thess. iii 10 *quis, cum famam compererit bonorum, eos uidere non* optet? 1 Tim. v 15 *ne eum putaremus* optare; 2 Tim. i 4 *tristitiam..., quam tua* opto *praesentia releuari.*

paganus: Rom. i 16; 1 Cor. xv 2; Gal. vi 10; Eph. vi 9; Phil. i 1; Col. iiii 6.

parco, used somewhat baldly, with the dative: Rom. ii 2; 1 Cor. x 1, 11 *bis*; Eph. v 6 *bis*; 1 Thess. ii 15; 1 Tim. v 20.

pasco: Rom. xiiii 4 *tres pueros leguminibus* pastos; 1 Cor. x 27 *non diuites* pascendos *esse, sed debiles*; 1 Tim. iiii 8 *ipsa uidua...* pasta *est.*

passibilis: 1 Cor. ii 8 *bis*; Eph. iiii 30.

perficio, with personal object, e.g. Eph. iiii 12; very frequently in the participle **perfectus**: Rom. v 4, 5; vi 2, 14; 1 Cor. i 10; ii 8; vii 7; xiii 2, 3, 9; xv 45; 2 Cor. i 4; ii 8, 9; iii 7, 8; v 8, 9, 16; vii 1; viii 14, 15; Gal. iii 11, 24, 25; v 5; Eph. i 23; Phil. ii 8; iiii 19; 1 Thess. arg.; i 7; iiii 4, 9, etc.: occasionally (illogically) the comparative **perfectior** is found: Arg. omn. epist.; Rom. xiii 11; 1 Cor. vii 38; xi 17; Phil. iiii 1. The adverb **perfecte** also occurs, Rom. iiii 22, 24; 1 Cor. xi 24; xiii 12; 2 Cor. ii 3; viiii 13; Eph. i 17; Phil. iii 10; 1 Thess. iii 2; 2 Tim. ii 4; Tit. ii 12, and the substantive **perfectio**, 2 Cor. viiii 12; Eph. iiii 12, etc.

persona (in non-theological sense): Rom. iii 2 *ex cuius* persona *respondetur*; Rom. vii 7 in persona *eius hominis* loquitur, *qui...*; Rom. vii 25 *unde probatur quia* ex *alterius* persona loquatur *apostolus, non in sua*; Rom. viii 30 *discretio non in* personis, *sed in tempore est*; Rom. viiii 20 *quibusdam uidetur et hoc adhuc* ex *ipsorum* persona dicere, *quia...*; Rom. viiii 26 *eos, qui haec non* ex *apostoli, sed* ex *Iudaeorum* persona dici *putant*; Rom. viiii 30

[1] The future occurs Eph. vi 5; perf. subj. Phil. iii 18.

si superiora ex persona *apostoli* dicuntur; Rom. xi 20 *nec adtendentes causam uel* personas; 1 Cor. xv 35 *ipse sibi* ex *contradicentium* persona *proponit*; 1 Cor. xv 55 *propheta* ex persona *iustorum* loquitur; 2 Cor. ii 10 *ego dono, non* in *mea* persona, *sed Christi, qui dixit*...; 2 Cor. iiii 6 in persona *Christi nos homines scientia luminamus*; 2 Cor. xii 2 *de se humilitatis causa* in *alterius* persona loquatur; Gal. i 8 *breuiter omni uoluit praeiudicare* personae; Gal. ii 6 *nec* persona (*praeiudicat*) *labori*; Eph. iiii 19 *in libro Sapientiae* dicitur ex persona *eorum, qui*...; 2 Tim. iiii 8 *non* personis *meritum, sed labori debetur.*

portendo: Rom. i 4; 1 Cor. xi 25; 2 Cor. iii 3.

postmodum (never *postmodo*): 1 Cor. x 4; 2 Cor. iii 3.

praeiudico: c. dat. Rom. viiii 6, 12; Gal. i 8; ii 6; 1 Tim. i 15; v 21: absol. Col. iii 11.

praeposterus: 2 Cor. viii 3: **praepostero** (verb) Rom. ii 24.

praesens. The adverbial phrase **in praesenti** occurs frequently, *in praesentia* once[1] only, 2 Cor. x 7: neither *in praesens*, nor Jerome's favourite, *in praesentiarum*, occurs. The examples of *in praesenti* are:—Rom. i 32; ii 4 *bis*; v 13; vi 22 *bis*; vii 9; viii 6, 39; xi 34; xii 6; 1 Cor. xiii 12, 13; xv 2 *bis*, 19; 2 Cor. i 4; vi 4; vii 7; xiii 4; Gal. vi 9; Phil. iiii 1; 1 Thess. ii 2; iii 12; Col. i 10; ii 17; iii 4; 1 Tim. iiii 8, 10; Tit. i 5.

praeualeo: absol. Rom. v 15; 2 Cor. xi 16; xi 33; Gal. iii 9; c. infin. Eph. iii 8; Phil. i 10; Col. iiii 2; c. dat. Rom. xvi 20; 2 Cor. xi 30.

principor: 1 Cor. xv 24 *nobis se sequentibus* principantur; Eph. iii 10 *qui rebus caelestibus*...principantur.

prior: Rom. i 4 *ut* prior *omnibus*...*resurgeret*; 1 Cor. xv 3 *uel a lege uel a* prioribus; Eph. i 12 *nos apostoli uel Iudaei, qui* priores *credidimus in Christo*; Eph. iii 5 *sciebant quidem prophetae* priores *gentes esse uocandas*; 2 Thess. i 11 priores *inuitati non erant digni*; 1 Tim. ii 14 *posteriores in factura sunt et* priores *in culpa*; 2 Tim. i 5 *Quia* prior *credidit.*

profectus (subst.)[2] Rom. i 8; xv 14; xvi 13; 1 Cor. i 4; ii 5; iiii 14; x 27, 29, 33 *bis*; xiii 11; xiiii 6, 19; xvi 14, 17; 2 Cor. vi

[1] Gal. iiii 18 is, of course, different.

[2] See the passages indicated earlier in this chapter, p. 70: Dr Alfred J. Smith shows that both *proficio* and *profectus* occur frequently in Origen-Rufinus *in Rom.* (see *Journ. Theol. Stud.* vol. xx (1918—19) p. 148 n.).

11 *bis*; vii 4, 9, 13, 14; viii 24; Gal. ii 11; iiii 21; Phil. ii 17; iii 13; 1 Thess. i 5; ii 20; iiii 1; 2 Thess. iii 1; 1 Tim. iiii 15[1]; Tit. i 10.

proficio is, as in Ambrosiaster[2], very frequent: (*a*) absol. Rom. xv 29; 1 Cor. i 19; v 10; xi 17; xiiii 5; xv 31; 2 Cor. ii 5; iii 7; vi 1; vii 7; Gal. iiii 11, 17; v 12; vi 4; Eph. i 10; iiii 2, 16; vi 21; Phil. arg.; iii 13; 1 Thess. arg.; i 7; ii 1, 8, 12; iii 9; Col. iii 23; 1 Tim. iiii 12; v 1; (*b*) c. **ad** (**in**) et acc. (in bad sense): Rom. iii 26; 1 Cor. xi 17; xvi 11; Eph. iiii 28; Phil. i 10; 1 Tim. vi 1; (*c*) c. **ad** (**in**) et acc. (in good sense): Rom. vii 4, 10; xi 15; xiii 4; xv 4, (29); 1 Cor. xiii 9; 2 Cor. iii 18; iiii 17; Gal. i 7; iii 10; Eph. iiii 28; vi 5; Phil. i 10; 1 Tim. iiii 8, 15; (*d*) c. dat.: Rom. xiii 4; 1 Cor. xiiii 10, 19; Col. iiii 3; 1 Tim. ii 2; (*e*) c. *contra*: Eph. iii 9; (*f*) c. *de*: Tit. iii 9.

propono: Rom. vii 15; viiii 14, 17, 30; xv 2; 1 Cor. viii 1; x 1; xiiii 6; xv 2, 35 *bis*; 2 Cor. arg.; v 16; vi 14; viii 19; 2 Tim. i 9; Tit. i 2; iii 3: the usual object is **exemplum**.

proprie: Rom. ii 22; 1 Cor. i 2; iii 3, 18; viiii 10; xii 6; 2 Cor. ii 15; vi 16; Eph. vi 2; Phil. iii 9, 11 (?); 1 Tim. ii 15; iiii 6; vi 16, etc.

prouoco[3]: Rom. i 8; xii 15; xiiii 15; xv 14, 27, 29; 1 Cor. i 4; vi 6; viiii 2, 21; x 33; xi 2; 2 Cor. vi 11 *bis*; vii 4; viii 1, 22; xiii 4; Gal. v 26; Phil. iii 13; iiii 18; Col. iiii 5; 1 Thess. arg.; 1 Tim. iii 1, 2; 2 Tim. i 16; iiii 6; Tit. iii 2.

pulchre: Rom. i 29 pulchre *homicidium inuidiae sociauit*; Rom. iii 29 pulchre *modum seruauit in uerbis*; Rom. xv 33 pulchre *in pace finiuit*; 1 Cor. x 4 pulchre *dixit*: 'consequenti petra'; 1 Thess. i 9 pulchre *ad deum uerum et uiuum a falsis dis et mortuis conuersi esse dicuntur*.

puto (in passive forms): e.g. Rom. ii 4 putatur *res humanas minime curare*; Rom. v 13 *ita* putabatur *esse peccatum*; Rom. viiii 10 *Rebecca* putatur *prima geminos edidisse*; 1 Cor. i 25 *quod stultum* putatur *dei*; 1 Cor. xv 6 *ne*...putarentur *esse mentiti*; 2 Cor. vi 3 *ne...nostrum uitium* putetur *esse*; 2 Cor. xii 20

1 In the scripture text of this verse the word occurs.

2 *Study of Ambrosiaster* pp. 129—132. The 'good' sense with *ad* (*in*) is found also in Tert. Ambr. Aug. Vincent.-Lirin.

3 See earlier in the chapter, p. 70.

ista nec putantur *esse peccata*; 1 Cor. xv 31 *non statim per puerum iurasse recte* putabor.

quale est, exclamatory: 1 Cor. vii 33 quale est *uxori magis uelle placere quam domino!* Eph. v 22 quale est *ut nouae uitae praedicator, nulla exsistente causa, hoc doceret quod naturaliter possidebant*[1]*!*

qualitas: Rom. iiii 25 *in ea* qualitate, *qua mortuus est, necessario resurgens apparuit*; Rom. xi 24 *radix* (*solet*) *ramorum* (*uim*) *in suam uertere* qualitatem; 2 Cor. xi 20 *Iudaica superbia...de generis* qualitate; Gal. iiii 3 (*elementa*) *fuerant eorum infirmitati necessaria* pro temporis qualitate; Gal. iiii 25 *de* qualitatibus *locorum uult intellegi diuersitatem testamentorum*; Eph. iiii 29 qualitatem *loquendi monstrauit*; Phil. iii 7 *utrumque* (i.e. *aurum, aeramentum*) pro temporis qualitate *necessarium*; 1 Thess. i 9 *et nostrae constantiae et uestrae conuersionis omnibus nota est* qualitas; 1 Tim. i 8 (*lex bona*) *ut a deo promulgata* pro temporis qualitate; 1 Tim. iii 13 qualitatem *ministerii praemium promereri*.

quanto magis exclamatory, occurs with a frequency usual in this period: e.g. Rom. i 20; ii 2; v 4, 9, 10; xi 4, 12; xv 7; xvi 19; 1 Cor. i 12; iii 5; vi 20; vii 31; viiii 12; x 11; xi 17, 27, 28; xiii 2; xiiii 7; 2 Cor. iii 3, 11; viii 10; viiii 4; xi 5; xiii 3; 1 Thess. iiii 16; Col. iii 8, 13; 1 Tim. iii 2; v 19; vi 2; 2 Tim. iiii 15. (*quanto minus* Rom. x 16; xi 21 etc.)

quantuslibet: 2 Cor. iiii 17; *quantumlibet* (adv.) Col. ii 19.

quantumuis c. subj.: Gal. iiii 30; Eph. v 6.

quasi si: Rom. v 20; viii 3; 2 Cor. vii 9; 2 Thess. i 6.

quisque = *quisquis*, as fairly frequently in late authors: Rom. xiii 10; 1 Cor. i 1; v 5; xi 25; 1 Thess. iiii 6; 2 Tim. iii 7.

non quo, introducing a rejected reason or view in the subjunctive, as in the best classical Latin[2]: Rom. xiiii 14; 1 Cor. vii 13; xii 23; 2 Cor. i 24; Gal. v 16; 2 Tim. iiii 17; where a second clause is added in contrast, it is generally in the form of a principal clause introduced by **sed**, but there is one example of the full-blown classical phrase **non quo...sed quia**, 1 Cor. i 21.

[1] Also relative, Rom. v 4; viiii 17 *tale est...*, *quale si*(*quis*).... For the exclamatory use, see Tert. *de fug. in persec.* 5, with Oehler's note, and Hoppe, *Syntax u. Stil des Tertullian* (Leipz. 1903) pp. 68, 82.

[2] Jerome and Augustine also preserve this use.

quoad usque: 1 Cor. xv 32; Col. i 24.

rationabilis: Rom. xvi 20; 1 Cor. viiii 21; Eph. i 11; Phil. ii 15; Col. i 23; **rationabiliter**: Rom. xii 1; 1 Cor. xii 8; Eph. vi 20; Col. iii 16; 1 Tim. iiii 6.

reddo uicem[1]: Rom. xii 17, 21; 1 Cor. iii 18; iiii 10 *bis*; Eph. iiii 2, 31; 1 Thess. v 15 *bis*; Col. iii 15; Tit. iii 2; (*rependere uicem* 2 Cor. v 14[2]).

replico: Rom. prol. *sed quid antiqua* replicamus...? 1 Cor. viiii 1 *suam illis* replicat *formam, quod etiam licita contempserit*; Eph. ii 1 *incipit collata beneficia* replicare.

ritu: Rom. v 12 *qui humano, non caelesti* ritu uiuebant; xiiii 14 *qui adhuc* ritu *Iudaico aliquid...arbitratur inmundum*; 1 Cor. ii 14 *quia animalium* ritu *uersatur*; 1 Cor. vii 39 *tantum ut infideli uel infidelium* ritu *non nubat*; 1 Cor. xv 47 *non naturae fragilis* ritu, *sed diuinae maiestatis nutu et conceptus est et enixus*; Eph. iiii 21 *ut...gentili* ritu uiuatis.

saepe is entirely absent, I think, as from many other late authors, being replaced by *frequenter*, etc.

sane occurs with frequency, sometimes as the first word of its clause, far oftener as the second: (*a*) in the first place: Rom. iii 30; 1 Cor. xii 8; 2 Cor. vii 7; Gal. vi 1; Eph. iii 1; (*b*) in the second place: Arg. omn. epist.; Rom. ii 26; iii 19, 24; vi 19; viii 3, 13; xii 8; xv 30; 1 Cor. ii 9; x 27; xi 27, 31; xiii 2, 3; xiiii 19; xv 28; 2 Cor. xi 13; Eph. ii 2; vi 5; Col. i 23; 1 Tim. ii 8; 2 Tim. iiii 7.

satio (verb): Rom. xv 24; 1 Tim. vi 9.

scilicet is an extremely favourite particle, *uidelicet* being very rare; the former occurs: Rom. vi 12; vii 17, 23; viiii 8; xi 26; xii 18; xiiii 20; xvi 15; 1 Cor. i 2, 30; ii 8; iii 21; vii 3; viiii 12; xi 8, 29; xv 8, 24, 25, 28; 2 Cor. i 17; ii 13; iii 5, 9; Gal. i 1; iii 21; iiii 24, 28; Eph. iii 18; iiii 22, 24; Phil. ii 6, 11; iii 3, 15; 1 Thess. ii 12; 2 Thess. ii 3; iii 11; Col. i 10, 23; iii 15, 16; iiii 6; 1 Tim. ii 14; iii 8; iiii 2; vi 13; 2 Tim. i 6, 9, 10; iii 2; iiii 5; Tit. i 2, 3, 7, 14, etc.

sector (usually metaphorically, with an accusative indicating

[1] See *Study of Ambrosiaster* pp. 146 f.: occurs in Tert. *pat.* 8; *carn. resurr.* 8; Hier. *epist.* 17, 1; Aug. *cat. rud.* 4 §7; Marcellin. ap. Aug. *ep.* 136, 1.

[2] Add to the passages in *Study of Ambrosiaster* p. 146, n. 2, Ambr. *expos. ps. cxviii* 14, 28, 1; 15, 15, 1.

the object of pursuit or desire): Rom. x 2; 1 Cor. vii 38; xii 31; xiiii 12, 39; 2 Cor. xi 12; Phil. iii 15; Col. iii 3; 1 Tim. iii 8; Tit. i 7.

secundum (preposition with accusative, far commoner than *iuxta*[1], which is very rare in this author): (*a*) with nouns: *historiam* Rom. x 8; 1 Cor. i 2; *legem* (Rom. ii 29); 1 Cor. vii 39; 2 Cor. xiii 1; Col. iii 18; with other nouns: Rom. iii 24; vii 3; viii 26; xiii 12; 1 Cor. i 23; iii 10, (23); vi 20; vii 3, 16; xi 3 *bis*, 12, 25; xii 2, 13; xv 24 *ter*, 2 Cor. i 17; v 19 *ter*; vii 9; viiii 7; xi 6; Gal. i 4; iiii 23; Eph. vi 1; Phil. i 20; ii 5 *quater*, 22; iii 5; 2 Thess. ii 3; Col. i 15 *bis*; ii 7; 2 Tim. i 13; Tit. i 8; iii 5; Philem. 16 etc.; (*b*) with pronouns: **quod**; Rom. i 8; ii 13, 16; iiii 3, 15; 1 Cor. xi 18; Phil. ii 5; Col. ii 23; 1 Tim. i 18; 2 Tim. ii 8, 24; *illud* 1 Cor. v 3; Gal. iii 4; Phil. iiii 5; *hoc* Rom. ii 16; Gal. i 1; *eos* Rom. viiii 21, 26; *illum* 2 Cor. v 8; *nos* 2 Cor. v 8.

sensus: especially in the phrase **hoc habet sensus**, but also in other phrases; e.g. Rom. viiii 28 *historia* hoc habet sensus; 1 Cor. i 19 hoc habet sensus *humanus*, ut...; 1 Cor. iii 1 hoc *solum* habere sensum *domini*, *quod*...; 2 Cor. i 11; iiii 15 hoc habet sensus, ut; in other connexions, e.g. Rom. viiii 29; 1 Cor. i 19; 2 Cor. viiii 5; proprio sensu, 1 Cor. viiii 8. In the plural, 1 Cor. vi 1.

similo intr. 'I am like': Col. iii 10, 15. (Rönsch, *Semas. Beitr.* III p. 76.)

non solum—sed etiam is almost invariable for 'not only'—'but also.' Once or twice we find *non solum—sed et.*

solum modo, 2 Cor. vii 12; 1 Tim. ii 5, 8, besides the classical *tantum modo*, which occurs e.g. Rom. xi 3; xv 24; Phil. ii 5.

subauditur (never *subintellegitur*): Rom. i 13; iii 27; v 18; (subaudias Rom. v 13); vii 4; x 19; 1 Cor. xi 17; 1 Tim. v 10.

subdolus, subdole: Rom. xvi 16 *non ficto uel* subdolo *osculo*; 2 Cor. i 12 *non* subdole *uel astute docentes*; 2 Cor. iiii 3 *noncredentes uel* subdoli; 2 Cor. xi 13 subdoli] subdolus *est, qui aliud fingit, cum aliud agit.*

su(b)scriptio (='postscript')[2]: 1 Cor. xvi 23; Gal. vi 18.

superfluus, superflue (never *superfluo*): adj. 1 Cor. viiii 20; xiv 7; xv 2; Gal. v 26; Tit. i 11; iii 9; adv. 1 Cor. vii 18; xv 2; Gal. ii 21; 1 Tim. vi 10.

taliter: Rom. iii 6; viiii 4; 2 Cor. ii 3; Gal. arg.; iiii 15, 24; Eph. vi 9.

[1] It occurs e.g. 2 Cor. v 19; vi 2; Col. i 15. [2] The verb *suscribo*, 2 Thess. iii 18.

tam...quam: Rom. ii 12; iii 20; iiii 24; xv 25, 30; 1 Cor. i 5; vii 14; viiii 21; xv 43; 2 Cor. ii 16, 17; vi 3; viii 23; viiii 9; x 5, 7; xi 13; Gal. iiii 26; v 26; Eph. ii 14; iiii 7; v 22; Phil. iiii 21; 1 Thess. i 1; iiii 15; Col. i 18; ii 23; 1 Tim. i 4; iii 2, 6; iiii 5; v 4, 7; 2 Tim. iii 8.

tango, exactly as in Ambrosiaster[1], whether the word bears the mild meaning 'allude to,' or the stronger meaning 'attack': Rom. i 16 *simul et illos haereticos* tangit; Rom. xv 5 *ut ipsos* tangat, *qui talia exercebant*; Rom. xv 20 *hic et* pseudo-apostolos tangit; 1 Cor. i 12 *sub nomine apostolorum* pseudo-apostolos tangit; 2 Cor. ii 17 pseudo-apostolos tangit; 1 Tim. v 6 *nostri temporis uiduas* tangit; 1 Tim. vi 17 *principalem eorum* tetigit *morbum*. (Cf. *taxo*, below.)

tantum ut: Rom. xiiii 9; 1 Cor. vii 39; 2 Cor. xiii 7; 1 Thess. v 22[2]. **tantum ne**: 1 Cor. vi 11; x 25; Gal. v 13[3].

taxo, taxatio: Rom. i 16 *hoc ad* taxationem *suptiliter pertinet paganorum*; Col. ii 11 *hic iam pseudo-apostolos* taxat. (Cf. *tango*, above.)

tempus, in the abl. **tempore**, contrasted with another category: cf. Rom. ii 11 'primum' *credulitatis* tempore, non honore; 1 Cor. xv 9 'minimus' tempore, non labore (contrast 1 Cor. xv 23 temporis *uel* honoris); Eph. iii 8 'minimum' tempore, non labore; Col. i 15 'primogenitus,'...non tempore, *sed* honore[4].

terrenus[5] (greatly preferred to *terrestris*, and opposite to *caelestis*): Rom. vi 6; 2 Cor. vi 10; viii 2; Eph. i 3; ii 3; Phil. ii 1; 1 Thess. v 12; Col. i 20; iii 1; 1 Tim. iii 8; 2 Tim. ii 10; Tit. i 7.

tolerantia (a favourite word of Augustine): 2 Cor. i 6; Phil. i 7; iiii 9; 1 Thess. i 3, 5; Col. iiii 18.

tolero: Rom. viii 18, 36; (xv 4); 1 Cor. viiii 12; Gal. iii 4; Tit. iii 3.

tollo c. acc. et dat. Rom. ii 14; xi 2, 33; xiii 10 (*tulerit*); xv 9; 1 Cor. xiii 3; Gal. ii 14; Phil. iii 13; 1 Tim. iiii 2.

[1] Cf. *Study*, p. 143.

[2] Also in the scripture of 2 Cor. iiii 13; Gal. vi 12.

[3] And the scripture of Gal. v 13.

[4] For the type of note, cf. Rom. xvi 13 *aetate, non partu*; cf. also 1 Cor. vii 3; 2 Cor. vi 17; Eph. v 31.

[5] See also under **nobilitas** above.

tracto (*a*) c. obj.: Eph. v 4; (*b*) c. *de*: Rom. xiii 8; 1 Cor. vi 12; xiii 3; xv 24; 2 Cor. viiii 2; 1 Tim. ii 15.

transitorie (a great favourite with Augustine): 2 Cor. viiii 5; 1 Thess. ii 2.

triplex (cf. *duplex* above) 2 Cor. vii 7; 1 Thess. iii 9.

tunc apodotic: (*a*) **tunc—si** Rom. iii 24; xii 11; xv 32; 1 Cor. viiii 17; 2 Cor. ii 3; vii 1; Eph. i 2; Phil. iiii 9; Col. i 23; 1 Tim. iiii 15; (*b*) **tunc...quando (quando...tunc)**: 2 Cor. viii 2; Eph. i 23; 1 Thess. v 3; Tit. i 3.

typus: Rom. ii 26; 1 Cor. x 2; Gal. iiii 24.

ualeo c. infin. Rom. viii 36, 39; x 8; 1 Cor. i 24; 2 Cor. xiii 3; Gal. ii 17; Eph. iii 4, 18; vi 17; Phil. i 20; 1 Tim. i 13; 2 Tim. iiii 5; (otherwise used, 2 Cor. x 4).

uere. Pelagius very much affects the use of this word: Rom. xv 1, 6, 12; 1 Cor. i 7, 10, 21; iiii 5; vii 15; viii 2; x 6; xi 10; xii 23; xv 2, 14; 2 Cor. i 19; iii 3, 6; vi 7; xi 1, 33; Gal. arg.; iii 1; iiii 19; Eph. ii 7; iiii 21 *quater*; Phil. iii 10; iiii 21; 1 Thess. i 6; 2 Tim. ii 9.

uindico, especially with **in** and the ablative[1]; Rom. iii 4 *bis*, 5; xi 22; 2 Cor. i 23; xiii 3, as well as in the classical construction *in* and the accusative; Rom. vi 16; 2 Cor. xiii 4; with *cum* and abl., 2 Cor. ii 10; and absol., 2 Cor. xii 19, 20; xiii 7.

usque[2] **dum** 2 Cor. iii 13; Gal. iii 19; **usque quo** Rom. xi 8; 1 Cor. iiii 19.

ut, quo modo..., ita (et): this collocation: Rom. i 17; vi 4; 1 Cor. xvi 24; Eph. i 3. He uses also *ut, sicut..., ita et* 2 Cor. viii 8.

uterque: the plur. **utrique** employed less exactly in the sense of *uterque*, a usage, which, according to one family of MSS, is found once even in Caesar[3]. The examples here are:—Rom. i 29; v 4; 1 Cor. xv 45; xvi 22; 2 Cor. vii 1; viiii 2; Gal. v 14; Phil. i 23. But though the author makes these slips[4], he knows the correct uses of the singular and plural quite well: e.g. *sing.* Rom. x 5; xiii 9; 1 Cor. viii 6 *bis*; 2 Cor. iiii 18; vi 8; vii 11; xii 2; Gal. iii 13; Eph. ii 14; v 24; Phil. ii 13; iii 7; 1 Tim. vi 16; *plur.* 2 Cor. ii 15; viii 14; Gal. v 19.

[1] So *uindicta in* 2 Cor. ii 15. In 2 Cor. iiii 4 *uindicare* has also an object.

[2] See *quoad usque* above.

[3] So *quique*=*quisque* 1 Tim. iii 1.

[4] Cf. Aug. *ep.* 126, 11.

utor libertate: cf. Rom. xiii 1 ita debere libertate *Christiana* uti, ut...; Rom. xiiii 16 *non ea* (libertate) ita debemus uti, ut...; 1 Cor. viiii 19 *cum possim* uti libertate mea; 1 Cor. x 29 ita utor libertate mea, ut; 2 Cor. i 24 *ne ipsa* libertate usi *fueritis in peius.*

Supplementary Note

While finally revising this chapter I noticed some other examples that might have been adduced in support of my argument. I add them here without references:

The following words or phrases introduce notes: *Hoc* (*totum*) *agit ut, Increpat, Modo, Plus, Praeuenit.*

A second quotation from the same author or book of scripture is introduced by *et iterum.*

The genitive singular of present participles like *confirmantis* is rather frequently employed.

It is not infrequently mentioned that some quality belongs *et mentis et corporis.*

The use of the following words, senses or constructions is also characteristic: *compello, confirmo, copulo, definio* (especially *definiuit*), *deprecor* (=*precor*), *dominor* (c. dat.), *duco* ('I think'), *expeto, fons* (metaph.), *gula* (metaph.), *inhaereo* (c. dat.), *permaneo, praecipio* (c. acc. et inf.), *putor* (c. gen., 'I am thought guilty of'), *suffragor.*

The Authenticity of the Prologue and Arguments

That the prologue and arguments are by the same author as the expositions themselves, will not be questioned by any one who has read through this chapter carefully. Those who desire to test the matter by itself for themselves, would perhaps find it simplest, in reading the prologue and arguments, to select any striking words or expressions, and then consult the preceding lists. The authenticity of prologue, arguments and expositions hangs together.

CHAPTER IV

THE BIBLICAL TEXTS USED BY PELAGIUS

Introductory

In this chapter an attempt will be made to describe the textual character of the Bible habitually used by Pelagius. An index of passages quoted shows his intimate acquaintance with scripture in every part; very few books of the Bible are left unquoted or unreferred to. It is true that from most parts of scripture the quotations are short, but even these may be instructive. To set over against this general brevity of quotation, also, we have received through him a complete, or almost complete, text of the Epistles of St Paul in Latin, and if we can only fix this text amidst the varying testimony of the MSS at our disposal, it will be no small gain to have in front of us what is substantially a Latin codex of the *Corpus Paulinum*, belonging to the latter part of the fourth, or the very beginning of the fifth century. Except for the still earlier codex which can be reconstructed from the Ambrosiaster commentary, we have nothing to compare with this in age till we come down to the famous *Codex Fuldensis* of Bp Victor of Capua, written in the middle of the sixth century.

The proper method to pursue in studying Latin Biblical texts, is to examine the extent of their divergence from the Vulgate. At first sight this may seem an easy matter, and so it is if by the Vulgate we mean the Sixto-Clementine Vulgate. But the labours of scholars during the past two centuries have made it clear that we can improve upon the Sixto-Clementine edition, though it is by no means a careless piece of work even from the textual point of view. If, however, we mean by the Vulgate the revision of the Old-Latin New Testament and the translation of the Old Testament as they respectively left the hands of St Jerome, we are face to face with considerable difficulties.

It is no very hard matter to identify a Vulgate Old Testament or the Vulgate Gospels. In the former case the fact that it was translated directly from the Hebrew marks it off from all earlier translations, quite apart from the presence of the prefaces by Jerome himself with which various parts are equipped; in the latter case the presence of the famous *Nouum opus facere me cogis* preface is a sufficient sign of what is Vulgate, what is not. But when we come to the Pauline epistles or other parts of the New Testament than the Gospels, how are we to say what is Vulgate and what is not? St Jerome thrice says that he revised the (whole of the) New Testament[1]; but if he did, his revision appears to have been perfunctory, and he evidently did not take the trouble to write prefaces to the Acts, Apocalypse, Catholic Epistles, or Pauline Epistles. And if he did indeed revise the whole, what proof have we that the text in the Sixto-Clementine edition, or even in the Wordsworth-White edition of *Acts* and *Romans,* has ever really passed through the hands of Jerome? May not his revision have perished altogether? He does not seem to have felt much interest in this New Testament textual work, or to have taken any steps to secure that it should be perpetuated. It began under compulsion of Pope Damasus, and Jerome's way of quoting the New Testament subsequent to the supposed date of his revision, appears absolutely to ignore his own work. The matter is yet further complicated by the fact that nearly every codex of the Pauline Epistles in the Vulgate text is provided with a prologue which is the work not of Jerome, but of Pelagius himself!

As some basis of investigation is absolutely necessary, it will be assumed in this book that the text published in the *Editio Minor* of Wordsworth and White's Vulgate New Testament[2] is really what we understand by the Vulgate, in the purest form at present attainable. The earliest fixed date at which the whole of the Vulgate New Testament is known to have existed, is the first half of the sixth century, the age of Cassiodorus[3]. Cassiodorus possessed a complete Old-Latin Bible and a complete Vulgate Bible. It was not till the ninth century, however, that the

[1] See *De Vir. Inl.* 135; *epist.* 71 § 5 (C.S.E.L. LV p. 6 l. 10); *epist.* 112 § 20 (C.S.E.L. LV p. 391 ll. 3—4).

[2] Oxonii 1911 (published Jan. 17, 1912).

[3] The genuine Augustinian *Speculum* provides a Vulgate text, and I believe that this work may be in the state Augustine left it, but some scholars still think that, in the form in which Augustine issued it, it was still partly Old-Latin.

Vulgate gained complete ascendancy. Down to that date pure Old-Latin, pure Vulgate, and mixed texts were in circulation. Wordsworth and White's text may be taken to represent the form which the Vulgate New Testament text had in the sixth century.

The presence of the Pelagian prologue in nearly all Vulgate MSS of the Epistles of St Paul is a sufficient proof that the Vulgate of these Epistles and the Pelagian commentary have in part a common history. How far the fact of that common history is due to the attribution of the commentary to Jerome in certain of its manuscripts, may be partially decided by the investigation that is to follow. But whatever may be the verdict of scholars as to the correctness of my view on the question of the text used by Pelagius himself, there will be furnished in these volumes such a body of entirely fresh evidence on the history of the Latin text of the Epistles of St Paul in the period between A.D. 400 and 800 as no other investigator has ever been privileged to publish, and I shall be well content if other scholars, using the evidence with which I provide them, are able to attain to truths hidden from myself in spite of all my strenuous endeavours to grasp them.

It is a working hypothesis[1] with investigators of the Biblical texts employed by ancient Christian writers, that if certain manuscripts of these authors' works offer the Biblical quotations in a text of normal character, such as the Constantinopolitan text in the case of Greek quotations and the Vulgate text in the case of Latin quotations, while other manuscripts give the quotations in an earlier form of text, the latter manuscripts are rather to be followed by the editor. I doubt if any one will be found to maintain the contrary: for it is hardly to be conceived that any scribe would put himself to the trouble of altering Biblical quotations, which were before his eyes in a normal type of text, back into an earlier type, for which for some reason he had a predilection. Similarly, if there are two manuscripts or two families of manuscripts, one of which more nearly approaches the normal in the character of its Biblical quotations than the other, the latter is the manuscript or family to be followed by the editor in constituting the text.

[1] Cf. the writer's *Text and Canon of the New Testament* (London, 1913) pp. 17, 85 f., as well as many other works.

§ 1. The Text of the Pauline Epistles

The investigation detailed in the second chapter resulted in the conclusion that two manuscripts alone present the Pelagian commentary in its original form, **A** Codex Augiensis CXIX (saec. VIII—IX) at Karlsruhe and **B** Balliol College MS 157 (saec. XV med.) at Oxford. We must start with the assumption that they also preserve the Pauline text in the form approved by Pelagius. We shall see, however, that these two manuscripts are far from showing the same exact agreement in Biblical text that they show in the part which is exposition. They share many non-Vulgate readings, but each on occasion supports the Vulgate reading against the other, and if we follow the rules stated above, we shall by their joint aid have to constitute a text that is as far removed from the Vulgate as possible. In other words, wherever one of these manuscripts reads with the Vulgate, the other against. we must at that point follow the latter, whichever of the two it may be. We shall of course have the weight of other manuscripts to help us, and may sometimes find that neither **A** nor **B** is right, but that we must follow some other MS whose text explains the aberrations of both. But before proceeding to the investigation proper, we can get some preliminary light on our problem from other considerations.

We shall discover in the course of this chapter that the quotations from every other part of the Bible than the Pauline Epistles are made according to an Old-Latin text. Nay more; the quotations from the Pauline Epistles themselves made in the course of the notes, apart from the lemmata altogether, and therefore much less exposed to alteration on the part of scribes, are also in the vast majority of cases made from an Old-Latin text, and in the few cases where they are not, there was perhaps no room for variation. I am of course not blind to the fact that a writer might employ more than one type of text, might, in fact, employ one type consistently for lemmata, and yet refer consciously or unconsciously to a different type in his notes. It is probable, for example, that Origen did so in some of his commentaries. It was also quite possible for a writer to employ a Vulgate text for one section of scripture, and a non-Vulgate text for another. Augustine, for instance, after about A.D. 400, uses the Vulgate of the Gospels when he seeks to quote *diserte* from the

Gospels, while he employs an Old-Latin text for the rest of the New Testament, and even for the Gospels (in this case akin to *e*)[1] when he is quoting from memory. Jerome, also, used his own Vulgate in commenting, for example, on Jeremiah, but for a number of Biblical books he consistently employs an Old-Latin text. The possibility that Pelagius used the Vulgate, or something very like it, for the lemmata, cannot at this stage be denied. Yet the presumption appears to be against this.

The parallel case of Ambrosiaster is instructive. No one doubts that this author employed an Old-Latin text for the lemmata of the Epistles, and yet in certain MSS, as Father Brewer informs me, the Vulgate text has been substituted throughout in the lemmata. The analogy of this case strongly favours the view that the great value of both commentaries, Ambrosiaster and Pelagius, created the demand for editions of these in which the Vulgate, with its growing influence and importance, was substituted for the text which the author employed. There can be no doubt that both Ambrosiaster and Pelagius arranged their work consistently throughout in the order:—(*a*) clause or clauses of text, (*b*) comment thereon[2]. At a later date, in the case of Pelagius at least, it became a practice to copy the whole commentary in the form of interlinear glosses, into a text of the Epistles already completely written, the Pelagian lemmata being either partially or entirely ignored. It is time, however, to pass from general considerations to a detailed examination of the question. And this we shall do under four heads: (*a*) occasional references to *variae lectiones* by Pelagius himself; (*b*) quotations from the Epistles made in the body of the notes; (*c*) the light thrown by the comments on the character of the text which lay before the author; (*d*) the testimony of the Vatican fragments and the interpolation in Ambrosiaster.

(*a*) *Occasional references to* variae lectiones *by Pelagius himself*

Rom. xii 13. He clearly prefers *necessitatibus*, though he refers to *memoriis* as a variant. Now *necessitatibus* is the Vulgate reading, with almost no Old-Latin support; *memoriis* is the Old-Latin reading,

[1] Cf. *J.T.S.* vol. XII (1910—11) pp. 154 f.

[2] This is proved for Pelagius in chap. ii p. 50.

supported by the one, but very important Vulgate codex, Amiatinus, which is however not backed up by Cassiodorus here.

1 Cor. x 22. He comments on *An aemulamur* (*adulamur*) *dominum?* He mentions a variant occurring in other manuscripts: *Ipsi me zelauerunt in non deo.* As no other Latin authority is known for this latter reading at this point, I think it probable that Pelagius is referring to the Old-Latin text of Deut. xxxii 21, from which verse this Pauline extract comes (αὐτοὶ παρεζήλωσάν με ἐπ' οὐ θεῷ).

2 Thess. ii 3. Here *discessio* was in his lemma, but he notes the variant *refuga*. *Discessio* is the Vulgate reading, definitely approved by Jerome himself (*epist.* 119 § 7 = C.S.E.L. LV p. 455 l. 12; also *epist.* 121 § 11 = C.S.E.L. LVI p. 53 l. 12): *refuga* is the most prevalent of various Old-Latin renderings of ἀποστασία[1].

Col. iii. 15. While reading *grati* with all other known authorities, he says that some copies have *gratia*. To the best of my knowledge, no other authority for *gratia* has turned up.

Such are all the definite references to various readings in Pelagius. So far as they go, they are not unfavourable to the view that the Vulgate was the basis of his comments.

(*b*) *Quotations from the Epistles made in the body of the notes*

As is hinted above, these appear to come from an Old-Latin source, but they must be studied in some detail. The method here followed is to compare each quotation with the Vulgate form, and to set down the word or words which show a real difference from the Vulgate. Then we search for other authorities in support of those readings. These where they are forthcoming, are arranged in three classes, first, manuscripts which rank as Vulgate MSS, described by the capital letters used by Wordsworth and White to indicate them; second, Old-Latin MSS, described by the usual minuscule letters; third, the names of Latin writers who quote according to that form, the names of these writers being indicated by the same abbreviations as are employed in the *Novum Testamentum Graece* (Oxonii, 1910, 1913, 1918) pp. xvii—xxii. An apology is due for any defects which may be noted in the enumeration of these authorities. The whole body of the authorities not

[1] See now the new fragments from Africa, published by Monsieur H. Omont, *Comptes rendus des séances de l'Acad. des Inscr. et Belles-Lettres*, 1918, pp. 241—250; cf. P. Alfaric in *Rev. d. Hist. et de Litt. relig.* VI (1920) pp. 62—98.

being accessible to me, it is proper to say that I have used Wordsworth and White's *Romans*; Nestle's *Novum Testamentum Latine* (Stuttgart, 1906); Wordsworth and White's *Novum Testamentum Latine: editio minor*; Dr Gwynn's *Liber Ardmachanus*; Buchanan's *Sacred Latin Texts: Nos* 1 *and* 2 (London; 1912, 1914); Tischendorf's *Codex Claromontanus*; Reichardt's *Codex Bœrnerianus* (Leipzig, 1909); Weihrich's *Speculum* (m); and Sabatier's great compilation, controlled in part by modern critical editions in the Vienna series, Rönsch's *Das Neue Testament Tertullian's,* Hans von Soden's *Das Lateinische Neue Testament in Afrika zur Zeit Cyprians,* personal study of Victorinus's text in Migne *P.L.* VIII, *The Study of Ambrosiaster*, Swete's *Theodore of Mopsuestia,* and the Toledan Lectionary (*Liber Comicus*[1]) etc. Where no authority is added, it means that I have found none.

Rom. ii 1	qui (*pro* in quo).
	alium iudicas.
	D (m) Aug.
v 20	peccatum (*alt.*).
	DF*L.
	d g.
	Iren.$^{\text{lat.}}$ Orig.$^{\text{lat.}}$ Ambst. Tycon. Hier. Aug.
vi 3	*om.* Iesu.
	Tert. Ambr. Orig.$^{\text{lat.}}$
vii 12	∾ iustum et sanctum.
viii 3	legi BDKUVWZ^{c} vg$^{\text{clem.}}$
	c d* g.
	Orig.$^{\text{lat.}}$ Aug. Vigil.
viiii 6	qui] + sunt.
	Orig. Tycon. Ambst. Aug.
x 12	deus.
xi 23	inseruntur (?) Hil.$^{\text{cod.}}$
xiii 10	caritas ($\frac{1}{2}$) (*pro alt.* dilectio) MZ$^{\text{post.}}$ (m) Ambr. Aug.
xvi 17	obseruate (d* g m).
„ 18	deseruiunt[2].
1 Cor. i 23, 24	*om.* quidem Ambr. $\frac{1}{2}$ Leo.
	uero (*alt.*) t.
	om. Iudaeis atque Graecis.

[1] Published by Dom Morin as *Anecdota Maredsolana* vol. I (Mareds. 1893).

[2] A favourite word of Pelagius: see chap. iii s.v.

1 Cor. ii 16 domini (*pro* Christi) D g r Ambst.
iii 3 homines (*pro* carnales).
v 4 cum (*pro* et).
om. cum uirtute domini Iesu.
8 et *alt.*] + in.
vii 7 ∾ esse omnes homines.
om. ipsum.
40 enim (*pro alt.* autem) $\frac{1}{2}$ D Ambst. Ambr. Vigil.
om. quod $\frac{2}{2}$ d g Tert. Ambst. (Greg. Illib.) Ambr. Aug. (Vigil.).
viiii 24 ut] + omnes ADO Ps. Cypr. Ambr.
x 32 Graecis d g Hil. Ambst. Aug.
33 ∾ omnibus per omnia DO.
d g $\frac{1}{2}$.
Tert. Cypr. Pacian. Ambst. Hier. Aug.
xi 32 ne (*pro* ut non) d Ambst. $\frac{1}{2}$ Aug. Gaudent.
xiii 2 habeam (*pro tert.* habuero) DO.
d g m t.
Cypr. Opt. Pacian. Ambst. Ambr. Aug.
mihi prodest (*pro* sum) D Ambr.
xiiii 14 orauero $\frac{2}{2}$ D (d *uacat*) g Ambst. Aug.
16 benedicas (d *uacat*).
25 occulta] + etiam $vg^{six.}$ d Ambr.
tunc (*pro* ita) D d Ambst.
∾ deus uere.
∾ est in uobis Ambr.
xv 31 per (*pro* propter) D^1Z^2 $vg^{clem.}$ d Ambr. Aug.
49 terreni] + ita Ambst. $\frac{1}{2}$.
om. et Hil. Instant.
2 Cor. v 15 illi (*pro* ei).
vii 11 castos d g$\frac{1}{2}$ r Ambst.
xi 1 sustinete (*pro* utinam sustineretis).
2 zelo (zelans) g$\frac{1}{2}$ Ambst. Hier. Rufin. Aug.
zelo (*noun*) g Ambst. Hier. Rufin. Aug.
23 seditionibus.
xiii 3 Christi $DF^2OZ^{corr.}$ g Ambst. (?) Faustin. Aug. (*non semper*).

[1] Gwynn's resolution of the symbol seems wrong here.

Gal. ii 4 ∾ nostram explorare subintroierant (-unt) libertatem.

iii 27 ∾ baptizati sumus in Christo.
induimus.

v 11 *om.* adhuc (1°) D d g Victorin. Ambst. Hier.

21 sicut] + et vg$^{codd.}$ d g t Iren.$^{lat.}$ Ambst. Hier. Theod.-Mops.$^{lat.}$

vi 1 praeuentus m Hil. Pacian. ½ Hier. ⅓ Arnob.-Iun.

2 inuicem (*pro* alter alterius) D
g½.
Tert. Pacian. Ambst. Aug. (*non semper*) Theod.-Mops.$^{lat.}$
onera] + uestra D
Tert. Pacian. Ambst. Hier. Aug. (*non semp.*) Theod.-Mops.$^{lat.}$

7 deridetur D
g½ m.
Tert. Cypr. Victorin. Ambst.

10 quod bonum est (*pro* bonum) D Cypr. Theod.-Mops.$^{lat.}$

12 qui Aug.
∾ in carne placere.
minime (*pro* non).

Eph. ii 5 mortui] + in Theod.-Mops.^{l}

v 8 fuistis Tert. ½ Ambst. Aug. *Promiss.*
aliquando *om.* **B**H_2, but **A**H_1 have it. Perhaps the omission is an accident.

27 sine macula Victorin. Macrob.-Don.

vi 6 quasi (*pro* ut) g Cypr.

Phil. i 1 diaconis D r.

23 cupio Tert. Victorin. Ambr. Hier. Aug. (*non semp.*)
∾ esse cum Christo D vg$^{clem.}$
(Tert.) Victorin. Aug. Cassiod.

ii 3 alter alterutrum maiorem aestimantes.
cf. alterutrum existimantes maiores D
inuicem existimantes superiores (uel maiores) g.

7, 8 ∾ exinaniuit se ipsum.

Phil. ii 8 se (*pro* semet) d g m t$\frac{2}{2}$.
Cypr. (Nouat. Hil. Lucif. Foebad.) Victorin. Faustin. (Ambr.) Aug. Theod.-Mops.$^{lat.}$

iii 12 si] + quo modo vg$^{clem.}$ Victorin. Macrob.-Don. Aug.

17 **cognoscite** cf. et cognoscite et seruate D (a doublet) ut.

21 transformabit (-uit) g$\frac{1}{2}$ Cypr. Hil.
conforme D.
g$\frac{1}{2}$ m.
Hil. (*non semper*) Ambst. Iren.$^{lat.}$ Ambr. Hier. Aug. *Promiss.* Fulg. Theod.-Mops.$^{lat.}$

1 Thess. ii 5, 6 ∾ fuimus in sermone adulationis aliquando.
cf. Gildas.
nec (*pro alt.* neque).

14 et uos (*pro* uos enim).
∾ fratres imitatores facti estis D Ambst.
om. in Christo Iesu.
eadem enim (*pro* quia enim).
om. et.
quae (*pro* sicut).
illi (*pro* ipsi).

2 Thess. i 2 *om.* nostro d.

6 ∾ his qui uos tribulant tribulationem.
Vigil. $\frac{1}{2}$ (cf. d Iren.$^{lat.}$ $\frac{1}{2}$ eis qui tribulant uos tribulationem, g eis tribulantibus uos tribulationem, Theod.-Mops.$^{lat.}$ his qui tribulant uos retribulationem).

ii 11 mittet CDGHOVZ^{2} vg$^{clem.}$
d g.
Cypr. Iren.$^{lat.}$ $\frac{1}{2}$ Ambst. Hier. Aug. *Promiss.*
spiritum (*pro* operationem).

12 quia (*pro* qui) (cf. O quod).

Col. ii 5 corpus ($\frac{1}{2}$) (*uacat* g).
om. sum (*uacat* g).
praesens (*pro* uobiscum sum) (*uacat* g).

iii 3 absconsa d Hil.
apud deum.

Col. iii 11 — Iudaeus et Graecus D Macrob.-Don. Faust. Ambr. Aug. (cf. d g Ambst. Hier. Grecus et Iudaeus).

iiii 17 — *om.* in domino m.

1 Tim. i 9 — data (*pro* posita) Greg.-Illib. $\frac{2}{2}$.

2 Tim. ii 12 — sustinemus AHOVZ.
    g.
    Ambst. Ambr. $\frac{1}{2}$ Theod.-Mops.$^{\text{lat.}}$
    (cf. toleramus D Cypr., toleremus d, sufferimus Tert.).

Tit. i 16 — ∾ deum confitentur se nosse d g $\frac{1}{2}$.
    (Ambst. Theod.-Mops.$^{\text{lat.}}$)

iii 8 — credentes (*pro* qui credunt).
    om. deo.

We may fairly conclude that passages in the above list where no other authority for the Pelagian readings can be adduced, are quotations from memory or paraphrases, and may therefore be left out of account. An examination of the others leaves no room for doubt that there is a special kinship between the copy of the Epistles used by Pelagius and D (*Book of Armagh*), in cases where the latter MS diverges from the Vulgate. A reference to Pelagius's note on the passage will show that the quotation from Phil. iii 17 is particularly significant. In the remaining passages above where Pelagius's quotation does not go with D, it goes with some copy of the Old-Latin; particularly of the European Old-Latin. It is often found in company with d and g, and where d and g diverge, rather oftener with g than with d. Now D is a composite text, partly Old-Latin and partly Vulgate[1]. It would seem therefore that the copy in Pelagius's hands was an Old-Latin text, representing throughout in absolute purity the particular Old-Latin element which only partially survives in D. We shall see later that this conclusion is confirmed. Dr Gwynn appears to regard the basis of D as Vulgate, and the Old-Latin elements as intrusions. May it not rather be that, as the basis of the Vulgate itself is Old-Latin, the basis of D is also Old-Latin, and the Vulgate elements are superimposed on its original from a copy of the Vulgate?

[1] See S. Berger, *Histoire de la Vulgate* (Paris, 1893) pp. 31 ff.

(c) *The light thrown by the comments on the character of the text which lay before the author*

The conclusions of such a paragraph as this must be received with some reserve. Pelagius, as we saw above[1], was acquainted with various readings, and it is not at all impossible that he may have consciously or unconsciously employed in a note a synonym of some word in the text, which synonym may or may not have really been in the biblical text on which he intended to comment. Yet some of the results of this paragraph seem indisputable.

Rom. xi 11. The comment on this verse, *Usque adeo illos* DILEXIT, etc. seems to indicate that he read in the text *dilecto*, not *delicto*. It may be remarked that there is no reference to a *delictum* in the note. *Dilecto* happens to be the reading of the first hand of Amiatinus. If my inference be unjustified, possibly Pelagius connected *delictum* etymologically with *diligo*: no one who knows anything of ancient etymology will doubt such a possibility.

Rom. xi 17. The note, RADICIS *patrum*, PINGVEDINIS *Christi* makes it almost certain that these words occurred in the same order in the lemma. As there is no authority for the order *pinguedinis... radicis* in the lemma except **A**, this is clearly a freakish error of **A**.

Rom. xi 32. The note has *quos inuenit* IN INCREDVLITATE. This suggests that we ought to read the same in the lemma, with a number of Vulgate MSS and Old-Latin authorities, but we cannot be certain on the point.

Rom. xii 2. The note is QVOD BONVM *sit et melius et optimum*. This suggests that we ought to read in the text *Quod bonum* [*est*] *et beneplacitum et* [*quod*] *perfectum* [*est*] with DO* d* g gue m Ambst. Orig.$^{lat.}$ Aug., and in fact our **AB** also.

Rom. xii 17. The note *ut non deo sed solis* HOMINIBVS *placere desideres* favours the idea that we ought to leave out *omnibus* in the lemma, as is done by **A** (def. **B**) in combination with DT d g gue m t Ps.-Cypr. Lucif. and some Greek authorities.

Rom. xiii 9. The note RECAPITVLATVR *omnis iustitia in proximi dilectione*, tempts one to read *recapitulatur* in the lemma, with g Hier. Orig.$^{lat.}$ Aug., but no Pelagian MS (def. **B**). It is possible that Pelagius took the word from Origen-Rufinus, which Dr Smith has proved that he used[2].

[1] Section (*a*).

[2] See *J.T.S.* vol. xx (1918—19) pp. 127 ff.: also below, pp. 188 ff.

Rom. xiii 12. The note *arma lucis, hoc est luminis opera,* INDVAMVS, suggests that we ought to read in the lemma *induamus arma lucis* with DFL* d g t Cypr. Orig.$^{lat.}$ Aug. Gildas etc.

Rom. xv 4. The note *ut per exempla patientiae et consolationis eorum quae scripta sunt, speremus* CONSOLATIONEM *et in praesentibus temptationibus* etc. seems to favour **A** in reading in the lemma *spem habeamus consolationis* with L^2, the Greek B and Clem.-Alex.

Rom. xv 16. The note SERVIENS *in euangelio; hoc est, reuocans ei seruos quosdam fugitiuos* favours the view that the lemma should read *ut sim seruiens* etc. with **AB**D d* g.

1 Cor. i 10. The note *si unum* SENTIATIS *et proferatis* rather favours the reading of the lemma thus: *in eodem sensu et in eadem sententia,* with **A**CDG^{1}O(Z) vg$^{clem.}$ Cypr. Hil. Aug. etc.

1 Cor. ii 3. The note *neque enim alio modo* DEVM *conuenerat praedicari* suggests that we should read in ii 1 *dei* (not *Christi*) with **A** (*om.* **B** altogether) d g r Ambst. Ambr. Hier. Aug. *Christi* seems in fact to be a real Vulgate reading.

1 Cor. viiii 5. The note *Non dixit* MVLIERES '*ducendi*'... *sed 'circumducendi,'* favours the reading *mulieres* in the lemma, with **A**. The other Pelagian MSS go wrong in giving *sororem mulierem* (= vg), but *mulieres* is supported by D g Tert. Hil. Hier.$^{codd.}$.

1 Cor. x 13. The note *Non uobis* VENIT *extrinsecus ista temptatio,* suggests that we ought to read *adprehendit* in the lemma with **A** d.

1 Cor. xi 10. The note *Velamen signum* POTESTATIS *esse declarat* suggests that we ought to read *potestatem* in the lemma, and in fact **AB** and nearly all the other Pelagian MSS do so: *potestatem* is also read by vg including DOZ, d g Tert. In fact Iren.$^{lat.}$. Hier. vg$^{six.}$. Aug. seem to stand alone in reading *uelamen.*

1 Cor. xi 34. The note AD *iudicium conueniebant* suggests that we ought to read in the lemma *ad iudicium conueniatis* with Ps. Hier. MSS (*def.* **B**), D d g Cypr.(?)[1] Aug.

1 Cor. xv 11. From the comment *et nos sic* PRAEDICAVIMVS *et uos similiter credidistis,* there is some probability that the lemma should read *sic praedicauimus et sic credidistis,* though **AB** Ps.-Hier. read *praedicamus.* In favour of *praedicauimus* are FO vg$^{six.}$. This, however, is a very doubtful case.

[1] Hartel gives L as reading *ad*; my report from a study of a photograph of L gives no prep.; von Soden reads *in*.

1 Cor. xvi 1. The comment *per singulas* ECCLESIAS favours *ecclesiis* in the lemma, and not *ecclesiae*, as is read by **B** Ambst.[codd.], and yet we cannot be quite certain.

2 Cor. i 4. The note on this verse, *non est minus* TRIBVLATIONE *solacium*, perhaps favours the reading of *tribulatione* in the lemma, though the synonym *pressura* is read there by **B** with D Ambst.

2 Cor. i 24. The note *credendo Christo* STARE COEPISTIS seems on the whole to favour the reading of *stetistis* in the lemma with **A**, one or two Ps.-Hier. MSS, (A)Z and seemingly other good Vulgate MSS.

2 Cor. vi 1. The note *gratiam dei* RECIPIT seems to favour the reading of *recipiatis* in the lemma with vg DOZ Ambst., but that this view is at least doubtful is suggested by the fact that **A** and one Ps.-Hier. MS read *excipiatis*, which is the reading of d.

2 Cor. vi 9 is a somewhat doubtful case. The true text of the comment would seem to be: IGNORATI *a perfidis et ingratis et* COGNITI [*a*] *fidelibus atque iustis*. This points to *ignorati* rather than *ignoti* in the lemma, where **A** has *sicut qui ignorati et cogniti*, with no authority known to me[1]. **A**'s reading would appear to be a revision of the reading of **B**, *ut qui ignoramur et cognoscimur*, which is supported by D[2] d g (Ambst.) Aug., and is no doubt right.

2 Cor. vi 9 (again). The note is a quotation from Prou. xvii 6, beginning with the words CASTIGANS CASTIGAVIT *me dominus*, which suggests that *castigati* was in the lemma (= vg Paul.-Nol.); but the agreement of **AB**D d g t Ambst. in reading *temptati* is difficult to get over, and we may explain the note by a knowledge of the other reading.

2 Cor. vii 4. At first sight the note *multam mihi* FIDVCIAM *dedistis loquendi* seems to favour the reading of *fiducia* in the lemma with vg, but *fiducia loquendi* corresponds so well to the *libertas* of **B**, supported as it is by Sedulius Scottus, that I have no doubt the latter was the Pelagian reading.

2 Cor. viiii 13. The comment uses the word MAGNIFICANTES twice here, which rather suggests that *magnificantes* was the word in the lemma. This supposition is confirmed by the fact that **B** reads *magnificantes* in the lemma with D d g Ambst.[3]

[1] But it should be noted that the first hand of t read *ut qui ignorati et cogniti*.

[2] *ignoremur* actually in D.

[3] See below on this rendering of δοξάζω.

Gal. ii 5. The comment shows clearly that the negative was absent from the text used by Pelagius, and this conclusion is confirmed by the fact that the negative is absent from **A** d with Tert. Iren.$^{\text{lat.}}$ Victorin. Ambst.$\frac{3}{3}$, as well as other authorities enumerated in my critical apparatus to the Greek New Testament.

Eph. ii 17. The comment here contains the expression *ad hoc* VENIT, which suggests that we ought to read *et ueniens euangelizauit* in the lemma, with vg DOZ d g (Cypr.) Hil. Ambst. Hier. Aug., Theod.-Mops.$^{\text{lat.}}$ in spite of the fact that **A** and one family of Ps.-Hier. MSS omit *ueniens*.

Eph. ii 22. The comment has HABITACVLVM *dei spiritale*, which confirms the reading *habitaculum* for the lemma, given by vg DOZ g Ambst. Hier. Aug. Theod.-Mops.$^{\text{lat.}}$, and all the Pelagian MSS[1].

Eph. iiii 24. The presence in the comment of the words ET SANCTITATE VERITATIS proves that these words occurred also in the lemma, supported as they are by **A** and one Ps.-Hier. MS, with vg OZ; in spite of the fact that the words are omitted by **B** and one family of Ps.-Hier. MSS. But the true reading in the lemma seems to have been *et sanctitate et ueritate*, supported as it is by the other family of Ps.-Hier. MSS, with D d g m Cypr. Hil. (Lucif. Ambr.) Theod.-Mops.$^{\text{lat.}}$; and lest it should be argued that the note confirms the form first mentioned, attention must be called to the fact that **B** reads the comment as ET SANCTITATE ET VERITATE. The omission of this phrase in the lemma of **B** must therefore be due to accident.

Phil. i 8 has in the comment *ita uos* DESIDERO, which suggests that we ought to follow **B** in reading the lemma thus: *quem ad modum desiderem*, as Ambst. Sedul.-Scott.; cf. D *dissiderauerim*, g$\frac{1}{2}$ Theod.-Mops.$^{\text{lat.}}$ *desidero*.

Phil. iii 13. The comment has *ad* PRIORA *festino*: we are thus encouraged to read in the lemma *quae sunt* [*in*] *priora*, as is indeed read by all the Pelagian MSS. The *in* is present in **A** and one family of Ps.-Hier. MSS, while the others omit it. The outside authorities are: (*a*) for the *in*: OZ Tert. Hil. Hier. Aug. *Promiss.*; (*b*) for the omission of *in*: vg D g Ambr. *In priore* is read by vg$^{\text{codd.}}$ d.

[1] *Tabernaculum* must in fact be due to the first editor of Pseudo-Jerome himself (Erasmus t. ix, 1516).

Phil. iiii 15. The comment PROFECTVS SVM favours the same reading in the lemma with all the Pelagian MSS except **B**, also with vg DOZ d g (r) Ambst. Aug. as against **B**'s *exiui*. Yet the very uniqueness of *exiui* (= *exii* Theod.-Mops.$^{lat.}$) is tempting.

Phil. iiii 17. The comment *abundans fructus* ORATIONIS *est* points to the necessity for *orationem uestram* in the lemma, as is in fact read by **A** and all Ps.-Hier. MSS, A^1Z. But **B** reads *uerbo uestro* with d, and this, as it gives the same sense as the other, may be in fact the true lemma.

1 Thess. i 6. The note *in passionibus uerbum* SVSCIPIENTES suggests that we ought to read in the lemma *suscipientes uerbum* etc. with **B**[1] Ambst. Theod.-Mops.$^{lat.}$ Were it not for the support of Ambst. and Theod.-Mops.$^{lat.}$, one might be tempted to regard the reading of **B** as an accidental assimilation to the preceding *suscipientes*.

1 Thess. i 9. The note has *deum* VERVM ET VIVVM in **A** and one family of Ps.-Hier. MSS, *deum* VIVVM ET VERVM in **B** and the other family of Ps.-Hier. MSS. But **A** and the same family of Ps.-Hier. MSS as agreed with it before, give *uero et uiuo* in the lemma, while **B** and its related Ps.-Hier. family of MSS give *uiuo et uero* in the lemma. Each MS and family is therefore consistent with its lemma. Outside we have no support for *uero et uiuo* except the Verona MS (Paris 653), but this seems enough to justify the inversion of the familiar order.

1 Thess. iii 2. The note has ADIVTORES *pro discipulis etiam uulgo dicuntur*. This suggests that we ought to read in the lemma *et adiutorem dei in euangelio Christi*, with **AB**, one family of Ps.-Hier. MSS[2], d g½[3].

1 Thess. iiii 11. The note *uel* PROPRII NEGOTII *cura et labore manuum* suggests that the word *proprius* should appear in the lemma instead of *uester*, and so in fact it does according to **B**, which reads *ut quieti sitis et negotii proprii et operandi* etc. The nearest form to this I know is d Theod.-Mops.$^{lat.}$ *et agere propria*.

1 Thess. v 23. The note reads *usque in* DIEM *iudicii*. We shall

[1] As corrected from *suscipies*.

[2] The other family has the doublet *adiutorem ministrum*.

[3] Curiously the similar word *auditor* is also sometimes an equivalent of *discipulus*: see Mayor on Juvenal *Sat.* I 1.

therefore not hesitate to read *die* in the lemma, with **AB** (one family of Ps.-Hier. MSS has *diem*). Ambr. $\frac{3}{3}$.

2 Thess. iii 1. The comment runs '*currat*' *afluentia*, 'MAGNIFICETVR' *auditorum profectu*. The character of this comment makes a strong case for *magnificetur* in the lemma with D^1 d g$\frac{1}{2}$: *glorificetur* is read by **B** with g$\frac{1}{2}$ Aug. Theod.-Mops.[lat.] Sedul.-Scott.: *clarificetur* by **A** Ps.-Hier. vg OZ Ambst. Max.-Taur.

2 Thess. iii 6. The words SEPARANT and SVBTRAHENDVM both occur in the note; so that it is a nice point whether in the lemma we ought to read *ut separetis* or *ut subtrahatis*. The former is read by **BD** g$\frac{1}{2}$ Macrob.-Don., the latter by all Pelagian MSS other than **B** and by vg OZ d m Theod.-Mops.[lat.] etc. We shall probably be right in adopting the non-Vulgate reading as lemma.

2 Thess. iii 6. The recurrence of the expression INQVIETVDO (on vv. 9, 10 etc.) suggests that the expression has occurred in some recent lemma. We find it in verse 6, where **B** has *inquiete ambulante* with (DF) d g m^2 Lucif. Aug.

Col. i 8. The comment, by reading CARITATEM, favours *caritatem* in the lemma, with **BD** g$\frac{1}{2}$. Theod.-Mops.[lat.]

Col. i 12. The note *plus uos* VOCATIO etc. shows that the lemma must have read *qui uocauit uos* with **AB**, one family of Ps.-Hier. MSS, (D) (d g m) Ambst. Vigil.

Col. ii 5. The comment on this verse is somewhat puzzling at first: *et* SVPPLENS *id quod de-est utilitati fidei uestrae*: uel litteris IMPLEO quod praesentia non possum. The real explanation is that down to *uestrae* the passage is not a comment at all, but a lemma, and a lemma very different from the Vulgate: cf. d *ut in quod de-est necessitatibus fidei uestrae* (*def.* g), Ambst. *et supplens id quod de-est utilitati fidei uestrae in Christum*, Aug. *et id quod de-est fidei uestrae in Christo*, Facund. *et id quod de-est utilitatis fidei uestrae*. Sabatier (after Latini[3]) acutely observes that these curious readings are due to **στερέωμα** in the Greek being miswritten or misread as *ὑστέρημα*. The *supplens* is clearly introduced to make sense. This one passage by itself would prove that Pelagius did not use the Vulgate as the basis of his comments.

[1] This is a case where D may be used to correct the errors of Pelagian MSS. There may be other instances also. See also 2 Cor. viiii 13 above, and pp. 139 f. below.

[2] The true reading: Weihrich is wrong here. [3] *Biblioth.* (Rom. 1677) p. 143 b.

Col. iii 5. The comment, *nihil prodest deo nomine et* IDOLIS *operibus deseruire*[1] gives just a suggestion that *idolorum* should be read in the lemma, and this suggestion derives support from the fact that *idolorum* is read there by one family of Ps.-Hier. MSS, with d g Cypr. Tycon. Ambst. Hier. Aug. Theod.-Mops.$^{lat.}$

Col. iii 21. The comment *ne exasperati* IRACVNDI *fiant* suggests that we ought to read *iracundiam* in the lemma, and this is in fact read there by **A** and Ps.-Hier. MSS, with FOZ g½ m$^{codd.}$ Ambr.

1 Tim. ii 10. The comment clearly points to CASTITATEM in the lemma, and this is in fact read by **AB** and one family of Ps.-Hier. MSS, with D (*pietatem et castitatem*, a doublet), m r Cypr. Seuer. Anon. ap. S. Paulin.

1 Tim. iii 15. The comment, *in qua sola nunc ueritas stat* FIRMATA, points on the whole to *firmamentum* in the lemma, and saves us from any temptation to read *fundamentum* with one family of Ps.-Hier. MSS, but with no outside support.

1 Tim. v 19. The comment on this verse suggests, what is confirmed by **A** and one family of Ps.-Hier. MSS, that the lemma was without the clause *nisi—testibus*. The clause is absent also from Cypr. Ambst. codd. latt. ap. Hier.

1 Tim. vi 9. The comment, *usque ad inferos* DEMERGVNTVR, suggests that we ought to read *demergunt* in the lemma, and that is what in fact we find in **B**, with D m Ambst.

1 Tim. vi 18. The word in the comment, COMMVNICARE, suggests the same word in the lemma (with Theod.-Mops.$^{lat.}$), but can hardly be regarded as decisive against *communicatores esse*, the reading of **B** g (*esse communicatores*) Ambst. (*libenter communicatores*)[2].

2 Tim. i 10. The occurrence of INCORRVPTIO in the comment commends *incorruptionem* as the reading of the lemma, but *aeternitatem* is read there in **B** with D Ambst.$^{rom.}$

2 Tim. i 17. QVAESIVIT in the note on the whole favours the same word in the lemma. There **A** reads *requisiuit*, with no outside support. I believe it is one of the instances of retouching which we find in this MS.

2 Tim. ii 4. The comment on this verse leaves it somewhat doubtful whether *deo* was present in the lemma or not. **A** omits

[1] For this expression, see also chap. iii p. 98.

[2] The comment renders these readings somewhat doubtful.

deo, with d, but I believe all other Latin evidence points to the nonsensical addition of *deo*.

This part of our investigation leads to the same conclusion exactly as the preceding, that a text akin to D was that which lay before our author. The case of Col. ii 5, as has been pointed out above, is in itself decisive against use of the Vulgate by the author.

(*d*) As the passage of time tends to obscure textual characteristics, it will not be out of place to ask what evidence, if any, as to Biblical text is furnished by the oldest Pelagian MSS at our disposal. These are the Vatican sixth century fragments, and the fifth or sixth century reconstructed interpolation from Pelagius in Ambrosiaster MSS. The method followed will again be to call attention to all variations from the Vulgate, and to append the other authorities which support the same readings.

Vatican Fragments

Rom. vii 10 in uita (in uitam **B** Aug. *saepe*).
in morte (in mortem **B** Aug. *saepe*).
11 occidit] + me **B**DW *cor. uat.** f.
13 super Aug.
∾ peccatum delinquens **B** g½ Aug.
mandatum] + legis **B**D.
14 autem **B**Θ Ambr. Orig. Aug.
quoniam t Orig.
viii 7 inimica est deo **AB**BDFKLUVW Ambst. Orig.
est subiecta **B**BDFKLVWZ^c Orig. Aug.

Here it is very significant that out of ten readings in all where the Vatican fragments disagree with the Vulgate, eight should be shared with the Balliol MS. It is only less significant that the *Book of Armagh* should agree with four of them.

Interpolation in Ambrosiaster[1]

1 Cor. xv 44 surget D g (*corr.*) (m) Ambst. Iren. Aug. Gaud. (surgit Ambst.^cas.).
om. si est—spiritale **AB**D m.

[1] As reconstructed in chap. ii pp. 51 ff.

1 Cor. xv 46 *om. alt.* est (*uersum om.* **A**) **B** d g m Tert. $\frac{3}{3}$ Iren. Ambr. Aug.
49 illius terreni **B**DZ Ambst. Ambr.
huius caelestis **B** (eius c. D) (illius c. O) Ambst. Ambr.
50 non possidebunt **B**DO g$\frac{1}{2}$ Tert. $\frac{1}{4}$ Siric. Greg.-Illib.
51 *om.* uobis **AB** Ambst.$^{codd.}$
om. sed **B** (m) (*habet* Ambst.$^{cas.}$).
52 *om.* canet enim **B** (m) (Ambr.).
53 incorruptionem DOZ d g m Tert. $\frac{1}{6}$ Cypr. Hil. $\frac{3}{3}$ Ambst. Ambr. (*non semp.*) Aug. (*non semp.*).
(incorruptelam Ambst.$^{cas.}$).
55 *pr.* stimulus tuus **B** d (g) (Tert. $\frac{3}{4}$) (Cypr.) (Iren. $\frac{1}{2}$) (Hil.) (Aug.).
alt. uictoria tua (*om.* **A**) **B** d g (Tert. $\frac{3}{4}$) (Cypr.) Iren. (Hil.) (Aug.).
56 ∾ est peccatum **B** Aug.
xvi 1 Nam de collectis **B**.
ecclesiae **B** Ambst.
2 *om.* ponat **B** Ambst.$^{cod.}$
3 ∾ fuero praesens (*uersum om.* **A**) **B** Ambst.$^{cod.}$
quoscumque **B**D d g Ambst.$^{cod.}$ Aug.
epistulam **B**.
om. in **B**.
6 *om.* apud—hiemabo.
ut—deducatis] nisi (+ si d) uos me duxeritis (*om.* **A**: deduxeritis g Ambst.$^{cas.}$) d g, ut uos me duxeritis **B**, nisi me uos deducatis D.
7 modo] nunc (*om.* **A**) **B** d g$\frac{1}{2}$ Aug.
mansurum (*om.* **A**) **B**D.
8 manebo **B**D Ambr.
9 enim] autem.
et *alt.*] sed **B**D Hier.
10 quia opus (nam opus D).
11 *om.* ergo **AB**DO d g.
12 fratre] + notum uobis facio quia **B** d cf. (nostro D) n. u. f. (faciam D) quoniam DFOZ, notesco uobis quia g significo uobis quia Ambst. (*uersum om.* **A**)

∾ illum rogaui (*om.* **A**) **B**D d (r) Ambst.
ut ueniret] uenire (*om.* **A**).
om. ei (*om.* **A**) **B**D d g Ambst.
oportunum (*om.* **A**) DF[1] **B** d g r Ambst.
1 Cor. xvi 15 Fortunati] + et Achaici (*uersum om.* **A**) **B**DO g.
∾ se ordinauerunt **B**D.
om. ipsos **B**D.
16 subiecti (*uersum om.* **A**) **B** d r.
talibus **B**D d g r.
laboranti] + in uobis **B**DO g.
17 adimpleuerunt **B**D.
18 enim] autem **B**.
om. qui **B**.
huius modi D.
om. sunt **B**.
19 ∾ Aquila multum **B** d r.
Priscilla **AB**DO d g Ambst.
ea quae in domo eorum est ecclesia **B** + apud quos etiam (et g) hospitor **B**D (a. q. inhospitor O) d g.
22 Dominum] + nostrum **B**DO.
23 Domini] + nostri **B**DOZ r.
om. Iesu **B** (*habet* Ambst.[cas.]).
2 Cor. i 1 ∾ Christi Iesu **AB**DOZ.
∾ sanctis omnibus **AB**ADFOZ d g r Aug. (omnibus sanctis Ambst.[cas.]).
2 *om.* patre—Christo **B**.
4 *om.* omni **B**.
pressura **B**D Ambst.
qui *alt.*] + sunt **B**D Ambst. Ambr.
angustia **B**D.
om. sunt **B**D Ambst. Ambr.
5 abundat] + etiam **B**D Ambst. Ambr. + et g.
6 angustiam patimur **B**, (*ex* angustiamur) Ambst.[cas.] (pressuram patimur Ambst.).

Nothing could be clearer than the meaning of this evidence. Here we find in the Ambrosiaster interpolation sixty differences from the Vulgate text. Of these sixty, no less than fifty-four are reproduced in the Balliol manuscript. Of these fifty-four instances, thirteen are supported by no other known authority. It is clear therefore that the complete Pelagian codex from which the interpolation was made exhibited already, in the period between A.D. 400 and 550, a Biblical text which is almost exactly reproduced in the Balliol manuscript. This complete Pelagian codex was almost certainly an older MS than that to which the Vatican fragments belonged. There is no reason to doubt that both these early MSS were Italian. Yet for the complete text to which they witness we are now dependent entirely on an Irish-Italian MS of the middle of the fifteenth century.

The net result of our investigation up to this point, is that the text of the Epistles of St Paul commented on by Pelagius is represented in its fullness by one manuscript only, the Balliol MS. It is not strange that here and there it bears traces of harmonization with the Vulgate, but these are as nothing compared to the systematic alteration in the same direction to which the Reichenau manuscript bears witness. We shall find on occasion, however, that the Reichenau MS helps us to recover the true text employed by Pelagius, where the Balliol MS has suffered this deterioration.

There is another striking fact to which attention must again be called at this stage, that is, the relationship of the *Book of Armagh* to the text employed by Pelagius. Of the sixty readings referred to above, thirty-one are found in the *Book of Armagh* (D) also, one being peculiar to Ambst.$^{\text{interpol.}}$ and D, namely *huius modi* (1 Cor. xvi 18). No other outside authority is so close. Even the Reichenau MS agrees only six times in this section with **B**, a fact which is however somewhat discounted by the omission of whole verses of scripture from the former manuscript. The real proportion of the agreements between **A** and **B** is better exhibited by the table of readings already published[1], where they agree in twenty-eight out of forty-four passages, against the Vulgate. Both the Reichenau MS and the *Book of Armagh*, therefore, exhibit Pelagius' Biblical text of St Paul's Epistles, after it has suffered harmonization with the Vulgate, but the harmonization is in each case independent of the other, and it is also partial, not complete. The Pauline text in the *Book of Armagh* is, then, in my view, taken out of a copy of

[1] *Brit. Acad. Proc.* vol. VII (1915—16) pp. 271—274 (Epistle to the Romans only).

Pelagius's commentary on the Epistles, after that text had been partially harmonized with the Vulgate. It will not be unsafe, therefore, to call in the help of D in doubtful cases.

In order to show as strikingly as possible the close relationship between the text in the *Book of Armagh* and that provided by the Balliol *codex* of Pelagius, it will be best to select the peculiarities of the Armagh text that have been signalised by two investigators, to whom our present problem was necessarily quite unknown.

Samuel Berger in his *Histoire de la Vulgate* gives a list of interpolations in the New Testament text of the *Book of Armagh* (D)[1]. I propose to repeat it here, adding the text of the Balliol MS of Pelagius (**B**) at each point.

Rom. iiii 18: tamquam stellae caeli et tamquam harena[2] quae est ad oram maris non denumerabitur a multitudine.

This is omitted both by **A** and **B** (= vg), which indicate an earlier stage.

Rom. xv 30: ut **solicitudinem inpertiamini** in orationibus **uestris** ad **dominum** pro me.

B reads: ac **sollicitudinem inpertiamini** mihi in orationibus **uestris** ad **dominum**. The *pro me* in D is doubtless taken from the Vulgate, which reads 'ut adiuuetis me in orationibus pro me ad deum.'

1 Cor. vii 35: ut sit frequens oratio uestra ad dominum sine ulla occupatione.

All this is absent from **A** and **B** alike; its origin is a matter of considerable interest, as it differs from the Vulgate 'et quod facultatem praebeat sine impedimento dominum obseruandi[3].'

1 Cor. xi 24: quod tradidi pro uobis.

B has quod pro uobis tradetur (= vg), **A** has simply pro uobis.

Gal. ii 2: qui **existimabantur esse maiores**.

This is a very instructive case. **B** reads qui **existimantur esse maiores**. The Vulgate has qui uidebantur simply.

Eph. ii 5: peccatis **et concupiscentiis** uiuificauit nos **in** Christo

[1] p. 32 n. 3.

[2] Actually *hariena* (Gwynn).

[3] This celebrated verse is the subject of a discussion by Jerome (*ad Iouin.* I 13), who blames the Latin MSS which, like our **A** and **B**, have no translation of the Greek here. See De Bruyne in *Revue Biblique* nouv. sér. vol. XII (1915) pp. 364 f.

cuius gratia sumus **salui per fidem facti**, et **simul suscitauit simulque fecit sedere.**

B reads peccatis conuiuificauit nos Christo (*om.* **A**) **cuius** gratia estis **salui facti per fidem** et **simul suscitauit simulque fecit sedem** (*sedem* is a palaeographical error, due to misreading of the insular script). The thick type indicates differences from the Vulgate, as elsewhere here.

Col. iii 8 **turpiloquium** de ore uestro **non procedat.**

B reads **turpiloquium** de ore uestro **non procedat**; identical[1].

1 Tim. ii 6 temporibus suis **datum est.**

B is here identical with D.

2 Tim. iiii 5 tu uero **sobrius esto**, in omnibus labora...iam enim ego **immolor.**

B reads tu uero uigila in omnibus...ego enim iam delibor (almost = vg).

Let us now examine Dr Gwynn's nine instances of 'singular readings of D[2].' Of these instances three have already come under our view above, namely Rom. iiii 18[3]; 1 Cor. vii 35 and Eph. ii 5. There remain, therefore, only six instances to consider:

Rom. i 27 **exercentes.**

B agrees: vg has operantes.

Rom. xii 9 **execrantes.**

B agrees: vg has odientes.

1 Cor. xi 4 **supra caput habens uelamen.**

Here all Pelagian authorities have uelato capite (= vg). It may be that we ought to put D's reading in the text of Pelagius.

2 Cor. vii 11 **sinceres.**

B agrees: vg has incontaminatos.

Eph. vi 18 **tolerantia** for instantia of vg.

B omits altogether the clause in omni instantia et obsecratione, but both D and **B** have a **semper** there which is absent from the Vulgate.

Phil. i 27 **certamen ineuntes cum** fide.

B has here conlaborantes fidei (= vg).

[1] Here Berger has gone badly wrong: he fails to give the *uestro* of D, and at the same time he adds *cum actibus*, which according to the Irish custom really belongs to *expoliate ueterem hominem.*

[2] *Liber Ardmachanus*, pp. ccxx f. Of the five dittograph readings (p. ccxxi) of D, **B** (or **A**) has three, of the six mere blunders only one, or rather a half of one.

[3] 8 is given by a slip for 18.

There can be no doubt of the close relationship of the two texts. In all, fifteen testing passages have been considered. In five of these passages **B** agrees with the Vulgate against D, and it may be that here D has preserved the true Pelagian text. In eight and a half[1] others the connexion between **B** and D is the very closest. In the remaining one and a half passages **B** and D differ from one another and from the Vulgate. In 1 Cor. vii 35 **B** clearly indicates a more primitive text than D, as it gives the true Old-Latin reading, and at Eph. vi 18 the omission of five words from **B** may be accidental.

External Confirmation of the use of the D type of text by Pelagius. Epistula ad Demetriadem

Having asked myself the question whether other works of Pelagius would shed any light on the type of Pauline text he used, I turned to the *Epistula ad Demetriadem*. This was at a time when I was fortunately in touch with a good manuscript of this work, namely *Codex Augiensis* CV (saec. IX in.) at Karlsruhe[2]. My friend Mr E. J. Turner[3] and I collated the MS as far as the middle of c. 26. In it the letter is attributed, as sometimes also elsewhere, to Julian, and it commences on fol. 15 a. It may be remarked incidentally that a critical edition of this letter will differ considerably from the published form, as like other heretical works, it has been neglected. Here I will call attention merely to one lengthy quotation from the Epistle to the Romans in c. 4, which reads thus according to the Reichenau manuscript:

Rom. ii 14—15 cum enim gentes quae legem
non habent
naturaliter quae legis sunt
faciunt
huius-modi legem non
habentes ipsi sibi sunt lex
qui ostendunt opus legis
scriptum in cordibus suis

[1] The 'half' is Eph. vi 18 where **B** and D agree in *semper*, but differ otherwise.

[2] Now described by Holder, *Die Reichenauer Handschriften* I Bd. (Leipzig, 1906) pp. 267 ff.

[3] Formerly Major Scholar of Trinity College, Cambridge, and long of H.M. India Office. The collation was made 16 Aug. 1906.

testimonium reddente **eis**
conscientia **eorum**
et inter se inuicem **accusan-**
tibus cogitationibus aut etiam
defendentibus.

What are the authorities for the non-Vulgate readings here? As given by Wordsworth and White they are:

huius T dem t Orig. $\frac{2}{4}$.
eis Orig. *ter*.
eorum c Sedul.[1]
'accusantibus cogitationibus' appears to be unique, but it is close to 'cogitationibus accusantibus' D g$\frac{1}{2}$ Orig. $\frac{2}{3}$ (Ambst.) Ambr. Hier. Aug. *bis* Sedul.[1]
defendentibus D Orig. $\frac{2}{3}$ g$\frac{1}{6}$ Ambst. Ambr. Hier. Aug. Sedul.[1]

The evidence here speaks for itself, I think. I have not pursued the matter further, but it will be quite instructive to compare the many quotations in the Letter to Demetrius, when once it is critically edited, with the Pelagian text as published in my second volume.

De Induratione Cordis Pharaonis

A tractate which circulated under this title in the Carlovingian period as a work of Jerome, has been recently rediscovered by Dom Morin in six manuscripts, of which four at least are British in origin. Dom Morin's edition will be published in the second volume of his *Études, Textes, Découvertes*. Meantime, we have to depend on a considerable account of the work which he has published in the *Revue Bénédictine*[2]. He considers it probable that the author of the tractate lived towards the beginning of the fifth century, as the Pelagianism it displays is in a very crude state. It will be of some interest to examine the character of its quotations from the Epistle to the Romans. Whether it be by Pelagius or not, it is interesting to observe that the word *induratio* is found also in the Pelagius commentary at 1 Tim. ii 4—*de induratione Pharaonis*[3].

If the suggestion made below, p. 148, is right, Sedul. = Pelag.

[2] Vol. XXVI (1909) pp. 163—188: see also his *Études, Textes, Découvertes* t. I (Maredsous and Paris, 1913) p. 24.

[3] See Benoist-Goelzer for other exx. (from Paucker).

Rom. vi 16 **oboedistis** (oboeditis vg) vg$^{\text{codd. pler.}}$ D c dem g r$_3$ t Orig. Ambst. Ambr. **B**.
viii 30 **magnificauit** (glorificauit vg) vg$^{\text{codd. mult.}}$ D c d* dem Ambst. **A** (honorificauit **B**).
32 qui **unico** filio suo non pepercit (qui etiam f. s. n. p. vg **A**) Orig. *semel* Aug. *semel* (qui filio s. proprio n. p. **B**).
viiii 11 bonum **uel** malum (bonum aut malum vg **A**) D Aug. *semel* **B**.
18 **cui** (cuius vg **A**) vg$^{\text{codd. mult.}}$ D c d Ambr. Orig. *ter* Ambst. Aug. *semel* Beatus **B**.
obdurat (indurat vg **AB**) DF$^{\text{mg.}}$R Ambr. Aug. (*semper*) Beatus Sedul.
20 **cur** me **ita** fecisti (quid me fecisti sic vg **AB** *epist. ad Demetr.*) unique.

This investigation does not seem to prove anything, but it can hardly be said to contradict the possibility that the *De Induratione Cordis Pharaonis* is the work of Pelagius himself.

Relation of the Pauline text used by Pelagius to the quotations in Gildas (A.D. 500—570)[1].

Rom. i 21 f. cognouerunt *with* **A**.
magnificauerunt *with* D**B**.
obcaecatum *with* D.
om. enim.
25 mendacium *with* D**A** Ps.-Hier.
om. amen *with* **AB** and one family of Ps.-Hier. MSS.
28 notitia *with* **A**.
29 inpudicitia fornicatione.
30 inoboedientes.
31 insensatos *with* **B**.
om. absque foedere *with* D**AB**.
sine misericordia sine adfectione.

I have used the edition of Mommsen in *Chronica Minora* vol. III (M.G.H. auct. ant. t. XIII) (Berol. 1898), not yet accessible to Haddan and Stubbs, *Councils and Ecclesiastical Documents*, etc. vol. I (Oxford, 1869) pp. 170—185. There is a reference to Gildas's Biblical quotations in *Zeitschr. f. celt. Philol.* Bd. IV pp. 572 f. by the late Dr Hugh Williams.

Rom. i 32 non solum] + qui *with* D**AB**.
faciunt ea *with* D**B**.
etiam *with* Ps.-Hier. as printed.
+ qui *with* D**AB**.
ii 5 tu autem secundum duritiam tuam *with* D.
cor inpaenitens *with* D**B**.
6 sua *with* D**B** Ps.-Hier. *cod.*
11 acceptio personarum.
12 *om.* et (*pr.*) *with* D**B** and one family of Ps.-Hier. MSS.
om. et *alt.*
vi 2 adhuc] iterum *with* D**B**.
viiii 3 *om.* ipse ego *with* D.
xi 3 *add.* et *ante* altaria *with* Aug.
xiii 12 adpropinquauit *with* D (def. **B**) and one family of Ps.-Hier. MSS.
induamus *with* D (def. **B**) and one Ps.-Hier. MS.
14 induite *with* **AB**.
concupiscentiis *with* D**B**.
1 Cor. iii 10 ff. alter *with* **B**.
om. autem *with* **B**.
om. positum est qui.
Iesus Christus *with* D.
superaedificet.
super *with* D[1].
om. fundamentum.
aurum] + et *with* **B**.
unum quodque (*pr.*).
enim] + domini *with* D**B** (def. **A**).
declarabit] + illud.
qui superaedificauerit (quod superaedificauerit D**B**).
om. ipse autem...per ignem.
(18) apud.
v 7 expurgate] + igitur *with* D and one family of Ps.-Hier.
10 exire *with* D**B** and one family of Ps.-Hier.

[1] I take it that Dr Gwynn has here wrongly resolved the insular symbol.

1 Cor. v 11	is qui] quis *with* D**B** and one MS. of Ps.-Hier.
	nominatur frater.
	] + et *with* D.
	huiusmodi *with* D.
	cibum] + quidem *with* D**B** and one family of Ps.-Hier. MSS.
2 Cor. iiii 1 f.	administrationem *with* **B** and one family of Ps.-Hier. MSS.
	deficiamus *with* D and Ps.-Hier. MSS.
	abiciamus *with* some Ps.-Hier. MSS.
xi 13 ff.	pseudo-apostoli] + sunt *with* D and one family of Ps.-Hier. MSS.
	magnum igitur.
	uelut ministri] ut angeli.
	eorum.
Eph. iiii 18 f.	uia *with* D.
	eorum Ps.-Hier. *codd. pler.*
	omnis inmunditiae.
	in auaritia] et auaritiae *with* D**AB** Ps.-Hier. *cod.*
v 17 f.	dei *with* D Ps.-Hier. *cod.*
	replemini *with* one family of Ps.-Hier. MSS.
	spiritu] + sancto *with* D and two Ps.-Hier. MSS.
Phil. i 8	cupimus unum quemque uestrum in uisceribus Christi esse (*cf.* cupio *with* one family of Ps.-Hier. MSS).
1 Thess. ii 5 ff.	fuimus apud uos aliquando.
	om. deus testis est *with* one family of Ps.-Hier. MSS.
	gloriari *with* one family of Ps.-Hier. MSS.
	possumus *with* some Ps.-Hier. MSS.
	honori *with* D and one family of Ps.-Hier. MSS.
	ceteri apostoli Christi *with* one family of Ps.-Hier. MSS.
	sicut paruuli (*with* one family of Ps.-Hier. MSS).
	tamquam] uel tamquam.
	paruulos *with* one family of Ps.-Hier. MSS.
	uobis tradere *with* one Ps.-Hier. MS.
	om. dei.

1 Thess. iiii 2 ff. dederim *with* most Ps.-Hier. MSS.
om. per dominum Iesum *with* **A** and one family of Ps.-Hier. MSS.
om. enim.
ut sciat] et sciat.
uas suum.
honore et sanctificatione.
(6) ut] et *with* one family of Ps.-Hier. MSS.
om. sicut...sumus *with* **A** and one family of Ps.-Hier. MSS.
inmunditiam *with* D**AB** and one family of Ps.-Hier. MSS.
sanctificationem *with* D**AB**.

Col. iii 5 f. libidinem] + et.
om. et auaritiam...seruitus (but not on p. 66).
super] in.
diffidentiae.

1 Tim. i 15 (iiii 9) sermo] + est.
iii 1 ff. desiderat 1°] cupit.
episcopum] huiusmodi *with* D**B**.
∼hospitalem ornatum
om. doctorem.
domum suam bene regentem *with* (s. d.) D.
adhibebit.
uino multum.
(10) *om.* Et.
vi 3 ff. sermonibus sanis.
superbus] + est *with* Ps.-Hier. as printed.
languescens *with* **B**.
erga *with* one family of Ps.-Hier. MSS.
(5) *om.* et *with* **B** and one family of Ps.-Hier. MSS.
17 ff. noli superbe s. uel (*cf.* D and **B**).
nobis] tibi.
omnia] multa.
om. ad fruendum.
adprehendant] habeas.

2 Tim. ii 4 f. placeat ei.
contendit.

2 Tim. iii 1 ff.[1] enim scitote.
periculosa] pessima ½.
et erunt] erunt enim.
semet.
om. sine pace criminatores (*om.* sine pace **B**).
uoluptatum ⅔ *with* **B** and some Ps.-Hier. MSS.
quidem speciem *with* **B** and one family of Ps.-Hier. MSS.
(8) autem] enim *with* one family of Ps.-Hier. MSS.
hi] isti *with* **B** and nearly all Ps.-Hier. MSS.
Tit. ii 8 sanum] + habens.
nullum malum habens *with* one family of Ps.-Hier. MSS.

These statistics are very significant, especially as Gildas's quotations are long, and therefore copied from a Biblical MS. There are out of 121 variants, 39 agreements with D, 13 with **A**, 33 with **B**, and 43 with one or more MSS of Pseudo-Jerome. It is quite evident that Gildas, about four generations after Pelagius, employed a text substantially identical with his and that of the *Book of Armagh*. Is it too much to argue that in Pelagius we find the textual form of the Epistles used in Britain in the pre-Vulgate period, and for long afterwards, that here we have the oldest form in which the Pauline Epistles were read in the British Isles, the missing British form of the Old-Latin?

A presumption having been established that the Pauline text employed by the Briton or Irishman Pelagius, by the Briton Gildas, and by the scribe of the *Book of Armagh*, is really a British text with definite characteristics of its own, it becomes a matter of no little interest to enquire whence this text came. The two recognised routes of travel from the Continent to Britain were by Boulogne and Richborough on the one hand, and from the Rhine to Colchester on the other[2]. It cannot be denied that there was also

[1] I purposely omit the quotation of these verses in the *fragm. epist. Gildae* published by Mommsen on p. 86 of his edition. Whether the fragment be by Gildas or not, it appears that the quotation is not taken from a copy of the Epistles, but from Jerome on Zephaniah, chap. ii (ed. Vallarsi, t. VI 713 A of the 4to edition).

[2] F. J. Haverfield in *Cambridge Medieval History* vol. I p. 370.

direct intercourse between Spain and Gaul on the one hand, and Cornwall, Wales and Ireland on the other, but the other routes were the most important. We have then to ask what continental texts are most likely to have been transmitted to Britain. If we try such Spanish texts as are accessible to us, those of *m*, *t*, 'Priscillian' and Gregory of Elvira, we shall not I think discover many notable coincidences between the Pelagian text and these. A comparison with the quotations in Hilary of Poitiers will be hardly less disappointing[1]. But when we come to the quotations in Ambrose, the situation is changed. It is a delicate question whether Ambrose used at Milan the type of scripture text in use in his native church at Trèves; but as he was brought up in a Christian family, it seems to me not improbable that this very ardent student of scripture used the text current at Trèves. It is indeed possible that there was no great difference between the Trèves text and the Milanese text. The resemblances between the Ambrose and Pelagius texts are set forth below. I have been careful to select, for the purpose of forming a judgment, only lengthy quotations from Ambrose in a modern critical text. I have gone through the six volumes of Ambrose already published in the Vienna series, and gathered together such passages as seem to have been copied straight from a Pauline *codex*, and then brought these quotations face to face with the Pelagian text, here denominated **B**. It will be seen that there are considerable differences between the two texts: I do not seek to argue for their identity. But what I think may be regarded as fairly established is this, that there is a real kinship between these two West-European Pauline texts such as one will seek in vain elsewhere. Each has its distinctive characteristics, but they spring from the same root. Is it too much, then, to hazard a conjecture that Britain got its Pauline text from the Rhine country viâ its oldest Roman *colonia*, Camulodunum (Colchester)?

An examination of the valuable lists in the introductory part of Dr Gwynn's *Liber Ardmachanus* shows a large number of passages

[1] Hilary, as a consummate Greek scholar, seems often to have translated direct from the Greek. Also, we lack a critical edition of most of his works with an index suited to modern requirements. So far as Pauline references in his commentary on the Psalms are concerned, I have endeavoured, in *J.T.S.* vol. XVIII (1916—17) pp. 73—77, to supply the want of an index in the Vienna edition.

where D has the support of Ambr., and if there be many where it has the support also of Sedulius Scottus, the reason for this is no doubt the adoption of Pelagius's Biblical text by Sedulius along with a large proportion of the Pelagian comments. In fact my investigations have led me to believe that anything in Sedulius's Biblical text that differs from the Vulgate is Pelagian, and that one might well substitute Pelag. for Sedul. in already published works that quote Pauline Latin *codices*. These works convey the impression that Sedulius in the ninth century used an Old-Latin text of his own. There is in fact in his *Collectaneum*, as I have proved, hardly one column of original matter[1]!

Ambrose's disagreements with the Vulgate, paralleled by Pelagius's text

		Vienna edition, vols. XXXII, LXII, LXIV.
Rom. i 15		
est promptus sum B	promtum est *vg*	fug. saec. pp. 173, 174.
Rom. ii 14		
si	cum *vg*	parad. p. 296.
Rom. v 4		
autem B	uero *vg*	ps. 118 p. 205.
Rom. vi 4–7		
in morte	in mortem *vg*	Iacob p. 52.
quem ad modum B	quomodo *vg*	parad. p. 303.
ille surrexit (Chr. s. **B**)	surrexit Christus *vg*	
morte	mortuis *vg*	
uirtutem	gloriam *vg*	
propriam suscitatus	patris *vg*	
eius gratia	in nouitate uitae *vg*	
resurgamus	ambulemus *vg*	
facti *om.* **B**	facti *vg*	
hoc *om.*	hoc *vg*	
confixus est cruci B	crucifixus est *vg*	
Rom. vi 16		
in mortem B	*om. vg*	Iacob p. 11.
Rom. viii 38 f.		
confido B	certus sum *vg*	ps. 118 p. 172. ps. 43 p. 288.
potestates $\frac{2}{2}$	principatus *vg*	
praesentia $\frac{2}{2}$	instantia *vg*	
separare nos poterunt (possint)	poterit nos separare *vg*	
domino nostro *om.* $\frac{1}{2}$	domino nostro *vg*	

[1] See *J.T.S.* vol. XVIII (1916—17) p. 228. I regret that I did not soon enough realise the significance of the lemmata in Sedulius Scottus, having my mind too exclusively concentrated on his commentary.

		Vienna edition, vols. XXXII, LXII, LXIV.
Rom. xi 1 f.		
hereditatem suam $\frac{2}{2}$	populum suum *vg*	ps. 118 p. 34. ps. 43 p. 281.
Rom. xi 25 f.		
Israhel contigit B	contigit in Israhel *vg*	ps. 118 p. 424.
Rom. xiii 4		
egit (*def.* **B**)	agit *vg*	Cain p. 391.
Rom. xiii 8 f.		
suum (*def.* **B**)	*om. vg*	ps. 118 p. 498.
scriptum est enim (*def.* **B**)	nam *vg*	
1 Cor. i 4 f.		
dei nostri	dei *vg*	ps. 118 p. 39.
ipso B	illo *vg*	
1 Cor. iii 18 f.		
sap. esse inter uos $\frac{3}{3}$ **B**	inter uos sap. esse *vg*	ps. 118 p. 493. ps. 36 p. 75. ps. 43 p. 263.
1 Cor. iiii 11—13		
ad	in *vg*	ps. 118 p. 153.
uapulamus	caedimur *vg*	
lustramenta	purgamenta *vg*	
"	peripsima *vg*	
1 Cor. vii 29 ff.		
et	ut *vg*	fug. saec. p. 199.
ita sint ac si non habeant B	tamquam non habentes sint *vg*	
hoc mundo utuntur	utuntur hoc mundo *vg*	
1 Cor. xii 23		
esse membra (*def.* **B**)	membra esse *vg*	de Noe p. 428.
honestatem abundantiorem (*def.* **B**)	abundantiorem honestatem *vg*	
1 Cor. xv 22 ff.		
sicut enim B	et sicut *vg*	ps. 118 p. 278.
qui in aduentum (-u B) eius crediderunt B	in aduentu eius *vg*	
dum	cum (2°) *vg*	
et uirtutem *om.*	*habet vg*	
1 Cor. xv 51 f.		
uobis *om.* **B**	*habet vg*	exam. p. 121.
non omnes autem (non omnes B)	sed non omnes *vg*	
in atomo in momento oculi	in momento in ictu oculi *vg*	
canet enim *om.* **B**	*habet vg*	
2 Cor. i 3 ff.		
omnis	totius *vg*	ps. 118 p. 225.
nos exhortatur	consolatur nos *vg*	
angustia	tribulatione *vg*	
nostra *om.*	*hab. vg*	
sunt in omni tribulatione (angustia B) B	in omni pressura sunt *vg*	
et ipsi aduocamur	exhortamur et ipsi *vg*	
(5) **et** *om.*	*habet vg*	
abundat etiam B	abundat *vg*	

		Vienna edition, vols. XXXII, LXII, LXIV.
2 Cor. vi 11 ff.		
coartamini B	angustiamini (2°)	ps. 118 pp. 124, 80, 154 etc.
2 Cor. vi 14		
et *ante* **nolite B**	*om. vg*	
portio $\frac{2}{2}$	participatio *vg*	
2 Cor. vi 16		
his $\frac{1}{2}$	illis *vg*	
deambulabo $\frac{2}{2}$	inambulabo *vg*	
+in ipsis $\frac{1}{2}$ **(his** $\frac{1}{2}$**)**	*om. vg*	
2 Cor. xii 3 ff.		
eius	huius *vg*	parad. p. 265 ps. 36 p. 102.
uerba ineffabilia $\frac{2}{2}$	arcana uerba *vg*	
(5) **huius**	eius *vg*	
non	nihil *vg*	
(6) **si enim**	nam etsi *vg*	
stultus B	insipiens *vg*	
nam ueritatem dico (B)	ueritatem enim dicam *vg*	
Gal. iii 16		
repromissiones $\frac{1}{2}$	promissiones *vg*	parad. p. 278 ps. 36 p. 118
tamquam $\frac{2}{2}$ **B**	quasi *vg*	
sicut $\frac{2}{2}$ **B**	quasi (2°) *vg*	
Gal. iiii 21 ff.		
sub lege uolentes esse B	qui sub lege uultis esse *vg*	Abr. p. 523.
quod B	quoniam *vg*	
habuerit	habuit *vg*	
sed is quidem qui (sed is qui B)	sed qui *vg*	
promissionem	repromissionem *vg*	
nam haec	haec enim *vg*	
quod est Agar	quae est Agar *vg*	
Gal. v 22		
patientia B +	longanimitas (*vg*) **B**	parad. p. 323 cf. ps. 36 p. 78.
bonitas *om.* $\frac{1}{2}$ (*om.* benignitas **B**)	*habet vg*	
fides *om.* $\frac{1}{2}$	*habet vg*	
dilectio (*in fine*) $\frac{1}{2}$ **B**	*om. vg*	
Eph. ii 14 ff.		
inimicitias B	inimicitiam *vg*	Abr. p. 585.
edictis	decretis *vg*	
conderet	condat *vg*	
ipso	ipsum *vg*	
uno nouo homine	unum nouum hominem *vg*	
ut reconciliaret Ps.-Hier. *codd.*	et reconciliet *vg*	
utrosque	ambos *vg*	
inimicitias B	inimicitiam *vg*	

		Vienna edition, vols. XXXII, LXII, LXIV.
Eph. vi 12		
principatus	principes *vg*	parad. p. 313 ps. 1 p. 33.
et	aduersus (3°) *vg*	cf. ps. 36 p. 113.
rectores huius mundi (**mundi huius rectores B** Ambr. ps. 1)	mundi rectores *vg*	
aduersus	contra *vg*	
nequitiam spiritalium ½	spiritalia nequitiae *vg*	
quae sunt ⅔	*om. vg*	
Phil. i 23 f.		
dissolui enim cupio	desiderium habens dissolui *vg*	ps. 118 p. 501 cf. ps. 47 p. 354 ps. 61 p. 390.
enim	magis *vg*	
Phil. ii 6 ff.		
esset in forma dei (etc.)	in forma dei esset *vg*	ps. 118 pp. 329, 414, 311, 454
specie	habitu *vg*	ps. 35 p. 53.
exaltauit illum deus ½	deus illum exaltauit *vg*	ps. 61 p. 382, etc.
dedit	donauit *vg*	
eius ½	Iesu *vg*	
Christus *om.* **B**	habet *vg*	
Phil. iii 7 f.		
lucra fuerunt B	fuerunt lucra *vg*	ps. 118 p. 154.
duxi B	arbitratus sum *vg*	
Christi Iesu B	Iesu Christi *vg*	
omnium	omnia *vg*	
passus sum	feci *vg*	
aestimor	arbitror ut *vg*	
Col. i 13 ff.		
claritatis (*Schenkl*, etc.: ?*errore pro* **caritatis B**)	dilectionis *vg*	exam. p. 232 ps. 118 pp. 52, 212 cf. ps. 36 p. 100.
redemptionem et	redemptionem *vg*	
inuisibilis et ½	inuisibilis *vg*	
ipse ½	qui *vg*	
uniuersae ½	omnis *vg*	
in quo	quia in ipso *vg*	
creata	condita *vg*	
omnia	uniuersa *vg*	
caelestibus	caelis *vg*	
siue uisibilia	uisibilia *vg*	
siue	et *vg*	
sedes B	throni *vg*	
Col. ii 18 f.		
uidet Ps.-Hier. *codd.*	uidit *vg*	ps. 118 p. 446.
extollens se B	ambulans *vg*	
mente B[1]	sensu *vg*	
omne	totum *vg*	
compaginationes	nexus *vg*	
colligationes B	coniunctiones *vg*	

[1] Cf. in this chapter, p. 154.

		Vienna edition, vols. XXXII, LXII, LXIV.
Col. ii 18 f. (*cont.*)		
copulatum B	constructum *vg*	
incrementum	augmentum *vg*	
Col. ii 21 ff.		
tetigeritis B	tetigeris *vg*	Noe p. 480.
ne adtaminaueritis $\frac{2}{2}$ **(con- B)** **ne gustaueritis** $\frac{3}{3}$ **B** } **B**[1]	neque gustaueritis neque contrectaueris } *vg*	ps. 118 p. 323 ps. 1 p. 23.
omnia *om.* $\frac{1}{3}$	*habet vg*	
ad corruptelam $\frac{3}{3}$	in interitu *vg*	
obseruatione religionis B (*om.* religionis)	superstitione *vg*	
humilitate cordis B	humilitate *vg*	
non in indulgentia corporis	et ad non parcendum corpori *vg*	
saturitatem et diligentiam B	saturitatem *vg*	
Col. iii 9 ff.		
uos *om.* $\frac{2}{2}$ Ps.-Hier. *codd.*	*habet vg*	ps. 118 pp. 53, 213.
induite $\frac{1}{2}$ **B** (**et induimus** $\frac{1}{2}$)	et induentes *vg*	
eum *om.* $\frac{2}{2}$ **B**	*habet vg*	
agnitione $\frac{1}{2}$ **B**	agnitionem *vg*	
2 Thess. ii 3 f.		
iniquitatis	peccati *vg*	ps. 118 p. 60.
] + **et**	*om. vg*	
interitus	perditionis *vg*	
1 Tim. vi 3 ff.		
languescens B	languens *vg*	ps. 118 p. 132.
sacrilegia	blasphemiae *vg*	
et	et qui *vg*	
a ueritate alienorum	ueritate priuati sunt *vg*	
Tit. iii 3 ff.		
et nos *om.* $\frac{2}{2}$	*habet vg*	ps. 118 p. 489 ps. 40 p. 245.
errantes in $\frac{1}{2}$ **B**	errantes seruientes *vg*	
dei *om.*	*habet vg*	
Philem. 12 ff.		
ut B	id est *vg*	ps. 118 p. 314.
sed sine B	sine *vg*	
autem *om.* **B**	*habet vg*	
uti *om.*	*habet vg*	

I should just add, in a word, that I have gone through the quotations adduced in my *Study of Ambrosiaster*, pp. 240—257, and have found that, side by side with certain coincidences, there are many signs of individual character in the Pelagius text.

[1] 'Die Wortfolge des Ambrosius, dass *gustare* erst an dritter Stelle, nach *attaminare* (oder *contaminare*, oder *contrectare*) steht, findet sich meines Wissens bei keinem unserer Zeugen, der Plural nur bei wenigen lateinischen.' (H. Rönsch, *Zeitschr. f. hist. Theol.* 1870, I p. 108.)

The Pelagian text being then an Old-Latin text, which when used by Pelagius was free from all contamination with the Vulgate, it is my duty to give some account of its Latinity.

There is a tendency to give the Divine name in full, where more correct texts give it more briefly, e.g. 1 Cor. v 4 b *domini nostri Iesu Christi* for *domini Iesu*; 1 Cor. v 5 *domini nostri Iesu Christi* for *domini Iesu*.

dilectissimus rather than *dilectus* or *carissimus*: Eph. vi 21; Phil. ii 12; 2 Thess. ii 13; Col. iiii 7. The use of the superlative, which has not necessarily got more value than the positive, is a feature of certain Old-Latin texts, where it is really a translation of the Greek positive. Cf. Burkitt, *Rules of Tyconius* p. xcii (*optimus*), p. xciv (*pessimus*), p. xcvi (*proximus*).

dilectissimus is early, being found in k of the Gospels, and Cyprian himself affects it[1]. It is also a feature of the African psalter[2], whereas the non-African have *dilectus*. The Latin Irenaeus has the superlative twice, the positive once.

facies (rather than *persona*) as a translation of *πρόσωπον*: 2 Cor. ii 10; Gal. ii 6; 1 Thess. ii 17.

hic mundus (rather than *mundus* simply). This point forms a good criterion in the study of Latin Biblical texts. Rom. v 13; 1 Cor. i 21, 28; ii 12; iiii 9; vi 2 *bis*; vii 33, 34; 2 Cor. i 12; Eph. ii 12; vi 12; Col. ii 8, 20 *bis*.

The addition of *hic* is on the whole un-African and un-Cyprianic[3]: but see Burkitt, *Rules of Tyconius* p. lxxxii.

inreprehensibilis (rather than *sine querella, crimine*, etc.): 2 Cor. vi 3; Eph. i 4; Phil. ii 15; Tit. i 7.

ipse as a rendering of *οὗτος* or *αὐτός*, preferred to *ille, is*: 1 Cor. i. 5 ; vii. 20; viii. 12; x. 10; (2 Cor. ii. 17); 2 Cor. viii 2; 24 etc.

There is some reason to regard *ipse* as late African[4]. Victorinus Afer's text of Ephesians shows a partiality for it. It abounds in the Latin Irenaeus.

[1] Watson, *Style and Language of St Cyprian* pp. 272 f.

[2] Capelle, *Le Texte du Psautier Latin en Afrique* pp. 100, 128.

[3] Hans von Soden, *Das Lateinische Neue Testament in Afrika zur Zeit Cyprians*, pp. 40 etc.

[4] Von Soden, *op. cit.* pp. 156, 302.

magnifico (rather than *clarifico, glorifico, honorifico, honoro*): Rom. i 21; viii 30; 2 Cor. viiii 13; Gal. i 24.

clarifico is definitely African[1], while *glorifico, honorifico* and *magnifico* are rather European. The Latin Irenaeus shows all, except *honorifico*, in about equal proportion. *Magnifico* is found twice in Tyconius (see the evidence in Burkitt, *Rules* p. lxxxix).

mens (rather than *sensus*)[2]: Rom. xii 2; Phil. iiii. 7; 2 Thess. ii 2; Col. ii 18.

nam (rather than *enim*): Rom. vi 2; vii 18; viiii 11; xiiii 3, 10, 15; 1 Cor. iii 3; (x 17; xvi 1); xvi 10; 2 Cor. iiii 17, (18); Eph. v 9; Phil. iii 18 etc.

A predilection for *nam* appears to be late African rather than early African[3]. Victorinus Afer often has *nam* where the Vulgate has *enim*. In the Latin Irenaeus *enim* is used almost to the exclusion of *nam*.

pressura (rather than *tribulatio*): 2 Cor. i 4 (1^{0}), 8; iiii 8, 17; Eph. iii 13; 1 Thess. i 6; iii 7; 2 Thess. i 4, 6.

Pressura is much more African than European[4]; the reverse is true of *tribulatio*. Dr Gwynn (*Liber Ardmachanus* p. ccxxi) notes that *pressura* is habitually preferred to *tribulatio* by D.

quasi (rather than *tamquam, quemadmodum, uelut, sicut, quomodo, ut*): 1 Cor. iii 1; iiii 9; 2 Cor. vi 10.

Quasi is the original equivalent in the African Bible[5], but *quemadmodum* and *sicut* are also found[6]. Victorinus Afer favours *quemadmodum*, as does the Latin Irenaeus, but the latter has also some examples of *quasi, sicut*; the others occur there hardly at all. Tyconius has *quasi* six times, *tamquam* four times, *uelut* seven times, *sicut* ten times, *quomodo* once (twice), *ut* twice (Burkitt, *Rules* pp. xcvi ff.).

quia (rather than *quoniam*, in reported statements, etc.): Rom. vii 21; 1 Cor. vi 19; 2 Cor. i 7; vii 8; xi 18; Eph. ii 11; Phil. iiii 10; 1 Thess. ii 8; 2 Thess. iii 7.

[1] Cf. von Soden, p. 239 n., etc.; Capelle, p. 30, etc.

[2] See W.-W. on Rom. i. 28.

[3] Von Soden, p. 233.

[4] Sanday, *O.-L.B.T.* II p. cxxi; von Soden, pp. 137, 142, 181, etc.; *J.T.S.* XIV (1912—13) p. 340; Watson, p. 289; Burkitt, *Rules of Tyconius* p. xcv.

[5] Von Soden, pp. 35, 82, 344.

[6] Von Soden, pp. 154 f.

This is as un-African as possible, *quoniam* being by far the most frequent in the early African Bible[1]. The latter is almost universal in the Latin Irenaeus and in Victorinus Afer. The same may almost be said of Tyconius, who uses *quia* about twenty times, but not nearly so often as *quoniam* (Burkitt, *Rules* p. xcvi).

uerbum (rather than *sermo*) is definitely European, and late African: Phil. iiii 17; 1 Thess. i 5, 8; ii 5; 2 Thess. ii 2, 15, 17; iii 1; Col. iiii 3.

Sermo is definitely African[2]. It is much more frequent in the Latin Irenaeus than *uerbum*. *Sermo* and *uerbum* occur with almost equal frequency in Tyconius (Burkitt, *op. cit.* pp. c, civ).

APPENDIX TO § 1

Pelagius and the Vulgate of the Pauline Epistles

If the preceding argument is valid, Pelagius made no use of the Vulgate of the Epistles of St Paul, and it cannot be proved that he had any knowledge of it. As, however, I was responsible for the statements, made at the end of 1906[3], that 'the text [in the Reichenau MS] on which the commentary is based is the Vulgate....If I am right about this Karlsruhe [Reichenau] MS...we are provided by it with an authority of the highest value for constituting the Vulgate text of Paul's Epistles. Perhaps it would not be wrong to say that we are thereby provided with the very highest authority which exists...,' it is right that I should explain how my view in regard to this matter came to change.

In the course of collating the Reichenau MS with the published Pseudo-Jerome, which is substantially Sixto-Clementine Vulgate, I was constantly impressed by the fact that the Reichenau MS supported either the *Amiatinus* or the *Fuldensis* of the Vulgate or both together, against the Sixto-Clementine text. The phenomenon recurred so frequently that at the middle of First Corinthians I ceased to note it. It was obvious that I was in presence of a very early form of the Vulgate text. There is no need to retract this opinion. Except in certain passages which approximate rather to D (*Book of Armagh*), the Reichenau MS of Pelagius provides an almost complete Vulgate text of the

[1] Von Soden, pp. 81, 154.

[2] Von Soden, pp. 71 f., 238; Capelle, pp. 31, 142.

[3] These remarks are quoted from the first of my two papers before the British Academy, delivered on Dec. 12, 1906, and printed in their *Proceedings* vol. II pp. 425 f.

Epistles in a very early form. Yet it was clear even in those days that Pelagius's text was not Vulgate throughout. I should now explain the Reichenau form of text as due to the almost complete substitution of a Vulgate text for the older type of text employed by Pelagius himself. But from internal evidence it is clear that the Reichenau MS must have been copied direct from a manuscript of the fifth or sixth century[1]. As early therefore as the fifth or sixth century the Vulgate must have been substituted almost throughout one MS of Pelagius's commentary for the text used by Pelagius himself. These substitutions will remain, therefore, an authority for the text of the Vulgate, and one, too, of the very highest value, at least as old as, and possibly a good deal older than the *Codex Fuldensis* (A.D. 546).

When I expressed my original opinion in 1906, my list of Pelagian manuscripts was almost as full as it is now. Naturally I deferred my examination of the latest MSS till I had already studied the earlier. It never occurred to me *then* that the character of two fifteenth century MSS whose existence in Oxford I had noted in 1905, could overturn my original opinion. As these MSS bore the name of Jerome, and the cataloguers had not observed that the text was considerably shorter than the published form, as well as seriously different from it in other respects, it was with the greatest surprise that in July 1913, on borrowing the MSS themselves, I discovered that they were of the same brevity as the Reichenau MS and offered an older type of Biblical text than it, in spite of the fact that they were vitiated by the name of Jerome in the title[2]. A complete collation of the Balliol MS made in 1914 revealed the character of the Biblical text used by Pelagius, and I tried to put myself right with the public at once by publishing a little note in the *Journal of Theological Studies* for October 1914 called 'Pelagius and the Pauline Text in the Book of Armagh[3].'

The mischief was, however, done. Scholars had been kind enough to support the view of my first paper, and my later discovery was made just too late to become available to Dr Gwynn for his *Liber Ardmachanus*. Yet I cannot altogether regret the mistake, because it has at least helped to give the impulse to a good deal of valuable publication by French and Belgian scholars, and it is the chief object of this note to call the attention of British students to their work.

There reached me in August 1914 a privately printed article by Dom Donatien de Bruyne, O.S.B. (who will always be remembered for his identification of the Latin Marcionite prologues to the Epistles of St Paul[4]), under the title: 'Étude sur les Origines de Notre Texte Latin de Saint Paul.' This

[1] See below for the proof, pp. 206 ff.

[2] The Merton MS 26 was examined by Dom Morin as long ago as 1888 (see *Anecdota Maredsolana* III 3 [1903] p. 194), and I gathered from him in 1913 that he had had some suspicion as to the facts.

[3] Vol. XVI p. 105. The Great War had already broken out.

[4] *Revue Bénédictine* XXIV (1907) pp. 1 ff.

article was afterwards published, with slight modifications, in the *Revue Biblique* for October 1915. In it Dom de Brüyne displays all the acute power of reasoning we have learned to expect from him. He reminds us how uncertain is the question of the Vulgate of the New Testament apart from the Gospels. We have Jerome's triple statement that he revised the whole New Testament, but we have no Hieronymian New Testament prologues except for the Gospels, and Jerome himself never, it seems, makes any use of the Vulgate of the Pauline Epistles. As Pelagius is the earliest author to use the Vulgate of the Epistles[1], and as the general Pelagian prologue appears in practically all Vulgate copies of the Epistles, sometimes under the name of Pelagius himself; as, further, a preface is the mark of an edition, the author of the Vulgate of the Epistles is none other than Pelagius himself!

It is not necessary to follow his argument further. It is based in part on a necessarily imperfect knowledge of the manuscripts containing the Pelagius commentary in one form or another, and is, in my opinion, as regards the three editions of the Vulgate, really fallacious. I feel, however, that I owe Dom de Bruyne and others an apology for the measure of responsibility that belongs to me.

Naturally, a sensational view like that of Dom de Bruyne was not allowed to pass unchallenged even in the midst of the Great War. The Abbé Eug. Mangenot, professor of the Institut Catholique at Paris, published in the *Revue du Clergé français* in 1916 an article entitled 'Saint Jérôme ou Pélage éditeur des Épîtres de Saint Paul dans la Vulgate[2].' His article is an able and learned exposition of what might be called the traditional view, that Jerome revised the whole New Testament[3]. Father M.-J. Lagrange of Jerusalem, author of two valuable commentaries, one on the Epistle to the Romans and the other on the Epistle to the Galatians (1918), has in recent years made a profound study of the Vulgate text of the Epistles of St Paul. Particular attention must be called to the article entitled: 'La Vulgate latine de l'Épître aux Galates et le texte grec' published in the *Revue Biblique* for 1917[4], which followed a corresponding article on the Epistle to the Romans in the same review for 1916[5]. Alive to the difficulties which Dom de Bruyne has posed afresh, he seeks to solve them by the view that Jerome is indeed the author of the Vulgate of the Epistle to the Galatians, but that its date falls between the date of Jerome's commentary on Galatians (384) and 392 (the date of the *De Viris Inlustribus*). Lagrange also shows from De Bruyne's own data that Pelagius employed an Old-Latin text of Galatians[6], and absolutely denies Pelagian authorship of the

[1] Here of course he depends on my 1906 argument.

[2] *Revue du Clergé français*, 1er Avril et 1er Mai 1916 (Paris, Librairie Letouzey et Ané). I owe a *tirage à part* to the author's kindness.

[3] He is inexact in saying (p. 20) that Holder 'signala un nouveau manuscrit de l'*Expositio* de Pélage': see below (pp. 203 f.) for the history of the discovery.

[4] *Nouv. sér.* t. XIV pp. 424—450.

[5] t. XIII pp. 225 ff.

[6] t. XIV pp. 447 f.

Vulgate, by referring to the type of text preserved in the Balliol manuscript. With the view Lagrange expresses as to the different Old-Latin texts employed by the commentators Ambrosiaster, Jerome, Pelagius, I should agree entirely. In the *Bulletin de Littérature Ecclésiastique de Toulouse*[1] Father Cavallera supports Lagrange's contentions in the *Revue Biblique* for 1917 (just mentioned) and 1918 (pp. 255 ff.). Cavallera concludes, as I believe rightly, that in 384 Jerome had issued a revision of the Gospels only, and that such revision of the Epistles of St Paul as he made was subsequent to that date. The texts cited by Jerome in his celebrated letter to Marcella, *epist.* 27 § 3 (A.D. 384), have in Cavallera's opinion the purpose of direct polemic against those that have been angered by Jerome's criticisms. The use of the subjunctive throughout, *legant*, etc., rather excludes the idea of an already existing translation of the Epistles by Jerome.

§ 2. THE TEXT OF THE OTHER PARTS OF SCRIPTURE

Pelagius's notes are short, and the quotations from scripture in them are also necessarily short. I have gone carefully through all that I could identify and compared the text with the Vulgate throughout. Having noted down all the differences, I have collected parallels to these from Sabatier and every other source I could think of. It is quite evident that Pelagius employed an Old-Latin Bible throughout, and the parallels between his quotations and other Old-Latin texts ought to be instructive. Considerations of space do not permit the complete publication of these data. Without them an induction would be unsafe, but it is not necessary to present the lists to the reader in full. It will be enough to select the more striking examples and to state briefly for each section of scripture the relationship with other texts that appears to emerge. It is hardly necessary to remind the reader that for all parts of scripture except the Gospels our supply of Old-Latin texts is scanty. Owing again to the war, I have not been able to avail myself of Pfarrer Denk's great work, which under happier conditions would now have been completely published. If a critical edition of the *Letter to Demetrias* had been available, the numerous quotations in it would also have been at my disposal. This is one of various directions in which the present work may be amplified by my successors.

[1] For my reference to this I depend entirely on Father Lagrange in the *Revue Biblique* nouv. sér. t. XVI (1919) p. 283.

The Heptateuch

Gen. xlviiii 10 **deficiet** *lugd. Nouat. Cypr. Hil. Hier. Greg.-Illib. Aug. Prom.*
auferetur *vg.*
princeps *lugd. Nouat. Cypr. Hil. Hier. Ambr. Greg.-Illib. Iren.*[lat.] *Aug. Prom.*
sceptrum *vg.*
ex *lugd. Hier. Ambr. Priscill. Aug. Prom.*
de *vg.*
nec *lugd.* (*Nouat.*) *Hil.* (*Hier.*) *Greg.-Illib.* (*Iren.*[lat.] *Prom.*).
et *vg.*
femoribus *lugd. Nouat. Cypr. Hil. Hier. Ambr. Greg.-Illib. Iren.*[lat.] *Aug. Prom.*
femore *vg.*

Exod. xxii 20 **sacrificans** (*def. lugd.*) *m Cypr. Ambst.* $\frac{2}{2}$ *Aug.*
qui immolauerit *wirceb.*[1]
qui immolat *vg.*
eradicabitur (*def. wirceb. lugd.*) *m Cypr. Ambst.* $\frac{2}{2}$ *Aug.*
occidetur *vg.*

Leu. vii 9 (19) **omnis** *wirceb. lugd. Cypr. Pacian.*
qui fuerit *vg.*
manducabit *wirceb. lugd. Cypr. Pacian.*
uescetur *vg.*

xxvi 12 **et inhabitabo in illis** (*def. lugd.*) *Ambr.* $\frac{3}{3}$.
ambulabo inter eos *vg.*

Deut. xxx 6 **in nouissimis diebus** *Cypr.*
om. vg.
deus (*lugd.*) *Cypr.* (*Aug.*).
dominus deus tuus *vg.*
ad...amandum *Cypr.*
ut diligas *vg.*

[1] For this, see below under 'Minor Prophets.'

Deut. xxxii 21 **zelauerunt** *cod. ap. Sabat.*
prouocauerunt *vg.*
non deo *cod. ap. Sabat. Tert. Ambr.*
eo qui non erat deus *vg.*

The agreement between the Lyons Heptateuch and Pelagius's text is almost perfect. The further agreement with fourth century quotations, and even with Cyprian, is very striking.

The Historical Books

1 Regn. xvi 7 **in facie** *m* (*Cypr.*) *Hil. Ambst. Hier.* (*Gaud.*).
ea quae parent *vg.*
deus *m Cypr. Hil. Ambst. Hier. Gaud.*
dominus *vg.*
in corde *m* (*Cypr.*) *Hil. Ambst. Hier.*
intuetur cor *vg.*
3 Regn. iiii (v) 25 (9) **sicut** *Tycon. Ambr.* $\frac{2}{2}$.
quasi *vg.*
maris *Tycon. Ambr.* $\frac{2}{2}$.
quae est in litore maris *vg.*

The situation here is like that in the Heptateuch. For the Historical Books Pelagius evidently employed an average fourth century text, which here again has real points of contact with Cyprian.

Psalms[1]

xxxi 5 **cordis** *m cod. Sangerm. psalt. Rom. Corb. al. Hil. Pacian. Ambr.* $\frac{3}{3}$ *Hier. Aug.*
peccati *vg.*
lxxiii 19 **animam confitentem** *cod. Sangerm. Aug. Prom.*
animas confitentes *vg.*
lxxxxiii 12 *om.* **homo** *Ambr.* $\frac{3}{5}$.
habet homo *vg.*
cxviiii 7 **qui oderant** ($\frac{1}{2}$) *Aug.* (*non semper*), *Prosp.*
odientibus ($\frac{1}{2}$) *psalt. Hebr. cod. Casin.*[2] *Hil. Tycon. Ambr.* $\frac{1}{2}$.
qui oderunt *vg.*

[1] On xlviiii 21 **ea**, see Rahlfs, *Septuaginta-Studien* 2 Heft (Göttingen, 1907) p. 65.

[2] *edidit* A. M. Amelli O.S.B. (= *Collectanea Biblica Latina* vol. I) (Romae, 1912).

The passages here given are not of average character. For the most part the quotations made by Pelagius from the Psalms agree with that form which is printed in the Vulgate, namely the 'Gallican' psalter, Jerome's second psalter. The above passages are selected out of fourteen phrases which seem to represent a slightly older text.

Sapiential Books

Prou. v 22 **funiculis**[1] *Aug.* $\frac{1}{3}$ *codd. Cassian.* $\frac{2}{2}$ *Fulg. Gildas* p. 85 *codd.* (see *Thes.* s.v. criniculus).
funibus *vg.*
unus quisque *Hil.* $\frac{1}{2}$ *Ambr.* $\frac{2}{2}$ *Hier.* $\frac{2}{2}$ *Greg.-Illib. Iren.*[lat.] *Aug.* $\frac{3}{3}$ *Cassian.* $\frac{2}{2}$ *Prom. Fulg. Gildas.*
om. vg.
viiii 8 **amabit** *m Pacian. Hier. Op. impf. Aug.*
diliget *vg.*
xi 26 **pretio grauans triticum** *m.*
qui abscondit frumenta *vg.*
populo *m.*
populis *vg.*
maledictus (*m Cypr. Ambr.* $\frac{3}{3}$).
maledicetur *vg.*
xiiii 6 **quaere[s]** *Hier. Cassian.*
quaerit *vg.*
apud malos *Hier. Cassian.*
derisor *vg.*
inuenies *Hier. Cassian.*
inuenit *vg.*
xvii 6 **gloria patris**[2].
corona senum *vg.*
eius qui fidelis est totus mundus diuitiarum *Hier.* (*Ambr.* etc.).
om. vg.

[1] The variants here are instructive: funibus *Hier.* $\frac{2}{2}$, restibus *Iren.*[lat.] *Greg.-Illib.*, uinculis *Hil.* $\frac{1}{2}$ *codd.*, *Ambr.* $\frac{2}{2}$ *Prom.*, criniculis *Aug.* $\frac{3}{3}$ *Gildas*, fasciis *Hil.* $\frac{2}{2}$.

[2] This is not the only place where Pelagius apparently provides the only existing Old-Latin evidence, in all cases unknown to Sabatier: cf. also Prou. xv 13, xviii 17 (below), xxviiii 27, (Iob xxx 25), etc.

Prou. xviii 17 **in primordio** *Ambst. Ambr. cod.* (C.S.E.L. lxii 73) *et saep.*
prior *vg.*
accusator est *Hil.* $\frac{2}{2}$ *Ambst. Ambr.*
est accusator *vg.*
ut statim cum coeperit aduersarius confundatur.
uenit amicus eius et inuestigabit eum *vg.*

xx 13 **detrahere** *m Cypr. Hier.*
somnum *vg.*
eradiceris *m Cypr. codd.*[1] *Hier.* (*Paulin.*) *anon. ap. Paulin.*
te egestas opprimat *vg.*

xxv 8 **uiderint** *Zosimus* (Rome A.D. 417—418).
uiderunt *vg.*
loquere *Zosimus.*
ne proferas *etc. vg.*

xxvi 12 **uidi** *m.*
uidisti *vg.*
uirum *m.*
hominem *vg*
qui sibi sapiens uidebatur.
sapientem sibi uideri *vg.*
habuit *m.*
habebit *vg.*
quam ille *m.*
illo *vg.*

Eccl. vii 5 **sapientis.**
sapientium *vg.*
in domo luctus *m Hier. Ambr.* $\frac{3}{3}$ *Aug.*
ubi tristitia est *vg.*

Cant. v 16 **fauces** *Ambr.* $\frac{5}{5}$.
guttur *vg.*
dulcedines *Ambr.* $\frac{4}{5}$ *Hier.*
suauissimum *vg.*

Iob viiii 28 **propter deum.**
om. vg.

[1] True text in *Cypr.* is *extollaris.*

Iob xxiiii 23 **illi.**
ei *vg.*
superbia *t.*
superbiam *vg.*
Sap.[1] v 2, 3 **salutis insperatae** (*t*).
insperatae salutis *vg.*
tunc
om. vg.
inter (*cod. ap. Sabat.*) *t Cypr. Lucif.*
intra *vg.*
per angustiam *t Cypr. Lucif.*
prae angustia *vg.*
Eccli. iiii 8 **sine tristitia** *om. m cod. ap. Sabat. Ambr. Aug.*
habet vg.
v 4 **accidit mihi** *Cypr. Lucif. Aug. Ps.-Vigil.-Taps.*
mihi accidit *vg.*
est enim altissimus *Cypr. Lucif. Ps.-Vigil.-Taps.*
altissimus est enim *vg.*
8, 9 **neque** *Aug. Paulin. Gildas.*
et ne *vg.*
uenit *m cod. ap. Sabat. Cypr. Vict.-Tonn. Gildas.*
ueniet *vg.*
eius *Gildas.*
illius *vg.*
xxi 1 **ne** *Aug. Fulg. Gildas.*
non *vg.*
xxxv 11 **et.**
om. vg.

In this section the parallels with *m* and *t* will not have escaped notice.

[1] It is perhaps necessary to remind the reader that Sap. Eccli. Bar. 1, 2 Macc. are in the Vulgate simply taken over from the Old-Latin. Pelagius's text of Sap. Eccli. differs considerably from that in *vg*, but where parallels to Pelagius's text are lacking, I have not thought it necessary to set it down here.

The Minor Prophets

Os iiii 5, 6[1] **nocti adsimilaui** *Priscill. Hier.*[2]
nocte tacere feci *vg.*
factus est.
conticuit *vg.*
tamquam.
eo quod *vg.*
habens (*Priscill.*) *Hier.*
habuerit *vg.*
viii 4 *om.* **ipsi** *w*[3] *Filast.* (*Hier. Gildas* $\frac{2}{2}$).
habet vg.
per *w Cypr.* $\frac{2}{2}$ *Hier. Filast. Gildas* $\frac{2}{2}$.
ex *vg.*
Ion. iiii 11 **pecora** *wirceb.*[4] *Ambst.* $\frac{2}{2}$ *Hier.*
iumenta *vg.*
Zach. ii 8 (12) **tangit** *m Faustin. Ambr. Fulg.*
tetigerit *vg.*
tamquam qui tangat (*Fulg.*).
tangit *vg.*
ipsius *m Faustin.*
mei *vg.*
Mal. ii 7 **exquirant (exquirent)** *Cypr.* (-ent) *Ambr.* (-unt).
requirent *vg.*
de ($\frac{1}{2}$).
ex *vg.*
omnipotentis ($\frac{2}{2}$) *Cypr. Ambr. Hier. Aug.*
exercituum *vg.*

The phenomena here are what we have become accustomed to in other sections.

The Major Prophets

Esai. i 22 **caupones tui** *Hier. Iren.*$^{\text{lat.}}$ *Greg.-Illib. Max.-Taur. Op.-impf.*

[1] Note the remarkable reading *resurgens* in Os. vi 3.

[2] *t* in the Prophets is almost pure Vulgate, as also in the Gospels.

[3] For *w*, see P. Lehmann, *Die Konstanz-Weingartener Propheten-Fragmente...* (Leiden, 1912).

[4] For *wirceb.*, see *Par Palimpsestorum Wirceburgensium*...E. Ranke (Vindob. 1871).

Esai. i 22 **miscent uino aquam** *Iren.* (comment) (*Max.-*
(*cont.*) *Taur.*).
uinum tuum mixtum est aqua *vg.*

vii 9 **nisi** *Tert.* $\frac{3}{3}$ *Priscill. Ambst. Greg.-Illib. Aug.* $\frac{2}{2}$.
si non *vg.*
nec *Tert.* $\frac{1}{3}$ *Ambr.* neque *Cypr.* $\frac{2}{2}$ *Ambst.*
non *vg.*
intellegetis *Tert.* $\frac{3}{3}$ *Cypr.* $\frac{2}{2}$ (*ap. Hier.*) *Ambst. Priscill. Greg.-Illib. Ambr. Aug.* $\frac{2}{2}$ *Prom. Fulg.*
permanebitis *vg.*

l 1 **peccatis** *Ambr.* $\frac{5}{6}$ *Hier. Rufin.*
in iniquitatibus *vg.*
uenundati *Hier. Rufin.*
uenditi *vg.*

liii 7 **uictimam** *Tert. Cypr. Ambr. Hier. Iren.*$^{\text{lat.}}$ *Gaud.*
occisionem *vg.*
ductus est *Tert. Cypr.*$^{\text{codd.}}$ *Hil. Ambst. Ambr. Hier. Iren.*$^{\text{lat.}}$ *Aug. Gaud. Prom. Vigil.-Taps.*
ducetur *vg.*

lxvi 2 **humilem** *m Cypr.* $\frac{4}{4}$ *Nouat. Hil.* (*Ambst.*) *Pacian. Hier. Ambr. saep. Iren.*$^{\text{lat.}}$ *Aug.* $\frac{3}{3}$ *Cassian.*
pauperculum *vg.*
quietum *m Cypr.* $\frac{4}{4}$ *Nouat. Hil.* $\frac{1}{3}$ *Pacian. Hier. Ambr. saep. Iren.*$^{\text{lat.}}$ *Aug.* $\frac{3}{3}$ *Cassian.*
contritum spiritu *vg.*
uerba *m Nouat. Hil.* $\frac{3}{4}$ *Ambst. Pacian. Ambr. saep. Aug.* $\frac{3}{3}$.
sermones *vg.*

Hierem. iii 15 **secundum** *Cypr.* $\frac{4}{4}$ *Lucif.* $\frac{5}{5}$ *Aug.*
iuxta *vg.*
cum disciplina *Cypr.* $\frac{4}{4}$ *Lucif.* $\frac{5}{5}$ *Aug.*
scientia et doctrina *vg.*

iiii 3, 4 **innouate** *m Tert. Greg.-Illib.*
nouate *vg.*
nouamen *Tert.* $\frac{3}{4}$.
nouale *vg.*
ne seminaueritis *Cypr.*
nolite serere *vg.*

Hierem. iiii 3, 4 (*cont.*) **in** *m Tert. Cypr. Macrob.*[1]
super *vg.*
circumcidite uos *Cypr. Ambst. Macrob.*
circumcidimini *vg.*
deo uestro *m Tert. Cypr. Macrob. Hier.*
domino *vg.*
circumcidite *m Tert. Cypr. Ambst. Macrob. Greg.-Illib.*
auferte *vg.*
praeputium *m Tert.* $\frac{1}{3}$ *Cypr. Ambst. Macrob.*
praeputia *vg.*
cordis uestri *m Tert. Cypr. Ambst.* $\frac{2}{2}$ *Macrob. Greg.-Illib.*
cordium uestrorum *vg.*

viiii 23 **sua sapientia** *m* $\frac{2}{2}$ *t Lucif.* $\frac{1}{2}$.
sapientia sua *vg.*
neque *t* (*Hil.*).
et non glorietur *vg.*
neque (*alt.*) (*Hil.*) *Lucif.*
et non glorietur *vg.*

xvii 16 **concupiui** *Hil. Aug.*
desideraui *vg.*

xxiii 24 **nonne** *wirceb. Cypr.* $\frac{3}{3}$ *Hil. Hier.* (*semel*) *Nicet. Fulg.*
numquid non *vg.*

Ezech. xviii 20 **ipsum** *m Iulian.-Aecl. Gildas.*
eum *vg.*

xxxiii 11 **peccatoris** (*w* illegible) *Tert.* (*Cypr.*) *Pacian. Ambr. Hier. Aug. Gildas* $\frac{2}{2}$.
impii *vg.*

Dan. ii 47 **ipse est deus** *Ambst.*
deus deorum est *vg.*

viiii 23 **concupiscentiarum**[2].
desideriorum *vg.*

The evidence for this section of the Bible is of the same nature as that which we have found for all the rest of the Old Testament.

[1] I.e. the Donatist, in the opinion of Harnack and Morin the true author of the Pseudo-Cyprianic *De Singularitate Clericorum.*

[2] On this important word see Rönsch, *Itala u. Vulgata* p. 49, *Thes. Ling. Lat.* iv 102 74 ff. It is real Old-Latin.

The Gospels

If my numeration be right, there are, for Matthew, 23 agreements with *h*, 22 agreements with *c*, 20 agreements with *g*, 19 agreements with *a*, 19 agreements with *b*, 15 agreements with *d*, 15 agreements with *q*, 14 agreements with *e*, 12 agreements with ff^2, 9 agreements with *f*, 8 agreements with *m*, 7 agreements with *k*, 4 agreements with *ff*, 4 agreements with *l*, 3 agreements with g^2, 2 agreements with *t*, against the Vulgate. In estimating the value of these figures, one must remember that not all these Old-Latin texts contain the whole Gospel. In fact *c*, *f*, *ff*, *g*, g^2, *l* alone seem to be complete. Pelagius obviously employed a real Old-Latin text in Matthew, and if we could say that *h*, so far as Matthew is concerned, is practically what Pelagius had before him, it would be a point gained. If we similarly compare the patristic authorities, we shall find that Pelagius agrees against the Vulgate with Augustine 17 times, Ambrose 15 times, Cyprian 12 times, the Opus Imperfectum 10 times, Hilary 9 times, Ambrosiaster 8 times, Tertullian 7 times, the Latin Irenaeus 6 times, Gildas 6 times, Chromatius 5 times. Here again it must be remembered that the Opus Imperfectum, Hilary and Chromatius are commentators on Matthew, also that Augustine's works are the most voluminous and he quotes very copiously from the Gospels. I attach most significance to the 15 agreements with Ambrose and the 8 agreements with Ambrosiaster. It is remarkable that we have also found Ambrose to have important points of contact with the *codex* of the Pauline Epistles used by Pelagius. Nor will the agreements with Gildas escape the reader's notice.

The Marcan agreements against the Vulgate are naturally very few, and do not merit mention, with the one exception of

Mark xvi 17 **credentes** *c* (*q*) *Ambr.* $\frac{3}{3}$ *Prom.*
eos qui crediderint *vg.*
haec signa.
signa...haec *vg.*

In Luke there are, against the Vulgate, 7 agreements with *a*, 6 with *d*, 5 with *e*, 4 with *c*, 3 with *l*, 3 with *r*. If we could go so far as to say that Pelagius employed the *a* text for Luke, it would be an interesting point of contact between him and Jerome[1]. One or two of the citations are of sufficient interest to be presented *in extenso*.

Luke vii 47 **cui plus dimittitur** {**amplius** / **plus**} **diligit.**

Cypr. codd. (**plus** in both places), Iren. (**plus** in both places), Ambr. $\frac{2}{2}$ (**plus** in both places in one citation, *multum* in the first place in another). The Armenian version has also this clause, which is wanting to the Vulgate, as it is to every extant Old-Latin MS. If Pelagius found it in his copy of Luke, then it was different from *a*. It is however possible that he got it from Cyprian. As he was himself the author of a book of extracts, he must have been quite well acquainted with Cyprian's *Testimonia*. Observe again the contact with Ambrose[2].

xx 36 **dei sunt.**
sunt dei *vg.*
Note that this clause is absent from most of the Old-Latin authorities.

38 **non est deus** *a Cypr. codd. Aug.*
deus non est *vg.*
illi uiuunt *adeir Cypr. Pacian. Aug.*
uiuunt ei *vg.*

xxi 34 *om.* **forte** $\frac{2}{2}$ *Ambst. Ambr. Adim. ap. Aug.*
habet vg.

In the Fourth Gospel there are 9 agreements with *a*, 8 agreements with *b*, 7 agreements with *e*, 7 agreements with *r*, 5 agreements with *c*, 5 agreements with *f*, 4 agreements with *d*, 4 agreements with *ff*[2], 4 agreements with *m*, against the Vulgate. This evidence appears to point to the Pelagian John as a fourth century

[1] Cf. the writer in *Journal of Theological Studies* vol. XII (1910—11) pp. 583 ff., and Hoskier, *The Golden Latin Gospels* (New York, 1910) pp. xxix, cxiv. The text of Luke xvi 3—14 in Hier. *epist.* 121 § 6 differs greatly from *a*, however.

[2] This Agraphon finds no place in Resch's *Agrapha*.

Old-Latin type of text. One or two verses will illustrate its character and relationship.

John viiii 39 ego *om.*
habet vg.
ueni in hunc mundum *a b c f q r Ambst.* $\frac{2}{2}$ *Hier.*
in hunc mundum ueni *vg.*
xii 35 **ne** *a e l m r Arnob.-Iun.*
ut non *vg.*
xvii 3 **unum** *a Nouat.* $\frac{2}{2}$ *Aug. Arnob.-Iun.*
solum *vg.*
24 **isti** *Ambr.* $\frac{2}{3}$ *Ambst.* $\frac{1}{3}$ ($\frac{2}{3}$?).
illi *vg.*

This last is a pretty example, pointing again in the direction of Ambrose.

Acts

The quotations from Acts are of a somewhat unsatisfactory meagreness, but we find 9 agreements with *d*, 8 with *p*, 7 with *e*, 5 with *gig*, 4 with *c*, and 4 with *dem*, against the Vulgate. Here the most significant fact is to be found in the agreements with *p*, which is Old-Latin for just half the Book of Acts. Out of 18 possible agreements there are thus 8 to be found. The relationship is not, therefore, very close. We cannot identify any existing Old-Latin MS as certainly the type employed by Pelagius. Of the patristic parallels, 7 are to be found with Augustine, and 4 with each of the following, namely Gregory of Elvira, Petilian, Ambrosiaster and Isidore: while in the case of each of the following parallels, Pseudo-Prosper, Latin Irenaeus and Niceta, Pelagius shares 3 instances against the Vulgate. The evidence suggests that the British text was related to those used in Africa and in Spain rather than any others. There are two parallels with Gildas.

Acts ii 3 **uisae sunt** *d Cypr. Greg.-Illib. Ambr.* (ps. 38 p. 196) *Aug. Petil. Prom. Vigil.*
apparuerunt *vg.*
eis (*d*) *e Aug.* $\frac{2}{4}$ *Petil. Prom. Vigil.*
illis *vg.*
uariae.
dispertitae *vg.*

Acts ii 3 **quasi** *Greg.-Illib. Aug.* $\frac{3}{4}$ *Prom.*
(*cont.*) tamquam *vg.*
super *d e* I *Greg.-Illib. Aug. Petil.*
supra *vg.*
iii 17 **hoc** CT (both Spanish MSS).
om. vg.
iiii 31 **omni uolenti credere** *d e* D etc. *Iren.* (cf. uni cuique hominum uolenti credere *lectionar. Schlettst.* [Morin, *Études* I p. 449]).
om. vg.
32 **unum** $\frac{2}{2}$ *c dem gig p* DW *al. Ambr.* ps. 47 p. 351, *Aug.*
om. vg.
34 **distrahentes** $\frac{2}{2}$.
uendentes *vg.*
35 **deponebant.**
ponebant *vg.*
ad *d p Aug. Petil.*
ante *vg.*
v 41 **apostoli** *d p Ambst.*
illi *vg.*
quia *d p.*
quoniam *vg.*
domini ($\frac{1}{2}$) (*e*) DΘ.
Iesu *vg.*
Christi ($\frac{1}{2}$) *p* CFT.
om. vg.
xiii 2 **segregate** ($\frac{2}{2}$) *c dem gig m p* etc. AKMOVW *Lucif. Ambst. Nicet. Isid.* etc.
separate *vg.*
Paulum ($\frac{2}{3}$) *m p Ambr.* $\frac{2}{2}$ *Nicet. Isid.*
Saulum *vg.*
ad *d gig Ambst. Nicet. Isid.*
in *vg.*
elegi *Ps.-Vigil. Isid.*
adsumsi *vg.*
xx 26—28 **ab omnium sanguine** *Gildas.*
a sanguine omnium *vg.*

Acts xx 26—28 (*cont.*) **uobis omne consilium dei** *e*, *Gildas* (mysterium).
omne consilium dei uobis *vg*.
uidete gregem.
adtendite...gregi *vg*.
conquisiuit.
adquisiuit *vg*.
episcopos ordinauit.
posuit episcopos *vg*.
xxvi 19 **caelesti uisioni** *c dem* (*e*) *gig p* (D)R*W *etc.*
caelestis uisionis *vg*.

These quotations may suffice to show the character of the Acts text used by Pelagius.

The Epistle to the Hebrews

The agreements with other texts are very scanty. Pelagius regarded Hebrews as Pauline, but hardly as canonical[1]. The text he used appears to have been somewhat different from any other known text; for out of thirteen differences from the Vulgate, nine are unparalleled. Let me give here those that are paralleled:

Heb. i 3 **imago expressa** (figura expressa D) (imago *d t* *Ambr*. ps. 38 p. 202) *Sedul*.
figura *vg*.
vi 4 **inluminati sunt** *d Tert. Ambr.*
sunt inluminati *vg*.
x 36 **repromissionem** Z *d*.
promissionem *vg*.
xii 25 **recusantes** om. *d*.
habet vg.

The situation might be reconciled with the view that Pelagius used a text like *d*, but quoted frequently from memory. It is interesting to note that he began the new sentence with *deficientes* (xii 3): to this I know no parallel.

Canonical Epistles

The quotations from James are hardly worth noting. Of six differences from the Vulgate, four are unparalleled. But in iii 14

[1] Cf. De Bruyne, *Rev. Biblique* for 1915, p. 373.

we find **si enim** with (*ff*) against quod si of *vg*, and in iiii 4 **deo** with DF against dei of *vg*.

In First Peter the following may be noted:

1 Petr. i 19 **inmaculati et incontaminati** A.
incontaminati et inmaculati *vg*.
ii 1, 2 **simulationem** *t Gildas*.
simulationes *vg*.
tamquam *Aug*.
sicut *vg*.
rationale *Hier*. $\frac{1}{3}$ *Prom*.
rationabile *vg*.
7 **incredulis** *Hier*.
non credentibus *vg*.
23 **qui percussus est et non percussit** (*Ambr*. $\frac{4}{6}$ *Max.-Taur.*).
om. vg.[1]
iii 9 **neque** D (*Aug.*).
uel *vg*.

Special attention must be called to ii 23. This point of contact with Ambrose and his fellow is important in view of what has been said about Pelagius's Pauline text in § 1.

For Second Peter only one quotation is of moment:

2 Petr. iii 9 **promissi** (?) G *m*.
promissis *vg*.
aliquem A *m Aug. Fulg*.
aliquos *vg*.
conuerti *Aug. Fulg*.
reuerti *vg*.

Here again, as in Acts, we are taken to Africa and Spain, but of course it must be remembered that the total evidence for the use of Second Peter is scanty.

Pelagius was rather fond of First John. A few examples of readings may be given from that epistle:

1 Ioh. ii 6 **Christo** ($\frac{2}{2}$) *Cypr*. $\frac{1}{4}$ *Hier*. $\frac{2}{3}$ *Aug*. $\frac{1}{2}$ *Fulg*.
ipso *vg*.

[1] Cf. C. H. Turner, *Ecclesiae Occidentalis Monumenta* fasc. I (1) (Oxon. 1899) pp. xvi, 33; Sanday, *Novum Testamentum S. Irenaei* (Oxford, 1922) p. 189.

1 Ioh. ii 6 **quo modo** ($\frac{1}{2}$) *Cypr.* $\frac{4}{4}$.
(*cont.*) sicut *vg.*
17 **fecerit** *Cypr.* $\frac{5}{5}$ *Lucif. Aug.* $\frac{4}{6}$ *Gelas.*
facit *vg.*
21 **de** *m Iren.*[lat.]
ex *vg.*
iii 16 **quia** *h r Ambst. Aug.*
quoniam *vg.*
debemus ergo et nos.
et nos debemus *vg.*
nostris *m.*
om. vg.
iiii 20 **si fratrem quem uides, non diligis** (*Ambr.*) *Aug.* $\frac{1}{2}$.
qui non diligit fratrem suum quem uidet *vg.*
uides *Ambr. Aug.* $\frac{1}{2}$.
uidet *vg.*
potes *Ambr.*
potest *vg.*

The text does not seem to have differed much from what would have been found in Africa in the fourth century.

Apocalypse

Only one reading need be mentioned. It appears that in vi 8 Pelagius read:

peccatum et mors (*vg* and all other authorities *mors* simply).

This is important, unless we are to regard it as a persistent lapse of memory on his part.

CHAPTER V

NOTES ON THE SOURCES USED IN THE COMMENTARY

THE question of the sources of any ancient work is complicated by the loss of so much of the old literature. The study of the sources of commentaries on the Pauline Epistles is above all hindered by the disappearance of the greater part of Origen's exegetical work. He was in a very real sense the father of Biblical exegesis, and every investigation of this kind suffers from that loss. In the present case the difficulty of the task is accentuated by the very brevity of the notes, which are the concentrated essence of much reading and meditation. There has been no serious attempt to analyse the Pseudo-Jerome commentary. Nothing has been written on the subject, so far as I know, except the few paragraphs of Richard Simon[1] and the list of parallels between Pelagius and the latinised Theodore of Mopsuestia drawn up by the late Professor Swete[2].

This neglect has not been altogether disadvantageous. Until the text of Pseudo-Jerome was purified of its thousands of textual corruptions, and was seen to fall apart into at least two portions, one written by Pelagius, the other by a Pelagian, it would have been premature and confusing to formulate any conclusions with regard to the sources. When it fell to me to make the necessary discoveries with regard to the form and character of the Pseudo-Jerome, I resolved to study also the possible Greek and Latin sources of at least that part which comes from Pelagius himself. But as the purely textual and linguistic work grew in my hands, and it became evident that the further task would delay publication for several years, I was glad to avail myself of the willingness

[1] *Histoire Critique des principaux Commentateurs du Nouveau Testament* (Rotterdam, 1693) pp. 236 ff.

[2] *Theodori Episcopi Mopsuesteni in epistolas B. Pauli Commentarii* vol. I (Cambr. 1880) pp. lxxiv ff.

of my former pupil Dr Alfred J. Smith[1], to undertake this part of the investigation. In the first instance he has confined himself to the most important part of the commentary, that on the Epistle to the Romans, and to the Latin sources of this part; but he hopes to complete the task later. Such work on the sources of the commentary as I have been able to perform myself, has been unsystematic, but it has been here incorporated for any worth it may happen to have. To Dr Smith will always belong the credit of being the first serious investigator into the sources of the Pelagian expositions.

Our best plan would seem to be to take, in chronological order, the Greek and Latin works which seem to have a close connexion at points with the commentary of Pelagius. An exception is made in the case of Origen, for it would appear that Pelagius knew, not the Greek Origen, but only the Latin of Rufinus's "translation[2]."

Before proceeding, however, to these details, it is necessary to remark that Pelagius makes no reference *by name* to any authority employed by him. In this respect he is only following the ancient practice. He does, however, not infrequently refer to the opinions of others by the vague terms *quidam, multi, alii, diuersi*, and it will help other scholars to supplement the serious defects of the present chapter, if I give here a list of the passages where these vague expressions occur. I am not without hope that those that really know patristic literature, as a mere Latinist can hardly be expected to know it, will be able to answer in many, if not in all cases, who the writers referred to are[3]. It seems probable that these authorities were for the most part recent, perhaps also for the most part Greek.

[1] M.A., D.Litt. (Aberdeen), at that time Classical Master in Robert Gordon's College, Aberdeen, Lieutenant, R.N.V.R. Dr Smith's articles are published in the *Journal of Theological Studies* vol. XIX (1917—18) pp. 162—230; vol. XX (1918—19) pp. 55—65, 127—177.

[2] Smith, in *J.T.S.* vol. XX, pp. 127 ff.

[3] Dr Smith has given the answer in certain cases. As the result of a somewhat cursory study I have formed the opinion that Tertullian, Cyprian, Novatian, Lactantius and Hilary (*on the Psalms*) are not among the *quidam* referred to except perhaps in these passages: Tertullian, *de pudic.* 13 (C.S.E.L. XX p. 245, Oehler, t. I p. 819) *colaphis...cohibebatur per* dolorem *ut aiunt auriculae uel* capitis, may be alluded to on 2 Cor. xii 7 *quidam dicunt eum frequenti* dolore capitis *laborasse*; Cyprian, *epist.* 54 § 3 (Hartel, pp. 622 f.) may be among those alluded to on 2 Tim. ii 20.

Quidam are referred to in the notes on:

Rom. ii 21	Rom. x 5	1 Cor. xv 28	Gal. iii 19
iii 28	xi 20	(also *multi,*	v 12
iiii 7	26	*alii*)	Eph. i 10
(also *alii*)	xiiii 2	2 Cor. ii 15	(also *multi,*
v 14	15	iii 6	*alii*)
viii 3	1 Cor. ii 9	v 13	iii 18
19	viii 1	vii 11	v 31
viiii 16	viiii 22	viii 22	vi 5
20 *bis*	xi 21	viiii 1, 2	Col. ii 14
(21)	27	(also *alii*)	2 Tim. ii 20
(26)	xiiii 19	xii 7	

Multi, diuersi are referred to in the notes on:

Rom. viii 19	Eph. i 10
viiii 17	ii 2
1 Cor. xv 28	Phil. ii 5
35	

AMBROSIASTER

It would have been very strange if Pelagius had made no use of the work of his remarkable predecessor, who in the period 365—380 issued a set of commentaries on the thirteen epistles of Paul. Who this predecessor was may be said to be still a subject of debate, even after the intensive study of his commentary which the last twenty years have seen. The most clamant need now is a reliable edition of the various ancient forms of the commentary. It would appear that the commentary on Romans was in the first instance issued by itself, possibly while Hilary of Poitiers was still alive. It was certainly known both in Africa and in Ireland under the name "Hilarius." At a later date the commentaries on the other epistles were issued: to these the name Hilarius was never attached, and the whole work, comprising an enlarged form of the commentary on Romans, circulated both anonymously and under the name of Ambrose in the succeeding centuries. The manuscript tradition is involved in various ways which it must be left for Father Brewer, the future Vienna editor, to set forth.

Pelagius may have been influenced by several motives to produce a new and complete Latin commentary on the Epistles. In the first place, the considerable length of the Ambrosiaster commentary, which probably filled two *codices* of the size fashionable in the fourth century, made a shorter exposition, which could be comprised in one *codex*, extremely desirable. In the second place, Ambrosiaster was a pronouncedly Western expositor, with a hostile attitude to Greek writers and manuscripts, while Pelagius seems to have known and valued Greek Christian writings. Quite apart from this difference of attitude, Pelagius definitely disagreed with certain opinions expressed in the Ambrosiaster commentary. We shall see, however, that he could not help using a work of such originality and importance. From Dr Smith's exhaustive account of the relations of the two commentaries in the Epistle to the Romans, I will borrow only the most striking coincidences.

Rom. i 8. Pelagius: '(Paulus) prudenter laudat, ut prouocet ad profectum.' Ambst.: 'hortatur ad profectum.'

Rom. i 22, 23. Pelagius: 'nec in hominis solum, sed in imaginis hominis' (*sc.* similitudinem). Ambst.: 'ut...non hominibus, sed quod peius est et inexcusabile crimen, in similitudinem hominum mutarent.'

'P.'s comm. on Rom. i shew throughout traces of the influence of Ambrosiaster[1].'

Rom. ii 14—16. Pel.: 'conscientia et cogitationes nostrae erunt in die iudicii ante oculos nostros.' Ambst.: 'gentes...per conscientiam iudicabuntur, si credere noluerint.'

Rom. ii 25. Pel.: 'quo modo ergo nihil est (*sc.* circumcisio), si prodest? sed prodest tempore suo. signum prodest, si iustitia cuius est signaculum, adsit; ceterum sine illa superfluum erit.' Ambst.: 'potest dici e contra: "si prodest circumcisio, cur praetermittitur? sed tunc prodest si legem obserues"' etc.

Rom. iiii 4. Pel.: 'debitoris enim est facere quae iubentur, et nisi paruerit, damnatur.' Ambst.: 'debitoris est enim facere legem, quia necessitas imposita est per legem, ut uelit nolit faciat legem, ne damnetur.'

Rom. iiii 5. Pel.: 'conuertentem[2] impium per solam fidem

[1] Smith, *J.T.S.* XIX p. 175.

[2] Here as present participle of deponent *conuertor*.

iustificat deus.' Ambst.: 'impius per solam fidem iustificatur apud deum.' Pel.: 'quo proposuit gratis per solam fidem peccata dimittere.' Ambst.: 'sic decretum dicit a deo, ut cessante lege sola fides gratiae dei proficeret ad salutem.'

Rom. v 15. Pel.: 'iniustum esse dicentes ut hodie nata anima non ex MASSA Adae tam antiquum peccatum portet alienum, dicunt' etc. Ambst. on Rom. v 12: 'manifestum itaque est in Adam omnes peccasse quasi in MASSA[1].' Note especially this extraordinary use of *massa*, which Augustine quotes from Hilarius (Ambrosiaster) in his *Contra duas Epistulas Pelagianorum* IV 4 § 7.

Rom. vii 8—10. Pel.: 'hic *peccatum* diabolum uidetur appellare, sicut et in Apocalypsi nominatur, scilicet ut auctor peccati.' Ambst. on Rom. vii 4 '*peccatum* quod est diabolus,' and especially on Rom. vii 11 '*peccatum* hoc loco diabolum intellege, qui auctor peccati est[2].' Pel. 'quod (*sc.* mandatum) custoditum proficiebat ad uitam, neglectum duxit ad mortem.' Ambst. 'quia (lex) oboedientibus proficit ad uitam.'

Rom. vii 18. Pel.: 'non dixit (*sc.* Paulus): "non est caro mea bona."' Ambst.: 'non dicit, sicut quibusdam uidetur, carnem malam.'

Rom. vii 22. Pel. on Rom. v 15: 'si anima non est ex traduce, sed sola caro, ipsa tantum habet traducem peccati et ipsa sola poenam meretur'; Pel. on Rom. vii 17: 'habitat (*sc.* in me peccatum) quasi hospes et quasi aliud in alio, non quasi unum, ut accidens scilicet, non naturale.' Ambst.: 'non in animo habitat peccatum, sed in carne quae est ex origine carnis peccati, et per traducem fit omnis caro peccati. si enim anima de traduce esset et ipsa, et in ipsa habitaret peccatum, quia anima Adae magis peccauit quam corpus....in carne ergo habitat peccatum quasi ad ianuas animae, ut non illam permittat ire quo uult: in anima autem si habitaret,

[1] This important coincidence between Ambrosiaster and Pelagius has not been alluded to by Dr Smith, because it is a coincidence between notes on different verses, but it has not escaped E. Buonaiuti, *La genesi della dottrina agostiniana intorno al peccato originale* (Roma, 1916) p. 15, n. 4, and was noted by the present writer a number of years ago. Cf. for this word Paris MS. 653 on Rom. xv 8, Aug. *Ep.* 186 § 4, Ambst. Rom. viiii 21, the proem to the *De induratione cordis Pharaonis*, published by Morin in *Rev. Bénéd.* XXVI p. 179 *duas* massas *humanae naturae, bonam et malam, a deo esse factas.*

[2] On a development of the text of Apoc. vi 8, personal to Pelagius himself, see chap. iv p. 173.

numquam se cognosceret homo: nunc autem cognoscit se et condelectatur legi dei.'

Rom. vii 24, 25. Pel.: 'homo carnalis duplex est quodam modo et in semet ipso diuisus.' Ambst.: 'duplex est homo carne concretus et animo.'

Rom. viii 2. Pel.: 'quae (lex) peccatoribus data est et mortificat peccatores. Siue: Ab ea lege, quam supra dixerat in membris esse.' Ambst.: 'lex peccati est quam in membris dicit habitare, quae suadere nititur aduersa: lex uero mortis Moysi lex est, quia mortificat peccatores.'

Rom. viii 20, 21. Pel.: 'uanitas est omne quod quandoque finitur.' Ambst.: 'quid est ergo in quo uanitati subiecta est, nisi quia quae generat caduca sunt' etc.

Rom. viii 24, 25. Pel.: 'fides per patientiam grandis est praemii.' Ambst.: 'credentes praemiis adficiendi sunt.'

Rom. viii 28—30. Pel.: **quos praesciuit**:...'quos praesciuerat credituros.' Ambst. on Rom. viii 21; 'quos scit deus credituros.' There are many parallels to these clauses in both writers. It is not too much to say that Pelagius, like Augustine, got his doctrine of foreknowledge from Ambrosiaster[1]. Pel.: 'discretio...in tempore est.' Ambst.: 'si...eligantur ad tempus.'

Rom. viii 35—37. Pel.: 'post tanta et tam praeclara beneficia.' Ambst.: 'Christi qui nobis tam magna et innumera praestitit beneficia.'

Rom. viii 38, 39. Pel.: 'pro certo confido quia nec si mihi quis mortem minetur nec si uitam promittat nec si se angelum dicat a domino destinatum nec si angelorum principem mentiatur nec si in praesenti honorem conferat neque si polliceatur gloriam futurorum neque si uirtutes operetur nec si caelum promittat et inferno deterreat uel profunditate scientiae suadere conetur, umquam nos poterit a Christi caritate secernere.' Ambst.: 'quid enim si mors inlata fuerit, nonne lucrum est maximum...? neque si praesens uita promissa nobis fuerit dignitate munita...nec quidem si se angelus nobis ostendat ad seducendos nos...neque si uirtus ab aliquo facta fuerit...neque si in altitudinem se nobis ostendat (*sc.* satanas)... neque si per fantasiam...profundum nobis ostendat horrore miran-

[1] Cf. Smith, p. 163 as well as pp. 201 f., and his note 13 on Augustine, where Aug.'s passages on foreknowledge are collected, and chap. iii above, p. 70.

dum, qua territi forte succumbamus illi...neque si futura nobis spondeat....'

Rom. viiii 1—5. Pel.: 'contra Iudaeos acturus primum illis satisfacit non se odii causa haec dicere, sed amoris, eo quod doleat illos Christo non credere.' Ambst.: 'quoniam superius contra Iudaeos loqui uidetur...nunc ut uotum suum et adfectum circa eos ostendat...ac per hoc dolet genus suum...quia incredulitate sua hoc...beneficio se priuarunt.'

Rom. viiii 14, 15. Pel.: 'hoc recto sensu ita intellegitur: illius miserebor, quem ita praesciui posse misericordiam promereri, ut iam tunc illius sim misertus.' Ambst.: 'eius miserebor, cui praescius eram quod misericordiam daturus essem, sciens conuersurum illum (cf. Pel. on vv. 11, 12 si conuerti uoluerit), et permansurum apud me.'

Rom. viiii 17. Pel.: 'tale est hoc quod in Pharaone gestum est, quale si medicus de cruciatu iam damnati rei multis inueniat sanitatem, causas inquirendo morborum....' Ambst.: 'hoc etiam genere antiqui medici in hominibus morte dignis uel mortis sententiam consecutis requirebant quo modo prodessent uiuis, quae in homine latebant apertis, ut his cognoscerent causas aegritudinis et poena morientis proficeret ad salutem uiuentis.'

Rom. x 4. Pel.: 'talis est qui Christum credidit die qua credidit, quasi qui uniuersam legem impleuerit.' Ambst.: 'hoc dicit quia perfectionem legis habet qui credit in Christum.'

Rom. xi 1, 2. Pel.: 'illam plebem non reppulit quam praesciit esse credituram.' Ambst.: 'quos fideles sibi futuros sciuit... quam praesciuit deus saluandam...hi quos praesciuit deus credituros[1].'

Rom. xii 13. Both Pel. and Ambst. mention Abraham and Lot as dispensers of hospitality.

Rom. xii 15. Pel.: 'ut siquid patitur unum membrum, conpatiantur omnia membra (1 Cor. xii 26).' Ambst.: 'hoc est quod alio loco dicit: "siquid patitur unum membrum, conpatiuntur omnia membra."' Pel.: 'cum uiderem homines in necessitate (Iob xxx 25)?' Ambst.: 'cum enim quis fideli solacio[2] est in necessitate.'

[1] See above, on Rom. viii 28—30.

[2] *Fideli* here is masc., while *solacio* is predicative dative (cf. Roby's *Grammar* vol. II p. liv *a*).

Rom. xiii 13. Pel.: 'comissatio est mensae collatio.' Ambst.: '(conuiuia) quae...collatione omnium celebrantur.'

Rom. xiiii 1—4. Pel. disagrees with the opinion of 'quidam' who think that Paul is here referring to the Jews. As this latter view is found in Ambst., he is clearly one of the 'quidam.'

Rom. xv 13 f. Pel.: 'bonus doctor laudando prouocat ad profectum, ut erubescerent tales non esse quales ab apostolo esse credebantur.' Ambst.: 'per laudem...prouocat eos ad meliorem et intellectum et uitam. qui enim uidet se laudari, data opera elaborat ut uera sint quae dicuntur.'

Rom. xv 20. Both commentaries refer to *pseudo-apostoli*. The frequency of such references is almost certainly due to the influence of the Marcionite prologues[1].

Rom. xv 22. Pel.: 'exposuit illud quod in capite dixerat: "et prohibitus sum usque adhuc (i 13)."' Ambst.: 'quod in capite epistulae memorat dicens: "quia saepe," inquit, "proposui uenire ad uos et prohibitus sum usque adhuc."'

Rom. xvi 4. Pel.: 'se periculis obiecerunt.' Ambst.: 'ut pericula pati pro eo non abnuerent[2].'

1 Cor. iii 17. Pel.: 'suum corpus peccando.' Ambst.: 'turpiter uiuentes corpora sua uiolando corruperant[3].'

1 Cor. viiii 5. Both Pel. and Ambst. are definitely of opinion that *mulieres* (*mulierem*) does not mean 'wives.' Pel.: 'mulieres, quae necessaria de suis facultatibus ministrarent.' Ambst.: 'mulieres...sequebantur apostolos ministrantes eis et sumptus et seruitia, sicut et saluatorem sunt secutae ministrantes ei de facultatibus suis.' It is only right, however, to point out that the same view is taken also by Jerome, *adu. Iouin.* I 26 (vol. II² p. 277 D Vall.): 'non uxores debere intellegi, sed eas, ut diximus (= *adu. Heluid.* 11?), quae de sua substantia ministrabant.'

1 Cor. viiii 20. Pel.: 'potest et ita intellegi quod Samaritanos dixerit "esse sub lege," quia legem tantum Moysi uidentur accipere.'

[1] Dr Smith is not responsible for this statement.

[2] From this point onward the brief notes are due to the author, as Dr Smith has confined his attention to 'Romans.'

[3] I have a note to the effect that Pelag. on 1 Cor. v 8 *in septem diebus—reuoluuntur* is paralleled in Ambst., but the nearest parallels I can now find are *Quaest.* 84 § 2, 95 § 2; *Anon. in. Math.* (*J.T.S.* v (1903—4) p. 236).

Ambst.: '"hi qui sub lege sunt" Samaritani noscuntur: legem enim solam accipiunt, id est quinque libros Moysi[1].'

1 Cor. xi 7. Pel.: 'uir ad imaginem dei factus est et idcirco liber est: mulier uero ad uiri similitudinem est formata; unde iubetur esse subiecta.' Ambst. on xi 8—10: 'mulier ergo idcirco debet uelare caput quia non est imago dei, sed ut ostendatur subiecta' etc.

1 Cor. xi 10. Pel.: 'uelamen signum potestatis esse declarat.' Ambst.: 'potestatem uelamen significauit.'

Gal. arg. Pel.: 'Galatas...pseudo-apostoli hac astutia subuertebant.' Ambst.: 'Galatae uel ei qui eos subuertebant.'

Eph. vi 5. Pel.: 'non uenit Christus condiciones mutare: nam seruitium non natura dedit, sed captiuitas fecit, neque ex maledicto Cham, ut quidam putant, cum ex eo reges legamus esse generatos. maledictum uero illud in filiis Cham impletum est, qui Istrahel sunt filiis subiugati.' Ambst. on Col. iiii 1: 'dum alter alterius fines inuadit, tunc captiuos ducit ingenuos....denique peccati causa Cham seruus audiuit: "maledictus puer Chanaan; seruus seruorum erit fratribus suis[2]."'

Phil. iii 2. Pel.: 'hinc contra pseudo-apostolos agit Christi euangelium lacerantes.' Ambst.: 'primum oblatrant, dehinc morsu saeuo male operantur in carnem.'

Phil. iii 19. Pel.: 'in circumcisione uerecundi membri.' Ambst.: 'gloriantes in pudendis circumcisis[3].'

Col. ii 21. Pel. and Ambst., with Ambr., regard these prohibitions as the Apostle's own: Pel.: '"ne tetigeritis neque gustaueritis neque contractaueritis (**A**)," illo tactu et gustu et contrectatione quo hi(?) qui in concupiscentiis abutuntur et diligunt pro aeternis.' Ambst.: 'prohibet omni genere ab spe mundanorum, quia inanis est' etc.

1 Tim. v 19. Pel.: 'iniustum est etiam aduersus laicum accusationem recipere, cum hoc nec saeculares iudices faciant: quanto magis aduersus domini sacerdotem!' Ambst.: 'quoniam huius or-

[1] It is to be noted that this view is found already in Origen (Cramer, *Catena* v p. 178), as I learn from Harnack, *Texte und Untersuchungen* Bd. XLII (4) [1919] p. 86, n. 3.

[2] On this passage of Ambst. cf. A. J. Carlyle, *A History of Mediaeval Political Theory in the West* vol. I (1903) p. 113: the scripture quotation is omitted by some MSS.

[3] In the case of Ambst. the scripture text was *gloria in pudendis illorum*, which is nearer to the comment, but there is no trace of this reading in Pelagian MSS.

dinis sublimis honor est (huiusmodi enim uicarii Christi sunt), idcirco non facile de hac persona accusatio debet admitti.'

2 Tim. ii 20. Pel. disagrees with 'quidam,' who define the 'magna domus' as the Church. Ambst. is one of these.

2 Tim. iiii 20. Pel.: 'hinc probatur quia non propter sanitatem carnalem tantum apostoli curabant, sed ut etiam signa monstrarent, quia hic suum discipulum non curauit.' Ambst.: 'quid est tamen ut praesente apostolo qui mortuos excitabat, Trophimus infirmaretur? sed signa propter incredulos facta sunt[1],' *etc.*

Jerome

A few parallels with passages in the works of Jerome written prior to our commentary, are here set down. There is no antecedent improbability, but rather the reverse, that Pelagius, as a resident in Rome, became acquainted with the works of this great Roman ecclesiastical figure. Some of the passages quoted are in all probability the origin of the Pelagian passages like them, and it does not admit of the slightest doubt, I think, that the third passage, cited from the *Aduersus Heluidium*, is the origin of the corresponding part of Pelagius's commentary. The order in which they are given is the presumed chronological order of the works of Jerome.

Epist. 18 B 4 (20) § 2 (A.D. 381[2]): 'ne uideremur aliquid praeterisse eorum quas Iudaei uocant deuterosis[3] et in quibus uniuersam scientiam ponunt.' Pel. in 1 Tim. i 4 *fabulis.* 'quas deuterosim appellant: unde in euangelio *docentes doctrinas hominum* condemnantur. *et genealogiis interminatis.* generationibus antiquorum in quibus sibi summam scientiae uindicant....'

Adu. Heluidium (about A.D. 383) Jerome first formulated the idea that 'brothers of the Lord' means 'cousins of the Lord.' Pel. on Gal. i 19 must therefore have got this view from Jerome[4].

[1] This topic is also discussed in Ps.-Aug. *Quaest.* app. 83 (pp. 476 f. of my edition).

[2] I accept Vallarsi's dates for the letters without question.

[3] Reference to the articles δευτέρωσις, *deuterosis* in the Greek and in the Latin *Thesaurus* respectively, will suggest other possibilities, but my view seems the most probable.

[4] This was pointed out by Lightfoot, *Galatians* (ed. 1865) p. 272, who acutely remarked 'unless his (*i.e.* Pel.'s) text has been tampered with here.' It has, but only to affirm the same view more definitely.

Adu. Heluidium 6 (t. II pp. 210 E, 211 A ed. Vall.[2]): 'nunc illud est ostendendum ut, quo modo ibi consuetudinem scripturae secutus est, sic etiam in DONEC eiusdem scripturae auctoritate frangatur, quae saepe certum tempus, ut ipse disseruit, in eius adsumptione significat, saepe infinitum, ut est illud quod deus ad quosdam loquitur in propheta (Esai. xxxxvi 4[1]): "ego sum, ego sum, et donec senescatis ego sum." numquid post quam illi senuerint, deus esse desistet?' Pel. in 1 Cor. xv 25: 'DONEC autem non semper finem significat, sicut est illud: "ego deus uester donec senescatis," et cetera talia.' It ought to be mentioned that in Jerome, shortly after the above passage, this very portion of 1 Cor. xv is quoted in its context; so that there is not the slightest doubt that Pelagius was indebted to Jerome's *Aduersus Heluidium.* By 'cetera talia' Pel. is referring to Ps. cxxii 2 (3) which Jerome afterwards quotes as a further illustration of this use of *donec.*

Comm. in epist. Gal. (about A.D. 386). Mangenot says: 'Il est à noter que Pélage a connu le commentaire de saint Jérôme sur l'Épître aux Galates[2].'

De uiris inlustr. c. 5 (A.D. 392): 'epistula autem quae fertur ad Hebraeos, non eius creditur, propter stili sermonisque dissonantiam, sed uel Barnabae iuxta Tertullianum, uel Lucae euangelistae iuxta quosdam, uel Clementis Romanae postea ecclesiae episcopi[3], quem aiunt sententias Pauli proprio ordinasse et ornasse sermone. uel certe quia Paulus scribebat ad Hebraeos et propter inuidiam sui apud eos nominis, titulum in principio salutationis amputauerat (scripserat autem ut Hebraeus Hebraice, id est suo eloquio disertissime), ea quae eloquenter scripta fuerant in Hebraeo, eloquentius uertisse in Graecum, et hanc esse causam quod a ceteris Pauli epistulis discrepare uideatur[4].' Pel. argum. omn. epist.: 'epistulam sane quae ad Hebraeos scribitur, quidam Pauli non esse adfirmant eo quod non sit eius nomine titulata, et propter sermonis stilique distantiam, sed aut Barnabae iuxta Tertullianum aut Lucae iuxta quosdam, uel certe Clementis discipuli apostolorum et episcopi

[1] Vall. ed. 2 wrongly 43, but Victorius before him rightly 46.

[2] *Revue du clergé français*, 1916, 1er Avril et 1er Mai, p. 28 n. 1 of *tirage à part.*

[3] Cf. Hier. *epist.* 129 § 3.

[4] With the tenor of this passage of Jerome cf. also Filast. *Haer.* 61 (89), and Isid. *Etymol.* VI 2 § 45 (from Hier.).

Romanae ecclesiae post apostolos ordinati....ipsius magis esse credenda est quae tanto doctrinae suae fulget eloquio...ne odium nominis fronte praelati...non est sane mirum si eloquentior uideatur in proprio, id est Hebraeo, quam in peregrino, id est Graeco, quo ceterae epistulae sunt scriptae sermone.' No case of borrowing could be clearer, and no mediaeval scholar could be blamed for attributing this 'argument' to Jerome.

Prologus Galeatus (about A.D. 392) (ed. Vall.[2] t. IX pp. 453, 454) 'Syrorum...et Chaldaeorum lingua...quae Hebraeae magna ex parte confinis est.' Cf. Pel. in 1 Cor. xvi 22 'magis Syrum est quam Hebraeum, tamen etsi ex confinio utrarumque linguarum aliquid Hebraeum sonat.'

Adu. Iouin. I 26 (after A.D. 392): for a possible borrowing from this work, see on 1 Cor. viiii 5, under the section dealing with Ambrosiaster parallels.

Epist. 52, 7 § 2 (A.D. 394): 'amare filiorum, timere seruorum est.' Pel. in Rom. viii 15: 'timere seruorum est, diligere filiorum.'

Epist. 74, 3 § 3 (A.D. 398): 'Mattheus quoque in καταλόγῳ apostolorum publicanus dicitur, non quo permanserit publicanus post apostolicam dignitatem, sed qui prius fuerit publicanus.' Cf. Pel. in Col. iiii 14: (Lucas) 'ex-medico erat, sicut Matheus iam apostolus adhuc dicitur publicanus.'

AUGUSTINE

At first sight the name of Augustine among the sources of Pelagius will seem even more incredible than that of Jerome, but we must remember that Augustine had been for some time before the close of the fourth century a writer of note, that he and Pelagius corresponded, and that it was only as the result of Pelagius's declared views that Augustine's developed in the course of controversy. Dr Smith's researches have shown that Ambrosiaster influenced Augustine as well as Pelagius, also that in Pelagius we find clear traces of the use of Augustine's *Expositio Quarundam Propositionum ex Epistula ad Romanos* and *Epistulae ad Romanos Inchoata Expositio,* both written about A.D. 394. The more striking of these we proceed to give.

Rom. i 18—19. Pel. quotes from Sap. xiii 5, while Aug. quotes from Sap. xiii 9.

Rom. i 24. Pel. quotes from Ps. lxxx 12: 'sicut in psalmo dicit: "et dimisi eos secundum desideria cordis eorum."' Aug. writes: 'quod autem dicit "tradidit," intellegitur "dimisit in desideria cordis eorum."'

Rom. v 14. Pel.: 'ut quidam dicunt: "forma" a contrario: hoc est: sicut ille peccati caput, ita et iste iustitiae.' Aug.: '"forma" autem "futuri" dictus est Adam, sed a contrario, ut quo modo per illum mors, sic per dominum nostrum uita.' Aug. is clearly referred to here in 'quidam.'

Rom. vii 2. Pel. says that by 'uir' Paul means the 'legis mandatum,' by 'mulier' the 'plebs' or the 'anima.' Aug. says that the 'mulier' corresponds to the 'anima,' while the 'uir' corresponds to the 'passiones peccatorum.'

Rom. viii 26 f. Pel.: '"postulat," quia postulare nos facit gemitibus qui enarrari non possunt, sicut temptare nos dicitur deus, ut sciat, hoc est, ut scire nos faciat, quales simus.' Aug.: 'gemere dicit spiritum, quod nos gemere faciat caritate, concitans desiderium futurae uitae, sicut dicit: "temptat uos dominus deus uester, ut sciat si diligitis eum," id est, ut scire uos faciat.'

Rom. viiii 15—21. Pel.: 'ita non uolentis neque currentis tantum, sed et domini adiuuantis.' Aug.: 'non sufficere dicit uelle nostrum, nisi adiuuet deus.'

Rom. xiiii 16, 22. Pel.: 'libertas quam habemus in domino, ut omnia nobis munda sint' (cf. v. 20, also Tit. i 15). Aug.: 'bona est haec fides qua credimus omnia munda mundis' (Tit. i 15) (cf. also Aug. on Rom. xv 8, 9).

The following refer to the *Inchoata Expositio*.

Rom. i 4. Pel.: 'non omnium resurgentium, sed ad Christum pertinentium, in ipso Christo resurrectionis forma portenditur.' Aug.: 'neque (praecesserat) ad exemplum omnium resurgentium... qui praedestinatus est filius dei ex resurrectione mortuorum suorum, hoc est, ad se pertinentium, in uitam aeternam.'

Rom. ii 2. Pel.: 'humanum iudicium multis modis corrumpitur; amore, odio, timore, auaritia saepe iudicii integritas uiolatur.' Aug.: 'nam et iudices mali praebent gratiam in accipiendis personis, aliqua cupiditate inlecti aut timore perterriti.'

Rom. vi 9. Pel.: 'iam non potestis iterum baptizari, quia Christus non potest pro uobis iterum crucifigi, sicut dicit ad

Hebraeos: "inpossibile est eos qui semel inluminati sunt," et cetera, quibus non paenitentiam negat, sed iterationem baptismi diffitetur.' Aug.: '...non posse deinceps eum qui peccauerit, iterum baptizando purgari; quo intellectu non intercluditur paenitendi locus...non enim possunt denuo baptizari qui semel baptizati sunt.'

It did not fall within the scope of Dr Smith's investigation to examine further works of Augustine. I must therefore myself call attention to another work of Augustine, namely *De Diuersis Quaestionibus ad Simplicianum* (assigned to the year 397), as certainly used by Pelagius[1]. This fact the following parallels will make clear.

Book i, quaestio 1, deals with Rom. vii 7—25.

Pel.: 'hinc in persona eius hominis loquitur qui legem accipit.' Aug. § 1: 'quo loco uidetur mihi apostolus transfigurasse in se hominem sub lege positum, cuius uerbis ex persona sua loquitur.'

Pel.: 'non dixit: "non habebam" aut "non faciebam," sed "nesciebam," hoc est, "nesciebam concupiscentiam" esse peccatum.' Aug. § 2: 'itaque non ait: "peccatum non feci nisi per legem," sed "peccatum non cognoui nisi per legem." neque rursus ait: "nam concupiscentiam non habebam nisi lex diceret: non concupisces," sed ait: "concupiscentiam nesciebam nisi lex diceret: non concupisces."'

Pel.: 'quia iam sciens praeuaricaui.' Aug. § 4: 'ut iam a sciente et praeuaricante peccetur.'

Book i, quaestio 2, deals with Rom. viiii 10—29.

Pel. and Aug. (§ 3) both quote 2 Tim. iiii 7 'cursum consummaui,' in this connexion. Pel. merely cites these words, while Aug. gives the whole of verses 7 and 8.

Pel. and Aug. (§ 10) both quote 1 Cor. viiii 24 'sic currite ut [omnes] conprehendatis.'

Pel.: 'non uolentis neque currentis tantum, sed et domini adiuuantis.'

Aug. (§ 12): 'uoluntas hominis sola non sufficit ut iuste recteque uiuamus, nisi adiuuemur misericordia dei.'

[1] The reader should consult the independent article of the theologian Batiffol in the *Revue Biblique* nouv. sér. t. xv (1918) pp. 5 ff.

ORIGEN-RUFINUS ON ROMANS

There is very little outward likeness between the Origen-Rufinus commentary on Romans (date about A.D. 405) and Pelagius. Origen as is well known, is discursive in this type of commentary and addicted to the allegorical method of interpretation. He comments on a group of verses at a time, while Pelagius deals with individual verses or clauses. Pelagius does not forswear the allegorical method, but he keeps it within bounds. His view about the matter is stated in his note on Gal. iiii 24 (cf. 2 Cor. iii 6); 'ut manente historiae ueritate figuras testamenti ueteris exponamus... praecepta uero difficile inuenies apostolum taliter exponentem, ne eorum uideretur eneruare uirtutem.' He approves allegory in the same limited way as St Paul himself. Origen of course believed in historical interpretation also, but Pelagius in the proportion in which he allows the two methods, approximates much more to the Antiochian point of view.

Yet there was a natural kinship of mind between Origen and Pelagius, as may be seen in their common attitude to Free Will. We should not be surprised to discover that Pelagius possessed enough Greek to tackle Origen's difficult style. The view, however, that Pelagius consulted the original Greek of Origen's commentary on Romans, has been rendered exceedingly improbable by the investigations of Dr Smith, who having proved use of Rufinus's 'translation' of Origen on Pelagius's part, is justified in appealing to the old maxim 'entia non sunt multiplicanda praeter necessitatem,' and arguing that Pelagius used Rufinus only. Dr Smith has also studied the surviving fragments of Origen's Greek in Mr Ramsbotham's careful recension[1], and has found no trace of their influence on Pelagius. It may therefore be taken as proved that it was Rufinus's adaptation[2] that was alone known to Pelagius. Incidentally this discovery enables us to be more precise with regard

[1] *J.T.S.* vols. XIII (1911—12), XIV (1912—13).

[2] On Rufinus's methods of translation, consult E. J. Kimmel, *De Rufino Eusebii interprete* (Gerae, 1838) pp. 80 ff., Bp Westcott's article 'Origen' in D.C.B., Engelbrecht's edition of Rufinus's Gregory of Nazianzus (C.S.E.L. 46) pp. xviii ff., Ed. Schwartz's art. 'Eusebios' in Pauly-Wissowa, *Real-Encycl.* Bd. VI Sp. 1406, Mommsen in Eusebius-Rufinus *Kirchengeschichte* Bd. III (Leipzig, 1909) pp. ccli f., Koetzschau in Origenes' *Werke* Bd. V (*De Principiis*) (Leipzig, 1913) pp. cxxviii ff., G. Bardy in *Revue Biblique* nouv. sér. t. XVI (1919) pp. 106 ff., t. XXIX (1820) pp. 229 ff.

to the date of Pelagius's commentary, if we may assume that he wrote the Romans portion first, an assumption which is *a priori* probable. The Pelagian commentary, then, belongs to the period 404—409 (inclusive).

Rom. i 1. Both commentators quote as examples of changed name, Abraham, Sara and Cephas, and both quote Phil. ii 7 in commenting on *seruus Iesu Christi*.

Rom. i 8. Both commentators refer to the expression 'God of Abraham,' and both suggest that the conversion of the Romans was matter for wonder.

Rom. ii 1, 2. Pel.: 'omnes norunt et innocentiam mereri praemium et malitiam habere supplicium.' O.-R.: 'communis professio est bonum non debere puniri nec malum consequi bona.'

Rom. ii 28, 29. Pelagius shows here undoubted acquaintance with the very long note of Origen-Rufinus, for example, with the symbolical view of circumcision, and the parallel between Joshua and Christ.

Rom. iii furnishes few parallels between the two commentaries. In iii 5 both contain references to the Deluge. At iii 13 Pel. has: 'aliud ore promentes, aliud corde uoluentes'; O.-R.: 'dolus est cum aliud quis lingua loquitur et aliud uolutat in corde.' At iii 15 Pel.: 'interficientes animas adulando': O.-R.: 'multo etiam uerius ille homicida dicendus est qui animam a uera uita separat.'

Rom. iiii 8. Pel.: 'quidam dicunt remitti per baptismum, tegi laboribus paenitentiae, non imputari per martyrium.' O.-R. in Rom. ii 2: 'sed requiritur si erga eos quorum remissae sunt iniquitates per baptismi gratiam, uel quorum tecta sunt per paenitentiam peccata, uel quibus imputandum non est peccatum per martyrii gloriam, secundum ueritatem uideatur deus seruare iudicium.' This instance alone, in the absence of any other evidence, would suffice to show use of Origen-Rufinus by Pelagius.

Rom. iiii 18. The question about Keturah which Pel. asks and answers here, was doubtless suggested by O.-R. on iiii 18—22.

Rom. v 8, 9. Pel.'s '*commendat*, amabilem facit' comes from O.-R.'s '*commendat* uel confirmat intellegitur uel amabilem facit pro beneficiis praestitis.'

Rom. v 12—14. Pel. points out that in saying 'omnes' Paul is exaggerating: O.-R. says that Paul makes it abundantly clear 'omnes homines et multos homines idem esse.'

Rom. vi 5—7. Pel.: 'hoc est, ut omnia uitia destruantur, quia unum uitium membrum est peccati, omnia corpus.' O.-R.: 'possunt autem membra ex quibus corpus istud peccati constat, illa uideri quae superius enumerauit apostolus,' followed by an enumeration of twelve sins. In his alternative explanation Pel. defines *corpus peccati* as 'corpus nostrum.' O.-R. says: 'si uero magis hoc corpus nostrum dixisse intellegatur.'

Rom. vi 7—9. Pel.: 'iam non potestis iterum baptizari, quia Christus non potest...iterum crucifigi, sicut dicit ad Hebraeos: "inpossibile est eos qui semel inluminati sunt," et cetera.' O.-R.: '"nos...qui semel inluminati sumus..."(non) exspectemus ut "iterum post lapsum renouemur ad paenitentiam, rursum crucifigentes in nobis ipsis filium dei[1]."' Both also quote Col. iii 3. Pel.: 'mortuus enim omnino non peccat': O.-R.: 'qui enim...existimat...mortuum se esse, non peccat.'

Rom. vi 13. Pel.: 'ut oculus qui ante uidebat ad concupiscendum, nunc uideat nudum ad uestiendum. sic etiam de reliquis membris aduerte.' O.-R.: 'circumspiciebant prius oculi mulierem aut alienum aliquid ad concupiscendum; nunc circumspiciant pauperes debiles egenos ad miserandum.'

Rom. vi 23. Pel.: 'non dixit similiter "stipendia iustitiae," quia *etc.*' O.-R. t. VI c. 1 p. 239 L.: 'unde idem apostolus in alio loco: "stipendia," inquit, "peccati mors," et non addidit ut similiter diceret: "stipendia autem iustitiae uita aeterna," *etc.*'

Rom. vii 1—6. Pelagius's notes here appear to be based on the lengthy discussion of Origen-Rufinus.

Rom. vii 7. Pel.: 'non dixit: "non habebam," aut "non faciebam," sed "nesciebam," hoc est, nesciebam concupiscentiam esse peccatum.' O.-R.: 'non dixit: "non habebam," sed ait: "nesciebam," tamquam quae esset quidem, ignoraretur tamen quod esset concupiscentia.'

Rom. vii 16. Pel.: 'cum lege sentio, quae mala et non uult et prohibet.' O.-R.: 'consentit legi dei quia bona est, quae prohibet malum.'

Rom. vii 18. Pel.: 'est uoluntas, sed non est effectus.' O.-R.: 'est talis quaedam infirmitas (*sc.* uoluntatis)...ut non statim uoluntatem sequatur effectus.'

Rom. vii 19. Pel.: 'sicut, uerbi gratia, siquis iam diu iurare

[1] See also Aug. above, pp. 186 f.

consueuit, etiam cum non optat, incurrit.' O.-R.: 'nec talis est quae dicat: "est, est: non, non," et ideo non potest operari quae uult, sed quae non uult.'

Rom. viii 1. Pel.: 'nihil in illis damnatione dignum est.' O.-R.: 'pronuntiat (*sc.* Paulus) in his nihil damnatione esse dignum.'

Rom. viii 3. Pel.: 'similem ergo ceteris hominibus carnem accepit, quantum ad naturam.' O.-R.: 'naturam quidem corporis nostri habuit.' On "et de peccato damnauit peccatum in carne" Pel. says: 'sicut hostiae quas **pro peccato** offerebant in lege, peccati nomine uocabantur...sic et Christi caro quae **pro** peccatis nostris oblata est, peccati nomen accepit'; O.-R. has '"et de peccato," uel—ut uerius habetur apud Graecos—, "et pro peccato damnauit peccatum in carne."' As Dr Smith points out[1], this is quite obviously an interpolation by Rufinus.

Rom. viii 9. Pel. and O.-R. both quote the list of fruits of the Spirit from Gal. v 22, 23.

Rom. viii 15. Pel. and O.-R. both quote Mal. i 6. Also, Pel.: 'qui uocat patrem, filium se esse profitetur': O.-R.: 'neque enim patrem alius quis nisi filius uocat.'

Rom. viii 19—22. Pel. interprets 'creatura' here in the sense of 'angeli'; and this is one of the views that O.-R. mentions. O.-R. and Pel. also both use the expression 'rationabilis creatura.'

Rom. viii 26 f. Both Pel. and O.-R. quote 1 Cor. xiii 12, and both also quote in illustration 1 Cor. xiiii 14 and 12: Pel.: 'hic gratiam spiritus spiritum nominauit'; O.-R.: 'dona uel gratias sancti spiritus multos spiritus nominari'...'spiritum suum dicens gratiam sancti spiritus.'

Rom. viii 28 ff. Here and elsewhere there is much common to the thought of Pel. and O.-R., even though resemblances in language are not easily found. Pel. was in some sense the inheritor and developer of Origen's position on various questions.

Rom. viii 31 ff. Both Pel. and O.-R. quote 1 Ioh. iiii 18.

Rom. viiii 14—19. Dr Smith indicates[2] that Pel. and O.-R. are here agreed on three points: (*a*) vv. 14—19 are put into the mouth of an opponent of St Paul: (*b*) both insist on the freedom

[1] *J.T.S.* vol. xx (1918—19) p. 156.
[2] *J.T.S.* vol. xx (1918—19) pp. 163 f.

of the will: (*c*) God's foreknowledge is foreknowledge of character. For a detailed comparison of the comments the reader is referred to Dr Smith's exposition. See also under Rom. x 15.

Rom. x 4—11. Pel.'s comment implies the view of O.-R. that 'God's righteousness' (v. 3) is the same as 'the righteousness which is of faith' (v. 6), while 'their own righteousness' (v. 3) is the same as 'the righteousness which is of the Law' (v. 5). O.-R. is probably one of the 'quidam' referred to later in Pel.'s notes.

Rom. x 15. O.-R. on this verse: 'isti sunt pedes quibus et Paulus "cucurrisse cursum se" dixit, et "sic currere ut comprehendat,"' recalls Pel. on Rom. viiii 16: 'si "non est uolentis neque currentis,"...quare et ipse cucurrit dicens: "cursum consummaui," et alios ut currerent adhortatus est dicens: "sic currite ut omnes conprehendatis"?'

Rom. xi 7—10. On v. 8 Pel. writes: 'scriptura dicit: "ante hominem uita et mors; quod placuerit ei, dabitur illi," ne libertas scilicet tollatur arbitrii.' O.-R. on Rom. i 24, 25, to which there is a cross reference from his note here, writes: 'seruatur ei (*sc.* animae) in omnibus libertas sui arbitrii, ut...quodcumque uoluerit ipsa declinet, sicut scriptum est: "ecce posui ante faciem tuam uitam et mortem, ignem et aquam."'

Rom. xi 17. Both Pel. and O.-R. use the striking phrase 'pinguedinis Christi.'

Rom. xi 25. Pel.: 'occasionem eis salutis etiam "caecitas" praestitit "Istrahel."' O.-R.: 'occasio...conferendae in uos misericordiae populi "Istrahel" incredulitas exstitit.'

Rom. xi 28. Pel.: 'inimici mihi sunt, quia uobis praedico Christum, sicut ipse alibi ait: "prohibentes nos gentibus loqui ut saluae fiant."' O.-R.: 'sed quod dicit: "propter uos," hoc est, quorum saluti scilicet inuident, "prohibentes" apostolos "gentibus loqui" et persequentes eos qui adnuntiant Christum.'

Rom. xii 3. Pel. and O.-R. both quote 1 Cor. xii 11 in illustration.

Rom. xii 6. Pel.: 'omnibus quidem credentibus gloria promittitur in futuro, sed qui ita mundum cor habuerit ut hoc mereatur, gratiam uirtutum accipit etiam in praesenti, quam deus ei donare uoluerit.' O.-R.: 'si enim in praesenti saeculo dat deus uni cuique gratiam "secundum mensuram fidei," sine dubio et in futuro dabit uni cuique gratiam pro mensura meritorum.'

Rom. xii 8. Pel.: '"qui praeest" ecclesiae uel fratribus, debet esse sollicitus.' O.-R.: '"qui" uero "praeest" fratribus, uel "qui praeest" ecclesiae, "in sollicitudine" esse debet.' Again Pel.: 'tristem (*sc.* datorem) sine dubio odit.' O.-R.: 'non uult in tali opere esse tristitiam.'

Rom. xii 17. Pel.: 'quod si tantae patientiae...fueris, non solum apud dominum, sed et apud omnes homines poteris probabilis apparere.' O.-R. on v. 19: 'patientia probabilis fit apud deum.'

Rom. xiii 3. Pel.: 'ipsa damnatio malorum laus est bonorum.' O.-R.: 'potestas omnis a deo data est "ad uindictam quidem malorum, laudem uero bonorum."'

Rom. xv 1—3. Pel.: 'si uere firmi estis, sic facite ut ego, qui "factus sum infirmis infirmus, ut infirmos lucri facerem."' O.-R.: 'uidetur in his Paulus firmum semet ipsum pronuntiare, sicut et in prima ad Corinthios dicit quia "factus sum infirmis infirmus, ut infirmos lucrarer."' Pel.: 'non a nobis ipsis, sed a proximis conlaudemur.' O.-R.: 'sed non ex hoc accipias eum quasi inmemorem mandati illius loci quo dicitur: "laudet te proximus tuus et non tuum os, extraneus et non tua labia." (Prou. xxvii 2.)' Pel.: 'sicut et alibi suum nobis proponit exemplum, dicens: "sicut et ego omnibus per omnia placeo, non quaerens quod mihi utile est, sed quod multis, ut salui fiant."' O.-R.: '...quod in aliis dicit: "sicut et ego omnibus per omnia placeo, non quaerens quod mihi utile est, sed quod multis, ut salui fiant (1 Cor. x 33)."'

Rom. xv 5 ff. Both commentators quote Matth. xviii 19.

Rom. xv 17. Both commentators quote 1 Cor. i 31.

Rom. xv 24. Pel.: 'ideo ex parte, quia nulla magnitudo temporis satiat caritatem.' O.-R.: 'quam tamen caritatem tantam praesentit futuram cui nec possit ex integro satis fieri.'

Rom. xvi 16. Both commentators refer to the kiss of Judas.

Rom. xvi 20. Both commentators quote the Gospel passage about stepping on serpents and scorpions.

Chrysostom

Long ago Simon declared: 'il [Pélage] suit d'ordinaire les interpretations des Peres Grecs, principalement celles de Saint Chrysostôme[1],' and recently Zahn has repeated the statement;

[1] *Histoire critique des...Commentateurs*, p. 242.

'Pel....griech. Ausleger, im Gal. besonders unverkennbar den Chrys., berücksichtigt hat[1].' There is no need to elaborate the proof of this: a few illustrations will suffice[2]. According to Zahn, Pelagius read in Rome about 404 the commentary of Chrysostom on Galatians, which was written before 398[3].

Pelagius's identification of 'Predestination' with 'Foreknowledge' (Rom. viii 29) is traced by Simon to the Greeks[4], but this statement must now be qualified by Dr Smith's discovery of this doctrine in Ambrosiaster and Augustine[5].

Pel. in Rom. viiii 16: 'hic interrogantis uoce utitur et redarguentis potius quam negantis': Chrys. (t. IX p. 614 B Bened.): *πάλιν ἑτέραν ἀντίθεσιν εἰσάγων, καὶ λέγων 'ἄρα οὖν οὐ τοῦ θέλοντος' κτλ....εἶτα πάλιν ἀντίθεσιν ἐπάγει· 'ἄρα οὖν ὃν θέλει ἐλεεῖ' κτλ.*[6]

Pel. in Phil. iiii 15: 'dantes carnalia et spiritalia accipientes.' Chrys. (t. XI p. 313 C Bened.) (*ἐκοινώνησαν*) *εἰς λόγον δόσεως τῶν σαρκικῶν, καὶ λήψεως τῶν πνευματικῶν.*

Pel. in 2 Thess. i 10: 'quia multi de die illo nostro testimonio credidistis.' Chrys. (t. XI p. 522 A): *μέλλων δὲ ὑπὲρ πάσης τῆς ζωῆς σου λόγον διδόναι, καὶ εὐθύνας ὑπέχειν, οὐδὲ ἄλλων σε ἀναμιμνησκόντων ὑπὲρ τῆς δίκης ἀνέχῃ; κτλ.* Both thus refer this clause to the Day of Judgment. See Swete on Theod.-Mops. *ad loc.* Pel. and Chrys. seem to be the only two ancients who regard *in die illo* as part of the preceding clause.

Pel. in 2 Thess. ii 3: 'nisi antichristus uenerit, non ueniet Christus. quod autem "discessio" hic dicit, alibi eum "refugam" appellauit in Latinis exemplaribus: utrumque autem ita intellegendum est quod "nisi uenerit refuga" ueritatis, siue sui principatus desertor, siue discessio gentium a regno Romano, sicut in Danihelo per bestiae imaginem dicit.' Chrys. (t. XI p. 525 B): *περὶ τοῦ ἀντιχρίστου ἐνταῦθα διαλέγεται, καὶ μεγάλα ἀποκαλύπτει μυστήρια. Τί ἐστιν 'ἡ ἀποστασία'; αὐτὸν καλεῖ ἀποστασίαν, ὡς πολλοὺς*

[1] Zahn, *Der Brief d. Paulus a. die Galater* 2 Aufl. (Leipz. 1907) p. 25.

[2] Incidentally a considerable number of agreements between Pel. and Chrys. will be found stated in the notes to Swete's *Theodore of Mopsuestia*.

[3] Zahn, *ibid.* [4] Simon, p. 242.

[5] *J.T.S.* vol. XIX pp. 201 f.

[6] Simon, p. 242, who here however cites the interpolator of Pel., who is much fuller than Pel. himself. Elsewhere also Simon's arguments are invalidated somewhat because he could not distinguish interpolations from the original Pelagius.

μέλλοντα ἀπολλύναι καὶ ἀφιστᾶν. Later Chrys. denies the identity of Antichrist and Satan. Theod.-Mops. and others follow Chrys.

Pel. in 1 Tim. iii 11 started in the West an interpretation which is found in Chrys. etc. The quotations are: 'similiter eas ut diaconos eligi iubet: unde intellegitur quod de his dicat quas adhuc hodie in oriente diaconissas appellant.' Chrys. (t. XI p. 605 A): *'γυναῖκας ὡσαύτως.' διακόνους φησίν...περὶ τῶν τὸ ἀξίωμα τῆς διακονίας ἐχουσῶν φησίν.* So Theod.-Mops.

Many more parallels between Pelagius and Chrysostom might be adduced, as is done by Swete in his notes to Theodore of Mopsuestia, but I have tried as far as possible to avoid mentioning cases where Theodore and others support Chrysostom's view. For our purpose it is necessary especially to collect instances that lack further Greek support. The fact that Pelagius was really influenced by Greek authors is nowhere more conspicuously evident than in his treatment of the difficult phrase in Phil. ii 6 *non rapinam arbitratus est esse se aequalem deo.* A reference to Lightfoot's well known catena of patristic opinion on this clause shows that Pelagius with his 'quod erat humilitate celauit, dans nobis exemplum ne in his gloriemur quae forsitan non habemus' belongs to the Greeks, and not to the Latins.

THEODORE OF MOPSUESTIA

Theodore of Mopsuestia, who lived till 428, held Pelagian views, was personally acquainted with Pelagius, and wrote in Greek a commentary on all the Epistles of St Paul. We should expect to find parallels between such a commentary and the exposition of Pelagius. Unfortunately Theodore's commentary, as a connected work, has perished, except in a Latin translation of the ten shorter epistles, Galatians to Philemon[1]. The preservation of even this portion is due to the happy accident that some mediaeval scholar possessed an imperfect Ambrosiaster, and somehow managed to complete it by acquiring an anonymous copy of the Latin Theodore, which he caused to be copied as a continuation of Ambrosiaster on Romans, First and Second Corinthians.

The fact that there are parallels between the Latin Theodore and the Pseudo-Jerome has naturally not escaped Professor Swete,

[1] Portions are preserved also in Isho'dad of Merv (Camb. 1916).

whose edition of the Latin Theodore is a light on the path of the investigator of patristic exegesis. Our task is greatly simplified by his labours, and nothing need be done to show that there is a relationship between the two commentaries, save to make a critical revision of his Pseudo-Jerome text and to add from his notes some instances which he refrained from quoting in his introduction[1]. It must, however, be remembered that Theodore was acquainted with the earlier work of Diodorus of Tarsus[2] and of Chrysostom[3], a fact which complicates investigation.

It is a more difficult question which of the two, if either, is the borrower. *A priori*, if borrowing there has been, it is more likely to have been on the side of the Latin Pelagius than of the Greek Theodore. But Theodore knew some Latin[4], and in view of the intimacy of the two men the other possibility cannot be denied. We have no information as to the date of Theodore's commentary to help us to a decision.

Gal. ii 2. Pel.: '"ne forte"...hoc non est dubitantis.' Theod.: 'nam quod dicitur "ne quoquo modo" non dubitationis causa dicitur.'

Gal. vi 11. Pel.: 'intellegite quam non timeam qui litteras mea manu perscripsi.' Theod.: 'designans quoniam neque ueretur eos, neque negat illa sua esse quae dicit.' (The Greek also survives.)

Eph. i 21. Pel.: 'quia unum est iam cum deo adsumptus homo.' Theod.: 'de suscepto homine id dicens, eo quod propter inhabitantem in eum naturam dei uerbi ab omnibus habet adorari.'

Phil. i 2. Pel.: 'hic "episcopos" presbyteros intellegimus: non enim in una ciuitate plures episcopi esse potuissent.' Theod.: '"episcopos" dixit illos qui nunc presbyteri dicuntur;...nec enim ordinis erat multos in una ciuitate esse illos qui nunc episcopi nuncupantur.'

Phil. ii 5 ff. Pel.: 'multi praeterea hunc locum ita intellegunt quod secundum diuinitatem se humiliauerit Christus..."formam serui" hoc est, naturam hominis induendo..."semet ipsum exinaniuit": quod erat humilitate celauit.' Theod.: 'deus uerbum talia sponte fecisse uidebatur ita ut pro aliorum salute praehonorandam omnibus existimaret humilitatem..."formam" autem "serui," ut dicat

[1] Vol. I pp. lxxiv—lxxvi. [2] See Swete, vol. I pp. lxxiii f.

[3] Swete, vol. I p. lxxii; Wohlenberg ed. of Pastoral Epistles (Leipzig, 1906) p. 76.

[4] As his note on 2 Tim. iiii 13 (μεμβοάνας) shows.

"naturam serui," humanam sic uocans naturam.'...'(τὸ οὖν "ἑαυτὸν ἐκένωσεν," ἀντὶ τοῦ οὐκ ἔδειξεν ἑαυτόν...τὴν ἀξίαν ἐκείνην ἀπέκρυψεν).'

Phil. ii 10. Pel.: 'ut omnes simul hominem cum uerbo adorent adsumptum.' Theod.: 'ut omnes illum adorent...propter illam copulationem quam habet ad unigenitum.'

Phil. iii 1. Pel.: 'eadem repetere quae iam praesens dixeram.' Theod.: 'non quia iam scripserat dicit...sed quia docuerat eos instantissime...frequenter uobis locutus sum.' (The Greek exists.)

1 Thess. ii 7. Pel.: 'id est, ut de euangelio uiueremus.' Theod.: 'magis enim erat ut et habentes potestatem quasi apostoli illa quae ad usus necesse habebant sibi acciperent' (μεῖζον γὰρ ἦν τὸ καὶ ἔχοντας ἐξουσίαν ὡς ἀποστόλους τὰ πρὸς τὴν χρείαν λαμβάνειν).

1 Thess. iiii 6. Pel.: 'in quolibet negotio nequis alterum fraudet.' Theod.: 'pudicissime quidem dixit "in negotio"' *etc.*

2 Thess. ii 1. Pel.: '"et nostrae congregationis in ipsum." quando a quattuor uentis caeli congregabuntur electi, ut, ubi fuerit corpus, illic concurrant et aquilae.' Theod.: 'hoc ergo dicit: "et nostram congregationem ad eum," dicit etenim Christi aduentum et congregationem nostram tunc ad eum futuram.' (ὅτι περὶ τῆς Χριστοῦ παρουσίας καὶ τῆς ἡμῶν ἐπ' αὐτὸν ἐκείνης ἐπισυναγωγῆς.)

Col. i 15. Pel.: '"primogenitus" secundum adsumpti hominis formam, non tempore, sed honore, iuxta illud: "filius meus primogenitus Istrahel."' Theod.: '"primogenitus" non tempore dicitur solum, sed et praehonoratione frequenter.' (The Greek exists.)

1 Tim. i 15. Pel.: 'quem omnes credant et omnium conscientiae uerum esse cognoscant.' Theod.: 'omnis quicumque fuerit ille recipiet, credens quia deus homines misericordia saluat...omnis autem quicumque ille delectatur in hisce sermonibus....'

1 Tim. ii 12. Pel.: 'publice non permittit: nam filium uel fratrem debet docere priuatim.' Theod.: 'neque uetabat mulieres ut impios maritos suos ad pietatem uel inuitarent uel docerent, aut pios inconuenienter conuersantes ad opera inuitarent uirtutum.'

1 Tim. iii 1. Pel.: 'ad boni operis desiderium eum prouocat, non honoris.' Theod.: 'bene "opus" dixit et non dignitatem.'

1 Tim. v 3. Pel.: 'necessaria praebendo uel solaciis fouendo.' Theod.: 'quod hoc in loco dixit: "honora," hoc est, diligentiam illis adhibe,' *etc.*

1 Tim. v 9: Pel. confuses between the orders of widows and deaconesses, and Theod. refers to those that fall into this error. Pel.: 'tales uoluit eligi diaconissas, quae omnibus essent exempla uiuendi.' Theod.: 'quidam uero non considerantes quam ob causam aetatem uoluerit significari, hoc statuerunt utrumnam mulieres diaconissas ante hanc aetatem ordinari minime conueniat.' If we could be certain that Theod. was here criticizing Pelagius, the question of priority would be settled. Then we might argue that Pel. had come into Theod.'s hands at a time when he had got through all the epistles down to Colossians; for it is from 1 Thessalonians onwards that parallels between the two begin to be fairly numerous. Other passages where Pel. and Theod. disagree, are 2 Thess. i 8—10; Tit. i 5—7, ii 14.

1 Tim. v 24—25. Pel.: '"*subsequitur* eorum in futuro iudicium"... "quae aliter se habent"...etiam quae ad tempus latent, non possunt diutius occultari.' Theod.: 'sicut delinquentium hominum et non recte uiuentium delicta manifesta sunt, quae necessarie illis in futuro saeculo poenas sunt prouisura, licet si et faciant aliqua quae multos latere poterunt' *etc.* (*ὥσπερ τὰ τῶν οὐκ εὖ βιούντων ἀνθρώπων πταίσματα πρόδηλά ἐστιν ἀναγκαίως τὴν ἐπὶ τοῦ μέλλοντος αἰῶνος τιμωρίαν αὐτοῖς ἐπάγοντα, εἰ καὶ* (*ὡς εἰκός*) *τινὰ παρ' αὐτῶν λανθάνει τοὺς πολλούς κτλ.*)

1 Tim. vi 6. Pel.: '"cum sufficientia" non luxuriae, sed naturae.' Theod.: 'necessitatibus nostris sufficientes.'

1 Tim. vi 20. Pel.: 'fidei "custodi depositum."' Theod.: '"custodi" fidem.'

2 Tim. ii 6. Pel.: 'ostendit eum primitias fructuum a populo debere percipere, praeter mercedem quam a domino messis accipiet in futuro.' Theod.: 'quae ad usum tuum necessarie pertinent, indiscrete adsequere a fidelibus qui praestant tibi,' *etc.*

2 Tim. ii 8. Pel.: 'hoc contra illos qui carnis resurrectionem negantes, consequenter etiam Christi negabant.' Theod.: 'ita ut nec resurrectio uera facta esse susciperetur; qui enim fieri poterat ut uera crederetur resurrectio, si caro uera ratione non fuisset sumpta?' *etc.*

2 Tim. ii 15. Pel.: 'ille "recte tractat" qui dicta sua exemplo confirmat.' Theod.: 'recto edoce instituto, et non pigeas laborem pro his subire.'

Tit. i 7. Pel.: 'ipsum dicit "episcopum" quem superius presbyterum nominauit.' Theod.: 'nam dum dicit: "ut constituas... presbyteros," et de presbyteris disputans adiecit: "oportet enim episcopum...."'

Tit. i 15. Pel.: '"coinquinati et infideles" sunt qui non credunt iugum legis a collo credentium dominum abstulisse.' Theod.: 'siquis uero per suam incredulitatem habet conscientiam coinquinatam, nihil mundum esse poterit illi qui talis est.' (Gk. also.)

Tit. iii 15. Pel.: 'qui nos fideliter amant. Siue: Qui fidei causa nos diligunt.' Theod.: 'qui per fidei familiaritatem cum eo iunctas amicitias habere uidebantur.'

Subsidiary Sources

This paragraph is intended to include merely a few notes that have occurred to me in the course of repeated readings. The first and second concern the subject-matter, the remainder have to do with the expression, and reflect Pelagius's reading of classical literature.

Pel. in Eph. ii 15: '"euacuans." per solam fidem iustificans et moralia sola decernens.' Severianus, quoted by Swete, *Theod.-Mops.* ad loc.: 'ἐν δόγμασιν τοῖς ἰδίοις [explaining these to be the principles of Christian morality].'

Pel. in 2 Tim. ii 18: '"cancer" esse dicitur uulnus quod in mammillis nascitur feminarum, quibus nisi cito subuentum fuerit, cum uirus ad cor serpendo peruenerit, nullum ultra remedium est.' This is evidently a quotation or a recollection of some medical work[1], cf. Aug. ciu. dei XXII 8 (p. 570, ll. 14 ff. Domb.[3]): 'Innocentia, religiosissima femina,...in mamilla cancrum habebat, rem, sicut medici dicunt, nullis medicamentis sanabilem[2].'

The following appear to be undoubted recollections of classical reading:

Lucretius: I 149—150 'principium cuius hinc nobis exordia sumet, | nullam rem e nilo gigni diuinitus umquam' (cf. III

[1] *Thes. Ling. Lat.* s.v. *cancer*, vol. III p. 231, esp. ll. 47 ff., has a number of references, going as far back as Ov. *met.* ii 825, to the incurableness of this disease.

[2] From which Isid. *Etym.* iv 8 § 14 comes.

417 seqq.): Pel. in Col. ii 8 'philosophos...dicentes ex nihilo fieri nihil posse': I 304 'tangere enim et tangi, nisi corpus, nulla potest res': Pel. in 1 Cor. vii 4 'corpus dicitur omne quod tangitur.' Knowledge of Lucretius is particularly interesting, for in the patristic period writers range between the exhaustive knowledge shown by Arnobius and the absolute ignorance shown by the majority. Tertullian also (*adu. Marc.* IIII 8, *De An.* 5) quotes this verse.

Virgil: IIII 174, 188 'fama, malum qua non aliud uelocius ullum...tam ficti prauique tenax quam nuntia ueri': Pel. in 1 Thess. i 8 'natura famae haec est, ut siue bonum siue malum nuntians ubique omni celeritate discurrat.' IIII 569—570 'uarium et mutabile semper femina': Pel. in 1 Cor. xvi 13 'muliebris omnis inconstantia et uarietas iudicatur.' All Latin writers posterior to Virgil show more or less of his influence.

Horace: epist. II 1, 250—1 'sermones...repentis per humum': Pel. in 2 Cor. iiii 2 'uerbo dei sermonem uilem admiscent et per terram repentem[1].'

Juvenal: 1, 142 'poena tamen praesens': Pel. in Gal. v 6 'praesentem metuit poenam[2].' (Cf. also Cic. and Plin., quoted by Mayor, and Sen. *Phaedr.* 162.) We know from Ammian that Juvenal was much read in the second half of the fourth century[3].

[1] A reference to *mulcere* in lexx. will suggest possible imitation of other poetical passages by Pel. in 1 Cor. xiiii 7.

[2] In his *epist. ad Demetr.* 25 (Migne, *P.L.* xxx 40 D) *uacuus uiator et nudus non timet latronis insidias* is an echo of Iuu. 10, 22 *cantabit uacuus coram latrone uiator.*

[3] Cf. Duff's *Juvenal*, p. li.

CHAPTER VI

THE MATERIALS FOR THE RECONSTRUCTION OF THE TEXT OF THE COMMENTARY, AND THEIR INTERRELATIONS

INTRODUCTION

CERTAIN of the existing authorities for the reconstruction of the text of Pelagius have already become partially known to the reader in the course of the discussion in the second chapter, but it is necessary to give here a fuller account of these, and at the same time to consider others. Further authorities, such as a number of late mediaeval compilations, based probably on some manuscripts of Pseudo-Jerome, it has not been possible to consider, for the simple reason that some limit must be set to these researches. I believe, however, that I have secured a broad and sound enough basis for the constitution of the text, in the authorities now to be described.

The first place rightly belongs to the two (three) manuscripts of the original form, with the Vatican and Freiburg fragments. Then we shall take the St Gall MS 73, the Paris MS 653, the two families of Pseudo-Jerome MSS, and Cassiodorus. Finally must come the Würzburg and other glosses, Claudius of Turin, Zmaragdus of St Mihiel, Sedulius Scottus of Liége, Haymo of Auxerre, and later authorities. An attempt will be made to show the interrelationship of various authorities and to estimate their relative value.

(*a*) THE MANUSCRIPTS OF THE ORIGINAL FORM

(1) *Codex Augiensis CXIX at Karlsruhe* (**A**)

The manuscript is thus described by the late Dr Alfred Holder in his great catalogue, *Die Reichenauer Handschriften beschrieben und erläutert, I*[er] *Band, Die Pergamenthandschriften* (Leipzig, 1906) pp. 303 f., as modified in *II*[er] *Band* (1914), pp. 666 f.

CXIX. 164 folia (2 columns, with 37, 36, 35, 33 lines to the page), measuring 302 by 221 mm., saec VIII ex.—IX in. Five hands:

the fifth scribe an old Irishman: written on the Continent; archetype Italian uncials[1] of the fifth or sixth century; folia 149—164 (1 column and 33 lines to the page), saec. X.

f. 1—8 = 1 quaternion I (a);

9 10 11 x 12 13 x | 14 x 15 16 x x 17 B;

18—33 = 2 quaternions CD;

34 x 35 36 37 | 38 39 x 40 41 U;

42—49 = 1 quaternion; 50—57 = 1 quaternion VII;

58 59 60 61 | x 62 63 64;

65 66 x 67 68 | 69 70 71 x 72 UIIII;

73 74 75 76 | 77 78 x 79;

80—87 = 1 quaternion; 88—95 = 1 quaternion XII;

96 97 x 98 | 99 100 101 102;

103—110 = 1 quaternion; 111—142 = 4 quaternions;

143 144 145 146 | 147 148 x x;

149—164 = 2 quaternions.

Pelagii commentarii in epistulas Pauli. Cf. Alexander Souter, *The Commentary of Pelagius on the Epistles of Paul* [from the *Proceedings of the British Academy*, vol. II (Ld. 1907)] pp. 15—18, 25—27. *The Journal of Theological Studies*, vol. VIII (1907) pp. 535—536.

[1] I should now rather say 'half-uncials': see below.

f. **3, 1.** Primum quęritur quare post euangelium: quae supplementum legis sunt et in quibus nobis exempla et pręcepta uiuendi plenissime digesta sunt uoluerit apostolus has epistulas ad singulas ecclesias destinare ut initią nascentis ecclesię nouis causis.... (**147′ 1**)...excipit apostolus quos salutet;

Explicit ad Titum incipit ad Philemonem.

Cui apostolus a Roma...debeamus.

Paulus uinctus...(**148, 2**)...fidei societate.

Exp*licit* ad Philimonem.

Expositio epistolae ad Hebraeos.

149. Incipit argumentum ad Hebreos.

Inprimis dicendum est cur apostolus...conposuit.

Multifarię multisque modis olim d*eu*s loquens patrib*us* in prophetis;

Ac si dicat per multos...(**164′**)...paenitentię et p*er*seuerentiae; Amen.

Finit expositio epistolae Pauli apostoli ad Hebreos. *above* in nomine s*anct*ae trinitatis semp*er* nobis cum amen trina maigestas d*omi*ni p*er* quem fiat fiat.

1′. ferur | ferunt | ferunt Ophyr conuexa.

2. omnia mihi licent sed non omnia expediu(nt).

3. lib*er* mon*asterii* Augie maioris.

Title on the cover Expo*siti*ones in epp*isto*las Pauli ad Ro*manos*, Cor*inthios*, Galath*as*, Ephe*sios*, Philippen*ses* Tesallon*icenses* Colocen*ses* Thimoth*eum* Titum Philomone*m* Ebreos.

Wooden cover, covered with grey leather; 2 leather clasps.

It is of some importance to show how Holder in 1914 arrived at certain of the conclusions stated above. Holder's catalogue of the Reichenau manuscripts at Karlsruhe was itself in MS for a considerable period before it was printed, and I had been privileged to handle and consult it at Karlsruhe in that form in 1901, when engaged on the Ambrosiaster *Quaestiones*. Early in 1905 Dr C. H. Turner was at Karlsruhe pursuing his own researches, but found time to note from Holder's MS catalogue that there was in the Reichenau collection an anonymous manuscript of "the Pseudo-Primasius commentary." I have in my possession the first proof (1905) of the printed catalogue, in which MS CXIX is described as such. I welcomed the information Dr Turner kindly gave me, and also the proof-sheet which my friend Holder sent me at my request. I saw immediately that the description of the MS was incorrect, and wrote to Dr Holder at once that his MS must be either a pure Pelagius or an anonymous Pseudo-Jerome. The loan of the MS, for which I asked, was refused by the Baden Minister of Public Instruction, and it was therefore necessary to consult it on the spot. A morning's work in July 1906 sufficed to show that a pure Pelagius had at last been discovered. I convinced Holder that his ascription was wrong, and in the first volume of the catalogue, as published in September 1906, the manuscript is described as: (s. IX):

Pelagii (Walahfridi Strabi) **commentarii in epistulas Pauli.**

During the interval between that date and 1914 he advanced yet further, put the date back from saec. IX to saec. VIII ex.—IX in., accepted my statements that five scribes wrote the MS on the Continent, of whom one was an Irishman, and that the archetype was an Italian uncial of the fifth or sixth century, and struck out 'Walahfridi Strabi' altogether.

These are the facts, and it has been necessary to state them exactly, because from the way in which the Abbé Mangenot writes, the reader would almost certainly infer that Holder had first described the manuscript in the published catalogue as Pelagius, and that then, and not till then, had I come to know of the manuscript as such: whereas my collation of it was complete at least two and a half weeks before the catalogue was published[1]. An apology is perhaps neccssary for insisting so strongly on a personal claim.

From the collotype of one page which was published in the seventh volume of the *Proceedings of the British Academy*[2], the reader will see that the script in which it is written is the ordinary pre-Caroline minuscule of the district Murbach-Reichenau-St Gallen-Chur, to which Traube has called attention[3]. It need not

[1] 'Holder signala un nouveau manuscrit de l'*Expositio* de Pélage, du IXe siècle... Alexandre Souter entreprit une édition critique' (Mangenot in *Revue du Clergé français* for 1916, p. 20 of *tirage à part*). The collation was completed on Aug. 14, 1906; the catalogue appeared in Sept. 1906.

[2] The frontispiece of my second paper in the *Proceedings* (p. 1=261).

[3] *Abhandlungen d. Kgl. Bayer. Akad. der Wiss., philos.-philol. u. histor. Kl.* Bd. XXV (2) (1910) p. 52.

be doubted that the MS was written at Reichenau itself about the end of the eighth or the beginning of the ninth century.

The scribes partition the work between them thus:

(1) ff. 3—33 (*gentium plenitudo ut*).

(2) ff. 34—59 b (*pater filius ad ettate*).

(3) ff. 59 va—100 a (*et ideo ipse paries ini-*).

(4) ff. 100 b—106 a l. 4 (*uere est in uobis*).

(5) ff. 106 a l. 4—148 b.

(3) is the most beautiful of all, (4) was possibly Irish, and (5) was, as has been said, Irish: the forms of the capitals *P* (e.g. f. 126 a), *B* (e.g. f. 133 va) and *S*, for example, are Irish, and there is an Irish *r* on fol. 124 a.

The scribes make very little use of abbreviation or contraction. The following list[1] must be approximately complete:

autem aū (first and third and fifth scribes), aūt (second and fifth scribes, corrector of fifth scribe)
Christus xp̄s
deus ds̄
dicit dic̄
dixit dix̄
dominus dom̄ (second scribe, six times), dn̄s
eius ēs[2] (ff. 111 vb, 114 b)
esse e͞e
est ē
fratres fr̄s (third scribe)
Iesus ih̄f
Istrahel isral̄ (second scribe, twice), isrl̄ (third scribe), irl̄ (fifth scribe, f. 126 vb)
meus ms̄ (fifth scribe, end of line)
uobis uob̄ (third scribe)
non n̄
noster N̄· = *nostrum* (f. 40 va) ·N̄· = *nostri* (f. 101 va)
nt̄ (third scribe, f. 65 b, 73 va, 74 vb, 76 a, 92 vb, also fifth scribe): so ut̄ (= 71 b)
nī, nm̄
nr̄m (rare), nr͞ae, nr͞as: so ur̄m, ur͞ae
nrūm: so urūm (fifth scribe only)
Nos (?) = *nostram* (f. 114 vb)
not̄ = *noster* (f. 119 va)[3]
omnes om̄
per ꝑ
post p’, p̓ (third scribe)
prae p̄ (third scribe only)
pro ꝓ
propter pp̄t (second and third scribes), pp̄ (third scribe, f. 70 a only)
quae q:· qu; q;·
que q; q: q̨ (second scribe only, f. 50 va, vb)
qui qͥ (third scribe only)
quod qd̄ (end of line three times, first scribe), q̑od (second scribe)
quoniam qm̄ (first scribe only, rarely), qn̄m (first and third scribes only), qūo (second, third and fifth scribes)
saeculum scl̄m
sanctus sc̄s
sicut sic̄ (first scribe)
spiritus sp̄s
sunt s̄
uel ul̄ (first scribe)
uero uō (third scribe, end of line)

[1] I should mention here once for all that the lists of abbreviations given in this book were put at the disposal of Prof. W. M. Lindsay for his *Notae Latinae* (Cambridge, 1915).

[2] The only instances known to Lindsay (*Notae Latinae*, p. xv); it is on the analogy of hs̄ (*huius*) c͞s (*cuius*).

[3] See Traube, *Nomina Sacra*, p. 234.

SYLLABLE SYMBOLS:

con c̄ (third and fifth scribes only)
en m̄ 'men' (first scribe only)
er t̄ 'ter,' ū 'uer' (third scribe only)
is b̄ 'bis,' l̄ 'lis' (third scribe only)
it c̄ x̄ (first scribe)
m suprascript stroke
rum ꝝ (second and third scribes), ꝝ (fifth scribe)
runt r̄ (first scribe)
ur t' (second, third and fifth scribes), (t^2 third scribe) (m̃r 'mur,' end of line)
us b; m; ' (third scribe) mꝫ (third scribe) l̄=lus (end of line, third scribe) lꝫ (f. 79 va) (third scribe)

Other palaeographical features of interest are these. The long i is never used. The ligature *ti* is used irrespective of the distinction between assibilated and unassibilated *ti*: thus in *inflati* and *generatis*, as well as in *gratiae*. The following combinations of letters are sometimes in ligature, the first and second very often: *ri*, *nt*, *at*, *an*: the second scribe puts *us* in ligature once at the end of the line: the ę for *ae* is quite often found. All the scribes employ a big Z, which lies on the line, with only the tail below.

Certain of these abbreviations shed light on the character of the MS from which the Reichenau MS was copied.

dōm̄ = *dominus* (ff. 36 va, vb, 37 va, 38 b, 40 va, 47 vb, 79 b) comes straight from the archetype, being almost obsolete at the end of the eighth, and the beginning of the ninth century. It is in fact a specialty of the fourth, fifth, sixth and seventh centuries[1].

n̄ = any case of *noster* (ff. 40 va, 101 va, 141 va) was rarely used after the middle of the sixth century, and never naturally after the seventh[2].

This evidence is borne out by instances of the preservation of really old orthography which had been given up long before the date of our MS.

The long forms *idololatria* etc. are rarely found in MSS of this date, but are almost invariable[3] in our codex (e.g. ff. 6 vb, 8 b, va, 9 a, 63 a). The solitary[4] MS of Lucifer of Cagliari (cod. Vatic. 133, saec. IX—X), the Laudian MS misc. 130 (saec. IX—X) of Augustine *De Baptismo*, also furnish it. There can be little doubt, I think,

[1] See Traube, *Nomina Sacra* (München, 1907) pp. 168 ff.

[2] The latest examples known to me (apart from those in Traube *op. cit.* p. 207, and one or two noted below) are Köln MS CCXII (saec. VII ex.) (Canons) in Chroust's *Monumenta Palaeographica* no. 298 where N̄ occurs for *noster* and *nostrum*, and Milan, Ambros. O 210 Sup. (saec. VI ex.) (*Acta Archelai*, ed. Beeson (Lpz. 1906) p. xx).

[3] An exception, f. 96 a. [4] But see now *Rev. Bénéd.* XXXIII (1921) pp. 124 ff.

that the syncopated form is not really ancient. It would be interesting to learn when it was first used by authors; hardly, I fancy, before the middle of the fifth century, at the earliest.

The form *Istrahel* (ff. 14 a, 15 a) is also very significant. It is the most ancient of all Latin spellings of this word, and was probably soon obsolete[1].

The second declension form *Danihelo* (f. 14 a, 123 vb) is very ancient and most reassuring[2] (cf. f. 69 b).

I should have little hesitation in assigning the archetype of our MS to the fifth or sixth century, and in view of its excellence, to Italy. Our *codex* is tentatively identified by Holder with no. 201 in the catalogue of the Reichenau collection, which was written between 842 and 850, and is now preserved at Donaueschingen[3]. Lest any one should doubt the probability of connexion between Reichenau and Italy, it may be pointed out that MS Augiensis LVII was written in North Italy in the second half of the eighth century[4]. There are also other indications pointing the same way[5].

A study of the textual corruptions in the manuscript suggests the character of its archetype:

(1) *a* for *u*: *totam, asu, auditas, intellegant, factas, negaturam,* instead of *totum, usu, auditus, intellegunt, factus, negaturum,* respectively.

(2) *u* for *a*: *intellectu, erunt,* for *intellecta, erant.*

(3) *e* for *o*: *deuteresis* bis, *macedene, salomene,* for *deuterosis* bis, *macedone, salomone.*

(4) *a* for *o*: *confundar, laboriase,* for *confundor, laboriose.*

(5) *a* for *tu*: *confirmear,* for *confirmetur.*

(6) *e* for *c*: *cheneris,* for *chencris.*

[1] See Traube, *Nomina Sacra,* p. 106. It must, however, be remembered that the abbreviations of this word are very frequent and disguise the spelling of archetypes.

[2] See C. H. Turner in *Journ. Theol. Stud.* vol. VI (1904—5) p. 253.

[3] *Die Reichenauer Handschriften* u.s.w., Bd. III (1) (1916) p. 100.

[4] Holder's article 'Der Isidorus-Codex Augiensis LVII der gr. Hof- und Landesbibliothek in Karlsruhe' in *Mélanges offerts à M. Émile Chatelain* (Paris 1910), of which article I possess by Holder's kindness a copy corrected in his own hand.

[5] The Ambrose MS, formerly at Reichenau, now at St Paul in Carinthia, an uncial of the period between 400 and 700, was perhaps written at Verona (*Die Reichenauer Handschriften,* Bd. III (2) (1917) p. 127). Also, Codex Augiensis CIX (saec. IX in.) was copied from a sixth century Beneventan original (*op. cit.* Bd. I (1906) p. 284).

(7) *u* for *o*: *bonus, -rus, nouatianus*, for *bonos, -ros, nouatianos.*

(8) *e* for *u*: *credentur* for *creduntur.*

(9) *o* for *u*: *mortuos* for *mortuus*, *infructoosi* for *infructuosi*, *uoluntariom* for *uoluntarium*, *obsequio* for *obsequium.*

(10) *c* for *g*: *cratiam, dilicatis*, for *gratiam, diligatis.*

(11) *p* for *f*: *reputent* for *refutent.*

(12) *r* for *s*: *redderemur* for *redderemus.*

Most of these corruptions can be best explained by the use of a half-uncial archetype: (10), however, would occur more easily at the uncial stage. We may therefore assume that the immediate ancestor of our MS was a double-columned manuscript in half-uncial writing.

A general study of the orthography of a manuscript like this leads one to certain conclusions as to the orthography of its original. If it be found that five pre-Caroline scribes agree in their spelling of a particular word, there is little doubt that the spelling they give was that of the archetype. There is in this codex a certain amount of consistency, combined with a certain amount of inconsistency. The following spellings, either because they are found everywhere in our MS, or because they are of such special excellence that they would not be known to the scribe apart from his exemplar, may be assigned with certainty to our Italian fifth- or sixth-century half uncial manuscript.

The usual final *d* in certain words appears almost everywhere as *t*: *aliquit, aliut, aput, athuc*[1], *illut, numquit, quitquit, siquit*; but *istud* (probably because of the preceding *t*).

Hiesus, thus written in full, is the form employed for 'Joshua' and for 'Jesus who is also called Justus': in contrast to the abbreviated form, employed for 'Jesus,' as a sign of sanctity[2].

suscribere (twice), *mercennarius, discidium, gluttire, balbuttire, afluere*[3] (and derivatives), *condicio* (less often than *conditio*), *solacium* (oftener than *solatium*), *haereticus* (whereas most MSS have the less

[1] Cf. *Dauit* at least once. The form *athuc* is not mentioned by the *Thesaurus*.

[2] Traube discovered that these sacred names were abbreviated as a sign of sanctity. A confirmation, not mentioned, I think, by Traube, is to be found in the N.T. Greek minuscules 118 and 209, which in Matth. xxvii 16 and 17 write the name *Jesus* in full in the case of Ἰησοῦν Βαραββᾶν.

[3] See the notable article s.v. in Nettleship's *Contributions to Latin Lexicography* (Oxford, 1889).

correct *hereticus* from ἑρετικός), *susurrio*, are perhaps the most notable cases of good ancient spellings.

It is necessary now to summarise the orthography of MS **A**, which is not in all respects consistent throughout, and the first matter to consider is that of assimilation or dissimilation of prefixes:

ad- adb. *adbreuiare.*

adc. *adcommodare*; but *accipere* (always).

adf. *adferre, adflictio, adfirmare* etc., *adfuit* (always), but *affectus, affligere.*

adg. *adgredi, adgrauare*; but *agnosco* etc. (always).

adl. never; always *allegere, alligare.*

adm. *admittere* always.

adn. *adnuntiare, adnectere* always.

adp. *adpendere, adpetere, adprehendere, adponere, adprobare, adplicare*; but *appellare.*

adq. *adquirere* etc.; never *acq-*, which perhaps did not survive the classical period.

adr. *adrogans* etc., *adridere*; but *arripere.*

ads. *adsistere, adscribere, adseuerare, adsignare, adsumere, adstruere, adsimilare, adsimulare, adserere, adstringere.*

adt. *adtemptare, adtendere, adtestari*; but *attendere* (generally).

con- conl. *conlaudare, conloquium*; but *colloquium, collocare, coligare* (or *-ere*), *collatus* etc.

conm. *conmendare, conmonere*; but *commemorare* etc., *communicare, commonere, commendare* etc.

conp. *conplacere, conparare, conprehendere* etc., *conprobare, conpungere*; but *comparare, comprehendere, compar, comprobare, comperire, compassio, compingere, complecti* etc.

conr. always assimilated, except in *conregno*:—*corroporari, corruere.*

in- (negative): *inmundus* etc., *inlicitus, inmoderate, inmensus, inpudenter, inreprehensibilis* (always), *inremediabiliter*; but *immundus, impius, impudicitia, irritus, immensus, immortalis.*

in- (preposition): *inrigare* (always), *inlatus, inluminare, inritare* etc., *inmittere, inponere, inpendere, inligare*; but *impugnare* (always), *implere* (always), *impetrare* etc. (always), *impendere, impedire, imputare, irritare, immammillis.*

ob- off. (always).

obm. (always).

obp. *obproprium*; but *optemperare* (very ancient).

obt. *obtulerunt* etc. (*obtare*), *obtundere*; but (*optare*), *optinere* (very ancient).

per- unassimilated, as far as used at all.

sub- *subportare*, *subponere*; but *suptilitas*.

exs- versus **ex**: *exsistere*; but *expectare* (always), *expoliare* (always).

On the whole the aspirate is correctly used in this manuscript, but we find exceptions, such as, in single instances: *abentem*, *aesitationibus*, *Iosep*, *exortari*, *catecizare*, *arena*, *pasca* on the one hand, and *hisdem* (twice), *cathecuminus*, *hactu*, *Thimotheus* (a very old spelling), *Sthephanus* (twice), *habundare*, *thorus*, *hillis*, *abhominabilis*, *henim*, *Thabitha*, *Machedonia*, *Honesimus* (twice) on the other.

Ae- and *e*- are confused in the following cases:

-ae for *-e*: *aequae*, *praemere*, *praetium*, *praetiosus*, *aepulari*, *cęlebrare*, *cęna*, *caena*, *speciae*, *depraecari*, *quaerella*, *caelare*, *cęlestae* (bis), *contrariaetas*, *uerae*, *praesbyter* (usually), *praessura*, *cęperant*.

-e for *-ae*: *penuria*, *-ate*, *enigma*, *lesio* (twice), *tedere*, *penitere*, *meror*, *emulatio*.

t for *c*: *audatior*, *mendatium*, *sotius*, *sotietas*, *pernitiosus*, *fallatia*, *iuditium*, *dilitiae*.

c for *t*: *eciam*, *nupciae*, *quociens*, *uicium*, *infancia*.

y for *i*: *Saphyra*, *Sapphyra*, *Helyas*, *elymosina*, *misteryo*, *cybus*.

i for *y*: *praesbiter*, *Listra*, *elymosina*, *elimosina*, *misteryo*, *martirium*, *praesbiterium*, *azimus*, *idolothitus*.

b for *p*: *deturbare*, *benetrare*, *probrius*.
p for *b*: *plasphemare*.
t for *d*: *impetiuit*.
} These confusions are perhaps Irish.

The reduplication of single consonants and the omission of one of a pair of double consonants may be regarded as an Irish, or at least an insular, symptom:

(*a*) *sabatum*, *presura*, *necesitas* (bis), *Philipenses*, *dificilis*, *positis*, *aparere*, *abysus*, but *sabatum* and *Philipenses* need not be so regarded.

(*b*) *Paralippomenon*, *Corrinthii*.

suuam and *euuangelium* are not to be so regarded, however, as they appear in Italy already in the sixth century.

Some spellings may be styled Merovingian, as they were frequent in that period, and were in great part cleared out by the Caroline reform. I refer to *sterelis, agnusco* (and *cognusco*), *crededi* (and such like: third scribe invariably), *mercis* (= *merces*, nom. sing.), *exestimare, prumptus, recipissemus* (and such like).

The interchange of *b* and *u* occurs once or twice.

The reader will find the orthography of this manuscript reflected, as far as possible, in my text. It may not be the orthography of Pelagius, but if it be not that, it is at least the orthography of the century succeeding his. For further particulars of the orthography of this and the other MSS, the reader is referred to the orthographical index in the second volume.

Orthography, particularly the orthography of proper names, and correctness of numbers, are perhaps the severest tests that can be applied to a Latin manuscript. This manuscript answers the former test well, and there is no opportunity to apply the latter. But in the fourth chapter we have already found that the text of the Biblical lemmata has been very thoroughly revised from the form which Pelagius used, and it may be that such revision has not stopped at the lemmata. Our manuscript was evidently copied, and carefully copied, from a clean manuscript, but behind that clean manuscript there must lie a rough copy into which harmonizations with the Vulgate had been inserted, while the original Biblical text was erased to make way for them. Or, if this was not the procedure, the scribe was instructed to keep his eye upon a Vulgate copy of the Epistles, placed in front of him simultaneously with the Pelagius, and to substitute the lemmata from the Vulgate for those which he found in his text of Pelagius. The substitution was not, however, completely made.

A careful study of the textual differences between **A** and **B** is not always to the advantage of **A**. There are cases where **A** is undoubtedly wrong; there are other cases where **A** is under suspicion of error. The differences between **A** and **B**, apart from the Biblical lemmata, are hardly of such moment as to suggest that we are dealing with representatives of two author's editions, as it were. It is safer to suppose that where **A**'s latinity differs from that of **B**, and at the same time lacks the support of any other manuscript, we are in presence of alterations made by some early mediaeval reviser in the interests of what he thought was better Latin. But the text of **A** is, also, on the whole shorter than that of **B**. There are a few passages in **B** which are absent from **A**. Here again, we could hardly suppose two author's editions, since the passages are not numerous, were it not for the fact that the Vatican fragments, where they survive, lack the same passages as are absent from **A**. It would appear then that after all **B** does, in this particular, represent a second (early) edition. In order that the reader may see clearly for himself what these passages are, I have caused all passages that are present in one of the two, but absent from the other, to be enclosed within square brackets.

At the following points, among others, portions are absent from **A** that are present in **B** (and other authorities).

In Rom. iiii 12, 16; vii 5, 6, 14[1], 22; viii 26 *bis*; viiii 16; xiiii 2, 23 *bis*; xv 4, 8; 1 Cor. iiii 12; vi 20; vii 4, 5; xvi 2 etc.; prol. 2 Cor.; 2 Cor. ii 7 etc.

In the following passages, among others, there are errors in the parts given by **A**.

In Rom. viii 17. Here the lemma is given twice, first as *ut et conglorificemur*, second as *ut simul glorificemur*. The first form is due to our Vulgate interpolator, being the Vulgate reading. The second is the Pelagian reading, being that of DF*W *d dem Lucif. Ambst. Ambr.* etc., given by Wordsworth and White.

In Rom. viiii 2. *nec eum mendacii reum* in aeterna *accusatione constituit* **A**, wrongly, for the true reading 'interna.'

In Gal. ii 10. *qui omnia sua* distribuentes *ad apostolorum pedes pretia deponebant* **A**, wrongly, for the true reading 'distrahentes' ('selling').

In Gal. ii 12. *ideo reprehensibilis erat quia se postea propter homines subtrahebat* **A**. This is editing. The true reading is 'non *ideo reprehensibilis erat* quia cum illis edebat sed *quia se postea propter homines subtrahebat*.' Probably the five words were accidentally omitted at some stage from homoeoarcton, and the *non* was then removed to make sense.

In Gal. iiii 25. *de qualitatibus locorum uult intellegi diuersitatem*

[1] Here the Vatican fragments join **A**.

meritorum **A**, for the true reading 'testamentorum.' It is a sort of haplography.

In Eph. i 17. *sapientiam a domino deprecatur: nouerat enim eam* adiutricem *omnium esse uirtutum* **A**. This is a very interesting case: **A** is supported by H_1, but the true reading 'matrem' is given by **B**VG and is supported by 'matrimonium' of H_2 (*corr.* C). It is quite in accordance with Pelagius's attitude that he should use the stronger expression: it is equally natural that a reviser should tone it down.

In Eph. i 18. *si diuitias hereditatis dei* uideretis, *omnis terrena nobis* horrebit *hereditas* **A**. The true readings are 'uideritis' (fut. perf. indic.) and 'sordebit,' with **B** and other authorities.

In Eph. iiii 7. *qui ad quam gratiam se aptauerit, ipsam* consequitur **A** etc. The sequence shows that the true reading is 'consequetur,' with V.

In Eph. iiii 22. *qui pristinos errores* desiderat *huius mundi* **AB** etc. The true reading, given by N, R m 3 etc., is 'deserat.'

In 2 Tim. ii 26. *non de dei bonitate dubitat, sed de accipientium* uanitate **A**. The others read rightly 'prauitate.'

(2) *Codex Collegii Balliolensis Oxon.* 157 (**B**)

MS 157 (Arch. E. 5. 2), 217 (219) folia (1 column with 33 lines to the page), measuring 405 by 292 mm., saec. XV med. in a beautiful Italian hand, of which fol. 15 r has been represented by photography, considerably reduced in size[1].

1 flyleaf + 7 (= x 1 2 3 | 4 5 6 7) + 16 regular quaternions

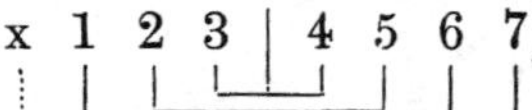

+ 82 leaves with which we are not strictly concerned + 1 flyleaf.

fol. **1** v. 'Ieronimus super ep*isto*las omnes pauli praeterquam ad hebraeos.'

'Hieronymus' 'Liber domus de Balliol in Oxoñ ex dono Willelmi Gray Eliensis epi.'

fol. **2** r. H 12 iudea: Eadem enim passi estis et uos a... manentem substanciam.

[1] *Proceedings of the British Academy* vol. VII (1916) opposite p. 17 of offprint (= p. 277).

EXPLICIT · PROLOGUS : OMNIUM · EPISTOLARUM : BEATI : PAVLI : APOSTOLI : ITEM : ARGUMENTUM : SOLIVS : EPISTOLAE AD ROMANOS (*red*) ⟨R⟩OMANI SUNT QVI :

ex iudeis gentibusque crediderunt

...(f. **2** v) et ad concordiam cohortatur.

EXPLICIT : ARGVMENTVM : EPISTOLAE · BEATI · PAVLI · APOSTOLI AD ROMANOS : INCIPIT EXPLANATIO SANCTI HIERONIMI IN :

(f. **3** r) ȨPISTOLA : AD : ROMANOS (*red*)

⟨P⟩AVLVS ; Querimus quare paulus...

(f. **134** v)...excipit apostolus quos salutet.

EXPLICIT : AEPISTOLA : AD. TITVM : INCIPIT ARGVMENTVM : AD : PHILEMONEM : FOELICITER (*red*)

⟨C⟩ui apostolus a Roma...debeamus

Paulus uinctus...(f. **135** v)...fidei societate.

EXPLICIT AEPISTOLA AD PHILEMONEM (*red*).

(f. **136** r) after five lines' interval begins genuine Jerome on the Epistle to the Galatians, which is followed by genuine Jerome on the Epistle to the Ephesians, which ends this superb codex, written in the most beautiful Italian style on the finest white vellum, with broad margins. It is unfortunate that in this, as in many another manuscript, the coloured initials were never filled in. At the very end occur these words:

Explicit liber beati hieronimi super ȩpistolas pauli apostoli.

One leaf is missing from the beginning, containing most of the *Primum quaeritur* prologue. This appears to be the only part of the MS itself that has perished, but we shall see later that at least two considerable portions of the archetype had perished before our copyist took it in hand.

The orthography of a manuscript like **B** shows three characteristics. It shares the orthography of its date, what may be called the humanistic or renaissance orthography. There are also in certain words affectations of antiquarianism such as some of the scribes of the latter part of the fifteenth century display. But, thirdly, there are certain undoubted relics of the orthography of the archetype. It is only these last that are of special importance to the editor, but for the sake of completeness we must take account of all three styles. I have caused those spellings which I think may be attributed to the archetype, to be printed in thick type: the affectations of antiquarianism are represented in italics. Most of the spellings are recorded in the orthographical index, and are therefore not repeated here.

spiritalis, quicumque, saltim, Arrius, Fotinus, holus, cotidie, Sarra, littera, oblitterare, secuntur, eundem, Eleazarus[1]**, zabulus, obprobrium, caelum, inmundus, inmensus, heremus, Philipus, Philipenses, Tessalonicenses, Colosenses, adtendere, discidium, Sostenes, ammirari, lacrima, inmunditia, scisma, cena, opor-tunus** etc., **carisma, commendaticius, quotienscumque, am-ministratio, abicere, coniti, inreprehensibilis, coartare, Grecus, obaudientia**[2]**, obauditio, obaudire, adsignare, inpetrabilis, in-pendere, arte** (adv.), **eicere, cohercere**[3]**, quicquam, hereditas, subplere, suplere**[4]**, conmilito** (noun), **allegere, alligare, ammo-nere, conlaborare, Filetus, conregnare, mammilla, locuntur, coniunx, temptare, ualitudo.**

quom, quoius, dissentio (noun), *-isare.* The very ancient forms *quom* and *quoius*, which were of course never employed by Pelagius, are an affectation of the scribes of this period, the second half of the fifteenth century[5]. It was a classical, not a theological scribe, who copied this MS to the order of Bp Gray, who visited Padua, Ferrara, and Florence, and who, when he could not obtain a manu-script, was able to pay a professional scribe to copy it[6].

Assimilation of prefixes is the rule: I think all the exceptions are in the list just given: *ti* and *ci* are both found as representatives of the assibilated sound, but *fatiunt, faties* etc. are almost invariable: *i* is often found for *y*, and *y* for *i*: we usually find the intrusive *p* in such cases as *condempnare*; even in *uerumptamen*: *marcesso* occurs for *marcesco.* All these may, I think, be regarded as examples of the average fifteenth century spelling.

[1] Where **A** has *Lazarus* (=vg).

[2] The scribe here betrayed himself by writing this word as two words: if he had imagined that it was another form of *oboedientia*, he would have written *obedientia*.

[3] So in archetype: corrupted to *coherere*.

[4] Cf. the Verona LI (49) uncial MS of Maximus of Turin etc. ed. C. H. Turner (*Journ. Theol. Stud.* vol. XX [1918—19] c. 6 l. 13 (p. 301), c. 11 l. 38 (p. 310)).

[5] Cf. A. E. Housman in the *Journal of Philology*, vol. XXI (1893) p. 180 n. 1, confirmed by A. C. Clark in a private communication to E. A. Lowe, whom I con-sulted.

[6] See the article on him in the *D.N.B.*

There is clear proof that the archetype of our MS was in insular, probably Irish, script, and it is an easy conjecture that this archetype was a Bobbio manuscript, Bobbio being the nearest place where such a manuscript was likely to be found.

The Balliol MS passed through an English hand, to which are due the 'non bene' in the margin opposite *in Rom.* v 4, where also an error is emended by the same hand; the 'quō sola fides sufficiat x̄pıano' in the margin of fol. 82 v; also headlines such as '2 co24,' and the occasional addition in the margin of the numbers of modern chapters. It is interesting to note that ꝗ = quod, while ꝗ = quid: sometimes errors are made in this connexion. A faint cross is often put over words that are corrupt in the manuscript (e.g. in 2 Cor. xiii 11).

The archetype was perhaps in double columns, each about 19 letters broad. This is suggested by the repetition of *membra iunguntur* after the second *corpus* in the comment on Col. ii 19. The manuscript seems to have been at times illegible through age or exposure: for not infrequently one or two words are omitted. Sometimes the omissions are more serious. The Balliol MS is thus written at *in Rom.* i 13 (f. 4 r):

Non enim arbitror ignorare uos fratres quia saepe proposui
uenire ad uos. Per commeantes enim fratres audire potuistis:
et proi
hibitus sum usque ad huc: proibitus hic: occupatus accipitur

Ut aliquid fructum habeam et in uobis...

Similarly at *in Rom.* i 18 (f. 4 v):

ex operibus legis. reuelatur ira dei de cęlo. Incipit ad partem

nouerunt enim homines et benefitia et plagas expectare de caelo:
in om

There is no doubt as to the meaning of this. On both sides of one leaf of the archetype there was a stain obliterating the equivalent of two and a half lines of writing of our MS, or a portion of that size had actually disappeared from the MS altogether[1]. The scribe of the Balliol MS has been very careful to represent the amount of the loss in each case by a blank such as is reproduced above. But these are not the only instances. Another case occurs later in the manuscript.

At *in Rom.* xi 28 (f. 28 v) the Balliol MS reads thus:

bis predico xp̃m. Prohibentes nos

quia deum non penitet abrahae semini promisisse: siue illi sine af-

and at *in Rom.* xi 33 f. (f. 29 r) thus:

cogitatio dispositionum eius. Quis enim cognouit sensum domini

aut quis eius consiliarius fuit ut eius nouerit archana sacramenta. Aut

This lacuna, which is rather longer than the last, is to be explained in the same way. The scribe of the Balliol MS was once again very careful to represent the extent of the loss.

It is quite evident that the archetype of our MS was in a defective condition. But the losses just pointed out are trifling in comparison with others which have to be mentioned.

In Rom. xii 17 'maxillam praebere—*in Rom.* xiii 12 abiciamus simul' had disappeared from the archetype, without leaving any sign in the Balliol MS. Here it is a matter of leaves, not of lines.

In 1 *Cor.* xi 28 'probet autem se ipsum—*in* 1 *Cor.* xv 3 secundum scripturas (*alt.*)' had also disappeared from the archetype, but here the Balliol scribe has written the word 'de est' at the beginning of the omission. A computation will show that this second omission

[1] Perhaps the best known instance of such a stain (and its consequences) is that of Cod. Bodl. Gr. Misc. 251 fol. 25 a, of Arrian's Epictetus (see the photograph in H. Schenkl's edition).

is four times as long[1] as the first. It is easy therefore to conjecture that in the second case a whole quaternion of the archetype had disappeared, and in the first case the two inmost conjugate leaves of another quaternion.

It is possible to tell more about this defective archetype, from a study of the errors in the Balliol MS.

n is written for **u**: some case of *noster* for the same part of *uester* (in the archetype of course in the contractions $\overline{nr}$, $\overline{ur}$, $\overline{ni}$, $\overline{ui}$ or $\overline{nri}$, $\overline{uri}$, so that there is really no confusion of *o* and *e*) on ff. 31 r, 57 r, 63 v, 69 r, 72 v, 79 r, 86 r, 94 r, 99 r, 105 r; *nos* for *uos* on ff. 39 v, 43 r, 49 r, 62 v, 73 r *bis*, 74 v *bis*, 84 r, 90 r, 112 *r*; *nobis* for *uobis* on ff. 79 r, 82 v, 119 v; *ne* for *ue* f. 93 v, *ant* for *aut* f. 116 r, *sine* for *siue* f. 54 v, *angures* for *augures* f. 26 v, *nolunt* for *uolunt* ff. 88 v, 90 r, *noluerit* for *uoluerit* f. 49 r, *boni* for *boui* f. 50 v, *nouit* for *uouit* f. 109 r, *senior* for *seuior* f. 111 v, *anniculo* for *a uinculo* f. 49 r, *ioninianum* for *iouinianum* f. 73 r, cf. *molatur* for *uiolatur* f. 99 v, *praemium* for *praeuium* f. 112 v, *amore* for *aiuniore*: *i.e.* 34 (37) cases.

u is written for **n**: *uos* for *nos* ff. 50 v, 57 v, 113 r; *uobis* for *nobis* ff. 61 r, 67 r, 74 v; case of *uester* for case of *noster* f. 106 r; *aliquo* for *alieno* f. 41 r, *peruitiosae* for *pernitiosae* f. 84 v, *iamues* for *iamnes* f. 112 v, *iusta* for *insta* f. 124 r, *auus* for *anus* f. 124 v, *autem* for *ante* f. 132 r, *siue* for *sine* on ff. 47 r, 50 r, 56 r, 127 r, *diuiuam* for *diuinam* f. 59 r, *ammoueri* for *ammoneri* f. 109 r, *commouet* for *commonet* f. 104 v, *commouentur* for *commonentur* f. 124 v, *scandalizauit* for *scandalizant* f. 41 v, *euacuauit* for *euacuant* f. 38 r: *i.e.* 23 cases.

u is written for **a**: *morabuntur* for *morabantur* f. 8 v, *exierunt* for *exierant* f. 24 v, *poterunt* for *poterant* f. 31 v, *dum querere* for *damnare* f. 32 v, *suum* for *suam* f. 33 r, *bonum* for *bonam* f. 33 r, *crediderunt* for *crediderant* f. 34 v, *seruatum* for *seruatam* f. 44 v, *cognoscunt* for *cognoscant* f. 47 r, *diuinum* for *diuinam* f. 49 r, *dicuntur* for *dicantur* f. 49 v, *terreus* for *terreas* f. 74 v, *solum* for *solam* f. 84 v, *edificandum* for *aedificandam* f. 94 v, *eum* for *eam* f. 97 v, *quom* (= *cum*) for *caro et* f. 98 v, *paulus* for *pro aliis* f. 115 v, *fuerunt* for *fuerant* f. 133 v, *secundum* for *secundam* f. 134 v, *corrigunt* for *corrigant* f. 134 v: 20 instances.

[1] At this stage I have only the copy of the text I wrote out for the printer to go by: in the first case the loss is represented by 105 lines of my writing, in the second by 421!

a is written for **u**: *ueram* for *uerum* f. 11 v, (*illas* for *illius* f. 14 v), *fractus* for *fructus* f. 17 r, *factum* for *fructum* f. 35 r, *dormierant* for *dormierunt* f. 56 v, *agant* for *agunt* f. 60, *mandanda* for *mundanda* f. 69 v, *perierant* for *perierunt* f. 96 v: 8 (9) instances.

r is written for **s**: *sustinemur* for *sustinemus* f. 21 r, *pro porci* for *propositi* f. 31 r: 2 instances.

s is written for **r**: *collaudemus* for *collaudemur* f. 33 r, *liberatus* for *liberatur* f. 35 r, *deus* (*ds̄*) for *dicitur* (*dr̄*) f. 42 r, *separare* for *reparare* f. 58 r, *prodest* for *prodere* f. 77 r, *ignorantes* for *ignoranter* f. 77 v, *conuersemus* for *conuersemur* f. 87 v: 7 instances.

t is omitted at the end of the third person singular and plural of tenses of verbs: *diligi* for *diligit* f. 3 v, *inpone* for *inponet* f. 19 v, *compleui* for *compleuit* f. 39 r, *moyses* for *mos est* f. 43 v, *admitti* for *admittit* f. 48 r, *ex causa* for *excusat* f. 61 v, *prodesse* for *prodesset* f. 81 r, *reuocare* for *reuocaret* f. 92 r, (*audere* for *audent* f. 100 v), *sin* for *sint* f. 108 v, (*terrena* for *terreant* f. 131 v), *pertinen* for *pertinent* f. 131 v: 9 (11) instances.

r is written for **n**: *redemptorem* for *redemptionem* f. 10 v, *arserit* for *manserit* f. 41 v, *audere* for *audent* f. 100 v; cf. *mittere* for *mitem* f. 130 v: 3 (4) instances.

n is written for **r**: *colentur* for *coleretur* f. 5 r, *uidentur* for *uideretur* ff. 84 v, 88 v, 97 r, *monituram* for *morituram* f. 116 v, (*quantitatis* for *caritatis* f. 106 r), cf. *sedem* for *sedere* f. 91 r, *insectarem* for *insectarer* f. 103 v: 5 (8) instances.

r is omitted after or before a vowel: *deseuio* for *deseruio* f. 3 v, *uetere* for *uertere* f. 28 v, *suppotauit* for *supportauit* f. 33 r, *factum* for *fructum* f. 35 r, *pe* for *per* f. 125 r: 5 instances.

r is added after a vowel: *hortandum* for *notandum* f. 30 r.

d is written for **t**: *de* for *te* f. 131 r.

t is written for **d**: *sanctum* for *secundum* f. 3 r (see below), *contemptamus* for *contendamus* f. 32 v.

c is written for **t**: *pro porci* for *propositi* f. 31 r, (*adduci* for *adducti* f. 33 v), *pace factum* for *patefactum* f. 36 v, *decrimento* for *detrimento* f. 44 v, *idolaticis* for *idolotitis* f. 49 r, *circa* for *terra* f. 58 r, *cedet* for *tedent* f. 61 r, *sic* for *sit* f. 61 v, *archeman* for *artheman* f. 134 v: 9 instances.

t is written for **c**: *sit* for *sic* f. 19 r.

c is written for **g**: *aucmentatur* for *augmentatur* f. 100 v.

nt is written for **m**: *sunt* for *sum* f. 38 r, *manifestent* for *manifestem* f. 119 r.

m is written for **nt**: *hesitabam* for *haesitabant* f. 59 r.

a is written for **o**: *coartar* for *coartor* f. 101 r.

h is written for **n**: *hortandum* for *notandum* f. 30 r, *barhabas* for *barnabas* f. 44 r.

li is written for **h**: *liuius* for *huius* f. 43 v.

t is written for **h**: *tunc* for *hunc* f. 35 r.

l is written for **i**: *lucidia* for *iudicia* f. 29 r.

c is written for **e**: *quom* (*cum*) for *eum* ff. 43 v, 77 v, 112 v, *aliquo* (*alicuo*) for *alieno* f. 41 r, cf. *coherenda* for *cohercenda* f. 87 v.

e is written for **c**: *diem* for *dicit* f. 79 r (*i.e.* diē for dic̄), *asmeritum* for *asincritum* f. 36 r, *aerore* for *ac(r)ore* f. 43 v, *eum* for *cum* f. 55 v, *eieę* for *eice* f. 86 r, *montem eum* for *monte cum* f. 101 v.

u is written for **ti**: *euam* for *etiam* f. 50 v.

u is written for **g**: *leuatione* for *legatione* f. 68 r.

s is written for **f**: *sit* for *fit* f. 96 v, *apocrisis* for *apocrifis* f. 112 r.

f is written for **s**: *fides* for *si des* f. 31 r, *fulcis* for *sulcis* f. 73 r, *inutile fiant* for *inutiles fiant* f. 98 r, (*inutili fuit* for *inutilis fuit* f. 135 v), *per infima* for *peripsima* f. 42 v.

o is written for **a**: *amotorem* for *amatorem* f. 109 r, *longuescens* for *languescens* f. 126 r.

a is written for **o**: *idolaticis* for *idolotitis* f. 49 r, *sodamitis* for *sodomitis* f. 96 v.

a is written for **it**: *lateris* for *litteris* f. 115 v.

n is written for **ti**: *ambulans* for *ambulatis* f. 40 v, *permanens* for *permanetis* f. 115 r.

r is written for **t**: *oblitterarum* for *oblitteratum* f. 14 v, *uidere* for *uidete* f. 59 r.

t is written for **r**: *reddat* for *reddar* f. 119 v.

The following may be classed together as confusions of letters in cases where these letters consisted mainly of short vertical strokes[1]; these suggest that the cross-strokes in the archetype were very faint:

petiuit for *petunt* f. 38 v, *uestiuit* for *uestiunt* f. 124 v, *finiunt* for *finiuit* f. 35 v, *proficuit* for *proficiunt* f. 95 v, *dubitanṭuit* f. 103 r.

in for *ut* f. 46 v, 121 r, 133 v.

[1] See also under *deus*, *dominus* in the following list.

inibant for *nubant* f. 46 v.

uni for *uim* ff. 38 r, 53 r, 104 r, *tribuni*[1] for *tribum* f. 83 v[2], *trophunum* for *trophimum* f. 132 r.

peremptus for *penitus* f. 62 v.

seruam for *seruaui* f. 75 v.

missum for *iussum* f. 98 v.

iouimanistis for *iouinianistis*[1] f. 104 v.

in for *hi* f. 111 v.

carnis for *carius* f. 112 r.

mutari for *imitari* f. 113 v.

m for *in* ff. 36 r, 123 r.

Other errors are due to ignorance or mishandling of abbreviations in the archetype:

sanctum for *secundum* (ꝫ) f. 3 r.

gloriam for *gratiam*[1] (grā interpreted as glā) ff. 13 r, 61 v, 66 r, 71 r, 79 v.

gratia omitted (grā again not understood) f. 118 v.

autem omitted (because in the form h) ff. 14 r, 48 v, 64 v, 75 v, 84 v *bis*, 110 v, 123 r, 125 v, 126 r, 131 r.

enim omitted (because in the form ꝉꝉ) ff. 78 r, 99 r, 101 r, 113 v, 124 r, 126 r, 133 r, 134 v.

enim written for *autem* (*i.e.* ꝉꝉ read for h) ff. 16 r, 34 v.

enim for *ergo* (*i.e.* ꝉꝉ for g̊) f. 57 v.

autem written for *enim* (*i.e.* h read for ꝉꝉ) ff. 42 r, 64 v, 78 v, 119 r.

igitur omitted (because in the form g') f. 14 r.

igitur written as *ergo* (because g' taken as g̊) ff. 94 v, 103 r.

ergo omitted (because in the form g̊) f. 14 r[3].

deus written for *dicitur* (because dr̄ confused with ds̄) f. 42 r.

secundum written for *saeculum* (sclm being in the archetype[4]) ff. 48 r, 52 r.

[1] These errors, combined with other facts (see p. 215 above), suggest that the scribe of the Balliol MS was a non-ecclesiastical scribe, accustomed to the copying of pagan texts.

[2] See also under *deum* etc. on p. 222.

[3] In cases where *autem*, *enim* etc. are interchanged in Biblical lemmata, it would not always be safe to assume error on the part of the scribe: the difference may be sometimes textual rather than palaeographical.

[4] The ignorance of the *saeculum* contraction supports the contention in the note above.

epistolas written for *epulas* (because he thought he saw ep̀łas in front of him) f. 55 r.

deum for *domini* (*i.e.* dm̄ for dn̄ī) ff. 55 v, 79 v, 100 r, 103 r.

dei for *domini* (*i.e.* dn̄ī confused with dī) f. 118 v.

dominus for *deus* (*i.e.* dn̄s̄ for ds̄) f. 57 r.

uult omitted (perhaps because written as *uul*[1]) f. 59 r.

peremptus for *penitus* is perhaps a dittography, f. 62 v.

uerbis is written for *uobis* (*i.e.* ub̄ was taken to be ūb̄) f. 63 r.

tantum written for *tamen* (*i.e.* tn̄ taken for tm̄) ff. 66 v, 115 r.

eius omitted (because in the unintelligible form ∅) ff. 67 r, 116 r.

ministrat written for *ministratur* (*i.e.* the ' or ² above the second *t* unobserved) f. 72 r.

per written for *pro* (*i.e.* ꝑ confused with ꝓ) ff. 74 v, 105 v, 108 v, 133 r *bis*.

pro written for *per* (*i.e.* ꝓ confused with ꝑ) f. 101 v.

quia written for *qua(m)* (*i.e.* q taken as q) f. 75 v.

uel omitted (because in the form ł) f. 80 v.

quod written for *quia* (because q misunderstood as q) f. 80 v.

est omitted (perhaps because in the form ÷) f. 81 r.

quom (*cum*) *dat* written for *condat* (because ɔdat was treated as c̄dat) f. 92 r.

aut written for *a* (the scribe mistook the accent over the *a* as the abbreviation sign: *i.e.* he took á for ā) f. 98 v.

homo omitted (because in the form hō) f. 102 r.

esse omitted (perhaps because in the form eē) ff. 38 v, 134 r.

aduersus written for *ad usus* (perhaps the scribe had *adūsus* before him) f. 134 v.

nostram omitted after *formam* (perhaps because in the form *nām*, which would make haplography easy) f. 60 r.

No one who has studied Latin palaeography will, I think, doubt where all this evidence points. The manuscript which the Italian scribe of our Balliol MS set out to copy, was in Irish pointed script not unlike that of the *Book of Armagh* to which it is textually related. As has been already hinted, this manuscript had probably been at one time in the library of St Columban's Irish foundation at Bobbio. Certain of the corruptions mentioned above, such as *u*

[1] This form is at least as old as the sixth century, and doubtless comes from an ancestor of the immediate original of the Balliol MS.

for *a*, *s* for *r*, *c* for *t*, may very well be inherited from a still earlier stage, the half-uncial stage. Another must, I think, be assigned to that stage, the confusion between *m* and *nt*; for this occurs most naturally in MSS where the transverse stroke following the vowel does double duty, *su*¯ being alike *sum* and *sunt*, and this usage seems to be unknown outside uncial and half-uncial script[1].

The descent of the Balliol MS may then, I venture to think, be thus sketched:

MS in half-uncial (saec. V—VI)
|
MS in Irish pointed minuscule (saec. IX in.)
|
B
(Italian minuscule [saec. XV med.]).

The reader will already have derived some knowledge of the quality of **B**, from what has been said about **A**, but as an impression may have been created that **B** is really superior to **A** elsewhere, as well as in Biblical text, some instances may be cited to show that **B** is on occasion inferior to **A**.

B interpolates the Marcionite prologue to First Corinthians.

Again, at 1 Cor. x 22 **A** is right with *ipsi me zelauerunt in non deo* (Deut. xxxii 21 αὐτοὶ παρεζήλωσάν με ἐπ' οὐ θεῷ), against **B** with *ipsi me zelauerunt in domino*.

Further, at Eph. iiii 13 **A** has *in unitatem fidei* rightly, while **B** has *homines sicut me*.

Other instances will readily be found by turning over the pages of the text.

(3) *Codex Collegii Mertonensis Oxon.* 26 (*saec. XV*) (O)

The manuscript numbered 26 in the collection of Merton College, Oxford, the gift of a former Warden, Richard Fitzjames, Bp of Chichester[2] (1504—1506) is, from the multiplicity of its contents, perhaps the most wonderful Jerome manuscript in existence. It is

[1] It seems to be very little known: see my edition of Pseudo-Augustini *Quaestiones* (C.S.E.L. vol. L [1908]) p. xxx n. 3, and add Codex Bezae (Rendel Harris in *Texts and Studies* II 1, 121 ff.), C.S.E.L. LIX p. lxv, and Cassiodorus (=Pseudo-Primasius) (Migne *P.L.* LXVIII, p. 587 ll. 44—5).

[2] As fol. 5 v records: as he is there called 'nuper Cicestriensis ep̄i,' the inscription may be assigned to the date 1506 or 1507.

true that there are many coeval manuscripts containing large collections of Jerome's letters[1], but to the best of my knowledge, there is no other single MS containing so many commentaries of Jerome on the New Testament. If I mistake not, it contains every genuine commentary of Jerome on a New Testament book as well as every New Testament exposition falsely attributed to him. Dom Morin elicited from it the genuine 'De Monogramma Christi,' which he published in 1903[2], and it has been used for Dr Haussleiter's edition of the works of Victorinus of Pettau, so far as concerns Jerome's revision of the latter's commentary on the Apocalypse[3]. It has been left to me to study the commentary on fourteen Epistles of Paul contained in it, falsely attributed to Jerome.

The manuscript 26 (B 3, 4) saec. XV (English hand) has on fol. 74 r the following title in red:

Hieronimi presbiteri breuiarium incipit feliciter; then in black:

Primum queritur quare post euangelia...meliorem et manentem substanciam; then in red:

Explicit prologus omnium epistolarum beati pauli apostoli. Item argumentum solius epistole ad romanos; then in black:

Romani sunt qui ex iudeis gentibusque...ad pacem et ad concordiam cohortatur; then in red:

Explicit argumentum epistole beati pauli apostoli ad romanos. Incipit explanacio sc̄i hieronomi (*sic*) in epistola ad romanos; then in black:

Paulus. Querimus quare...gloria honor in secula seculorum amen.

(*red*) Explicit epistola ad romanos incipit argumentum prime epistole ad corinthios.

(*black*) Corinthii sunt achaii...scribens eis ab epheso.

(*red*) Explicit argumentum incipit epistola prima ad corinthios.

(*black*) Paulus quod nomen preponit...super tuam benedictionem.

[1] I made an inventory of the contents of all, or nearly all, MSS in Britain containing letters of Jerome for Dr Isidor Hilberg of Czernowitz, the Vienna editor.

[2] *Anecdota Maredsolana* vol. III pars 3 pp. 194 ff.

[3] The collation was made by the present writer: see *Victorini episcopi Petavionensis Opera*...rec. Joh. Haussleiter (=C.S.E.L. 49) (Vindob. 1916) pp. lxix—lxx.

So with 2 Cor., Gal., Eph., Phil., 1 Thess., 2 Thess., Col., 1 Tim., 2 Tim., Tit., Philem.

(*red*) Explicit Epistola ad philemonem. Incipit argumentum ad hebreos.

(*black*) Inprimis dicendum cur apostolus...greco sermone conposuit.

(*red*) Explicit argumentum. Incipit Epistola ad hebreos feliciter.

(*black*) Multipharie multisque modis....Per multos inquit prophetas.

Expliciunt annotaciones super epistolam ad hebreos (fol. 141 v).

Then three blank leaves:

Then genuine Jerome in Gal. Eph. Tit. Philem., which end the codex.

That the portion of this manuscript down to the end of the first commentary on the Epistle to Philemon, is a copy of the Balliol MS, immediate or mediate, is evident from the following facts:

Its text agrees with that of the Balliol MS throughout, and this is true of no other existing MS; but absolutely irrefragable proof of the descent is furnished by the lacunae referred to above in the account of the Balliol MS[1].

The first lacuna, where two lines and a portion of a third are carefully left vacant in the Balliol manuscript, is represented in the Merton manuscript by the blank of half a line only. As we know what the missing words are, it is clear that the Merton manuscript is secondary to the Balliol manuscript.

The second lacuna, also of 2 + lines in the Balliol MS, is represented again by half a line in the Merton MS.

The third lacuna is three and a half lines long in the Balliol MS, but the scribe of the Merton MS was content to indicate the gap by about a fifth of a line. His vellum was more precious to him than was that of the Italian scribe.

The fourth lacuna measures exactly three lines in the Balliol manuscript, but only half a line in the Merton manuscript.

The Merton manuscript is therefore secondary, and in consequence is not employed in this edition, except for the text of the general prologue which has almost entirely disappeared from

[1] pp. 216 f.

the Balliol manuscript owing to the loss of its first leaf. Fortunately the Merton MS was written before this loss occurred, and here takes the place of the Balliol manuscript.

(4) *The Vatican Fragments* (𝕽)[1]

The two Vatican leaves belonged to a MS in half-uncial writing of about the sixth century, which was taken to pieces, at least as early as the eleventh or twelfth century, to make guard-leaves. No doubt the manuscript was already defective before it was deliberately broken up. The leaves are mutilated, scribbled over and cut down, and some nineteenth-century bookbinder did not improve their condition by separating them unskilfully from some unknown MS or printed book.

The leaves are conjugate, but not consecutive. They are in fact the third and sixth leaves respectively of a quaternion, thus:

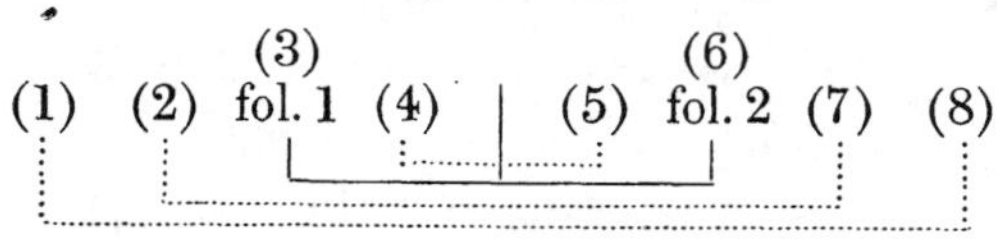

The vellum is good, if somewhat coarse, and has been ruled with a hard point on the softer and whiter side, both horizontally at even intervals and perpendicularly to govern the commencement and the course of the lines of writing. On the external margin of fol. 1 some of the punctures still remain, which were placed there to make the lines equal.

The margins and some lines of writing being absent, it is not possible to fix the exact size of the leaves in their complete state. Dr Mercati would reckon the written part of the page as approximately 20 × 12 cm., and the whole page as at least 25 × 15—the dimensions, that is to say, of a good-sized MS in octavo. The existing fragments are unequal, and measure roughly speaking the one 177 × 118 mm., the other 178 × 140 mm.

The writing is regular and compact, and keeps to the horizontal lines: both from its own size and from the amount of space left blank between the lines it gives the impression of a certain richness

[1] See also chap. ii pp. 48 ff. I am almost entirely indebted to Dr Mercati's description (*J.T.S.* vol. VIII [1906—1907] pp. 529 ff.).

and magnificence. There are no initial letters larger than the rest, but at every new section—and a new section begins with every new *stichos* of the apostolic text to be commented upon[1]—a commencement is made two letters outside the line, and the same in every succeeding line (except in fol. 2 r line 19, 2 v, l. 8) until the lemma from the sacred text is concluded. Thus the text stands out at the first glance: and to ensure this effect two perpendicular lines are ruled down the page, one to serve for the beginning of the lines of the lemma, the other, further in the page, for the lines of the commentary. From this method of emphasizing the text, it results that part of the preceding line is sometimes left unoccupied; and, conversely, the line is, in such cases, sometimes prolonged further than usual, and the letters made smaller than usual, in order to end off the comment, as can be seen on fol. 2 r line 17, without beginning a new line. In filling up the lost ends these unequal contents of different lines must be borne in mind: the lines vary from 23 letters (or even less) up to 36, the average being about 26.

Punctuation by the first hand is rare, and is distinguished by being placed neither at the top nor at the bottom, but towards the middle of the letters. Abbreviations too are rare, and only the most common occur: ds̄ dn̄s sp̄s xp̄s sc̄a, and at the end of the line a stroke for *n* and *m*[2]. q. for -que does not occur. One single ligature, the well-known one for -unt, is found on fol. 2 v line 20. Noteworthy divisions of words are subs|tantia, cons|tructus, fol. 2 r lines 5, 23.

Between the *recto* and the *verso* of each extant leaf three whole lines and part of a line have been cut away, so that the whole page consisted of twenty-six lines. Whether the lines which have completely fallen out stood at the foot or at the head of the page, cannot be stated with certainty[3]. As has been pointed out above, the two inner conjugate leaves of a quaternion separated the two leaves which have survived, and these two inner leaves had the flesh sides inmost, as was usual.

[1] This fact is very important as testifying to the original arrangement of text and commentary: cf. also above, p. 50.

[2] For *m* besides the stroke there seems to be also a point ∸, fol. 1 v, line 2: but the point may be one of punctuation, and not part of the abbreviation of *m* found in other MSS.

[3] At the top of fol. 1 v Dr Mercati seemed to make out the tail of some letter in the preceding line.

Two later hands dealt with the MS. One of them, who used a dark ink similar to that of the text, is practically contemporary with the original scribe: he added dots for punctuation, placing them level with, or even above, the tops of the letters, and in four instances corrected or supplemented the text (fol. 1 r lines 4, 12; 1 v line 5; 2 v line 15), probably from a second MS which in two cases gave the readings of the Migne text of Pseudo-Jerome. Whether we should attribute to this or to the first hand the erasure in eg*o (doubtless egeo was written at first), fol. 1 v line 12, is not clear. The third, somewhat later, hand has confined its activity to marking the beginning and ending of the verses of the Apostle with a big stroke something like a bracket, making use of a dirty sooty ink. This hand's work can safely be neglected.

Finally, after the two leaves had been already taken from the MS, various uneducated hands have touched up the ink of letters here and there, and have scribbled roughly across the page letters of the alphabet and the words *probatio penne, proba, probatio inconstri, ave cuius* (saec. XI—XII?). One of them, in between the lines but upside down, has signed himself 'Ego dn̄s (the profanity of the man!) adobad' cleric' plebis valliis (or 'vallus') renovata' (*sic*). The name of the valley in question is quite unknown either to Dr Mercati or myself[1].

The fragments contain text and commentary for Rom. vii 9—15 and viii 3—7, with certain slight gaps which are recorded in the critical apparatus. Short as these fragments are, they are most welcome; first, because they show the way in which Pelagius arranged his work: second, because they give a Biblical text which is not Vulgate, which is in fact distinctly more Old-Latin than that furnished by the Reichenau MS: third, because, while their Biblical text is nearer to that of the Balliol MS than to that of the Reichenau MS (cf. Rom. vii 13, 14, 15), the fragments agree with the Reichenau MS in omitting at Rom. vii 14 a portion of exposition which is furnished by the Balliol MS.

For these reasons the Vatican sixth century fragments are, so far as they extend, the most valuable *testis* we have for the text of Pelagius' work.

[1] I regret very much that I omitted to take the opportunity of consulting the late Dr H. M. Bannister on this point.

(5) *The Freiburg Fragments* (K)

Two conjugate leaves of a Latin manuscript, discovered by Dr Flamm of the Stadtarchiv at Freiburg im Breisgau, Baden, came under the eyes of Professor J. M. Heer there, who most courteously forwarded rotographs of them to me in 1912. The leaves had been in use for many years as the cover of the accounts of a professors' gawk club[1] at Freiburg, and are now preserved in the Stadtarchiv there.

The writing may be safely assigned to the first quarter of the ninth century, and to a South German *scriptorium*[2]. Certain of its palaeographical characteristics may be mentioned. Open *a* is invariable. The diphthong *æ* is never so written; generally it is represented by *e* merely, once or twice by *ę*. In the last lines the following letters are sometimes provided with long tails, reminiscent of legal documents: *f*, *p*, *q*, *r* and *s*. The short stroke is sometimes used both for *m* and for *n*, both in the middle and at the end of a word or line. The letter *r* is sometimes highbacked, and a low *ſ* is characteristic. The *y* is of rather peculiar shape and is dotted; the *z* is short, and stretches half below the line. The following ligatures occur: *ec*, *et*, *ex*, *nt* and *ri*. Punctuation is rare, and is of three kinds: the simplest is that of the dot placed half-way up above the line, the most emphatic is that of two dots in a line and a comma midway between them underneath, while the medium strength is represented by the semi-colon. The interrogative sign is entirely absent, though there is at least one place where the sense is interrogative: the absence of the interrogative sign is unfortunate, as its presence would greatly facilitate an answer to the question of the provenance of the MS. The presence of scripture quotations in the text is sometimes indicated in the margin in the usual way. The MS is carefully and neatly written; there is no attempt to save space. The separation of words is fairly advanced. The number

[1] *Gesellschaft zum Gauch*, stupidly rendered by me 'goose-club' in *Journ. Theol. Stud.* vol. XIII (1911—1912) pp. 515—519, where I published a diplomatic text of the contents of the leaves. The leaves enclosed vol. 55, the accounts of the club for the year 1592—1593.

[2] I was fortunate in afterwards securing Dr Alfred Holder's agreement with this view.

XVI, indicating a *capitulum*, appears at 1 Cor. x 25. This is a matter of some importance, as 1 Cor. x 25 is regularly the beginning of *capitulum* L or LI: the question of what system of capitulation is here used must be left to experts. The scribe was somewhat addicted to the omission of syllables—*euan⟨ge⟩lizare, ce⟨te⟩ris, idol⟨i⟩o, immola⟨ti⟩cium*, and he was not always sure of his vowels—*potet* for *putet*, and *parte cipo* for *participo*.

The following are all the abbreviations and contractions that occur: aū, dm̄, dn̄i, ē, e̅e̅, f̅r̅s̅, n̄, ꝑ, ꝓ, p̄pter, q; (= quae), qđ, s̅c̅a̅, x̅p̅i̅. The following syllabic suspensions occur: b; (= bus), t̄ (= ter), t' (= tur), at end of line.

The contents are text and commentary for (*a*) 1 Cor. viiii 15—17, (*b*) 18—20, (*c*) 1 Cor. x 24—27, (*d*) 27—31, with lacunae equivalent to six lines of MS, first between (*a*) and (*b*) and second between (*c*) and (*d*). That is, six lines of writing have been clipped away from the tops of the four pages right across. As the pages now contain 17 lines each, they must have contained originally 23. A calculation of the matter lost between (*b*) and (*c*) shows that eight pages are missing, and that our leaves are therefore the second and seventh of a quaternion.

We must now consider the textual quality of the fragments. There are four cases where they go with **A** and **B** combined:

potero immutare **AB**K(G): *poteram mutare* V: *potest immutari* **H**.
exemplo apostoli **AB**KG, (-um) V, (Cassiod.): *apostoli exemplo* **H**.
prosunt **AB**KGV Cassiod.[ed.] : *prosint* **H**, Cassiod.[cod.] (recte).
infideli **AB**KG Sedul.: *alia* V**H** Cassiod.[ed.] (= vg): *aliena* Cassiod.[cod.].

In the case of 1 Cor. x 27 the omission of *ad cenam* is supported by **A**KV Cassiod. (= vg), while *ad cenam* is present in **BH**. This is a somewhat difficult case. K agrees with **B** in *amplius aliquid* for *aliquid amplius* of the others.

But if these examples show that the Freiburg fragments keep good company, the text is nevertheless characterized by considerable errors: *abstinere* repeated after *salutis* (viiii 15), *nec adnuntiem* after *adnuntiem* (viiii 18), *quod* after *licet* (x 24), *esse* after *conscientiam* (x 25). The following omissions occur: *legem* after *qui* (viiii 20), *ut* after *fratres* (x 24). These readings are wrong: *in* for *me* (viiii 15), *fecisse* for *fecistis* (viiii 16), *immolarē* for *immolate* (x 25).

If we compare the Freiburg text with **A** and **B** in some detail, we shall find that in fifteen cases it disagrees with their joint evidence: in at least fourteen of the cases, it is undoubtedly wrong[1]. But there are three and a half cases where K agrees with **B** against **A**. They are *amplius aliquid* (1 Cor. viiii 16), *enim* omitted (1 Cor. x 26 = vg), *ergo* (1 Cor. x 30), *parte cipo* (1 Cor. x 30 = vg *participo*) where **B** has *participor*.

In these cases the full evidence is:

amplius aliquid **B**KG: *aliquid amplius* **A**V**H**.

enim omitted **B**KV**H** Cassiod. (= vg): *enim* **A**G Sedul.

ergo **B**KGM, N (*corr.*) R (*corr.*) Sedul.[ed.]: *ego* **A**VHC Cassiod. Sedul.[codd.] (= vg).

parte cipo (*participo*) KV**H** Cassiod. Sedul. (= vg): *percipio* **A**: *participor* **B**G.

In the first case, K is probably right, as it is the *lectio difficilior*, and we can see why the alteration was made in the others. In the second it is natural to regard the non-Vulgate reading as right, especially as the Psalm itself also lacks the *enim*, and *enim* is a word which is apt to be omitted: also γάρ appears to be everywhere present in the Greek. The next case is rather more difficult to judge. No doubt *ergo* is an incorrect reading, whether it be an anticipation of the *ergo* of verse 31 or a mere palaeographical mistake, as Tischendorf conjectured. But it is not easy to say whether the reading is Pelagian or not. Sound criticism will, in the fourth case, I think, hold to *participor*: *percipio* is one of those aberrations of **A** to which reference has been already made. In only one of the four places, therefore, is K with absolute certainty right. There are no places where K agrees with **A** against **B**.

It is a misfortune that so little of this manuscript survives; also it is to be regretted that what does survive should belong to a part where Pseudo-Jerome has made no interpolations. It is really impossible, therefore, to deny that the complete Freiburg codex was a Pseudo-Jerome, but on the whole the evidence, I think, favours the view that we have here the scanty relics of another Pelagius of the original extent, not very closely related to any MS of which I have knowledge.

[1] The possible exception is *aliut quid* (1 Cor. x 31) for *aliquid*.

(*b*) Manuscripts of Interpolated Forms

(1) *No.* 73 *in the Stiftsbibliothek at St Gall* (G)

The manuscript is thus described by the late Dr G. Scherrer in the *Verzeichniss der Handschriften der Stiftsbibliothek von St Gallen* (Halle, 1875) p. 31:

'73. Pgm. 2°. s. IX incip.: 262 pages[1], double columns, with corrections. **Glossae incerti auctoris in epistolas sancti Pauli** (Incip. pag. 3: Paulus. expō. Querimus·quare Paulus scribat etc.).'

To this it may be added that it measures 35 × 25 cm., that it was written by two scribes, and that there are commonly 37 lines to the page, though on page 13 there are as many as 47. The real beginning of the MS on page 1 is INCIP*IT* OMNIUM EPISTOLARUM. Primum queritur quare...discipuli apostolor*um*, page 2 being blank.

The first sheet contains now only six leaves (twelve pages)

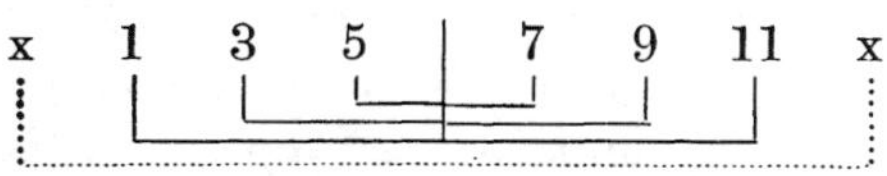

the second is a normal quaternion, lettered B at the foot of the second column: so with quaternions C, D, E, F, G, H. The next sheet I is a trinio signed at the end (foot of p. 136): K and L are normal and signed at the end. M takes this form:

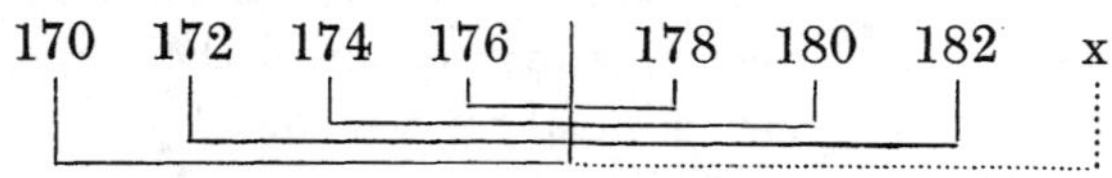

That is, the last leaf has been cut out, but a different scribe has signed the second last leaf M: N, O, P are normal. The end of P coincides with the end of the exposition of Philemon (p. 230 a): p. 230 b is blank, and the exposition of Hebrews commences at the top of the new quaternion Q (p. 231 a). The last quaternion of all is unsigned.

The initial words are as described above. The closing parts are:

230 a crescit quoties loquitur et auditur. FINIT EPISTOLA PAULI AD PHILIMONEM.

231 a INCIPIT ARGUMENTUM AD HEBREOS. In primis dicendum

[1] The St Gall MSS, like those of Ghent, are numbered by pages, not folia.

est cur...**260 a** baptismi, pęnitentiae et perseuerantiae. FINIT EXPOSITIO EPISTOLE PAULI APOSTOLI AD HEBREOS. Follows alien poetical matter. Page 262 is blank.

Titles on the cover are Appostolus paulus glosatus *and* Epistole B. Pauli glossatae. *Strong wooden boards, covered with leather.*

Besides the modern signature 73 on the outer cover, there are to be found (fol. 1) the bookplate with *Sig. Monaste. sanc. galli* and also the old shelfmark *D. n.* 23, under which the new one has been added in red letters. On page 2, which is otherwise blank, a fifteenth century hand has written *Apostolus paulus glosatus n* 4.

There can be little doubt that Zimmer is right in identifying this manuscript with that referred to in the old St Gall catalogue of about the year 850, preserved in manuscript 728 of the St Gall library, as

Expositio pelagii super omnes epistolas pauli in uolumine I[1].

But Zimmer makes a curious mistake about this entry. He states that it was added to the original catalogue along with two items *Tractatus Origenis in Genesim, Exodum et Leuiticum in uolumine I* and *Item Tractatus Origenis super epistolam ad Romanos uolumen optimum.* As a matter of fact, personal examination made it clear to me that, while the second Origen entry is certainly later, the Pelagius entry is part of the original catalogue[2]. Zimmer's argument that the Pelagius manuscript was incorporated in the library between 850 and 872 thus falls to the ground, and there is nothing to hinder us from assigning it to the first half of the ninth century, to which palaeographically it belongs.

The manuscript is written in a continental hand, by more than one scribe. As Zimmer has pointed out[3], one scribe wrote quaternions A—D, N—P, and another E—M, Q—R; or, in other words, the first wrote the expositions of Romans, Colossians, 1, 2 Thessalonians, 1, 2 Timothy, Titus, Philemon, while the other copied the exposi-

[1] The catalogue published in G. Becker, *Catalogi Bibliothecarum Antiqui* no. 22 pp. 43 ff., P. Lehmann, *Mittelalterliche Bibliothekskataloge Deutschlands und der Schweiz...* I Bd (München, 1918) p. 76 l. 6.

[2] I am now confirmed by Lehmann, *loc. cit.* Zimmer's error, derived from Becker, is repeated by Koetschau, *Origenes Werke* Bd V (Leipzig, 1913) p. lii, whose discussion is vitiated by another error of Becker's, the attribution of catalogue no. 15 to St Gall, whereas it belongs to Reichenau (see *Die Reichenauer Handschriften* Bd III (Leipzig, 1916) pp. 97—103).

[3] Pp. 238 ff.

tions of 1, 2 Corinthians, Galatians, Ephesians, Philippians, Hebrews. No doubt these two scribes worked concurrently, in order to get their task finished as quickly as possible, and there is no reason to suppose that the *scriptorium* where the manuscript was executed, was any other than the St Gall *scriptorium* itself. A third hand writes occasional passages, e.g. p. 40 a, ll. 21—25, *Radicis patrum* to *per te stant*. A fourth hand, perhaps to be identified with the corrector of the codex wrote pp. 55 b, l. 1 to 56 a, l. 3 (end of Romans).

The orthography of the manuscript as well as the abbreviations show many Irish[1] symptoms such as we expect to find at St Gall. We shall consider the orthography immediately in an endeavour to trace the ancestry of the manuscript. The abbreviations employed are these:

apostolus apōs (dat.) (abl. p. 223 b), apƚ (corr.) (S-L[2]), apoƚs, apƚs (S-L), apƚsts (corrector), apƚsls (p. 47 b)
apud ap̄
aut ā (once) (S-L)
autem aū nearly always (S-L), aut̄ very rare (S-L), ħ also very rare, and only above the line in additions
capitulum ƙ
carissimi crm̄i, cm̄i (corrector km̄i), km̄i (S-L)
cetera c&
Christus xp̄s
cum c̄
Dauid đđ (S-L)
de đ
deus ds̄ (S-L)
dicimus dm̄s
dicit dic̄ (S-L), dit̄ (S-L), dt̄
dicitur dr̄ (S-L)
dicunt dn̄t
dicuntur dn̄r
dominus dn̄s (S-L)
ecclesia ecƚa
eius ꝫ (once only, s.l.) (S-L)
enim ꝉꝉ (S-L)
episcopus {epīs (accus. sing.), epōs (accus. plur.) / ep̄s etc.}
epistula epīs, epƚa, epƚ
ergo g̊
esse ēē (S-L)
est ē (S-L), ÷ (S-L)
et 7 (corrected at least once to *et*)
explicit expƚi etc.
expositio exp̄, expōs, exp̄o
frater frt (S-L), ff̄ 'fratre,' frm̄ 'fratrem,' frs̄ (S-L), ff̄, fras̄ (rare) (S-L), fs̄, frf̄ all for 'fratres.'
haec h̄ (altered once by a corrector to hec) (S-L)
hoc ḣ, h̄
hoc est ho ÷ (S-L)
Iesus ih̄s
Johannes ioh̄, ih̄
Israhel isrƚ (S-L)
item it̄ (very characteristic)
meus m̄s (S-L)
mihi m with i above
misericordia mīa (S-L)
nomen nōē, 'nomine'
{*noster* nm̄, nr̄m 'nostrum' etc. (S-L both)
uester ur̄, 'uester,' ur̄a etc. (S-L)}
nunc nc̄
omnipotens omp̄s (S-L)
omnis om̄s (S-L) (p. 160 b, corrected by corrector to omīs (S-L)), om̄l(?); om̄ (S-L), om̄s (S-L) 'omnes'; om̄a (S-L), omīa (S-L) 'omnia'

[1] See also Zimmer, pp. 232 ff.

[2] The letters S-L are added to those abbreviations which are definitely attested for St Gall MSS in Fr. Steffens, 'Die Abkürzungen in den lateinischen Handschriften des 8. und 9. Jahrhunderts in St. Gallen' (*Zentralblatt für Bibliothekswesen*, Bd xxx [1913] pp. 477—488); W. M. Lindsay, 'Note on the Preceding Article' (ibid. pp. 488—490). These scholars did not use MS 73.

Paulus paū
per ꝑ (S-L)
post p' (S-L)
prae p̄ (S-L)
presbiter pr̄bi 'presbiteri'
propter ꝑt (twice), pp̄ (S-L) (once, altered by corrector to pp̄t (S-L))
quae q: q· q̄· (first and second S-L)
quam numq̃ 'numquam'
quando qn̄ (expanded once by corrector) (S-L)
que q: (S-L) q· (S-L)
quem q̃ (several times) (S-L)
qui qⁱ (S-L)
quia q̄ꝃ, qꝃ (S-L), q
quod qđ (S-L)
quoniam qm̄ (S-L), quō (very rare) (S-L), qnm̄ (rare) (S-L), q°m (once)
reliqua rq̄, rel̄, req̄, rl̄, rel̄iq, rl̄q, rel̄q
saeculum scl̄a 'saecula' (S-L), sacl̄o 'saeculo'
sanctus sc̄s, etc.
secundum secđ (S-L), scđm (S-L), sđm
sed s· (very characteristic) (Swiss, perhaps from Italy)
sicut sic̄ (S-L)
significat sig̃, sign̄ (both end of line)
spiritaliter spītaliter
spiritus sp̄s, spūs 'spiritus' (genit.) (S-L), spūm 'spiritum'
subauditur sub̄
sunt s̄, st̄ (S-L both)
tamen tn̄ (S-L)
tantum tm̄
tempore tep̄°
tunc tc̄ (S-L)
uel ł (very characteristic) (S-L)
uero u°
uersus uers̄, ur̄[1]

SYLLABLE SYMBOLS:

bunt b̄t, bt̄ (S-L), b̄n+
con c̄ (corrector only, except p. 142a) (S-L)
e đ 'de'
en m̄ 'men' (S-L)
er b̄ 'ber' (S-L), t̄ 'ter' (S-L), ū 'uer' (S-L)
is b̄ 'bis' (S-L)
it dic̄ 'dicit' (S-L)
m suprascript stroke (S-L)
n suprascript stroke (S-L)
os see *us*
ri suprascript i; pⁱ 'pri' (S-L)
rum ꝝ (S-L)
runt r̄ (S-L), rt̄ (S-L)
ur m² 'mur,' t' (S-L) 'tur,' t² (second scribe) (S-L)
us cui' 'cuius'
b: (S-L), b' 'bus'; m' (S-L), m̃, m; 'mus'
n+ 'nus' (S-L)
also for *os*: p'sidebit 'possidebit,' p'tea 'postea,' etc. (S-L)

The instances to which the letters (S-L) are added are sufficient to show that MS 73 is a product of the St Gall *scriptorium*. Certain of the others have been taken over inadvertently from the archetype, and may give us indications of the ancestry of our manuscript. There can be little doubt that the symbols for *apud, autem* (third), *cum, dicimus, dicit* (third), *dicunt, dicuntur, ergo, et, hoc, mihi, nomen, nunc, quam, quia* (third), *secundum* (third), *tantum, uero,* employed in this manuscript, were copied from an immediate ancestor in Irish script, which lay before the scribe. But I think traces of two earlier copies also show themselves. The symbols for *apostolus* (last two), *de, ecclesia, item*[2] on the whole favour the idea of a Visigothic strain.

[1] Wrongly interpreted by Zimmer (p. 382) as 'urbe.'

[2] See *Notae Latinae*, p. 115 for another St Gall example. The standard works on abbreviation are this and the earlier work of Traube, *Nomina Sacra* (München, 1907).

What I conceive to have been the case is that the immediate parent of the Irish MS was Visigothic, and there is nothing antecedently improbable in this view. The connexion between Ireland and Spain was very considerable. But we can go I think even behind this Visigothic manuscript which probably belonged to the period 600 to 800. Certain of the abbreviations take us a stage farther back still; I refer to such as those for *apostolus* (the first), *episcopus* (the first), *epistula* (the first), *presbiteri*. In the first, second and third cases the abbreviation by suspension recalls a very early stage of transmission, perhaps a half-uncial of the sixth century. Farther back than this we cannot go. These arguments drawn from the abbreviations employed can be powerfully reinforced from the orthography and from corruptions present in the St Gall MS.

Zimmer has already collected instances from the manuscript of what he considers Irish orthography[1]. I do not regard all of them as equally cogent, and have therefore studied the matter independently. But some of them at any rate will stand. Confusion of vowels is one of the most striking characteristics of Irish manuscripts, and of this we find plentiful illustration. The most common confusions, abundantly exampled in this manuscript, are *a* for *e*, *e* for *a*, *i* for *e*, *e* for *i*; less common, but yet frequent are *o* for *u*, *u* for *o*, *a* for *o*, *y* for *i*; others, which need not be specially Irish, and are still less frequent, are *o* for *a*, *u* for *a*, *a* for *u*, *e* for *o*, *o* for *e*, *e* for *u*, *u* for *e*, *u* for *i*, *i* for *y*. Another characteristic of Irish MSS is the doubling of single consonants, and the 'singling' of double consonants. Of these phenomena the following examples occur among many others: (*a*) *abssens*, *circumcissus*, *cassibus*, *conmissistis*, *pertulli*, *iddolis*; (*b*) *posunt*, *corumpit*, *nulius*, *comutare*, *comouere*, *mitatur*. The following spellings may be safely attributed to the Irish exemplar: *plasphemus*, *ponis* (for *bonis*) (p. 135 b), *spalmus* (for *psalmus*), *tetinere* (for *detinere*), *contempnare* (frequent for *condemnare*): possibly also *redient* (for *redigent*), *neglientia*, and *exiere* (for *exigere*)[2].

[1] Pp. 234 f. I propose to use some of them to indicate Visigothic ancestry. My own lists are quite independent of his.

[2] This last type of spelling is very common in C of the Pseudo-Augustinian *Quaestiones*, which appears to be a copy of an Irish exemplar (*SB. der Kais. Akad. der Wiss. in Wien*, Bd CXLIX [1905] (1) p. 9).

That an Irish original was in front of the scribes of St Gall 73 is also amply proved by certain misreadings of the exemplar. Only in reading an Irish (Insular) script could the following confusions arise:

n for *r*: *con* for *cor* (p. 80 b); *condelectante* for *corde laetante* (p. 94 a); *ina* for *ira* (p. 162 a).

r for *n*: *deperderent* for *dependerent* (p. 45 b); *liberter* for *libenter* (p. 170 a); *oppiniorum* for *opinionum* (p. 229 b).

ri for *n*: *tripherium* for *triphenam* (p. 54 b), etc.; *m* for *ri*: *comparam* for *comparari* (p. 142 b); *rm* for *m*: *erminentem* for *eminentem* (p. 177 a).

g for ʒ: *baptigentur* (p. 85 b), *baptigantur* (p. 102 b), *euangeligabant* (p. 171 b).

ʒ for *g*: *euanʒelium* (p. 70 b), *euanʒeliʒet* (p. 137 b), *euanʒeliʒat* (p. 139 a), *euanʒeliʒaui* (p. 144 b).

There are also errors which could arise only from a neglect or misunderstanding of Irish abbreviation symbols. Such are *in* for *autem* (h͛) (p. 163 b); the frequent omission of *autem* (h͛) and *enim* (††), and the substitution of one for the other; the omission of *eius* (ɔ) (p. 226 b); the use of *quod* (ꝗ) for *quia* (ꝗ) (p. 174 a); *quam* (ꝗ) for *quod* (ꝗ) (pp. 52 a, 228 a); *uel* (ł) for *id est* (·i·) (p. 131 b); *prae* (p̄) for *per* (p͛) (pp. 105 b, 150 a)[1].

That Visigothic influence lies behind the Irish influence is suggested by the following symptoms: *bebet* for *bibit* (p. 87 a), *pobulus* for *populus* (p. 86 b), *suberbia*; *ocultus* (regular in this MS); *abdicaberint*; *accipiad*, *uenissed*; *facillantes* for *uacillantes* (p. 160 b), *defortium* for *diuortium* (p. 165 b)[2]; *simulagrorum* (p. 92 a), *fugata* for *fucata* (p. 170 b); the wrong presence of *h* before a vowel, especially at the beginning of a word, as in *haccubitus*, *hapud*, *haudeo*, *helimosina* (*helymosina*), *herudieris*, *hodium*, *homnis*, *horans*, *hostendo*, *husque*, *adholatio*, *exhistimo*, as well as its absence where it ought to be present, as in *abere*, *eres*, *omo*, *ora*, *umanitas*, *subtraebat*, *distraere*[3]; *quohabitatio* for *cohabitatio*, etc.; *aceruitate*,

[1] *quo* for *quō* (=quoniam), p. 4 a, is against alike an Irish and a Visigothic exemplar. Probably our scribe has simply forgotten to write the cross-stroke.

[2] These instances are valuable as illustrations of Prof. Lindsay's *deuoret* for *deforet* of the Visigothic and other MSS of a fragment of Lucilius in Isidore, *Etym.* XIX 4 § 10 (cf. *Classical Quarterly* vol. v (1911) p. 97).

[3] I am well aware that these phenomena are not confined to Visigothic MSS, but that they are specially characteristic of these, there seems to be no doubt; see an excellent example in A. E. Burn's *Niceta of Remesiana* (Cambr. 1905) p. lxxxviii n. 2.

adorauit, seruauimus, separauit, liuertas (p. 88 a) on the one hand, with *brebi* for *breui, donabit, seruabit, debitum* for *diuitum* (p. 64 b), on the other[1]. The confusion between semi-consonantal *i* and *g* is also to be traced to Visigothic influence[2]: *proienie* for *progenie, iuium* for *iugum* on the one hand, and *gam* for *iam, geiunis* for *ieiuniis* (p. 85 b), *agunt* for *aiunt, geiuniis* (p. 132 b), *agit* for *ait* (p. 176 a), if *agit* be not the true text, as it is on p. 186 a. It is perhaps hardly safe to call *cartelarium* on p. 223 a (=*cartularium*) a Spanish symptom, but the spelling is not otherwise recorded. Finally, *per* and *pro* could only be corrupted from a Visigothic exemplar, for it is in Visigothic alone that the symbol which indicates *pro* elsewhere, has the value of *per*; we find *per* for *pro* on p. 195 b, and *pro* for *per* on pp. 120 a, 153 a, 229 b.

It is strange to find any distinct characteristics of the very early period, after the blighting influence of a Visigothic and an Irish scribe has worked its will on a text; yet it appears that a few such traces remain, in the following venerable spellings, which must have passed unscathed through the various stages: *Danihelo* (once or twice), *Danielum*; *Eleazarus* (for the ordinary *Lazarus* of Luke xvi); *Isac* (nearly always); *prode est* (pp. 95 a, 102 b, 103 a); *unianimis* (always); *uul* (for *uult*) (pp. 81 b, 127 b). The numerous confusions between *r* and *s* may have occurred either at this stage or at the Irish stage.

I venture to think, then, that a study of the abbreviations and orthography of our manuscript shows that it was copied from an Irish exemplar, which in its turn was a copy of a Visigothic exemplar, and that this Visigothic exemplar was copied from an early manuscript, say a semi-uncial of the sixth century. Whether the whole text as we have it was contained in this very old copy, is a question somewhat hard to answer. It is quite possible *a priori* that certain accretions took place at the Visigothic or at the Irish stage or at both.

Some idea of the contents of this manuscript has already been given in the second chapter of this book. The *codex* contains

[1] Zimmer (pp. 234 f.) classifies these last as Irish spellings, perhaps rightly; but both views may be correct.

[2] See E. A. Lowe in *SB. K. Bay. Akad. Wiss.* 1910 (12) pp. 14 ff.; H. W. Garrod, *Classical Review* xxxv (1921) p. 40.

nearly the whole of the real Pelagius, but in addition it contains most of the interpolations we have learned to associate with the Pseudo-Jerome form, particularly with this form as it appears in the longer branch of that family (H_2). It contains, however, on the one hand more, and on the other hand less than Pseudo-Jerome. As Zimmer has observed, it generally omits, in the exposition of First Corinthians, one of the two explanations given by Pseudo-Jerome[1]. In the case of that Epistle it corresponds almost exactly to the manuscripts of the uninterpolated form with one exception. It interpolates the chapter headings generally found in Vulgate manuscripts[2]. On the other hand, from the Epistle to the Ephesians onwards, it is interpolated from the genuine commentaries of Jerome on that Epistle, the Epistle to Titus and the Epistle to Philemon[3]. It is interesting to observe that Jerome's commentary on Galatians was not used. This fact suggests that the interpolator had only the other three at his disposal. In this connexion I ought to point out that several MSS of Jerome in Eph., Tit., Philem. together, without Gal., are still in existence. They are these: Karlsruhe, Codex Augiensis LXXXI (saec. IX in.); St Gall 129 (saec. IX); Köln LVIII (Darmst. 2052) (saec. IX); Wolfenbüttel 13 Weissenb. (saec. X); Florence Laur. plut. XVIII dext. cod. IX (saec. XIII)[4]. What inference can we draw? This, I think. As all the places to which the earlier manuscripts belong are within the zone of Irish influence, it was the compiler of the Irish exemplar of our manuscript who extracted them from a manuscript of Hier. in Eph., Tit., Philem. in his possession, and added them to what he found in the Visigothic codex. In other words these interpolations were absent at the Visigothic and the earlier stages. In addition to portions of genuine Jerome[5], our manuscript contains extracts from Augustine[6] and Gregory[7]. It is probable that these emanate from the same Irish interpolator as added the passages

[1] Zimmer, pp. 246 f. [2] See Zimmer, pp. 249 f.

The passages are indicated in Zimmer's footnotes from p. 357 onwards.

[4] I made a list for my projected Vienna edition.

[5] To which I must add one from epist. 28 §§ 4, 5, unidentified by Zimmer, on p. 229 b, which is shared with the longer Pseudo-Jerome form.

[6] 'ut augustinus (*ex* agustinus) dicit,' p. 165 a; 'augustinus dicit,' p. 201 a (=*in* 2 *Thess.* ii 8), 205 b, 'beatus augustinus dicit,' p. 207 b.

[7] 'gregorio dicente,' p. 222 b.

from genuine Jerome. If this be so, the date of the Irish MS must be post-Gregorian, and there can be little doubt that it belongs to a date not earlier than the middle of the seventh century. The Jerome quotations are added without the name of Jerome[1], a fact which suggests that the Irish scribe found the whole work under Jerome's name, and therefore did not add the name to extra notes derived from other works by the same author. If this be so, then our manuscript is a (modified) member of the second family of Pseudo-Jerome MSS (H_2), to which it is otherwise closely related, as Hellmann contended against Zimmer[2].

The St Gall MS is like the second family of Pseudo-Jerome MSS in two other respects; it gives the Epistles in the normal order, and it contains an (un-pelagian) commentary on the Epistle to the Hebrews, whereas the first family contains none. This commentary is not, however, identical in both cases. The St Gall commentary cites Cyprian, Augustine, Gregory of Nazianzus, and Gregory the Great, and is therefore not older than 650. Zimmer is no doubt right in regarding it as an Irish production[3]. The St Gall commentary on Hebrews is also preserved by itself in a manuscript at Wolfenbüttel, as Riggenbach was the first to point out. This is the MS already mentioned, 4097, Weissenb. 13 (saec. X), but the part already referred to is really quite a different MS that has been bound up with the commentary on Hebrews[4]. Riggenbach has also proved that, though not identical, the Hebrews commentary in the St Gall MS is very closely related to that in the second family of Pseudo-Jerome MSS[5], and, further, he has done a great service to our studies by showing that the Pseudo-Jerome form is often primary and the St Gall form secondary. His conclusion is that they are both revisions of one and the same original, and he points out that in Pseudo-Jerome

[1] With one exception, p. 201 a, not from a commentary *ad loc.*: 'secundum iheronimum dicentem.'

[2] *Sedulius Scottus* (München, 1906) pp. 153 ff. Hellmann, however, knew only the shorter form of Pseudo-Jerome (H_1), as published, which makes his discovery all the more acute.

[3] Zimmer, p. 276.

[4] Riggenbach, *Die ältesten lateinischen Kommentare zum Hebräerbrief* (=Zahn's *Forschungen zur Gesch. des nt. Kanons*, VIII Teil) (Leipzig, 1907) pp. 12 f.

[5] *Op. cit.* pp. 202 ff.

no name of a Father occurs. Later in the same book he shows a close relationship between Sedulius Scottus's compilation on Hebrews and that of the St Gall MS.

The textual character of the St Gall MS has already been illustrated by Zimmer and Hellmann with the aid of such materials as were at their disposal. I propose now to study their lists[1] in the light of the fresh materials now accessible. The general effect of the new evidence is to clarify the situation. We shall follow the ordinary maxim that community of error implies community of origin.

Further Agreements of G (*St Gall* 73) *with* **H** (*Pseudo-Jerome*) *where both are wrong:*

Rom. i 3 *addendum* G**H***V Sedul. : *addendo*[2].
exclusit G; *excludit* **H** : *extinxit.*
21 *recedentes* G**H** Cassiod. : *recedens.*
iiii 1 *adhibeatur* G**H** : *id habeatur.*
vi 14 *estis* G**H** : *eritis.*
xiii 1 *libertatem Christianam* G**H*** : *libertate Christiana.*
xiiii 4 *legi* G**H** Sedul. : *lege.*
22 *salutem* G (*salute* H_1 *saluti* H_2) *infirmi* : *infirmi salutem.*
xv 21 *ostenditur* G**H** : *uidetur.*
1 Cor. xiiii 1 *proficiatis* G**H** : *profetetis.*
2 Cor. x 1 *delicti* G**H** : *uindicandum.*
4 *Item cognitiones*—
—*destruendas dicit* G**H** : om.[3]
Eph. iii 18 *diligant* G**H** : *eligant.*
2 Tim. iiii 15 *resistit* G**H** : *restitit.*

Agreements of G *with* H_1 *where both are wrong:*

Rom. i 4 *est* GH_1 : *portenditur* (*pertendit*[*ur*] H_2).
vii 8 *obliuione*[*m*] *erat* GH_1 : *obliuionem ierat.*
viii 6 *parat* GH_1* Cassiod. : *parit.*
xvi 24 *commoneret* GH_1 : *commemoraret* (*commemoret* H_2).
1 Thess. iiii 6 *fratri* GH_1 : *pari.*

[1] Zimmer, pp. 230 ff., 243 ff.; Hellmann, pp. 153 ff.

[2] The evidence for the true readings will be given in vol. II *ad locos.*

[3] The examples of that type of error which consists in interpolation are very numerous.

Agreements of G *with* H_2 *where both are wrong:*

2 Cor. iii 5 *se nihil* GH_2 : *nihil se.*
rusticani GH_2R : *rustici.*
Gal. v 18 *lex uobis* GH_2 : *uobis lex.*
Phil. i 20 *et uita nostra—pertinet Christi* om. GH_2 : legendum.
22 *si uiuere—operandi* om. GH_2 : legendum.
ii 22 *ut qualis sit nouerítis* om. GH_2 : legendum.
23 *modo enim incertus sum* om. GH_2 : legendum.

From all this evidence it is clear that the St Gall MS is considerably different from Pseudo-Jerome. Before we pass on to compare it with other MSS, we can dispose of other differences not already mentioned. It gives the famous note on Romans v 15 *Plus praeualuit* etc., which is wanting from every Pseudo-Jerome manuscript[1]. It has the Pelagian *Primum quaeritur* prologue, somewhat mutilated, and the Pelagian prologues to First Timothy and Titus. It has the Marcionite prologues to First Corinthians, Galatians, First Thessalonians and Philemon, and the Pseudo-Marcionite (catholic) prologues to Second Thessalonians and Second Timothy. Of the remaining epistles, Second Corinthians has the Pseudo-Marcion *plus* the Balliol prologue with some differences, Ephesians has the Marcionite *plus* a portion of Jerome, Philippians has the Marcionite *plus* the Pelagian prologue, Colossians has no preface, Hebrews has the usual Vulgate preface found also in H_2. From this it is clear that the basis of our manuscript was a copy of the Epistles or of Pseudo-Jerome, fitted with the usual Marcionite or Pseudo-Marcionite prologues.

This last suggestion is supported by a partial stichometry incorporated with the arguments.

2 Cor. { DCCC·LXX[2]
LI

[1] Here and elsewhere of course I except the Balliol MS, which is in a sense a Pseudo-Jerome. It is convenient to treat it by itself, as it differs so greatly from the longer manuscripts.

[2] Probably this has become displaced and really refers to 1 Cor. It is given at the beginning of 2 Cor., whereas the other is given at the end of 2 Cor.

Phil.[1] {CCXV / CCL}
2 Thess. CXCIII
1 Tim. CCXXX
2 Tim. CLXII
Tit. XCVII

It is obvious that this stichometry is in part corrupt, even if there are not traces of two systems here. There is some relationship between it and that which is given by the second family of Pseudo-Jerome manuscripts[2], though only in two cases, Phil. (b) and 1 Tim., are the numbers absolutely identical. Both omit stichometry in five cases, only eight numbers being given in each case, and on the whole the same epistles are alluded to in both. It would be of the utmost importance to fix the date and place of origin of the stichometrical system here employed, but in the present state of our knowledge I am unable to do so. Meantime we must return to the consideration of the textual relations proper of our manuscript.

Agreements of G *and the Würzburg glosses*[3] *where both are wrong:*

Rom. i 21 *imaginem* GWb : *magnitudinem.*
2 Cor. x 16 *ad alios* GWb; *alibi* Cassiod.[txt.] (*om.* Cassiod.[cod.]): *alio.*

The two also share various interpolations, e.g. at Eph. v 14[4].

Agreements of G *and the Vienna glosses*[5] *where both are wrong:*

1 Tim. vi 2 the interpolation *in baptismo* GWn : om.
Philem. 25 a considerable interpolation GWn : om.

Agreement of G *and Cassiodorus where both are wrong:*

Rom. viiii 10 *nati* G Cassiod. : *generati.*

The question of the Biblical text employed in the St Gall manuscript must now be considered. It is not pure Vulgate, but it approximates much more closely to the Vulgate than does

[1] The first is given at the beginning, the second at the end.
[2] See below, p. 270. [3] See below, pp. 326 ff.
[4] Zimmer, pp. 262 ff., 270 f.: cf. also his notes on the Hebrews commentary (p. 275).
[5] See below, pp. 328 f.

either **A** or **B**. Let us examine, for instance, Romans i and v 12—21 with the aid of Wordsworth and White's apparatus. The following differences from the Vulgate occur in these sections:

Rom. i 10 *semper* om. with **B.**
11 ~ *uobis gratiae* **B**Ḋ[1] etc.
13 *enim* vg. codd. **A.**
17 *autem.*
18 *et* om.
ueritatem dei **B**D etc.
iniustitia dei.
20 *intellectu.*
~ *uirtus eius* D etc.
et **AB**D etc.
21 *qui* with d*.
23 *incorruptibilis* om.
24 *efficiant.*
25 *mendacium* **A**D etc.
amen om. **AB** etc.
27 *in* (alt.) om. **AB**D etc.
28 *ea quae* vg. codd. etc.
29 *repletos*] + *enim.*
iniquitate] + *et* **B.**
fornicatione] + *et* **B.**
32 *solum*] + *qui* **AB**D etc.
et] + *qui* **AB**D etc. (D however om. *et*).
v 13 *hoc mundo* **B**D etc.
15 *gratia* (alt.) **AB**D etc.
16 *iudicium*] + *quidem* **B**D etc.
17 *in* (pr.) om. vg. codd. **AB.**
uitam **A**D etc.
18 *in* (pr.) eras. vg. codd. Sedul.
et om. Aug. ter.
in (tert.) eras. vg. codd. Sedul.
19 *oboedientiam* **B**D Sedul. etc.
constituiuntur (sic) : *constituuntur* vg. codd. etc.
20 *superhabundabit*[2].
21 *et* om.

[1] For the meaning of these symbols see chap. iv.
[2] See p. 238, above.

The variants unparalleled in other authorities may safely be regarded as merely graphic, or inspired by such intelligence as the scribes possessed. It will not escape notice that among the remainder, twenty-five in number, there are ten shared with A, fifteen shared with B, and thirteen with the *Book of Armagh* (D), which we have discovered to be in close relationship with the text used by Pelagius himself[1]. The St Gall text is then, no doubt, like others which will come before us, and like the text in the Reichenau MS (A), the original Pelagian text as considerably revised to bring it into harmony with the Vulgate. If the commentary in the St Gall MS was really built round a separate copy of the Epistles, then this copy may very well have been an Irish text, which would naturally show relationship with the *Book of Armagh*. It has been shown above that Gildas used such a text, and the evidence, alike that already given, and that which is yet to be provided, shows that Sedulius the Irishman's text was of the same kindred. But more probably our MS represents what was a good Pseudo-Jerome at the Visigothic stage, and the other comments were added in the margin of our 7th or 8th century Irish copy of it. (See further under Pseudo-Jerome.)

(2) *No.* 653 *in the Bibliothèque Nationale at Paris* (V)

The wonderful manuscript now numbered 653 in the Latin collection of the Bibliothèque Nationale, bears also three earlier shelf-marks, the earliest of all being DLXXXVIII, the next in age 628 (belonging to the year 1645), and the next 3939 (belonging to the year 1682)[2]. It reached the Bibliothèque Royale from Italy during the reign of Henri II (1547—1559), whose arms it bears on the elaborate binding of that date, to which the gilding of the leaves may also be assigned. It belongs to the end of the eighth or the beginning of the ninth century[3]. It now contains only 296 folia, though from errors in numeration it appears to

[1] See chap. iv, pp. 126 etc.

[2] I am indebted to Monsieur H. Omont's kindness for the dates of these shelf-marks.

[3] So Dümmler, *Poetae Latini Aevi Carolini* (Mon. Germ. Hist.) tom. I pars prior (Berol. 1880) p. 89; and E. A. Lowe, *Studia Palaeographica* (SB. Bay. Akad. Jhrg. 1910 [12 Abh.]) p. 86; W. M. Lindsay, *Notae Latinae* (Cambr. 1915) p. 471, 'saec. VIII'; so also M. Mellot in *Nouveau Traité de Diplomatique* t. III (Paris, 1757) p. 65.

contain fewer still, namely 292. The leaves measure 27 cm. by 18 cm., the written part 224 mm. by 12—14 cm.

The quaternions are regular up to and including XIIII (ending on fol. 112 v), and are signed thus: ||||II||||| in the middle of the foot of the last page of the quaternion. Then follows a quinion arranged thus:

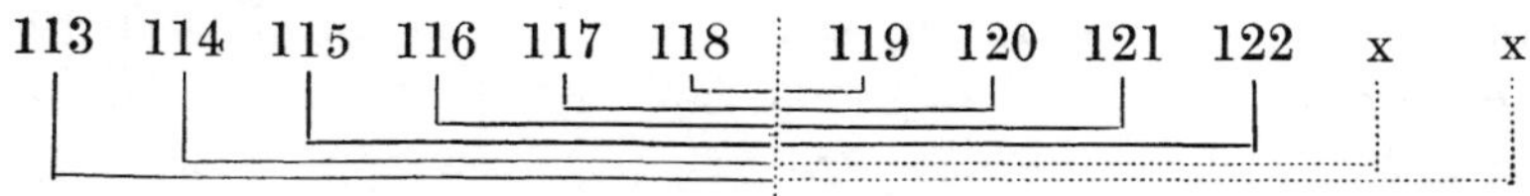

This is signed I; then there are regular quaternions signed II, III; then five leaves together thus, and unsigned:

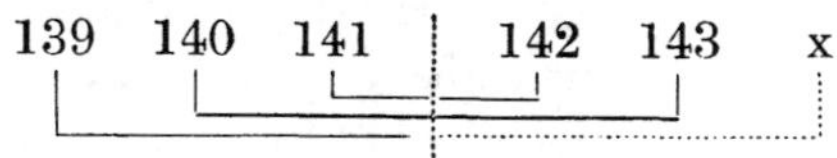

then regular quaternions signed |||I||||–, ||||II|||||, ||||III||||, etc., till we reach ||||VIIII|||| (ending on fol. 212 v); then a binion unsigned, and then an ordinary quaternion signed ·I· at the right lower corner of f. 224 v; then:

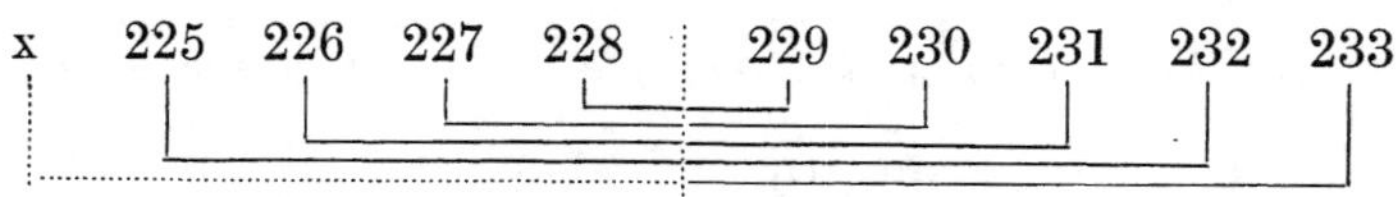

signed II at the right lower corner; then a set of regular quaternions, III, IIII, V, VI, VII, VIII, VIIII (f. 288 v); then a binion unsigned,

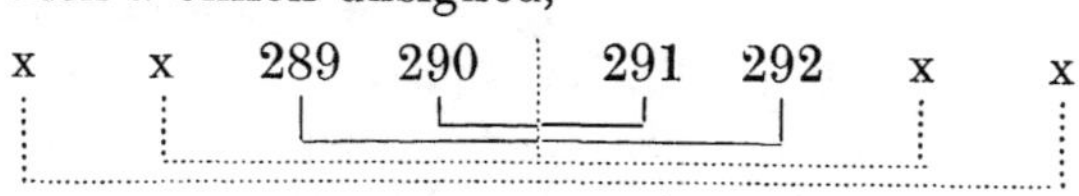

which finishes the codex, which is imperfect, two outer conjugate leaves having been lost from the last quaternion now represented[1]. The number of extant leaves, then, may be computed thus:

$$112 + 10 + 16 + 5 + 72 + 4 + 8 + 9 + 56 + 4 = 296.$$

[1] This loss is very old, probably older than the time of Henri II, and certainly prior to the saec. xv—xvi (?) foliation, which numbers fol. 288 by pp. 8 and fol. 289 by pp. 9. The folia themselves were numbered by Arabic numbers, probably in the seventeenth century.

There is a fol. 169 and a fol. 169 *bis*, a leaf is unnumbered between fol. 183 and fol. 184, another is unnumbered between fol. 189 and fol. 190, and yet another is unnumbered between fol. 287 and fol. 288. We thus see how the numerator is four folia short with his 292 ff.

Fol. 1r contains a short poem addressed, it appears, to Charlemagne himself[1], and the authors of the *Nouveau Traité* make the probable conjecture that this volume was a present to that Emperor. He was certainly active in Italy in the encouragement of learning from A.D. 776 at least[2].

On fol. 1v there is the following table of contents (in uncials):

HAEC INSUNT · PAULI · APOS (*red*)
TULI · EPISTVLAE · NUMERO · XIIII
AD ROMANOS
AD CORRINTHIOS II ·
AD GALATAS
AD EPHESIOS
AD PHILIPPENSES
AD COLOSSENSES
AD THESSALONICENSES II
AD TIMOTHEUM II
AD TITUM
AD PHILEMONEM
AD HEBREOS[3].

Fol. 2r begins with the shelf-marks already referred to: DLXXXVIII stroked out by the hand that wrote 628: *Primum quaeritur* prologue—ending on the middle of fol. 3v, the rest of which is occupied with the *Romani sunt* argument in uncials; fol. 4r—fol. 5r (middle) contain the *Romani ex Iudaeis* prologue; fol. 5r another version of the *Romani sunt*; then a tractate beginning *Verbum caro factum est* and ending *esse non desinit*, and (f. 6r)

[1] This poem was published in the *Nouveau Traité* t. III (Paris, 1757) p. 78, and by Dümmler in *Poetae Latini Aevi Carolini* tom. I p. 1 (Berol. 1880) p. 98.

[2] W. Wattenbach, *Deutschlands Geschichtsquellen im Mittelalter...* I Bd 7 Aufl. (Stuttgart and Berlin, 1904) p. 168. He died 11 Jan. 802.

[3] This table disguises the fact that in the body of the MS the epistles are in the Pelagian order: Phil. 1, 2 Thess. Col.

another beginning *De numero apostolorum* and ending *partis meritum repperitur* (fol. 6 v)[1]. Then, after a fourteenth century hand's insertion of the words '*Incipit expositio in epistola ad romanos*' the commentary proper begins. After the commentary on Romans comes the Marcionite prologue to First Corinthians, and then in succession the following: EXPOSITIO ARGUMENTI : *Corinthus metropolis est Achaiae; et idcirco quod Corinthis* (sic) *scribit, Achiuis omnibus scribit*; commentary on First Corinthians; Pseudo-Marcionite argument to Second Corinthians, followed by the prologue to that epistle printed in the Benedictine (Migne) edition of Ambrosiaster, and found also in the interpolated MSS of that author[2] as well as in our B; commentary on Second Corinthians; Marcionite argument to Galatians; Pelagian prologue to Galatians; commentary on Galatians; Marcionite argument to Ephesians; Pelagian prologue to Ephesians; commentary on Ephesians; Marcionite argument to Philippians; Pelagian prologue to Philippians; commentary on Philippians; Marcionite argument to First Thessalonians; Pelagian prologue to First Thessalonians; commentary on First Thessalonians; Pseudo-Marcionite argument to Second Thessalonians; Pelagian prologue to Second Thessalonians; commentary on Second Thessalonians; Marcionite argument to Colossians; Pelagian prologue to Colossians; commentary on Colossians; Pelagian prologue to First Timothy; commentary on First Timothy; Pelagian prologue to Second Timothy; commentary on Second Timothy; Pelagian prologue to Titus; commentary on Titus [down to c. ii v. 11 where, after *crapula*, the first two leaves of a new quaternion are gone: these contained the rest of the Titus commentary, the prefatory matter to Philemon, and the Philemon commentary down to *gaudium enim* (v. 7)]; commentary on Hebrews [lost after c. iv v. 3]. This bald enumeration gives little idea of the multiplicity of the contents, which we shall have to consider later.

The conjoint opinion of palaeographers who have seen this manuscript is that it was written in Italy. 'Ainsi il paroît venir d'Italie' is the verdict of the authors of the *Nouveau Traité*

1 These tractates were published by me in *Proc. Brit. Acad.* vol. II pp. 435 f.
2 See chap. ii p. 57.

(accepted by Dümmler)[1]. Dr E. A. Lowe calls it 'a north Italian MS of about 800 A.D.[2],' and assigns it hesitatingly to a Verona scriptorium[3]: Lindsay's attitude is identical[4].

The signatures of the quaternions suggest that at least three scribes took part in writing the *codex*. As a matter of fact, I believe there were four, and that they distributed the work thus:

1st scribe: fol. 1r (the Charlemagne poem), fol. 6v—114v.
2nd scribe: fol. 1v—6v (end of prefatory matter).
3rd scribe: fol. 115r—142v.
4th scribe: fol. 143r—end (296v).

The writing of the first scribe 'shows cursive traditions: it uses i-longa, ꞓ (for soft ti), the ligatures of *ri, st* etc. Characteristic is the *r* with the shoulder extending over the following letter. The second scribe lacks i-longa, ꞓ, ligatures of *ri, st* etc. and represents the more modern tendency[5].' To this it may be added that the third scribe uses the i-longa, both as the initial letter of a word and as representing the semi-vocalic i, also the ꞓ (soft ti) symbol, the ligatures of *st* etc., and the *r* with the shoulder extending over the following letter: the fourth scribe shares all these characteristics[6].

The following abbreviations occur in the manuscript. Where they are already attested for a Veronese scriptorium, I have added the letter V in brackets[7].

aliter aĺ āl al˜ aĺi (ff. 71r etc.) aĺt (f. 146v) alitē (f. 103r)
apostolus apōslū 'apostolum' (f. 177r)
autem aū (very frequent) (V) aü (f. 116v) (autē f. 16v)
caput cap̄ (end of line f. 117v)
Christianus xp̄ianis 'Christianis,' etc.
Christus etc. xp̄s etc.
Colosenses 'colosenss' (f. 264v)

[1] References above. *Nouveau Traité* vol. III, opposite p. 65, gives a plate representing the subscription at the end of 1 Cor. and the title at the beginning of 2 Cor. of fol. 143r. The authors also had enough intelligence to realise that the MS, though anonymous, contains 'l'exposition ou les commentaires de Pelage sur les épitres de S. Paul.'

[2] *Studia Palaeographica* p. 5 n. He also publishes a facsimile of a portion of one page (plate 2), given him by Prof. W. M. Lindsay.

[3] *Op. cit.* p. 43.

[4] *Notae Latinae* p. 471. He thinks Paris B. N. 9451 (which I have not seen) is from the same scriptorium.

[5] Lowe, *op. cit.* p. 86.

[6] The Trustees of the Revision Surplus Fund in Oxford very kindly defrayed the cost of over 400 rotographs of this MS.

[7] 'Abbreviature nel Minuscolo Veronese' by Antonio Spagnolo in *Zentralblatt für Bibliothekswesen* XXVII Jhrg. (1910) pp. 531—548 (with W. M. Lindsay's note, pp. 549—552) as corrected by the author in XXVIII Jhrg. (1911) pp. 259—261.

Corinthii corint̄ 'Corinthios'
deitas dītate 'deitate' (f. 108 r)
deus etc. ds̄ etc.
dominus etc. dn̄s etc.: note dnm̄ dnis dn̄o̅s (of secular lords once or twice, e.g. ff. 46 v, 213 v)
ecclesia aeccl̄a (ff. 80 v, 101 r)
episcopus ep̄i 'episcopi,' ep̄m̄ 'episcopum' (ff. 287 r, 287 v *bis*), ep̄o̅s 'episcopos' (f. 270 r *bis*) (V)
epistula ep̄is (ff. 264 v, 279 r, 287 r, 289 v)
est ÷ (ff. 62 v, 103 v *s.l.*, 142 v, 145 r etc.) (V) pot ÷ (end of line, f. 153 r) 'potest'
et &
explicit expt̄, exp̄, expl̄
expositio exp̄o (f. 291 r *bis*)
fratres fr̄s (V) ff̄ (ff. 122 r, 129 r etc.) (V)
gloria gl̄a (f. 118 r, and six other times) (V), gl̄ā (f. 290 v) 'gloriam'
hic deest hd̄ (in text f. 141 v)
hic pone hp̄ (in margin f. 141 v)
id est id̄ (f. 153 v, end of line) (V)
Iesus etc. ih̄s etc.
ih̄ū 'Iesum' (f. 216 r)
ihūs (ff. 164 r, 176 r, 197 v)
incipit inc̄p̄, incp̄t, inc̄ (f. 289 v)
Israhel ih̄l (V), ihl̄is 'israhelis'
Israhelita ih̄lita (f. 52 r etc.)
Israheliticus ih̄litico 'israhelitico' (f. 201 v)
item it̄ (V)
meus m̄s (fourth scribe only, but frequently) (V)
mihi never abbreviated[1]
misericordia mīā 'misericordiam' (f. 238 r) (V)
mā̄ē 'misericordiae' (f. 261 v), mā 'misericordia,' mā̄ 'misericordiam' (used only by fourth scribe, and sometimes expanded by another hand) (V)
{*nobis* nob̄ (V)
{*uobis* uob̄ (V)
non n̄ (V)

noster often written in full, with other divine names contracted, thus: dn̄i nostri ihū xp̄i
n̄ 'nostro' (f. 203 v)
nēr 'noster' (ff. 66 r, 109 r) (V)[2]
nor̄is 'nostris' (f. 178 r), nōrę 'nostrae' (f. 145 v), nor̄i 'nostri' (f. 229 v)
ns̄r̄ (five times, fourth scribe) (**Spanish**)
nī 'nostri' (f. 221 r etc.), nm̄ 'nostrum' (f. 230 r, and often), nā 'nostra' (f. 149 v etc.); this type used by fourth scribe only, except that it occurs also f. 31 r
nr̄i 'nostri,' 'nrāe 'nostrae,' etc. (V)
uester uer̄i 'uestri' (once), uer̄a 'uestra' (f. 77 r only)
uā 'uestra,' uīs 'uestris' (each twice by fourth scribe)
ur̄i 'uestri,' ur̄o 'uestro,' etc. (V)
omnipotens om̄ptis 'omnipotentis' (f. 269 v) (V)
omnis om̄s 'omnes' (V), 'omnis' (ff. 164 v, 165 r, 178 r, etc.) (V)
om̄a 'omnia' (f. 278 v, and five times later) (V)
paenitentia pęnitiā 'paenitentiam' (f. 175 r)
per ꝑ (V)
prae p̄ (V)
pro ꝓ (V)
propheta ꝓph̄ (f. 10 v, mg)
propter prop̄ (very frequently, beginning with f. 206 v) (V)
pp̄r (f. 216 v)
(propt̄, end of line)
(ꝓpt̄, end of line) (V)
ꝓter (ff. 118 r, 126 v)
psalmus psl̄ (once, f. 116 v)
que q: (V)
q; (V)
ꝗ (end of line, f. 209 r) (V)

[1] I mention this because mh̄ is a characteristic Veronese abbreviation (Lindsay's note on Spagnolo [see p. 249, n. 7 above] p. 549).

[2] These appear to be the oldest known examples of this Italian abbreviation (see Lowe, *Beneventan Script* [Oxford, 1914] p. 208).

qui ꝗ (m 2 mg) (V)
quod qđ (once) (V)
quoniam qm̄ (V)
qn̄m̄ (f. 133 r) (V)
saeculum saeƚi 'saeculi' (f. 142 v)
scƚm (V), scƚi 'saeculi' (f. 290 r) (V), scƚa 'saecula' (V), scƚrū (f. 286 v only)
sanctificatio sc̄ificationis 'sanctificationis,' etc.
sanctifico sc̄ificaret 'sanctificaret' sc̄ificatis 'sanctificatis'
sanctitas sc̄itatem 'sanctitatem,' sc̄itatis 'sanctitatis'
sanctus etc. sc̄s etc.
sc̄or̄ 'sanctorum' (f. 247 v)
secundum sec̄ū (f. 158 r)
spiritalis etc. sp̄alis etc.
sp̄ilis 'spiritalis' (f. 169 r), sp̄ilia 'spiritalia' (ff. 115 v, 129 v)
sp̄itali 'spiritali' (f. 146 v), sp̄italem 'spiritalem' (f. 128 r), etc.
spirituliter sp̄aliter
spiritus etc. sp̄s etc.
spūm 'spiritum' (f. 123 v)
sunt s̄t (end of line once, f. 177 v, and twice in a correction, f. 114 v)
uel uƚ (near end of line) (V)

Syllable Symbols:

ae ę (V)
er t̄ 'ter' (V)
is b̄ 'bis' (f. 61 v, 70 v, 71 v, 112 r etc. etc.) (V)
it dilig⁀ 'diligit' (f. 127 r) (V)
m suprascript stroke (V)
n suprascript stroke (V)
u the v form superposed after q, as also in half-uncial script, e.g. q̌i (fol. 2 v)[1]
um ꝶ 'rum' (V)
ur t̄ 'tur' (ff. 44 r, 281 v) (very rare) (V)
tꝛ 'tur' (end of ff. 158 r, 204 r, 205 v)
us b; (V)
bꝫ (V)
pˢ (f. 120 v) eiˢ (ff. 137 v, 194 r, 197 r) b, (ff. 187 r, 200 r) mˢ (ff. 144 v, 153 r) tˢ (ff. 177 r, 203 r) lˢ (f. 209 r, end of line) (V)

The orthography of this manuscript is of great excellence. This does not mean that it is absolutely consistent throughout. We always find *adb-*, but on the contrary always *acc-* and *arr-*. Apart from these there is no consistency: we have *adf-* and *aff-*, *adgr-* and *agn-*, *adl-* (rare) and *all-*, *adm-* and *amm-*, *adn-* and *ann-* (*an-*), *adp-* and *app-*, *ads-* and *ass-*, *adt-* and *att-*. We find *conburo* and *conregno*, but *conl-* and *coll-*, *conm-* and *comm-*, *conp-* and *comp-*, and *corr-* (always, except for *conregno*, *conresuscito*). There is hardly a trace of consistency in regard to either *in-* (negative) or *in-* (preposition), even in the case of the same word. Thus we have *inmanis* and *immanis*, *inmundus* and *immundus*, *inpune* and *impune*, *inperitus* and *imperitus*, but I believe always *inl-*; and yet we find *irritus*, *impius*, *impie*, *impietas*. The case is similar with the other *in-*, though there the unassimilated or uneuphonic forms greatly predominate. *Impleo* is regular, but *inl-* is even

[1] This is not, of course, a real abbreviation. I know no complete discussion of its use.

invariable, while we have *inpertio* and *impertio, inpedio* and *impedio, inpendo* and *impendo, inpugno* and *impugno, inplico* and *implico, inpono* and *impono, inbecillitas* and *imbecillitas*; *inrideo, inrogo,* but *irritatio. Obm-* is (except once) invariable, but so is *occ-*; yet we find *obf-* and *off-*, *obp-* (rare) and *opp-*, *obt-* (rare) and *opt-*. *Per-*, as far as used, is unassimilated, and the assimilated (euphonic) forms are almost invariable in compounds with *sub-*: thus we have *sumministro, supplicium, suppono, supporto, supter, suptiliter, suptilitas, suscribo,* while *subtilitas* occurs, I believe, only once. *Exs-* is much less common than *ex-*, and the following inconsistencies occur: *exsisto* and *existo, exspecto* and *expecto, exsurgo* and *exurgo.* The following forms are consistent: *exsupero, exsequor* on the one hand, *execror, expolio, extasis, extinguo, exulto* on the other.

There are probably fewer traces of uneducated spelling in this manuscript than in any other with which we have to do. I have gathered together all the instances, and classify them here. They are, most of them, such as might be found in any MS of that date:

aspirate omitted: *exibeo, geenna, ebreus, aruspex, ospes, ospitor, ospicium, istoria, istoricus, odiernus, ostia, ipocrisis, ortor, ymnus, retrao* (twice).

aspirate added: *habii, habundo, habundanter, habundantia, herastus, honus, humor.*

i for *e*: *accīpi, abolire, aduliscens* (etc.), *cathecuminus, debit* (several times), *discendo, distruo, dibilitas, discritio, diuis, dificio, diffirentia, dispero, deuterisis, distituo, elimosina, elimentum, erubisco, famis, gentis, habit, hospis, herimus, innotisco, inrepraehinsibilis* (6 times), *licit, magistas, manit, mercis, oportit* (several times), *obmutisco, onisiphorus, pinguido, peripsima, penticusten, paraclitus, profitia, redigerit, reuiuisco, senix, scilicit, uidelicit, uilisco, uiri,* etc.

e for *i*: *ancella* (4 times, Italian), *accepio, agonezari, aures, bestea, crededi, collego, dilego, dedici, dessideo, eretis* (twice), *excesseremus, homecidium, intrensecus, porrego, possedeo, praesteti, perdedi, reddedi, sterelis, suscepio, tradedi, ueletis* etc., and particularly in verb forms of second person plural: *lapidastes, legistes, recessistes, correxistes, probastes, fecistes, coepistes, seruetes, uelites, suffertes, coegistes, habuerites,* etc.

o for *u*: *absordus, adolor, adolatio, emolatio, consolo, costodio, copolo, capitolum, curso, discipolus, luxoria, popolus, stimolus, uolocres* (twice), *nabochodonosor, uulto, stodio, oror, saecolo, cocurrem, testimonio, commodo, com, actos,* etc.

u for *o*: *apostulus, apostulatus, auditur, diabulus* (nearly always), *cognusco, consuletur, furtunatus, humicidium, lucutus, lurica* (twice), *mundu, nundum, praeuaricatur, prumptus, pulire, pulluere, penticusten, parabula, scurpio, subrius, nullus, solus.*

y for *i*: *dygamus*, *aelymosina*, *hytoria* (sic), *hyspania*, *paralypomenon*, *paraclytus*, *sapp(-ff-)yra*, *synapis*, *syna*, *satellytibus*, *sybilla*.

i for *y*: *azima*, *hiperbatum*, *ipocrisis*, *idolotitus*, *misterium*, *neophitus*, *proselitus*, *praesbiter*, *sybilla*, *syntiche*.

ae for *e*: *conpraehindo*, *caena*, *caeler*, *cotidiae*, *depraecor*, *depraessus*, *aepistula*, *aecclesia* (nearly always), *aeua*, *aerubesco*, *aelymosina*, *ęlymosina*, *aepulae*, *aeloquentia*, *aebrietas*, *aesca*, *aegredior*, *aegere*, *ędo*, *aelisaeus*, *faemina*, *haebreus*, *inrepraehinsibilis* (6 times), *interpraetor*, *laeuissimus*, *laquaeus*, *paenitus* *praessura*, *praeces*, *praetium*, *praetiosus*, *praesbiter*, *quaem*, *quaerella*, *repraehindo*, *saeueritas*, *terraestris*.

e for *ae*: *adhereo*, *aggeus*, *egrotus*, *enigma*, *emolatio*, *ledo*, *letus*, *longeuu* , *meror*, *penitentia*, *prestetit*, etc.

t (intervocalic) for *c* (intervocalic) : *amititia*, *conspitio*, *capatior*, *mendatium*, *offitium*, *pernitiosus*, *solatium*, *sotius*, *speties*, *initiam*.

c (intervocalic) for *t* (intervocalic): *diucius*, *hospicium*, *ospicium*, *malicia*, *preciosus*, *perdicio*, *pacientia*[1].

Much more significance attaches to the following:

qu for *c*: aliquius, **quum** (at least five times), quoaequare (twice), quur (eight times), quoheres[2], quoram, loquutus, quuius (four times), sequuntur, sequuturus, persequutio (twice).

c for *qu*: alico, corundam (twice), co, condam.

g for *c*: apogryphus, collogo, **gregus**, **obsegro** (seven times), **uagare**, negare.

d for *t*: cedera, confidens, gradus, dubidare, confideatur, gradanter, heredicus (twice), **hospidem**, refudo, tradidi, tradidurus. These intervocalic instances have, I think, more significance than the elsewhere frequent final *d*, found here in quod, inquid.

t for *d*: impetit, potest (*for* prodest), canditatus, sordito, nutus, gratus (twice), excitant, expetit, etc.

b for *u*: abia, coacerbauunt, minorabit, mutabit.

u for *b*: coacerbauunt, inuistigauilis, furaueris, suscitauit, multiplicauit, adimpleuites, habeuit, gubernauit, cessauit.

Such forms as **anuntio**, **aplaudo**, **apello** (twice), **acommodo**, aministratio, **asensus**, **atemto**, **atendo**, **afirmo**, **suportare** must I think be grouped with the phenomena just mentioned, as well as adibiscor (for adipiscor), obrebit, probrius (for proprius), praecebit (twice). But to no forms should I attach greater significance than to:

guila (seven times) for gula, and **menime** (ten times).

[1] These may be due to a misreading of *t* in a Visigothic MS: cf. Lowe, *Studia Palaeographica* (München, 1910) p. 20 n. 1, p. 51 n. 2.

[2] *In Rom.* viii 17 has *quoheredes*: Wordsworth and White's only authorities for this spelling are CT, both Spanish manuscripts.

Guila has recently been produced from a Spanish manuscript (Madrid, Bibliot. Acad. Hist. 44 (saec. VIII—IX) = Table 16[d] (twice) in C. U. Clark's *Collectanea Hispanica*[1]), and Mr Robert Weir quotes me *gyilosus*, *guilosus* from the 'Abolita' glossary (*C.G.L.* IV 81, 24), which is of Spanish origin (W. M. Lindsay in *Journal of Philology* XXXIV (1918) pp. 268 f.[2]). The forms just given prove that our manuscript was copied from a Spanish original. Lest any one should doubt the cogency of the reasoning, I must point out that Paris 653 is by no means the only North-Italian product which was copied from a Spanish original. Some of the oldest and best manuscripts of Isidore of Seville's *Etymologiae* are of North-Italian provenance, for example three Bobbio MSS of the eighth century (Lindsay's AKL) and a Veronese MS (Lindsay's Phill.) coeval with our own[3]. Beeson's lists of early Italian MSS of Isidore's other works tell the same story[4]. Verona still houses a Visigothic MS which may have been written before A.D. 732[5]. Direct communication between Spain and Italy was quite frequent in the seventh century[6], at which date the original of our MS was probably brought there. The remarkable character of that original is quite consistent with the conjecture that it was an autograph compilation of Isidore himself. Sedulius Scottus had a commentary on the Epistles in his possession, which he calls 'Isidore[7].' Though the extracts thus labelled come really from Cassiodorus (Pseudo-Primasius), we may attribute this ascription to a current tradition that Isidore had really compiled a commentary on the Pauline Epistles.

[1] *Transactions of the Connecticut Academy of Arts and Sciences* vol. 24 (Paris, 1920). My attention was called to the form *guilae* in the above-mentioned MS by a review of P. Lehmann in *Philologische Wochenschrift* XLI (1921) p. 324. It is instructive to compare Clark's lists (pp. 100 ff.) with the peculiarities noted on the preceding page or two.

[2] See also Th. Birt in *Rh. Mus.* Bd LI (1896) pp. 98 f., referred to by Goetz.

[3] See the 'praefatio' to Lindsay's edition (1912) in *Oxford Classical Texts*, and *Classical Quarterly* v (1911) p. 46; also C. H. Beeson, *Isidor-Studien* (München, 1913) pp. 9 ff.

[4] *Isidor-Studien* pp. 23 f., 29, 45, 66, 74, 127 f.

[5] Bibl. Capit. LXXXIX (Clark, *Collectanea Hispanica* pp. 63 f.).

[6] Traube, *Vorlesungen und Abhandlungen* II (München, 1910 [dated 1911]) p. 21; Wilmart, *Bull. d'anc. litt. et d'archéol. chrét.* IV (1914) p. 187.

[7] See below, p. 338.

The scribes, as we have hinted, were very careful; but they had one failing not uncommon among scribes, the omission of syllables, especially where two similar or identical syllables come together in a word. I have noted these examples: *homi⟨ni⟩bus, contend⟨end⟩i, prophet⟨et⟩is, ⟨de⟩leo, cred⟨id⟩istis, si⟨di⟩gnum, st⟨at⟩e, hort⟨at⟩ur, aedif⟨ic⟩ationem, sollic⟨it⟩ior, dil⟨ig⟩it, oboe⟨die⟩ntibus, habun⟨dan⟩tius, infir⟨mi⟩tate, euan⟨ge⟩lizo, tolle⟨re⟩tur, pecca⟨ta⟩, beat⟨it⟩udo, huma⟨na⟩, de⟨ne⟩gemus, restau⟨ratu⟩m, mand⟨at⟩orum, libid⟨in⟩em, euang⟨el⟩io, nit⟨it⟩ur, ex⟨em⟩plum, ostend⟨end⟩o.*

There are very few examples of the opposite mistake. I have noted these: *abs[tin]entibus, ad[in]uenticius, empt[at]ionis, ambi[gi]t, bapti⟨s⟩mum[um], inmortali[tali]tatem.*

The kernel of the commentary is of course the original Pelagius, but it has become greatly expanded in various ways, in the case of all the thirteen epistles except First and Second Timothy, Titus and Philemon. In the first place, it contains a number of additional short notes the style and language of which suggest that they are by Pelagius himself, and that they go back to the author's own copy, to which he added notes from time to time. This author's copy must somehow have come into the possession of our Spanish compiler. He was not, however, satisfied with the increased size of the original commentary. Being in possession of a Pseudo-Jerome also, he has added a large number of the new notes he found in it, in a text purer than we can otherwise find, because quite independent of the corrupt Insular tradition to which we owe our copies of Pseudo-Jerome. From the lists in my second chapter the reader will get a fair idea of the type of both these classes of additional notes[1]. A third class of note consists of unacknowledged borrowings from Jerome *Against Jovinian* on 1 Cor. vii. But the most interesting of all the accretions are a number of long extracts quite unsuited in character to the glossarial Pelagius as originally composed. These are the following:

(*a*) *Verbum caro factum est.* Sic accipimus quod—esse non desinit [f. 5 r, v: anonymous[2]].

[1] Pp. 37 ff., 46 ff., 51, 59 f.

[2] Published in *Proc. Brit. Acad.* vol. II pp. 435 f.

(*b*) De numero apostolorum quaeritur—meritum repperitur [f. 6 r, v: anonymous[1]].

(*c*) Hieronimus: Ecce quod non uult—implere non posse. Pelagius: O uocem temerariam—uirtutum uincit exemplo [ff. 41 v—42 v: an extract from genuine Jerome followed by a long extract from the third book of Pelagius's *De Libero Arbitrio*, of which only the last part was hitherto known, and that from a quotation in Augustine, *De Gratia* 39 § 43[2]].

(*d*) De eo uero quod solent dicere—anterius posteriusue non recipit [ff. 108 v—110 v: an anonymous tractate on the Divinity of the Son, undoubtedly by the same author as (*f*) and (*h*), this author being probably either Fulgentius of Ruspe (*ob.* A.D. 532)[3] or some other African of his date and circle].

(*e*) Hieronymus: 'qui nouit,' inquid,—quaecumque uultis, illa faciatis. Pelagius: ut autem ex hoc quoque—ut ultra non seruiamus peccato [ff. 191 r—192 v: an extract from genuine Jerome, followed by a long extract from Pelagius's *De Libero Arbitrio*, otherwise unknown[4]].

(*f*) Non autem ignoramus quae—uoce absolutissima pronuntiatum [ff. 221 v—224 r: an anonymous extract, by the same author as (*d*) and (*h*)[5]].

(*g*) Hieronymus: 'unde et apostolus,' ais,—non esse contentum. Pelagius: si tuam hoc quoque loco—mihi corona iustitiae [ff. 228 r—229 r: probably from the same work as (*c*) and (*e*)[6]].

(*h*) Quod autem eiusdem sit—credere uelle quod non lego [ff. 242 v—247 v: an anonymous tractate on the Holy Spirit, by the same author as (*d*) and (*f*)[7]].

These and all other additions to the original extent of the commentary have already been copied out for press, but their publication as part of the present work is inevitably deferred till happier times.

[1] Published in *Proc. Brit. Acad.* vol. II p. 436.

[2] Published in *J.T.S.* vol. XII (1910—11) pp. 34 f.: the location of the extract is due to Dr F. Loofs (private communication of 12 Aug. 1912).

[3] Published in *J.T.S.* vol. XVII (1915—16) pp. 133—136.

[4] Published in *Proc. Brit. Acad.* vol. II pp. 437 f.

[5] Unpublished at the time of writing.

[6] Published in *Proc. Brit. Acad.* vol. II pp. 438 f.

[7] Published in *J.T.S.* vol. XIV (1912—13) pp. 482—488.

The numerous doublets in the commentary are best explained by the supposition that the compiler used both a pure Pelagius and a Pseudo-Jerome, without taking sufficient precaution against duplication. Examples of this occurrence are these:

In Rom. v 15—16 *Adam solam formam—exemplum uiuendi* (see pp. 38—39). It really belongs to v 16, but Ps.-Hier. has it also under v 15: V gives it in both places.

In 1 *Cor.* xiii 2 *Hinc intellegitur magna fides esse quae in euangelio grano synapis comparatur, quod non propter modicitatem, sed propter integritatem uel uigorem appositum est. notandum sane quod inter cetera etiam omnis fides quae montes transferat, sine caritate non prosit....unde intellegitur perfectam fidem grano sinapis comparari, et hoc non propter exiguitatem, sed ob integritatem eius appositum....notandum quod inter cetera etiam omnis fides sine caritate non prosit.*

In 1 *Cor.* xiii 3—4 *Sed non propter deum, sed propter gloriam fiat humanam. uel certe siquis in ipso martyrio aduersus fratrem retineat iram, contemnens eum qui iussit nos maliciam proximi obliuiscere, et in ipsa etiam morte praeuaricatur existens....*[first clause of verse 4]. *Quis non propter deum, sed propter gloriam fiat humanam. uel certe siquis in ipso martyrio aduersus fratrem retinet iram, contemnens eum qui iussit nos malitiam proximi obliuisci, et in ipsa etiam morte praeuaricatur existens* [follows now second clause of verse 4]. Similar cases occur at *in* 1 *Cor.* xi 2—3; xv 24, 25; *in* 2 *Cor.* xii 12; *in Phil.* iiii 3; *in* 1 *Thess.* iii 5. The infrequency of these cases shows that the scribes were on the whole very careful to avoid the snares into which the abundance of their material might lead them.

A very considerable number of passages have been rewritten: I have counted some fifty. The variations will be recorded in my critical apparatus, but a few may be selected here to show their nature. Sometimes they are mere variations of language; in other cases the differences are more serious. The attentive reader will have observed that on *Rom.* v 14—15 this form of the Pelagian text lays stress more than once on the responsibility of Eve[1], while the others leave her alone.

[1] See pp. 47 f. above.

In 1 *Cor.* iiii 20

(Original Text.)	(Paris 653)
Hic ostenditur nihil prodesse doctrinam absque iustitiae operibus ei qui non faciat quae facienda persuadet.	Ostendit hic nihil prodesse absque iustitiae operibus scientiam et doctrinam, nouum scilicet testamentum.

In Gal. ii 10

Hoc est quod in omni paene scribit epistula.	Hoc est quod in omni pene epistula gentes sollicite commonet et[1] hortatur.

In Eph. iii 8

'Minimo' tempore, non labore, simul notandum quod inter sanctos se humiliando fecerit gradus.	[Tempore, non labore *in the margin only.*] Est ergo minimus et maximus inter sanctos: quamuis enim se humiliauerit, tamen est res in qua se humiliat unus quisque.

Ibid.

quas sensus humanus adprehendere nisi reuelatione non praeualet.	'inuestigauiles' humano sensui sine reuelatione diuina.

In Eph. v 5

Contra illos agit qui solam fidem dicunt posse sufficere.	Contra illos agit qui solam fidem dicunt ducere ad regnum posse caelorum.

In Eph. v 7

Si in peccatis iudicium desperantium participes fueritis, eritis et in poena consortes[2].	Si in peccatis participes fueritis dei iudicium non timentes, eritis et in poena consortes[2].

In Eph. vi 15

Cum fiducia incedentes intrepide praedicate.	Ut sicut calciati pedes fiducialiter ambulant, ita et uos intrepide praedicetis.

In 1 *Thess.* iiii 10—11

Hoc est, etiam ignotos quosque diligatis.	Etiam peregrinos amando. Siue: Manibus operando, cum accipiendi habeant potestatem.

[1] *Commonet et* is my conjecture for *commoneret* of the MS.

[2] There is perhaps some primitive corruption here (read *dei spernentium* for *desperantium*?), but cf. iiii 19: Cassiodorus's pupil has neither *iudicium desperantium* nor *dei iudicium non timentes*, but has all the rest!

Some at least of these alterations seem to be by Pelagius himself. The character of such passages, and the style and language of many of the additional notes, as is mentioned above, have led me to the conclusion that the basis of the text in this wonderful manuscript was the author's personal copy revised by him and added to from time to time.

That this copy is based, at least in part, on a continuous codex of the Epistles apart from the Pelagian original text and commentary, is proved by a number of instances of bad division of the scripture text. (Pelagius himself always made his division at suitable points.) Examples of this characteristic are these:

In 1 *Cor.* xi 23 *Quoniam dominus Iesus in qua nocte.* Iam hinc quasi oblitos commemorat quam magnum sit huius mysterii sacramentum. *Tradebatur accepit panem.* Iam passurus etc.

In 1 *Cor.* xii 15 *Si dixerit pes: Quoniam non sum.* Pes ecclesiae dici potest, qui ad intercedendum egreditur. *Manus, non sum.* Manus ille qui operatur. *De corpore, non ideo non est de corpore.* Dicebant etc.

In 1 *Cor.* xvi 18 *Refecerunt enim.* Circa meum obsequium. *Et meum spiritum et uestrum.* Meum spiritum etc.

In Gal. i 15 *Cum autem placuit ei.* Non supra omnes, ne iactantiae putaretur. *Qui me segregauit* etc.

In Phil. i 19—20 *Et sumministrationem spiritus Iesu Christi secundum.* Quia ad meam omnia salutem gubernat. *Expectationem et spem meam.* Quia de omnibus etc.

In Phil. ii 15 *Et simplices sicut filii dei sine repraehinsione in medio nationis.* Sicut uos deus fecit. considerate enim cuius filii sitis, quia cum in omnibus purus ac sanctus sit, filios non potest habere degeneres. *Prauae et peruersae.* Quae omnem etc.

In 2 *Thess.* ii 7—8 *Donec dimidium fiat et tunc reuelabitur ille iniquus quem dominus Iesus interficiet.* Regnum quod etc. *Spiritu oris sui et destruet.* Celeri imperio etc. *Inlustratione* etc.

It has been already noticed in chapter ii that a number of the notes are given in the margin[1]. These notes are generally genuine, and belong to the commentary in its original form. It does not seem possible to conclude that they are taken from a separate codex. It appears to me that they were put there simply to save

[1] Pp. 47, 59 f.

space. They are in nearly every case very short notes that do not encumber the margin unduly. It is possible, however, that they were overlooked at first, and added afterwards.

I have noted over two hundred places where the biblical text is 'interesting,' or in other words differs from the Vulgate. An extended examination of these is not possible here, both from considerations of space and lack of the necessary materials for comparison. Already in the second British Academy paper[1] I had occasion to compare the biblical text of our MS in Romans with that of other authorities, in over forty passages. The net result goes to show that out of forty-three passages where the Reichenau MS differs from the Vulgate, in twenty-nine it is supported by the Balliol MS, and in twenty-five by the Paris MS 653.

Here I will take Romans as a whole, and compare its readings with the materials collected by Dr H. J. White. If my numeration be correct, there are in all 333 differences, great and small, between his text of the Vulgate and the text furnished by the Paris MS 653. In the following cases the Paris MS furnishes a reading which appears to be hitherto unknown:

		Paris MS 653	Vulgate
Rom.	i 10	*om.* semper (so Ball.)	semper
	27	femineo	feminae
	32	faciunt illa	ea faciunt
	ii 5	cor sine paenitentia	inpaenitens cor
	24	in (*corr.*) gentes	inter gentes
		scriptum est enim	sicut scriptum est
	29	circumcisio	in circumcisione
	iii 25	fidei per fidem	per fidem
	iiii 4	inputabitur	imputatur
	18	contra spem naturae[2]	contra spem
		in spem potentiae dei[3]	in spem
		add sicut stellae et arena	*om.*
	19	non considerabat	considerauit
		emortuum *om.*	emortuum
	21	quoniam	quia
	v 18	sicut *om.* (*add mg*)	sicut
	vi 16	obaudistis	oboeditis
	vii 7	nam	sed
	13	est *alt. om.*	est
	viii 19	filiorum *om.*	filiorum
	22	autem	enim
	24	uidit	uidet

[1] *Proceedings*, vol. VII (1915—16) pp. 271 ff.

[2] *naturae* is perhaps a gloss which has got into the text.

[3] *potentiae dei* is perhaps a gloss.

	Paris MS 653	Vulgate
Rom. viiii 11	qui cum	cum enim
21	potestatem *om.*	potestatem
32	offendit	offenderunt
x 4	credendi	credenti
15	quomodo	quomodo uero
19	moses primus	primus moses
20	autem *om.*	autem
	palam apparui	inuentus sum
	inuentus sum	palam apparui
xi 12	mundo	mundi
23	et illi autem	sed et illi
25	nolo autem	nolo enim
	ex parte *om.*	ex parte
26	et *om.*	et
34	eius consiliarius	consiliarius eius
xii 5	corpus *om.*	corpus
20	si sitat	si sitit
xiii 1	estis	est
5	stote	estote
9	in hoc uerbo *om.*	in hoc uerbo
12	appropriabit	adpropiauit
xiiii 6	et 1° *om.*	et
xv 6	uno ore *om.*	uno ore
	honorificemus	honorificetis
12	exsurgit	exsurget
19	in uirtute signorum et prodigiorum *om.*	in uirtute signorum et prodigiorum
21	quia	sed sicut scriptum est
24	spero quod praeteriens *om.*	spero quod praeteriens
	uobis *alt. om.*	uobis
xvi 5	epemen	epaenetum
10	aristobolim	aristoboli
17	discensiones	dissensiones

Eliminating these fifty-four passages, we find that there are 279 differences to which parallels can be produced. I have gone through the Wordsworth-White apparatus and counted the authorities for these, in order to discover with which of them our Paris MS is most closely related. It is obviously necessary to confine our attention to those that are extant for the whole Epistle[1], but I have included Augustine, because a fairly complete copy of the Epistle could be constructed from his writings. In paying regard to the readings of Ambrosiaster and Origen-Rufinus, it must be remembered that neither is as yet edited according to modern critical requirements, and that the same is true of a large portion of St Augustine. The authorities are arranged in the order of

[1] I have ignored *e* and *f* because of their well-known connexion with *d* and *g* respectively.

their closeness to Paris 653, the number of agreements being added in each case.

d (the Latin side of the Old-Latin Codex Claromontanus, saec. VI, which appears to have been contaminated with the Vulgate in Romans and the other long Epistles[1]): 150 agreements, of which 79 are with *d*, 62 with *d**, and 9 with d^3.

L (Paris MS 335, saec. IX[2], written in Beneventan script, therefore native to S. Italy or Dalmatia): 109 agreements, of which 78 are with L, 10 with L*, 3 with L^1, 13 with L^2, 2 with L^3, and 3 with L^4.

D (*Book of Armagh*): 105 agreements.

g (the Latin side of the Old-Latin Codex Boernerianus): 89 agreements, of which 85 are with *g*, 3 are $g\frac{1}{2}$, and 1 is g^c.

F (codex Fuldensis, saec. VI): 89 agreements, of which 66 are with F, 21 with F*, 1 with F^1, and 1 with F^c.

O (codex Oxoniensis, Laud. lat. 108, saec. IX): 79 agreements, of which 39 are with O, 36 with O*, 2 with O^c, and 2 with O^3.

Ambst. (Ambrosiaster's lemmata): 79 agreements.

Z (codex Harleianus 1772, saec. VIII—IX): 77 agreements, of which 29 are with Z, 31 with Z*, and 17 with Z^c.

Orig. (the lemmata in Origen-Rufinus): 71 agreements.

Aug.: 69 agreements.

W (codex Sarisburiensis, saec. XIII): 66 agreements.

The others may be mentioned more summarily: M (56); H (55); T (55); U (52); G (50); C (49); R (49); Θ (46); B (44); K (44); *c* (42); V (41); A (25); *dem.* (20)[3].

We saw reasons above to conclude that our Paris MS comes from a Spanish original. It is therefore somewhat surprising to find that the Spanish Vulgate MSS C and T are not represented by more readings than they are. The large number of agreements with D is gratifying, seeing that we have shown this MS to be nearest of all to the text used by Pelagius himself[4]. The great preponderance of agreements with *d* shows that there are many early European elements represented: this type of text is as old

[1] *Study of Ambrosiaster* p. 214.

[2] Lowe, *Beneventan Script* (Oxford, 1914) p. 356 and passim.

[3] Note also that the Spanish authorities *m* and *t*, which cover only a part of the text, have 24 and 20 agreements respectively; *gue* (8), *r* (4), r_3 (3), *p* (1). If *m* and *t* were complete, this would give about 80 with the former, and 44 with the latter.

[4] See chap. iv p. 126 etc.

as Lucifer of Cagliari († 371). The very large number of agreements with L is the real surprise of our investigation. I cannot find that this MS, written as it was on Italian soil, had anything but Italian ancestors. The next MSS on our list, *g* and F, are also Italian in text. It would therefore seem that the text of Paris MS 653 represents the Pelagius text, after it has been brought into partial harmony with an Italian Vulgate text retaining many Old-Latin elements. This text was not closely related to the Cassiodorian Amiatinus. It may be, therefore, that we are really dealing with a text that, though Italian in origin, was actually in use in Spain. Yet the possibility must be kept open that our text belongs to the locality to which the MS itself belongs, namely the district of Verona.

The value of this manuscript for the restoration of the original comments by Pelagius is very great. This is clearly shown by passages already adduced by Zimmer and Hellmann for a different purpose, Paris MS 653 having been quite unknown to them:

Rom. i 3 extinxit **AB**V Cassiod. Sedul.: exclusit G, excludit **H** (cf. in Eph. vi 16).

21 recedens **A**V Sedul.: recedentes **BGH** Cassiod.

29 intentio **AB**V**H** Isid. Sedul.: contentio G: animositas Cassiod.

iiii 1 *ut quod* in initio constiterit, id habeatur *in toto*, read by **AB**; also by V, except that V has constituerit with H_1: **H** has *adhibeatur* for *id habeatur*.

xv 21 uidetur **AB**V Cassiod. Sedul.: ostenditur G**H**.

xvi 24 commemoraret **A**V Sedul.: commemoret **B**H_2: commoneret GH_1.

1 Cor. xiiii 1 profetetis **A** (*def.* **B**) V Cassiod. Sedul.: proficiatis G**H**.

Eph. iii 18 eligant (**A**)**B**V Cassiod. Sedul.: diligant G**H**.

19 perficiamini **AB**VGH_2 Cassiod. (*def.* Sedul.): efficiamini H_1.

Col. iii 10 similare **A**V**H***: similari Cassiod.: simulare GH_1 *corr.* Sedul.: simulari **B**.

An even better test is to choose places where some of our leading MSS are wrong, and see what help we get from V.

Eph. i 17 *nouerat enim eam* (i.e. *sapientiam*) adiutricem *omnium esse uirtutum* **A**H_1 Sedul.
matrem **B**VG, C (*ex corr.*).
matrimonium H_2.

matrem is clearly the original reading, which was purposely modified to soften the hard statement.

Eph. i 18 *si* sciretis *ad quantam spem uocati estis, omnem spem saeculi facile* contemneretis, *et si diuitias hereditatis dei* uideretis, *omnis terrena uobis* horrebit *hereditas* **A**GH_1 (*exc. quod* contempnitis H_1).
scieritis...contemnetis...uideritis **B**VH_2 Cassiod. Sedul.: sordebit **B**V (*non* H_2) Cassiod.

iiii 7 *qui ad quam gratiam se aptauerit, ipsam* consequitur **AB**GH_1.
consequetur V.
consequatur H_2.

There can be no doubt that V is right here, against all others.

Eph. iiii 22 *qui pristinos errores* desiderat *huius mundi* **AB**VG***M**.
disserat R m 1, S.
dixerat E.
deserat N, R *corr.*
et desideria C.
deserit G (*ex corr.*).
repudiat Cassiod.

We have here to do with a primitive corruption *des[id]erat*, which part of the second family of Pseudo-Jerome MSS has rightly emended. It is quite clear that even the Cassiodorus copy was corrupt, for his pupil has altogether ignored the *ductus litterarum*.

Phil. ii 7 *discipulis* autem *seruiendo* **A**.
discipulis etiam *seruiendo* V, rightly.
seruiendo H_1 (seruando R).
om. **B**GH_2 Cassiod. Sedul. (*cum toto contextu*).

2 Tim. i 15 philegus **A**G phylegus V.
filetus **B** philetus N.
figelus E Cassiod. phygelus R phigelus MC (=D) fugulus S.
phylogelus R *corr.*

The common corruption in **A**GV here seems a compromise between *filetus* and *figelus*.

THE PSEUDO-JEROME MANUSCRIPTS (**H**)

The Pseudo-Jerome manuscripts divide themselves into three classes:

(*a*) *The uninterpolated or almost uninterpolated class, to which* **B** *and the Merton MS belong.*

It is impossible for us to say whether the name of Jerome has adhered to this form from the very first or not. In favour of the view that it has, is the reference in the well-known chapter of Cassiodorus, who distinctly says that he had left a copy of a brief commentary which some attributed to Jerome[1]. This can hardly have been anything but a Pseudo-Jerome of some sort[2]. There is also some relationship[3] between **B** and the longer, what we shall call the Irish, recension of Pseudo-Jerome (H_2), suggesting that Jerome's name was attached to the **B** class from the first. There is, however, the other possibility that the **B** and Merton form got the name of Jerome added to it because some mediaeval scholar saw its kinship with the longer form that he had come to know under the name of Jerome. Whichever of the two views be the right one, it is convenient to treat the **B** form as something quite apart, and to apply the name Pseudo-Jerome only to the other two classes.

These other classes have a common root with the St Gall MS and also with one another. A signal proof of the close connexion of the St Gall MS with both, is a case of a repeated note observed by Dr Alfred J. Smith in the published Pseudo-Jerome. The following words occur twice in all these MSS, first as a note on Rom. xi 17, and second as a note on Rom. xi 24:

> Item: [Hoc] Contra naturam gentilem populum insi-
> tum dicit in radice[m], hoc est, in fide[m] patriarcharum,
> et non secundum naturam arborum quasi
> insertum proprii generis fructum ferre, sed boni-
> tatem radicis sequi in qua[m] insertus es. [*or* insertum est][4].

As the note properly belongs only to verse 17, it is clear that its

[1] See p. 16 above.

[2] It cannot have been the compilation (still unprinted) which is handed down to us in the following MSS: Berne (formerly Micy) 344 (saec. IX); Paris B.N. 1764 (saec. X—XI); Paris nouv. acq. lat. 1460 (saec. X); Dublin, Trin. Coll. 254 (saec. XV) (?). This compilation is made from the genuine works of Jerome, and the places are indicated. It is probably not earlier than Cassiodorus's time.

[3] Shown in the 'packing' of verses in some of the shorter epistles, etc.

[4] Minor variations of text are reserved for my third volume.

repetition at verse 24 is due to an error in the archetype of the St Gall and Pseudo-Jerome MSS. This error could only have arisen, I fancy, from the fact that the note was written in the space between two columns of a glossed[1] MS of the Pauline Epistles, in which verse 17 was in the left hand column and verse 24 opposite it, in the right hand column. A copyist, not remembering that he had copied the note at verse 17, mistakenly copied it again at verse 24, and from the faulty copy thus made all our manuscripts of Pseudo-Jerome and the St Gall MS come. There can be no doubt also that the faulty copy was in insular script.

How far back can we trace the Pseudo-Jerome interpolations, or any of them? That they, or most of them, come from a Pelagian, cannot be doubted, even though the identity of that Pelagian may never be discovered. I have sometimes wondered whether Caelestius himself was the interpolator: difference of style precludes Julian of Aeclanum. But that some at least of the interpolations are very old is proved by certain passages in Arnobius Junior, the author of *Praedestinatus*. Von Schubert, in his monograph, *Der Sogenannte Praedestinatus*[2], has produced three (or four) parallels to the interpolations in the printed Pseudo-Jerome. They are *Praed.* III 14 (Migne, *P.L.* LIII 653 B) = Ps.-Hier. *in Rom.* vii 18; ibid. (653 D) = Ps.-Hier. *in Rom.* vii 22; *Praed.* III 2 (634 A) = Ps.-Hier. *in Rom.* viiii 12. About the cogency of the first and second some doubt may be felt; about the third none whatever:

Ps.-Hier.	Praed.
In Geneseos libro dictum est: Duae gentes etc. Ergo prophetia non de his est qui secundum carnem sunt Iacob et Esau, *sed* [et] *de* his qui futuri erant ex operibus esse boni et mali	*In Geneseos libro* de Rebecca *dictum est: Duae gentes etc. Prophetia ergo non de his est qui secundum carnem* nascebantur, *sed de* duobus populis Iudaeorum et gentium

Some of the Ps.-Jerome interpolations are then older than the date of *Praedestinatus*, and according to the generally accepted view the third book of this work, among other parts, is the work of Arnobius Iunior[3]. The date is perhaps not later than 439, and the place of writing possibly Rome.

It is probable that there are strata in the interpolations, that

[1] Glossed, I mean, with Pelagian and Pseudo-Hieronymian notes.

[2] *Texte und Untersuchungen*, N.F. IX[er] Bd (Leipzig, 1903) pp. 35 f.

[3] See Morin, *Études Textes Découvertes* t. I (Maredsous and Paris, 1913) pp. 316 f.; Schanz, *Gesch. d. röm. Litt.* IV[er] Teil (2) (München, 1920) pp. 533 ff.

there is this early element, contemporary or almost contemporary with the author himself, and that there are one or two later strata. The earlier of the later strata is perhaps to be found in the interpolations preserved by H_1. Certainly some of the interpolations in H_2 must be quite late, such as the extract from Jerome's 28th epistle to which allusion has been made[1]. Again, Pelagius himself, according to the **A** text, says nothing of the identity of the 'propheta' in Tit. i 12, but the **B** text (with **GH**[2]) has 'Parmenides siue Callimachus.' This can hardly be anything but an interpolation from Jerome on Titus ad loc.[3]: 'Dicitur autem iste uersiculus in Epimenidis Cretensis poetae oraculis repperiri....Sunt qui putent hunc uersum de Callimacho Cyrenensi poeta sumptum, et aliqua ex parte non errant...uerum, ut supra diximus, integer uersus de Epimenide poeta ab apostolo sumptus est, et eius Callimachus in suo poemate est usus exordio....Epimenides siue Callimachus' etc. It is not so likely to be taken from Jerome, *epist.* 70 § 2, 2, where he says: 'Paulus apostolus Epimenidis poetae abusus uersiculo est scribens ad Titum...cuius heroici hemistichium postea Callimachus usurpauit[4].' Jerome doubtless got his information, at least partly, from Origen, who in turn may be indebted to Clement[5]. The interpolation, with the corruption 'Parmenides' for 'Epimenides' is an ugly blot on **B**'s text. Investigation may show that there are other interpolations of this sort, justifying to some extent the attribution of the commentaries to Jerome[6].

The history of the use of the Pseudo-Jerome as 'Jerome' in the middle ages would be an interesting topic, were space available to pursue it. I will merely call attention to the fact that Abelard (†1142)[7], the *Glossa Ordinaria*[8] and Hervaeus Burgidolensis (†after 1150)[9] cite it as 'Jerome.'

[1] P. 239, n. 5.

[2] The MSS of H_1 agree in the more deeply corrupt text 'parmedissidiae challimacus,' to which the first editor gave the form 'Callimachus scilicet.' H_2 also contains a doublet after 'consecuntur': 'Item Epimenides dixit hunc uersum.'

[3] Ed. Vall.[2] t. VII (1) pp. 706—708. [4] Ed. Hilberg (C.S.E.L. LIV p. 701).

[5] References are Athenag. 30; Clem. *Strom.* I 59, 2; Orig. *c. Cels.* III 43 (cf. Geffcken, *Zwei griech. Apologeten* [Leipz. and Berl. 1907] pp. 227 f.).

[6] Cf. the same feature in V (p. 255).

[7] See the index to Migne, *P.L.* CLXXVIII. I think Prof. Lehmann first called my attention to this fact. [8] Cf. p. 6.

[9] Migne, *P.L.* CLXXXI. Another MS (not alluded to by Denifle, *Luther und Luthertum*[2] I Bd. 2 Abt. [Mainz, 1905] p. 54) is Rome, Vallicell. E 5 (saec. XII).

It does not seem profitable to fill space with a discussion about the Pseudo-Jerome biblical text. It is very doubtful, in fact, whether there was any original Pseudo-Jerome biblical text from which all the Pseudo-Jerome *codices* ultimately derive. We shall see that R sometimes goes its own way. We also argue that H_2 is based upon a separate *codex Paulinus*, which may have had nothing to do with the biblical text that can really be reconstructed from the representatives of H_1. I may in fact have to content myself with presenting the evidence for the various forms in the critical apparatus. It seems probable, however, at this stage, that the person who first built the exposition in H_2 round the *codex Paulinus* of which we have spoken, really believed that it represented Jerome's Vulgate text, and it will not be without interest to the Benedictines to examine this claim, as the date at which it was done was relatively early.

The interpolator occasionally airs a slight knowledge of Greek by verbal quotations, a practice alien to Pelagius[1]: the passages are these: in Rom. viiii 20; in 1 Cor. xii 31; in 1 Cor. xv 31, 51.

(*b*) *The shorter or Anglo-Saxon interpolated form of Pseudo-Jerome* (H_1).

This form, which I call Anglo-Saxon because its oldest representative is in Anglo-Saxon script and it has also other connexions with England, is that which has become in part known through Erasmus's edition of Jerome (vol. IX, 1516), and other subsequent editions of the works of that Father. It is nearer to the original Pelagius in various respects than the longer form can claim to be. It has the Epistles in the Pelagian order, Phil., 1 Thess., 2 Thess., Col., and it furnishes no exposition of the Epistle to the Hebrews. The practice of 'subnotation,' also, as defined on page 50, is maintained throughout. It is, however, defective in two main respects. It lacks the true Pelagian prologue to all the Epistles, and in its place furnishes a forged letter to 'Heliodorus.' This fraud is so far ingenious that St Jerome really had a correspondent of this name, to whom the epistles now numbered 14 and 60 are addressed. There are no arguments to Romans, First or Second Corinthians, any more than there are in MS **A** of the original form.

[1] 2 Cor. vii 11 and 2 Thess. ii 16 are hardly exceptions.

Second Corinthians ends with the stichometry *Scripta de Macedonia: uersus DXCI.* Galatians is introduced by the Marcionite argument. Ephesians begins with the genuine Pelagian argument, as do Philippians (here the Munich MS is somewhat curtailed), and all the remaining epistles, that to Philemon being slightly curtailed. There are frequent interpolations, introduced by *Item* or *Item alia* (*expositio*). In this class we not infrequently find Vulgate chapter headings intruding, as at 2 Cor. v 15—16. At Rom. v 14—15, apart from one or two notes introduced by the usual *Item*, there is a short note added on verse 14, while for the long incriminating note on verse 15 a short note is substituted[1].

Other peculiarities of less moment are shared by the members of this class, as will be shown on every page of the apparatus. Such are the following readings:

in Rom. viiii 21	*eos* true text:	*eius* H_1
xi 13	*uult ostendere se ad Iudaeorum salutem magnopere festinare* true text:	*uult ostendere ad Iudaeorum salutem magnoperis festinare* H_1

(*c*) *The longer or Irish interpolated form of Pseudo-Jerome* (H_2).

The whole character of the MSS of this longer form gives the impression that they go back to an original which was at first merely a copy of the Pauline Epistles in Latin, but afterwards had the Pelagian and other notes inserted, for the most part, at least, between the lines of the Pauline text. This view, and this alone, will account for the constant inversion of order by which the comment precedes the verse or clause which it was written to explain. As the basis of this recension is a biblical MS, we find in it the prefaces and lists of chapter headings proper to such a MS. In the two oldest representatives of the class there is also an almost unique set of canons which may have formed part of the archetype. Other notable characteristics of the class are the normal order of the Epistles, Phil., Col., 1 and 2 Thess., which, as we have seen, is not the Pelagian order, and the presence of the Epistle to the Hebrews with a short exposition. In the account of the St Gall MS it was

[1] See p. 35 for the text.

shown that it contains many of the interpolations present in this class, but absent from H_1.

The exact contents are:

1. [Canones, confined to M and N].

1. [*Epistulae ad Romanos causa haec est* argument, confined to the other members of the class[1]].

2. *Omnis textus uel numerus* prologue.

3. *Primum intellegere nos oportet* etc. (a variant opening of the genuine Pelagian *Primum quaeritur quare*).

4. *Romani ex Iudaeis* etc.

5. Capitula headings to the Epistle to the Romans.

6. *Romani sunt in partes Italiae: hi fidem habentes*, etc.

7. Then begins the commentary proper, with the heading:

IN NOMINE $\overline{\text{DI}}$ SVMMI INCIPIT EXPLANATIO $\overline{\text{SCI}}$ HIERONIMI IN QVATTVORDECIM EPISTOLIS(-AS) $\overline{\text{SCI}}$ APOSTOLI PAVLI.

8. Long argument to First Corinthians, beginning *Corinthus metropolis ciuitas Achaiae est*, published by De Bruyne from biblical MSS[2].

9. Capitula headings to First Corinthians.

10. Marcionite prologue to 1 Cor., *Corinthii sunt Achaici.*

11. Commentary on First Corinthians;

and so on with each of the Epistles to the end of Hebrews. I have already called attention to the passage added anonymously at the end of Philemon from one of the genuine epistles of Jerome[3], in this family of MSS and in the St Gall MS. A partial stichometry is found in these MSS, very imperfectly in the later ones. It is as follows:

1 Cor. DCCCXI.
2 Cor. DXCI.
Eph. DXCIII.
Phil. CCL.
2 Thess. CVIII.
1 Tim. CCXXX.
2 Tim. CLXIIII.
Tit. XLII.

This stichometry is unfortunately corrupt, and is, so far as I know,

[1] See Wordsworth and White's *Epistula ad Romanos* (Oxon. 1913) for the text of these prefatory documents.

[2] *Revue Bénédictine* t. XXIV (1907) pp. 257 ff.

[3] See p. 239, n. 5.

not identical with that of any biblical MS published, though it must come from the biblical original I have postulated.

The situation in Romans v differs in this class of MSS from that which we have found in the other class. Here also the incriminating passage is wanting, but there is a further double loss (not shared by the St Gall MS), which serves as a means of classification of authorities. The first loss is that of the words *sicut Adam* (in Rom. v 14) down to, and including, the words *eum cupientibus* (ibid.): the second is that of the words *dimittitur amplius* (in Rom. v 20) down to, and including, the words *iustitiae actionem* (in Rom. v 21). The first omission measures rather over nineteen lines in Migne, and the second rather over ten. In M, the vellum of which is at this point quite normal, $13\frac{1}{2}$ lines are left blank in the first case, and $11\frac{5}{6}$ in the second. From this fact we gather that the missing passages were no longer legible in the *exemplar* from which M was copied, and that the scribe left blanks of adequate length, in the hope that he might be able to supply the gaps from another MS of this work. In this hope he was disappointed. N wants the same passages, but leaves no gaps, and the only sign there that anything is wrong is in a much later addition at the foot of the page, in the second case only, in which the missing words of scripture are given, but without any comment. The other three MSS of this family are also without the missing portions, but they have adopted the drastic, and at the same time much more interesting course of inserting at both places the corresponding portions of the Cassiodorus (Pseudo-Primasius) commentary, not however without marginal notes to the effect that the passages thus inserted were wanting in the *exemplar*. These marginal notes are absent from the late and degenerate Cambridge MS.

The text of this class considerably exceeds that of the other class in bulk. Many of the additions are present also in the St Gall MS, and can meantime be studied in Zimmer's collation of that MS. Yet there are also intentional omissions, for example, of comments on the eucharistic section of 1 Cor. xi. Perhaps the theologians will be able to locate this tendency.

It is of considerable interest, in view of palaeographical considerations which will be stated in their place, to point out that this family has got a real connexion with documents of Spanish origin. The long prologue to First Corinthians to which allusion has just been made, is not known outside this family except in (*a*) certain Biblical MSS: Épinal 45 (saec. IX), closely related to our Épinal 6; Paris, B.N. 9380 (Bible of Theodulf—a Spaniard) (saec. VIII—IX); Bâle B. I 6 (saec. X)[1]: (*b*) the unpublished commentary of Claudius of Turin (a Spaniard), written about A.D. 820, whose prologue, as contained for example in the contemporary MS, Paris, B.N. 2392, copied by me, consists of the prologue in question combined with Ambrosiaster. Thus the oldest external evidence for this prologue points to Spain as its place of origin.

DESCRIPTION OF THE MSS OF THE SHORTER FORM, WITH A DISCUSSION OF THEIR RELATIONSHIP

(3) *Paris, B.N.* 9525 (*saec. VIII ex.*) (*formerly of Echternach abbey*) (E)

This manuscript has 222 folia[2], with one column and 26 lines to the page. It measures 287 × 193 mm. and was written about the end of the eighth century. The arrangement of quaternions is for the most part normal. The guard-leaf is not counted, and the first quaternion is therefore signed on fol. 9 v. Quaternions 10 and 11 are signed thus respectively · q̄ · X · and · q̄ · XI. This is a sixth century fashion, and would seem to have been imitated from the archetype. The twenty-second quaternion consists of five leaves only, but none of the epistle is lost. The following six quaternions are, like the preceding, normal, though the twenty-eighth is signed on the seventh leaf, because the eighth is only half a leaf: the reverse of fol. 222 is blank.

The contents of the manuscript are as described above.

On fol. 3 r the former Paris shelf mark 'Suppl. lat. 752 A' is twice given, a previous (non-Paris) shelf mark having been removed. Below a line which has been erased the same page bears in a fourteenth century hand, the words, '*Contínet íeronímū ín o̅e̅s̅ XIIII eptas paulí*[3].'

[1] See De Bruyne, *Revue Bénédictine* t. XXIV (1907) pp. 257—262.

[2] The numerator has mistakenly given it 223, because fol. 106 was misnumbered as 107.

[3] The XIIII is a mistake: the MS never had more than thirteen Epistles.

Immediately following on the close of the text, that is, after the words 'Explicit epistola adphylimonem,' and without any break, the same scribe continues:

> exsolutio omnium finita est pauli epistolarum quae
> ameriano[1] papiaui puerculo[2] malo atque laborioso
> scripta est atromento[3] uertente anno post obitum
> duorum[4] idest helisęi[5] adsalamonis[6] regum
> quis[7] hoc opusculum legat cum caritate
> emendet et excusatum me habeat qui paruo fru-
> itus sum ingenio :7 :7 :—AMEN.

It is clear that this most interesting 'subscription' does not refer to the MS itself, but is copied from the archetype. It occurs also (with certain slight variations) in the sister manuscript S, with which we are next to deal[8]. The young scribe of their common original calls himself 'Merian of Powys' and dates his production as belonging to the year after the two (Welsh) kings Elisha and Solomon died. If our knowledge of Welsh history were more precise, we could date the archetype exactly, but the most that the authorities can suggest is that the Elisha is identical with a king of Powys who lived between 700 and 750[9]. Merian's MS was probably executed, therefore, in the early part of the eighth century.

After this subscription certain words of the text (*simul autem—uice sit,* i.e. Philem. 22) are repeated, in Caroline minuscule. This passage is followed by these words, in capital letters:

LIBER ADONIS ABBATI.

This subscription, unlike the other, was observed by earlier students of this manuscript, and shows that the book once belonged to Ado, Abbot of Echternach, A.D. 796—817[10].

Some comparatively late matter is bound up with the MS proper at the beginning and the end. I refer to fragments of a treatise of scholastic philosophy, which seem to have been written towards the end of the thirteenth century. On the blank portions of these pages there are various notes in a German hand of the first half of the

[1] ameridiano S. [2] pierculo S. [3] atramento (*ex* atromento) S.
[4] *ex* duonum S. [5] peliri S. [6] ad (*corr.* ac) solomonis S.
[7] qui S. [8] The preceding notes record the variations.

[9] Monsieur J. Loth in a note on my original publication of the subscription in the *Revue Celtique* t. XXXII (1911) pp. 152 f.

[10] Traube and Ehwald, 'Jean Baptiste Maugérard' (*Palaeographische Forschungen* Bd. III pp. 336—7).

sixteenth century (fol. 125 verso). Monsieur Léon Dorez, to whom I am deeply indebted also for a photograph of one page, has very kindly deciphered these fragments for me:

in (*?an?*) *dem erberen vesten...de Hans von*(*?*) *friburg sol mir* XX *lib. s. d.*

On the verso of fol. 223 (the last), we read in a hand of the fourteenth century (perhaps earlier):

Filius Henrici regis de nomine quartus | *Rex puer imbellis sed ad hoc utilis armis* | *Defuncto patre sub presule coloniense* | *Anno cui nomen proprio tutore manebat* | *Qui presul donec puer hic ad sceptra valeret* | *Investituras regni provisor agebat.* | *Comperit hic ergo post quam de famine tanto* | *treveris ecclesie pastore suo viduate.* | *Usus consilio minus ut*(*?*) *patet expirante* | *discreto quendam consanguinitate nepotem.* | *Nomine Cunonem puero quoque rege favente* | *Sed qui treburice ter*[*r*]*e*(*?*) *investivit honore.*

I leave it to students of German history to determine the exact references here. For readers of this book the chief interest lies, I think, in the word *friburg* in the first extract, and the reference to the church of Trèves in the second, as will appear presently.

There need be no doubt that this manuscript remained in the Echternach library for seven hundred years after it was written, and that it did not travel till early in the sixteenth century. Erasmus was then busy with his edition of Jerome. It needed very little study to observe that there is a relationship between Erasmus's *editio princeps* of Pseudo-Jerome and this MS. Being anxious to discover whether there was in existence any evidence as to the identity of the '*codex quidam obsoletae uetustatis, Gotthicis*[1] *characteribus exaratus* etc.[2],' which was the only copy of Pseudo-Jerome in his hands, I naturally turned to Mr P. S. Allen, Fellow of Merton College, Oxford, the accomplished editor of Erasmus's Epistles. He very kindly directed me to the Amorbach correspondence, preserved in the University Library, Basle, and only in part printed. There I found three letters which have a bearing on the question, and which I must now quote:

(G I 15 p. 9º.)

Sept. $\overline{\textit{XXI}}$ (*?* $\overline{\textit{XXIV}}$) *Anno* $\overline{\textit{MDXIII}}$. Bruno Amorbachius in Basel to his brother Bonifacius in Freiburg.

'*Commētarios hieronymi in paulum accepi*[3].'

[1] The humanists meant by this word 'Middle-Age, barbarous, and in general difficult to read' (Traube, *Vorlesungen und Abhandlungen* I (Munich, 1909) p. 25).

[2] See p. 6 for the following words.

[3] Dr Bernoulli, at the instance of my friend Prof. Ed. Riggenbach, helped me with the decipherment of this letter.

This may of course refer to the genuine commentaries of Jerome on four epistles, and even to a printed edition[1] of these, but the probabilities are otherwise. It must be remembered that Bruno Amorbach signs the preface to the volume containing Pseudo-Jerome, and in it makes reference to the Pseudo-Jerome codex. It is probable that Bruno copied out the text of the venerable MS for press.

(G II 29, letter 152.) Gregory Reisch in Freiburg to John (and Basil) Amorbach, 10 Oct. 1513.

†

'*felicitatem in domino consequi perpetuam, amantissime frater. quid agatur de S. Iherom̄ scire cupio. misi nuper martyrologium ipsius in littera antiqua, ad quod conferre poteris martyrologium in treueri excopiatum, et sic remittere illud antiquum. mitto et nunc Cōmētariola eiusdem diui Iherom̄ in omnes epistolas pauli, quae esse Iherom̄ testatur glossa ordinaria ad Ro.* 1, *allegans S. Iheron in expositione super eamdem ep̄tam. ponit uerba eadem quae reperiuntur in isto codice. etiam facias quaeso librū per filios tuos excribi. item ipsum una cum martyrologio remittam ad locum unde accepi sub Chyrographo. In quo loco continentur Omelie S. Iherom̄ super cantica, quamquam initium et finis discordant ab his quae impresse habentur. quae uere non sunt Iherom̄ sed potius origenis. etiam optime uiue.*

Scriptum ex cartusia friburgensi, altera post dyonisii 1513.

fr gregorius
friburg.'

(G II 29, letter 151.) Gregory Reisch in Freiburg to Bruno and Basil Amorbach, 12 Aug. 1514[2].

'*Prestantissimis artium liberalium magistris Brunoni et Basilio Amorbachiis fratribus in Christo charissimis.*

S.P.D. Venerabiles ac charissimi magistri, attulit impressor nonnullos quaterniones opera et diligentia vestra castigatos. Et quantum quod angustia temporis nunc videre licuit, optime placent omnia. placeret autem summopere ut ubicunque Iheronimus ab expositione litterali ad anagogen(?) *et* [one word] *digreditur, hoc ipsum in margine signaretur, sicuti et concordantiae signantur. Id ipsum non dubito uniuersi desiderarent lectores. miror si ego in exemplari nostro praeter* [one word] *quoque* [one word] *ex initio*(?) *ita signari decreueram fixi insuper ubi verba textus* LXX *per minutas litterales* [one word] *est ad expositionem quae res et utilis est et opus decorat. Ideo consulo ut in antea similiter*

[1] Say that of 1497—1498, published at Venice by Johannes and Gregorius de Gregoriis.

[2] Kindly copied for me by Dr Carl Roth of the University Library, Basle, at the instance of Dr Bernoulli. The script is very difficult, and certain words must be left doubtful, even with the aid of Dr Roth's tracings.

fiat. Ego quidquid ad inventarii collecturam pertinet adiutorio patrum meorum conplebo. similiter Excopiata commentaria in epistulas Pauli ex antiquo volumine, cum misse fuerint, ad exemplar [one word ?*emendandas*] *curabo. prior in Yttingen*[1] *optime notus in sancto Gallo de Job similiter prouidebit.*

Cum iam in nundinis [one or two words] *bibliothecam in* [one word] *percurrerem, inueni psalterium littera armenica pulchre scriptum. bene valete. raptim ex cartusia friburgensi. Sabbato ante assumptionis anno* 1514.

Fr. Gregorius
p. Cartusie friburgensis.'

From the relevant parts of these letters it is clear that Erasmus and the Amorbachs received help for the great edition of Jerome from Gregory Reisch, as is in fact acknowledged in the prefaces to the fifth and sixth volumes of the edition itself[2]. Reisch was at the time Visitor of the Carthusians in the province of the Rhine, having been previously, if not also concurrently, Prior of the Carthusian house of the Mount of St John Baptist, near Freiburg[3]. It is obvious that such a man, interested in Jerome as he was, would be of the greatest help in discovering important manuscripts, and obtaining the loan of them. From the letters just printed we see that he obtained from some place not definitely named by him, a '*martyrologium Hieronymi in littera antiqua*' which he sent to the Amorbachs, and that he shortly afterwards (10 Oct. 1513) sent them, from the same place, a '*commentariola Hieronymi in omnes epistolas pauli*': for both of these he had signed a receipt. From the preface to Erasmus's edition of Pseudo-Jerome we know that the MS of the Pauline expositions was also in old and difficult characters. Now, there was one library, and perhaps one only at that time, which contained very old manuscripts of these two spurious works, and that was the library of Echternach. Both manuscripts still survive. They are:

Paris, B.N. 10837 (saec. VIII in., Anglo-Saxon large minuscule) and Paris, B.N. 9525 (saec. VIII ex., Anglo-Saxon minuscule).

The first contains the 'Martyrologium,' the second the expositions of the Epistles of St Paul. The reader will recall that the word 'friburg' occurs on a flyleaf of the latter MS, and it may be a part

[1] This Yttingen or Ettingen is said to be in Canton Thurgau, near the Lake of Constance (P. S. Allen, *Opus Epistolarum Des. Erasmi* t. II [Oxonii, 1910] p. 211).

[2] Allen, *loc. cit.*

[3] Allen, *op. cit.* p. 27.

of the very receipt signed by Reisch. It will be proved later by textual evidence that the former Echternach MS (now Paris, B.N. 9525) is the very MS from which, and from which alone, Erasmus derived the text of Pseudo-Jerome. After Reisch had duly returned it to Echternach Abbey, it does not seem to have been disturbed till the Napoleonic period, when, as Traube believes, Maugérard stole it, as well as its old travelling companion the 'Martyrologium' and many other Echternach books, and sent them to Paris, where they were received on 26th December, 1803[1].

The manuscript is written in rather pointed Anglo-Saxon minuscules[2]. That they are Anglo-Saxon, and not Irish, is proved by the frequency of the ꝉ symbol (= *tur*), which is almost the only infallible test[3]. If I am right, at least five scribes took part in copying this manuscript: the first and second wrote the first four quaternions: the second also from f. 50 r etc.: the third scribe begins with the fifth quaternion (f. 34 r *nolens noceo aliena desidero*) and also did part of f. 50 r: the fourth scribe does from f. 57 v (*siue misericordia*), but is soon interrupted by the second, after which interval he does all f. 58 r (beginning of quaternion VIII), to be soon superseded again by the second, who resumes in f. 58 v (after *praeciso*), only to be succeeded again by the fourth at the top of f. 59 r (*atque salutem*); this alternation continues for some distance down to the end of f. 67 v: there appear later traces also of a fifth and a sixth scribe, and the total number may have been as many as eight. The manuscript has also been annotated by an English hand of the latter part of the thirteenth or the early part of the fourteenth century. The notes are for the most part marginal, and are generally titles of the subject-matter. The book has been disfigured by the frequent insertion of paragraph symbols and occasional

[1] I have not access to A. Reiners, 'Les MSS de l'ancienne abbaye d'Echternach conservés à la Bibl. Nat.' (*Publications de la Société historique de Luxembourg* XL (1889) pp. 13—52), or his article in *Studien u. Mittheilungen aus dem Benediktiner- und Cistercienser Orden* IV (1) (1884) pp. 429—432, or to *Publications de la Section historique de l'Institut Grand-Ducal*, vol. LII (1911) pp. 412—478, where perhaps further information may be found. Traube's article is in his *Palaeog. Forsch.* Bd. III p. 331.

[2] Two pages photographed in *New Palaeographical Society*, fasc. VIII (1910) plate 184.

[3] Lindsay, *Revue des Bibliothèques*, t. XXII (1912) p. 428; *Notae Latinae*, pp. 373 f.

labels like 'textus' and 'glo(sa),' to distinguish text from comment[1]. The numbers of capitula are only sporadically indicated in the margin or the text, the earliest being XXXIII[2] of Romans (xi 11). The lemmata, which are sometimes in neat uncials, have .., opposite them in the margin on the left. A portion of fol. 117 has been burnt out, and various torn leaves have been most carefully repaired by sewing.

The orthography of the manuscript is excellent, and division of words is regular. The abbreviations are collected below. They agree for the most part with those in the Breton Orléans MS 193 (221) of Canons[3], and are paralleled by those in the oldest Welsh MSS[4]. While our manuscript shows one or two traces of its continental surroundings, such as *eius* (second symbol), *est* (first symbol), *omnis* symbols, the main body of the symbols is Anglo-Saxon and may well have been copied direct from the *exemplar*: a few, like *apos̄*, may go back earlier still. In view of the Merian subscription, the argument for a Welsh (Cornish, Breton) stage in its ancestry need not be laboured.

aliquando aliqn̄ (f. 142 v)

apostolus apostl̄s (ff. 17 v, 44 v), aposl̄s (ff. 25 v, 45 v, 48 r, 54 v), aposl̄ (ff. 53 v, 72 v end of line, 56 r in middle)
apl̄r 'apostolorum' (f. 17 r)
apl̄s (f. 49 r)
apol̄i 'apostoli' (f. 113 v)
ap̄ 'apostolus' (f. 124 r, doubtful)
apo̅s̅ 'apostolo' (f. 125 v), 'apostolis' (corr. m 2, f. 126 v), 'apostoli' (f. 142 r)
apl̄ 'apostolus' (corr. rec. apl̄s) (f. 210 v)

autem ħ (f. 27 v first, erased), au̅t̅ (ff. 57 r, 70 r), aū (ff. 61 v, 179 r)

carissimi km̄i (f. 37 v), (perhaps only three times)

Christus[5] xp̄s etc.
x with i above 'Christi' (f. 78 r, doubtful)

cum c̄ nobisc̄ 'nobiscum' (near end of line, f. 205 v)

deest d̄ (f. 67 r)

deus ds̄ etc., dītas 'deitas' (f. 101 v)

dicit dt̄ (ff. 125 v, 142 v), dic̄

dicitur dr̄ (f. 94 v *ter*)

dicunt dn̄t (f. 125 v), di̅n̅t̅ (f. 126 v)

dixit dx̄ (f. 191 r, end of line)

dominus dn̄s etc.

eius ɔ (f. 118 r, end of line, f. 212 r), ei' (f. 137 v)

episcopus epīs 'episcopus' (f. 185 v), 'episcopis' (or '-os') (f. 178 r)
epi̅ 'episcopi' etc., eps̄ 'episcopos' (corr. epo̅s̅)

epistula epistl̄ (f. 72 v), epsl̄ (f. 193 v), epl̄ (f. 213 v), epl̄a

[1] See the published photographs.

[2] Doubtless an error for XXXVI of the ordinary numeration.

[3] For which see Lindsay in *Zentralbl. f. Bibliotheksw.* XXVII (1912) pp. 264—272.

[4] See Lindsay, 'Early Welsh Script' (*St Andrews Publications* no. 10) (Oxford, 1912).

[5] *Christiani* written in full (f. 91 r).

esse ee̅
esset eēt (f. 213 v)
est ē ÷ (first f. 36 v, end of line f. 65 v, crushed in f. 98 r)
et 7 (not frequent, sometimes crushed in where *et* omitted at first)
explicit expl̄, explc̄ (f. 193 v), explc̄t (f. 213 v)
expositio exp̄o
fratres fr̄s
ff̄ 'fratres' (f. 70 v), 'frater' (f. 91 r)
frās (f. 142 v)
hic h̄ (corresponding to đ 'deest,' f. 67 r)
hoc ḣ (f. 141 r)
id est ·i· (f. 123 r and often after)
Iesus etc. ih̄s etc.
Iohannes ioh̄; (end of line)
Israhel irl̄ (ff. 43 r, 127 v), isrl̄ (regular)
item it̄
meus m̄s (four times), mm̄ 'meum' (five times)
{*nobis* nob̄
{*uobis* uob̄
nomen nom̄
noa⁻ 'nomina' (f. 185 v)
non n̄
{*noster* nr̄ 'noster' (f. 66 r first), nrm̄ 'nostrum,' nr̄a 'nostra'
nm̄ 'nostrum' (four times)
{*uester* urā 'uestra,' ur̄ę 'uestrae,' ur̄is 'uestris,' ur̄s 'uestras' (f. 97 v)
omnis om̄s 'omnes,' 'omnis' (corr. m 2 omīs f. 17 v)
omīs 'omnis,' om̄i 'omni'
omā 'omnia'
om̄ 'omnes' (four times)
Paulus, paū 'pauli'
per ꝑ
prae p̄
presbyter prb̄m 'presbyterum' (f. 210 v)
pbr̄m 'presbyterum' (f. 219 v), pb̄ri (f. 219 r), pb̄ris (*ibid.*) 'presbyteris,' pbr̄s (*ibid.*) 'presbyteros,' prsbtri 'presbyteri' (f. 3 r)

pro ꝓ
propter ꝓr̄ (ff. 142 r, 143 v) (ꝓpt̄ f. 42 r)
psalmus psal̄ 'psalmo' (f. 52 r)
quae q̄ q̄: (f. 35 v *bis*, f. 20 r m 2), q: (ff. 47 v, 48 r, 48 v)
quam q̄ (ff. 124 v, 126 v, 127 r, 128 r, 142 v *bis*)[1]
(*quando* abbreviated only in *aliquando*)
quare qͣre (f. 143 r)
que q; (f. 48 r), q; (f. 18 r, end of line), q: (f. 47 v, etc. corr. to q̄), 7 (f. 188 r)
quem q̄: (f. 188 v)
{*quia* q (f. 122 v, 142 v), q (f. 126 v) (what is q (f. 124 r)? The true text is *quo*), q (ff. 95 r, 100 r[2])
{*quod* qđ q (f. 37 r, eras. et corr. quia, 142 v, 143 r), q (f. 130 r)
quoniam qūo (the prevalent form) qm̄
reliqua rl̄q (f. 139 v)
saeculum scl̄o 'saeculo' (f. 130 r), scl̄a 'saecula' (f. 204 v)
secl̄i 'saeculi' (f. 99 r), saecl̄i (f. 121 v)
sanctus sc̄e 'sancte' etc.
sc̄s 'sanctos' (f. 140 r)
secundum secđ (f. 132 r), ꝯ (f. 143 v)
sed s; (f. 64 v, end of line), s. (f. 140 v etc.)
sicut s̄ (f. 125 v, 142 r), sic̄ (f. 126 v)
spiritus sp̄s etc.
spū (=spiritus gen. sing., thrice at least, e.g. f. 68 r twice)
spūm 'spiritum' (f. 172 r)
sometimes written in full (f. 30 v)
sunt st̄ (once end of l.), so posst̄ 'possunt' (f. 37 v)
tamen tm̄ (f. 140 v)
tempore tempor̄, tempr̄ (ff. 15 v, 18 v, 114 v)
uel l̄ (f. 41 v and later)
ul̄ (105 r and later) ul̄it 'uelit' (f. 147 v)

[1] See Lindsay, *Notae Latinae*, p. 218.

[2] Also f. 37 r, where erased and corrected by first hand to *quia*. The scribe evidently ought to have used this symbol for *quod* only.

SYLLABLE SYMBOLS:

bunt bt̄
con ɔ (ff. 141 r, 155 v, 188 r [with flourish])
en m̄ 'men'
er t̄ 'ter,' b̄ 'ber,' ū 'uer'
is b̄ 'bis,' l̄ 'lis'
it b̄ 'bit,' c̄ 'cit,' d̄ 'dit,' p̄ 'pit,' ū 'uit,' x̄ 'xit' (credt̄ *irregular for* credit, f. 19 r)
m suprascript stroke, sometimes beyond the letter in the manner of very early MSS, e.g. etia⁻ (f. 57 v)
n suprascript stroke
rum r̄ (apostolor̄ 'apostolorum,' f. 138 r, end of line; uer̄ 'uerum' ff. 141 r, 220 r; so mear̄, persona2+ (f. 197 r))
runt r̄, rt̄
ur t with suprascript r 'tur' (f. 9 v, 24 v), t̀ (f. 58 r), ꞇ (ff. 36 r, 36 v, 39 r, 41 r, 42 r, 43 r etc. etc.[1]) expanded by m 2 very often
t̄ (?) (f. 144 r)
us b: 'bus,' b; 'bus'
d̄ 'dus' (grad̄ 'gradus,' f. 138 r, laudand̄ 'laudandus,' f. 102 v)

The manuscript behind Merian's transcript may not have been in a state of great textual purity, but there is still enough good in the descendants of the archetype of this family to show that the archetype must have been a good text. The Echternach MS, however, swarms with errors, and for these Merian is far from being entirely to blame, as is proved by the text of the Salisbury MS, alike descended from his. There is a mass of errors special to the Echternach MS among our *codices*. Chapters 1 to 4 and chapter 10 of Second Corinthians are very corrupt. Perhaps the immediate original of E had become very much faded, and was badly worked over by a later hand. Of all the errors of E perhaps the most interesting in its consequences falls to be mentioned when we come to the *editio princeps*, but two others may be mentioned here:

In Rom. iiii 17 *quamuis in principio uocauerit quae non erant, et statim esse coeperunt, tamen hic, quia iam non erant eis tempora generandi.* Such is the true text, and such is the main text of E, but the first hand has added a *d(eest)*, and at the foot of the page after *h(ic)* has written the words *de filii di* (corr. al. man. *de*) *sperata conceptione significat.* These words are an interpolation from the Cassiodorus (Pseudo-Primasius) commentary at that point, and there is no trace of them anywhere else except in the Würzburg glossed MS, where however the words are: *de insperata conceptione dixit.*

In 1 *Tim.* iii 2 *si enim omnes uult scire quo modo omnibus debeant respondere, quanto magis sacerdos, de cuius ore legem exquirent*....This is the true text, but the first hand of E reads *si*

[1] It may be seen in the *New Palaeog. Soc.* facsimile, no. 184.

enim omnes uota scire...quanto magis sacerdus uel uxore legem exquirent, which the thirteenth century corrector alters to *si enim om̄*(?) *uota scire uolunt uel debent*(?) *respondere, quanto magis sacerdos uel ab uxore legem exquirent.*

(3^b) *The Editio Princeps*

Except the spurious letter to Heliodorus the prefatory matter in E is ignored by the *editio princeps*. This fact does not, I venture to think, overthrow the preceding argument that E was the manuscript used by Erasmus, and it remains to clench the argument by alluding to certain textual phenomena.

In Rom. i 8 (interpolated passage) ed. pr. reads: *ostendit quō Romanorum fides omnibus ecclesiis cognita sit.* What Erasmus intended by *quō* I do not know, but the later editors expand to *quomodo.* E gives exactly what ed. pr. gives, and the true expansion is of course *quoniam* (M *qn̄m* N *qūo* ∗ [∗ fuit *d*] RC *qm̄* S *quod*).

In Rom. i 19 (interpolated passage) is exactly parallel in every way, except that here ed. pr. actually reads *quomodo.* So again at Rom. i 32 (interpolated passage); iii 9 (interpolated passage); 1 Cor. vi 18 (interpolated passage). The first editor seems gradually to have come to know what the symbol *quō* really meant, for, where the cross stroke is actually absent and the true reading is *quo*, he expands to *quoniam* at Gal. iiii 6.

But the crowning instance occurs at 2 Tim. ii 24 where the true text is *secundum quod de eo propheta praedixit.* For the harmless *de eo* E offers *doe.* This the *editio princeps* ingeniously alters to *Doeg*. One of the later editors then asked himself the question whether Doeg also was among the prophets, and having ascertained that he was not, read *Doeg* [*Isaias*], and that is what you find in Migne. The reference is, of course, to Isaiah xlii 2[1].

It is only just to point out that, despite these errors and multitudes of others, the *editio princeps* is the best published edition of Pseudo-Jerome. In proof of this it will be sufficient to refer to one or two passages, without attempting to assess the merits of the succeeding editions. Victorius and Martianay are accurate enough,

[1] At 1 Cor. x 4 E has *paulus edixit*, while ed. pr. has the true reading *pulchre dixit.* This may have been arrived at by emendation, or by the consultation of another MS.

and the earlier Vallarsi edition only less so, but the later Vallarsi edition on which Migne depends, has many errors. The later editors did something in the way of identifying scripture quotations, and they improved the orthography somewhat, but Vallarsi is really degenerate. Probably the later Migne is also a degeneration from the earlier Migne. Here follow some instructive passages.

EDITIO PRINCEPS	LATER MIGNE
In Rom. ii 9 (interpolated part)	
Idcirco autem Iudaeus gentili antefertur, quoniam praeter naturalem legem et Moysi legem scriptam habet	*om.* legem et Moysi
In Rom. ii 12	
Sine lege literae, in lege naturae	*om.* literae, in lege
In Rom. ii 26	
ideo circumcisio carnis, indiget cordis, circumcisio autem cordis non indiget carnis	*om.* circumcisio carnis, indiget cordis
In Rom. xii 16	
qui non dolemus de acie nostra uiros fortissimos corruentes[1]	qui non dolemus de acie nostra uiros fortissimos currentes
In Rom. xv 24	
nulla magnitudo temporis saciat caritatem	nulla magnitudo temporis faciat caritatem
In 1 *Cor.* vii 26	
praesentis uitae sollicitudinem[2]	praesentis uitae solitudinem

Portions of text and notes at 1 Thess. iii 5, Tit. i 15, Philem. 17, which are entirely absent from Migne, are present rightly in the ed. pr. It must also be observed that ed. pr., for the sake of brevity, often omits the latter part of a lemma, and prints 'etc.': the later editors have filled this out, probably from a printed Vulgate! The misleading consequences of such a procedure may well be imagined.

[1] Martianay is still right here; Vallarsi introduced the *currentes*.

[2] Martianay still right.

(4) *Salisbury, Cathedral Library, no.* 5 (*formerly* CLVII 70) (*saec.* XII *in.*) (S)[1]

This manuscript has 119 folia numbered, but contains in reality 121, because there is a blank unnumbered leaf, and fol. 36 *bis* has not been counted. It has one column of writing and forty lines to the page. It measures now 293 × 195 mm., and was written about the beginning of the twelfth century. The top and outer margins at least have been clipped[2]. The MS has also suffered from damp, and is in an unworthy cloth binding of the nineteenth century. No traces of numbers now appear on the quaternions, but they are quite normal in character. On fol. 119 (flyleaf) there is no writing except on the recto side. We find there a paragraph mark, the upper part of which has been clipped off, and there are also traces of the feet of two letters. Below this occurs AMurKAt(r)is, and to the right above, these words: H(enricus) rex Angl(orum) et dux Nor(mannorum) et Aquit(anorum) et com(es) And(egavorum). Will(elm)o de * * *[3] bello ca(m)po[4] sa (*cut off*). The particular Henry referred to is doubtless Henry II (1154—1189)[5]. The curious subscription common to E and S is in this manuscript written twice, but on the second occasion the scribe is a different (contemporary) scribe. The contents of the manuscript are precisely those of E, except for the omission of *In* 2 *Cor.* x 8 (*et non destructionem*) to xi 17 (*si hic*), without any sign: this part may have been so blurred in the original as to be illegible.

The script of the manuscript is the Caroline type usual in the south of England at that date, and the whole book appears to have been executed by one scribe, with the exception above mentioned. The second scribe appears to have written also four lines on fol. 93 v. The orthography is, like that of E, very good[6], and it will presently be made clear that the manuscript was copied from an early exemplar in insular script.

[1] I have to thank Rev. J. F. Shepherd, now of Halifax, for assisting me with the collation of the MS, which the Salisbury Cathedral authorities most kindly sent to Aberdeen twice for my use.

[2] E.g. fol. 83 r, only half of the first x of XXVIII remains.

[3] Three (or four) letters lost through a tear in the vellum.

[4] This Beauchamp was Sheriff of Worcester (1155 to 1170). (J.A.R.)

[5] I have to thank my colleague Prof. W. L. Davidson, for help in the identification.

[6] For instance *aput* is nearly always found.

It has certain of the insular abbreviation symbols: s; (= *sed*) on fol. 49 v, end of line, å (= *aut*) on fol. 51 r, ħ (= *autem*) on fol. 50 v; and tēpr (= *tempore*) on fol. 67 r is not inconsistent with the theory of an insular exemplar[1]. The frequent wrong division of words favours an early rather than a late archetype. This manuscript suffers more than most of our MSS from homoeoteleuton. The scribe has sometimes failed to complete a word he began near the end of a line, and has sometimes also begun the word again at the beginning of the next line. Where words in the archetype proved illegible or incomprehensible, he was apt to leave a vacant space of the exact length required.

That the manuscript from which ours was copied was insular of the close of the eighth or the beginning of the ninth century is made absolutely clear by the following evidence. *Autem* is frequently omitted in our MS, because the symbol ħ was not understood: for a corresponding reason we find *con-* (ɔ) once at least omitted, *dicimus* (dm̄s) once omitted, *eius* (ɜ) often omitted, *enim* (⫲) often omitted[2], *est* (÷) often omitted[3], *hic* (h with vertical stroke above the shoulder) once omitted, *mihi* (m with i above) once omitted, *uel* (ł) once omitted. The following corruptions also tell their own story. Quō (= *quoniam*), which is really Anglo-Saxon rather than Irish, is found corrupted to *quo, quod, quomodo*, quā (= *quam*). The following corruptions enable us to fix the date of the exemplar:

ad dn̄m̄ for ad nm̄ (*in* 1 *Cor.* i 28)
non (nō) for *nostro* (nō) (*in Rom.* vi 23)
nā (*nam*) for nā (*nostra*) (*in Rom.* viii 26).

These corruptions were impossible unless the scribe had before his eyes an abbreviation system which became extinct about A.D. 815[4]. He was not to blame for not always understanding it. After the period mentioned, the nr̄a, nr̄m̄ system held the field. We find also (p̄) for *per* (p'), *plus* (pl') for *post* (p'). The frequent corruption of *quia* to *quę* (q·) and suchlike is due to pardonable ignorance of the value of the insular symbol ꝗ. We find *saecula* (scła) for *secunda*

[1] See Lindsay, *Notae Latinae*, p. 308.

[2] We also find *autem* (ħ) for *enim* (⫲), and *enim* for *autem* sometimes. On this confusion see especially P. Lehmann in *Philologus* LXXIII (1914—1916) pp. 543—548.

[3] Omission of the continental ē is also possible, of course.

[4] Lindsay, *Notae Latinae*, pp. 148 f.

(scđa) (*in* 1 *Thess.* iiii 11): scłm is an Anglo-Saxon rather than an Irish symbol[1], and if our scribe was accustomed to it in the exemplar, the mistake is natural. The *sed* symbol (s̄) was also misread by him as *si*, *se*.

The confusions between letters point the same way as the errors due to misunderstood abbreviation:

a was misread as *u* (very frequently), *o* (about six times), *cu*, *eo*, *ec*, *co*. This was possible only if *a* had the open form, and the open form belongs to early rather than to late minuscule.

c misread as *t* (possible already at semi-uncial stage).
ec „ „ *a*.
m „ „ *nt* (may go back to semi-uncial stage), *r* (once).
n „ „ *h* (several times), *r* (several times).
nt „ „ *m* (may go back to semi-uncial stage).
r „ „ *n*, *s* (often; oftener than the opposite), *u*.
s „ „ *r* (often), *n* (once).
u „ „ *n*.
z „ „ *g*.

The final *t* is sometimes omitted in verbs, e.g. *opta* for *optat*, *falla* for *fallat*, and we often find single letters for double, e.g. *asero*, *acuso*.

The immediate ancestor of the Salisbury MS was an Anglo-Saxon manuscript of the end of the eighth or the beginning of the ninth century. Though contemporaneous with the Echternach MS, this ancestor was not the Echternach MS, nor even strictly speaking a sister MS. A curious analogy to the relationship between the Echternach and Salisbury MSS is to be found in the relationship between the other Echternach MS already alluded to (the Martyrology), and the Ricemarch MS recently edited by Dr Lawlor[2]. The Ricemarch MS, now Trinity College, Dublin, MS A. 4. 20, was written in Cardiganshire, South Wales, about A.D. 1079.

S is, in fact, on the whole, a better MS than E. Taking a few places at random, we find S right where E is wrong:

In Rom. v 6 *an tam benefico et sancto aliquid praeponendum sit*, where E has *aut* before *aliquid*.

In 2 *Cor.* i 6 *obtinent* : *obtent* E.

„ „ „ 13 *me* : *meum* E.

[1] Though of course common elsewhere.

[2] *The Psalter and Martyrology of Ricemarch*, edited by H. J. Lawlor, vol. I (H.B.S. vol. 47) (London, 1914) especially pp. xiv, xviii ff., xxv ff.: 'R is closely related to E' (p. xxv).

S is really independent of the special errors of E. There is also some extent of difference where the advantage is on the side of E. Neither E nor S can be a direct copy of Merian's manuscript. For on the one hand we have found E swarming with errors which are not to be found in S, and on the other hand we have found that the immediate ancestor of S belongs to as late a date as saec. VIII—IX[1]. We shall therefore not be far wrong in constructing the following stemma.

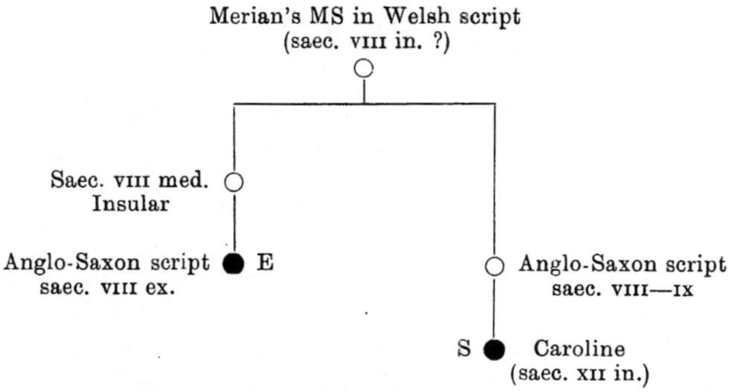

If we seek to penetrate behind Merian's production to the MS which he was copying, we may conjecture that it was a half-uncial of some sort of either the sixth or seventh century.

(5) *Munich, Staatsbibliothek, lat.* 13038 (*saec. IX in.*) (*formerly of St Emmeram in Ratisbon*) (R)

This manuscript has probably 390 folia, not counting a fifteenth century guardleaf at the end. It has two columns to the page, and 26 lines to the column. It measures 315 × 235 mm.[2] Each column is rather over 24 cm. long and rather over 8 cm. broad. In the opinion of the great palaeographer, Professor Paul Lehmann of the

[1] It seems impossible to say where this ancestor came from, whether from an English or a continental centre. I am greatly indebted to Canon Christopher Wordsworth of Salisbury for a number of detailed notes as to the connexion of Old Sarum with the Province of Rouen and the diocese of Bayeux, as well as with Lisieux, Coutances, Bec, Fontenelle, Caen, Jumièges, Mont St Michel, and St Wandrille. I lack the necessary knowledge to follow up these interesting facts.

[2] The MS was once taller: the binder of saec. XV—XVI has clipped off a whole line at the top of fol. 183 recto and verso, and also parts of lines at the top of f. 201 v, f. 217 v.

University of Munich, it can hardly be of earlier date than A.D. 810. The writing is a large dark Caroline minuscule of the South German type. The arrangement of quaternions is far from regular throughout. The first and second quaternions are an afterthought, due to another scribe, who, as we shall see, did his best to remake this manuscript into a member of the other Pseudo-Jerome family. They bear no signatures, and fol. 14 v is quite blank.

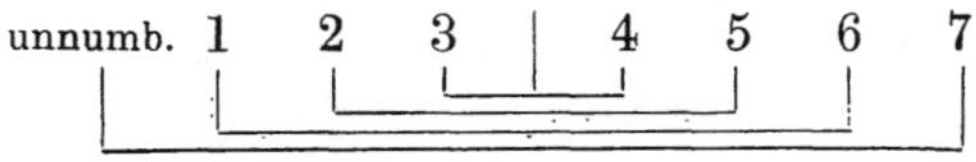

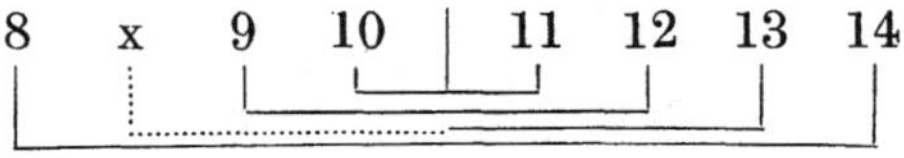

The codex began originally with what is now the third quaternion:

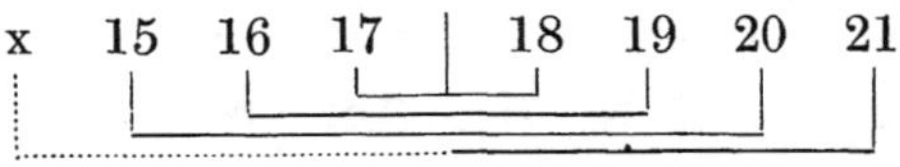

This is signed on the lower right corner of fol. 21 v: I. The next is signed II in the same position (fol. 29 v): III (signed in the same way on fol. 35 v) is a ternion of very thick vellum. IIII (signed so on fol. 45 v) is thus constituted:

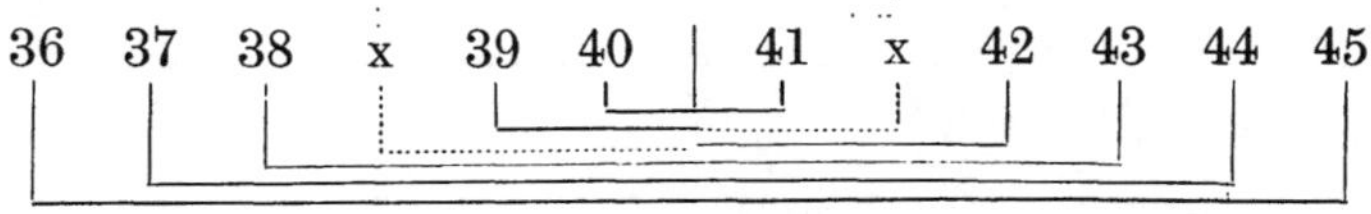

V (signed so on fol. 53 v) is thus made up:

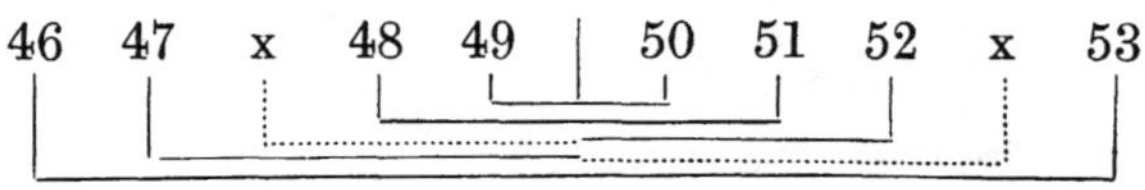

VI (signed so on fol. 61 v):

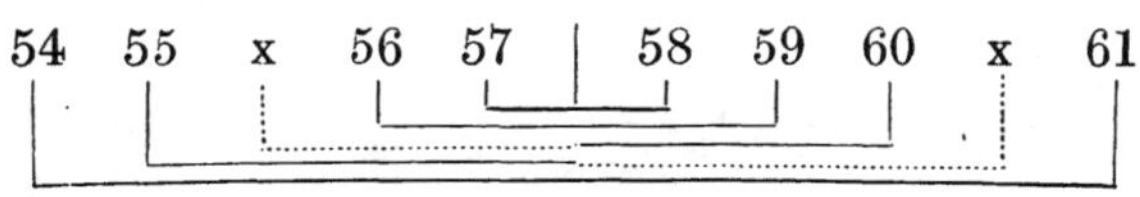

VII is normal, but is signed on fol. 67 v, because leaves after 65 and 66 have been overlooked in the numbering: VIIII (fol. 83 v), XI (fol. 99 v), XII (fol. 107 v), XIII (fol. 115 v), quaternion XV (unsigned), XVI (last I partly erased, because XV was unsigned, f. 139 v)[1], XVII (f. 147 v) are all normal: but VIII (signed f. 75 v) is made up thus:

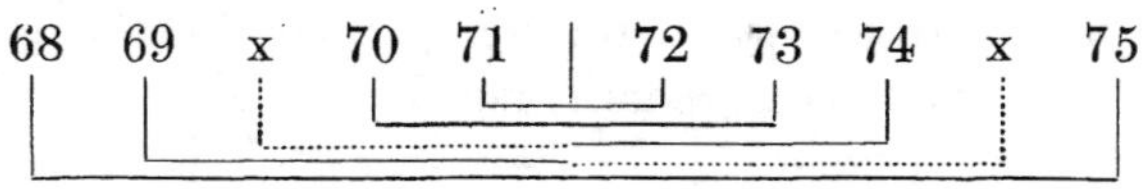

X (signed 91 v) thus:

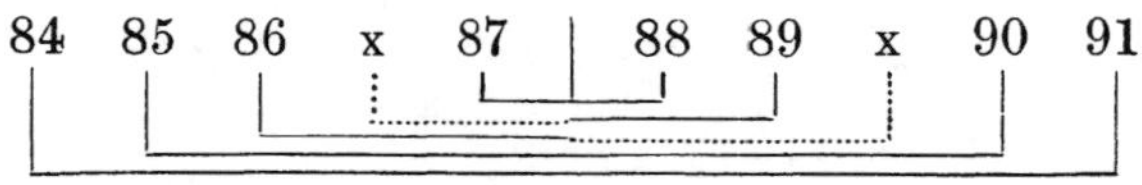

XIIII (signed 123 v) thus:

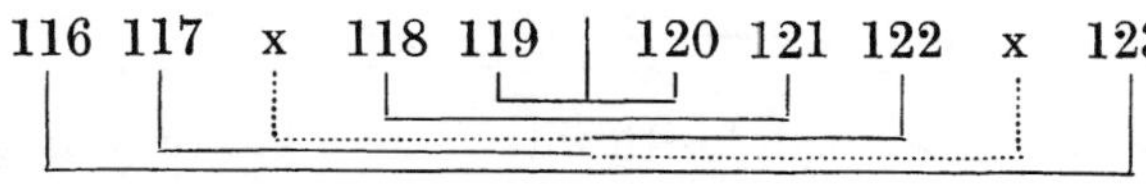

XVIII (signed 157 v) thus:

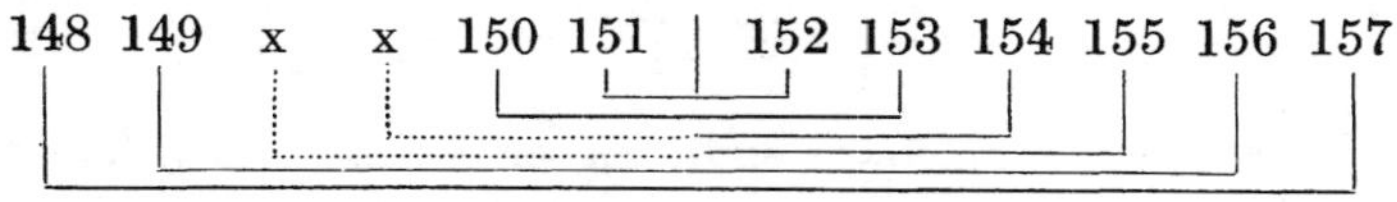

XVIIII (signed 165 v) thus:

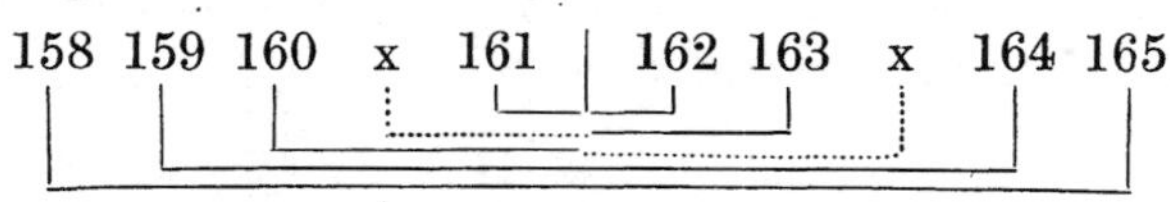

XX (signed 173 v) thus:

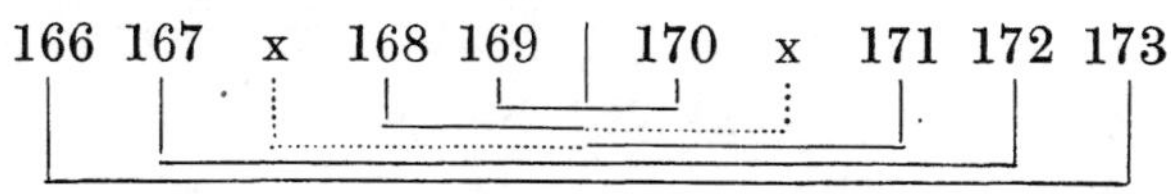

XXI (signed 181 v) thus:

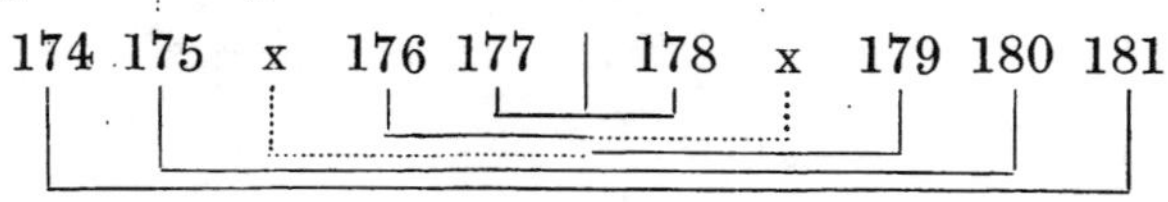

XXII (signed 189 v):

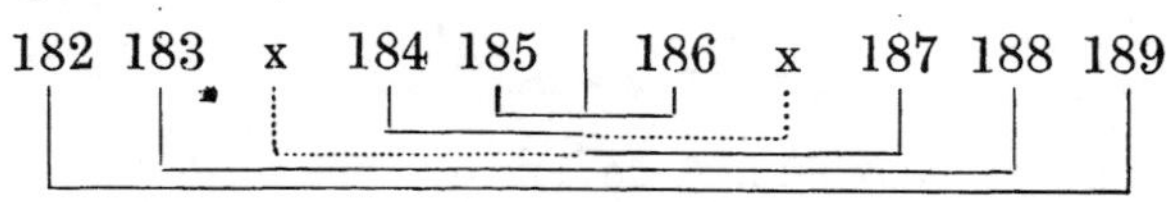

[1] XVI (at fol. 132 a) begins like a fresh codex, and is by a different scribe from the latter part of XV. At the very top of f. 132 is 'IIII · pars hruommano.'

23 is unsigned (197 v):

XXIIII (f. 203 v) is a perfect ternion. 25 is unsigned (210 v) thus:

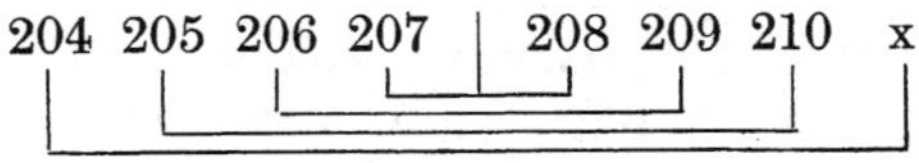

After fol. 210 several leaves have been cut out; they bore writing by the first hand and marginal additions by the leading corrector. They were then cancelled, the corrector writing all. XXVI (signed 220 v):

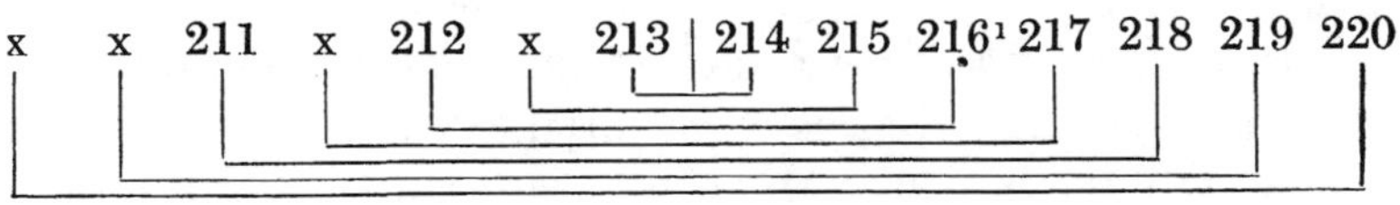

XXVII (f. 228 v) and XXVIIII (f. 243 v) are perfect, but XXVIII (signed 235 v) is thus made up:

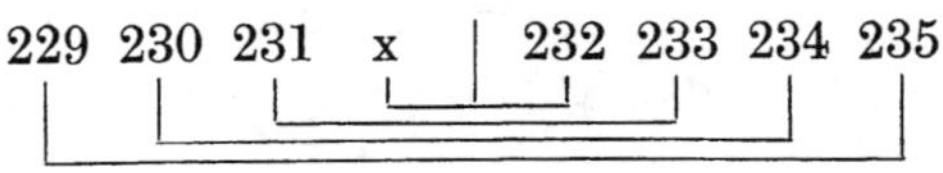

ff. 244—247 are a perfect binion, and f. 248 would seem to end the codex proper (end of exposition of Philemon: Hebr. begins on f. 249 r). f. 265 v is signed XXX, which indicates that all is confusion at this point, the MS being made up of patchwork, the outward sign how difficult was the task of altering a MS of the short recension into a MS of the longer. The rest of the MS, with which we are not really much concerned, is for the most part made up on a regular plan, the signatures being found on the following leaves: 273 v (XXXI), 281 v (XXXII), 289 v (XXXIII), 297 v (XXXIIII), 305 v (XXXV), 313 v (XXXVI), 319 v (XXXVII), 327 v (XXXVIII), 335 v (XXXVIIII), 343 v (XL), 351 v (XLI), 359 v (XLII),

[1] 216 is only half a folium, the recto half bearing no writing.

367 v (XLIII), 375 v (XLIIII), 383 v (XLV): 387 v finishes the codex.

In A.D. 1462 a scribe went over the whole MS, underlining black lemmata with red, adding modern chapter numbers and headlines etc. He himself furnishes the date of his activity in red letters on fol. 387.

1. **Pseudo-Hieronymi in epistulas Pauli.**

f. **1 r.** In nomine (*later addition*) INCIP PROLOGVS · IN EPISTOLIS BEATI PAVLI APŁI S̄C̄Ī HIERONIMI PRESBITERI (*red*) Litteras tuas... EXPLICIT PROLOGVS · INCIPIT ARGVMENTV̄ EPISTOLARV̄ (*erasure*) PAVLI (*eras.*) APOSTOLI. Omnis textus uel numerus...emendatus melior factus. EXPLICIT. INCIPIT PROLOGVS S̄C̄Ī HIERONIMI PRESB̄Ī · (*red*). Primum quęritur quare...(f. **3 r a**) manentem substantiam. EXPLICIT. INCIPIT ARGVM̄TVM SOLIVS EPISTOLĘ AD ROMANOS. Romani ex iudęis...concordiam cohortatur (f. **4 a**) FINIT. INCIPIVNT CAPITVLA I. De natiuitate dn̄i secundum carnem...(LI)...uero ipsius reuelatio. EXPLICIT (f. **5 v a**) INCIPIT ARGVMENTVM Romani sunt in partibus italiae...ab athenis. EXPLICIT ARGVMENTVM (f. **5 v b**) INCIPIT ARGVMENTV̄ EPŁA AD CORINTHIOS PRIMA. Corinthii sunt achaię similiter...ab epheso. INCIPIVNT CAPITVLA. I. De plenitudine diuitiarum...(LXXII) eos qui credunt dn̄o ihū. Then capitula to 2 Cor., argument to 2 Cor.; argument to Gal., capitula to Gal.: so with Eph., Phil., 1 Thess., 2 Thess., Col., 1 Tim., 2 Tim., Tit., Philem....luca adiutoribus pauli. EXPLICIVNT.

f. **15 r** (beginning the original codex) INCIPIT PROLOGVS IN EPISTOLIS BEATI PAVLI ĀP̄L̄Ī SCI HIERONIMI PRESBITERI. Litteras tuas (*corr. al. man.*)...p̄dicant EXPŁ PROLŌḠ; INCĪP̄ CORPVS · ĒP̄Ī S̄: AD ROMĀN̄: The MS proceeds like the others of its family, and would have ended (f. **248 v a**) like them, save for the Merian subscription, had not the patchwork process already referred to been carried out... (f. **249 a**) INCIPIT PROLOGVS AD HEBREOS. Haec nos de intimo hebreorum...(f. **262 a**) caesę uictimae non remittunt. EXPLICIT EXPOSITIO S̄C̄Ī HIERONIMI IN QVATTVORDECIM EPISTOLIS BEATI PAVLI APOSTOLI.

2. **Hieronymus in epistulas Pauli ad Ephesios, ad Titum**[1].

Title on the cover: 42. | 57. | in epistolas D. Pauli Com̄ent. | · PS

[1] The text of these genuine commentaries appears to be good, if a cursory inspection may be trusted.

(*monogram*) · *paper label.* Rat. civ 38. *Paper label* Cod. lat. 13038. XXXXII (*old*). *Old wooden boards: clasps gone*[1].

The following abbreviations occur:

apostolus apl̄s, apstl̄s (twice), apostl̄s 'apostolus,' apl̄ 'apostoli,' apostl̄i 'apostoli,' ap̄s (corrector frequently)
autem aūt (aū corrector once)
Christus xp̄s
cum c (uob̄c, uobc̄, nob̄c)
Dauid dd̄
deus ds̄
dicens dic̄s
dicit dic̄, dīt (end of line)
dicitur dr̄, dir̄
dominus dn̄s
ecclesia ecl̄a (corrector)
eius ei'
enim ꝉꝉ (once only? above the line)
episcopus epōs 'episcopos' (corrector)
epistula epīs, epl̄a, epl̄
esse ēē (also eēs, eēnt 'esses,' 'essent,' etc.)
est ÷ (twice, once above line, once by corrector)
et 7 (once only, where *et* missed out)
euangelium euangl̄o, eugl̄o 'euangelio'
frater frt̄ (twice)
gloria gl̄a
gratia gr̄ā
hoc h̄ (corrector)
homo hō
id est ·i· (once, corrector)
Iesus ih̄s
Iohannes iohāes
Israhel isrl̄, irl̄, isrhl̄ (end of line, thrice)
item it̄
meus m̄s̄
mihi mⁱ
nisi nⁱ
{*noster* nl̄, nm̄, nō, nis̄ etc.
nr̄s, nrā (corrector)
ntr̄, ntr̄m, ntr̄a etc. etc. (most frequent)[2]
uester utr̄, utr̄m, utr̄o etc. (t twice erased)
uīs 'uestris'}

{*nunc* nᶜ
tunc tᶜ, t' (once each)}
oblatio obl̄o (end of line)
omnipotens omp̄s, omnipt̄s
omnis omn̄s 'omnes'
omā, omēs, omībus, omīs
omm̄ 'omnem'
ōnem 'omnem,' ōnes 'omnes'
populus ppl̄i 'populi'
post p̄'
presbyter prb̄os 'presbyteros' (corrector)
propheta pph̄, ꝓph̄
propter pp̄, ꝓpt̄
{*qua* qᵃ
quo qᵒ}
quae qᵛę
que q; q; (expanded once by corrector)
qui ꝗ (corrector alters to qui or qⁱ) ꝗ;
quia qꝃ
quod qd̄
quoniam qm̄ (rarely qnm̄, quō)
reliqua rel̄q (rl̄ corrector)
saeculum scl̄a 'saecula'
secl̄a, sęcl̄i
sanctus s̄c̄s̄
scilicet s· (? a later hand)
secundum secd̄, scd̄m, secund̄ (often), scd̄
sequitur seqr̄, seqt²
spiritus s̄p̄s̄
sunt s̄, st̄
tamen tm̄ (corrector, should be *tamen*)
tempore tempr̄, tempr̄e
uel l̄ (rare), ul̄
uero uᵒ

[1] The MS was kindly sent to Karlsruhe for my use in July 1906: the collation was made at Munich seven years later in the Arbeitssaal of the Universitätsbibliothek, by kind permission of the authorities of both libraries.

[2] Traube (*Nomina Sacra*, p. 225) had noted this speciality of this manuscript.

SYLLABLE SYMBOLS:

bis b̄ (uerb̄ 'uerbis,' expanded by corrector)
bunt bt̄
con ɔ (corrector)
dum d̄ (mod̄ 'modum,' cremand̄ 'cremandum,' etc. see *secundum*)
en m̄ 'men'
it ostend̄ 'ostendit'
mus, nus m', mʒ, m;, n' (see *eius*), n; (corrector corrects to n'), nʒ, *bus* b; *pus* p;
ra, ri etc. suprascript a, i, etc. (supᵃ 'supra,' pⁱmis 'primis')
rum ꝝ
runt r̄
ter t̄
tur t t

The long *i* is found usually at the beginning of words, whether the letter be vowel or semi-vowel. The ligatured *ti* is also indiscriminately employed.

These abbreviations are for the most part the regular abbreviations of a Ratisbon scriptorium, which was of course under Anglo-Saxon influence. It is not very easy to determine exactly which of the abbreviations were taken over unaltered from the exemplar. That the exemplar was itself insular is hardly to be doubted. But a few of the abbreviations, such as apstls, apostls, gla, grā, suggest that at some stage of the transmission it was represented by a Spanish copy.

That there was a Spanish stage in transmission is also suggested by the habitual use of *-quu-* in words like *loquutus, consequutus, quur,* for the usual *locutus, consecutus, cur.* But this Spanish stage must have preceded the insular. The omission of *ergo* (g̊) at least twice, and of *autem* (h) a good number of times, as well as the writing of *enim* (H) for *autem* (h), are proof sufficient of an insular exemplar in front of our scribe. This view is backed up by the confusion between *r* and *n* which occasionally appears: the confusion between *a* and *u* is witness to an 'open' *a* in the exemplar, as we should expect at the date when it was written.

R has many corruptions absent from E and S, for example: *In Rom.* i 24 iudices R; uindices ES: *in Rom.* i 25 est deus benedictus R; est benedictus ES: *in Rom.* ii 4 cum R; cur ES: *in Rom.* ii 11 sibi quid R; sibi quia E; sibi qui S; quidem sibi H_2; true text 'sibi' (alone): *in Rom.* ii 17 uerum esse R: esse uerum ES.

This MS sometimes agrees with E against S, more often perhaps with S against E, as we should expect. Two examples of the latter occurrence will suffice: *In 2 Cor.* v 16 neminem nouimus carnaliter circumcisum—exemplum *om.* RSH_2, *habet* E: *in Gal.* iiii 24 nos uero praeter auctoritatem RS; nos uero praeter caritatem E.

In some cases it appears as if an ancestor of R had rewritten the text, for example: *In* 1 *Cor.* vi 11 in tali delicto R; ut adsolet E; ad haec S: *in* 2 *Tim.* ii 24 eiulauit R; clamauit ES.

Yet R is an undoubted member of the H_1 family. In view, however, of the many differences from E and S, and the entire absence of the Merian subscription from R, it is on the whole probable that R is not descended from the MS executed by Merian, but belongs to a collateral branch; thus:

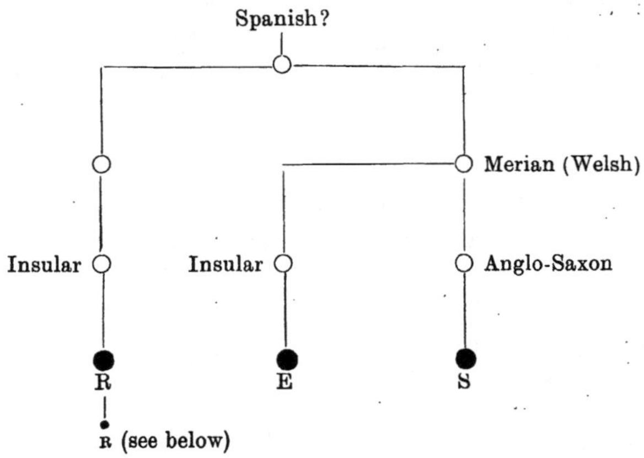

The work of the special corrector of R is more properly referred to in the part of this chapter concerning the other recension.

In Biblical text and prologues this MS has distinct points of contact with the Biblical MS M (= Clm 6229 saec. VIII) used by Wordsworth and White in constituting the text of Romans.

(6) *Munich, Universitätsbibliothek, Cod. MS in folio* 12 (*saec. XV ex.*) (R)

This manuscript is a paper MS of the years 1490 and 1491 containing 253 folia. It comprises all Pseudo-Jerome as well as the commentary on Hebrews, and the genuine Jerome on Galatians, Ephesians, Titus and Philemon. Preceding the Pseudo-Jerome part is a sort of alphabetical index of topics in the Epistles of St Paul, beginning *Abrahae filii sunt gal* 3 *g*: then the *Omnis textus*, the *Romani sunt in partibus italiae*, the *De natiuitate domini* capitula, also the prologues and capitula to the other Epistles as in Clm 13038 (order 1 Thess. 2 Thess. Col.). The *Litteris tuis* is followed by the commentaries on the Epistles (order 1 Thess. 2 Thess. Col.). Much space is saved by giving frequently only the initial letters of words in verses. I convinced myself that for Pseudo-Jerome at least this MS was copied from the older Munich MS. It must of course have got the genuine commentaries on Galatians and Philemon from some other source. The cover has the following inscription inside: 'Hunc librum legauit fratribus minoribus dominus Achacius Haiswasser predicator In Elpogen[1] anno dn̄i 1516.' Another inscription reads: '...tunc rector scolarium ratisbone recessurus tamen ad ange reminiscere ad susceptum statum ad S Judocum landtzhuete[2].'

I have naturally made no use of this MS in constituting the text.

Description of the MSS of the Longer Form, with a Discussion of their Relationship

(7) *Paris, B.N.* 1853 (*saec.* viii—ix[3]) (M)

Older shelfmarks are preserved as follows 'Cod. Colb. 2065 Regius $\frac{3990}{3\cdot 3}$, 1853 Jac. Aug. Thuani.' It is absolutely certain that the MS belonged in the sixteenth century to the first library of the Jesuits at Paris, formed before 1594, which was pillaged by De Thou about the end of the sixteenth century[4].

The MS consists now of 255 ff., but once had at least 256. The canons at the beginning are arranged in two columns to the page, but elsewhere there is one column only to the page. Each page contains 25 lines, and measures 295 mm. by 191 mm., while the

[1] In Bohemia, as I learn from Prof. Paul Lehmann, to whom I am also indebted for the knowledge that the Munich University Library contains MSS and for the decipherment of certain difficult parts of these notes of ownership.

[2] The modern Landshut (62 km from Regensburg [Ratisbon]).

[3] As to the date, various palaeographers have favoured me with their opinions: C. H. Turner, last quarter of saec. viii; W. M. Lindsay, saec. viii; E. A. Lowe, saec. viii—ix; A. Holder and H. M. Bannister, saec. ix incip.

[4] This information I owe to a kind examination of the MS which Monsieur H. Omont undertook on my behalf. The pressmark of the Jesuit library has been erased. Cf. also Delisle, *Cabinet des Manuscrits* t. i p. 437; Traube, *Vorlesungen und Abhandlungen* Bd. i p. 17 n. 1.

written part measures 233 mm. by 135 mm. (approximately). Not fewer than twenty scribes took part in the production of this manuscript, which is for this and other reasons of great palaeographical interest. It is difficult to give the precise arrangement of the quaternions because of the manner in which the manuscript has been bound[1]. The earliest signed quaternion of which the signature is now visible is XIIII on the right inner lower corner of fol. 111 v. The existing series is as follows[2]:

XIIII	on	fol.	111 v	(right inner lower corner)
XVI	„	„	127 v	(middle foot)
XVII	„	„	135 v	(„ „)
XVIII	„	„	143 v	(„ „)
XVIIII	„	„	151 v	(„ „)
XX	„	„	159 v	(„ „)
XXI	„	„	167 v	(„ „)
XXII	„	„	174 v	(„ „) (leaf cut out between 172 and 173)
XXIII	„	„	182 v	(middle foot)
a XXIII]	„	„	190 v	(„ „)
XXV	„	„	198 v	(„ „)

Leaves have also been cut out as follows: two between ff. 89 and 90, one between ff. 244 and 245, one between ff. 245 and 246 (containing a portion of the Philemon commentary and part of the Hebrews argument and capitula), and one between ff. 248 and 249. Only in the one specified case does this mean any loss of text: the others are merely cases of cancelled leaves.

The contents are as described on an earlier page, but the title of the commentary proper may be repeated here (fol. 12 r)

IN NOMINE DĪ SV̄MI INCIP EXPLANACIO SCI HIERONIMI IN QUATUORDECĒ EPISTOLIS SCI APOSTOLI PAULI.

Such a grandiloquent title is not confined to the MSS of the second family of Pseudo-Jerome. I am unable to produce

[1] It belongs (like Paris B.N. lat. 2709) to a group of MSS bound superbly in crimson morocco about the middle of the nineteenth century, but the sheets have been so tightly bound that the volume does not open easily and one cannot see the inner edges of the sheets.

[2] A number appears to have been erased on fol. 7 v.

another instance of this precise phraseology, but parallels are not uncommon[1].

To the best of my belief, no photograph of any part of this extraordinary manuscript has been published. A study of the MS from the palaeographical point of view may be commended as a most interesting piece of work, which ought to be accompanied by a carefully selected series of photographs designed to show the writing of each scribe. The lamented Abbé Liebaert had taken photographs of folia 12, 23 v (1, 2), 78 v, 94 v, 115 v, 185 v, 205, 206 v, 222 v, as I learn from Professor Lindsay's list[2]. The present writer possesses beautiful rotographs of ff. 137 r, 159 r, 159 v, 177 r, 177 v, 178 r, 184 r, 245 v, selected for their textual rather than their palaeographical importance. The scribes, with the exception of the last, use a pre-Caroline minuscule, which for the most part slopes in an extraordinary way, the upper part of the letters falling some degrees to the left of the perpendicular. Dr H. M. Bannister, to whom I showed the MS, was struck by the crowd of ignorant scribes, all taught to write in the same way. He thought that the last scribe, who wrote in Caroline script, came perhaps from elsewhere, and filled in the letters with red ink. The question of the *scriptorium* in which this manuscript was produced will be discussed after the numerous abbreviations have been recorded.

apostolus apostł 'apostolus,' apostłi, ap'tłi 'apostoli,' apostł, ap'tło 'apostolo,' 'apostoli' (f. 226 r), ap'tulū
apostłs, ap'tłs 'apostolus'
āp̄ 'apostoli'
ap̄s
ap̄stolo 'apostolo'
apstło 'apostolo,' apstłi 'apostoli'
apł 'apostolo,' 'apostolus'
apsł 'apostolus,' 'apostoli'
apo̅s̅ 'apostolus,' 'apostoli,' 'apostolo'
apłs 'apostolus,' apło 'apostolo,' apłos 'apostolos,' apłis 'apostolis'
aposٙt̄ 'apostolus'
apo̅s̅l, aposłi, ap'łi, 'apostoli,' ap'ło 'apostolo'

apud ap̄, apđ

autem aū, au̅t̅ (rare), h̶

[1] For example, Metz 134, Oxford, Bodl. Auct. T. II 24 (saec. X—XI) (*Corp. Gloss. Lat.* IV p. XXXV), Paris B.N. 12289 (Fleury), Einsiedeln 131 (saec. X) (E. v. Dobschütz, *Das Decretum Gelasianum*, p. 16), Chartres 31 (saec. IX) (*ibid.*), Laon 273 (saec. IX ex.) (C.S.E.L. XXIII p. 231), St Gall 158 (saec. IX) (C.S.E.L. LI p. XV), Brit. Mus. Harl. 1772 (saec. VIII—IX) (ed. Buchanan), Paris B.N. 12,125 (saec. IX) (Corbie) etc. (*Origenes' Werke*, Bd. V [Leipzig, 1913] p. lix), show such titles as *In Christi nomine*, *In nomine domini*, *In nomine domini nostri Iesu Christi*.

[2] Copies of these may be obtained from Sig. Pompeo Sansaini, Via Antonio Scialoja 3, Rome.

capitulum etc. cap̄, capil̄, cap̄l
caput capđ (on analogy of *apud*)
carissimi km̄i, km̄s 'carissimus'
cetera c&, c&er̄, caet̄, cet̄
christianus xp̄iano 'christiano'
Christus xp̄s, xpo (*sic*, f. 109 r)
Colosenses colosen̄s, coll̄os̄, col̄os̄
consolationibus consl̄
Corinthios corint̄, chorint̄, corin̄, cor̄, chorinth̄s
cum c̄
Dauid đđ
de đ (prep. and syll.)
deus etc. ds̄ etc.
diaconii (*-atus*) diacon̄
dicere dr̄e
dicimur dm̄r
dicit dic̄, dit̄, dt̄
dicitur dr̄
dicunt dn̄t
dicuntur dn̄r
dixit dix̄, dx̄
dominus etc. dns etc.
ecclesia aecl̄a, aecl̄m 'ecclesiam'; aecl̄ae, ęccl̄ę 'ecclesiae'
eius eī (once ēi, f. 178 v) ei; e; (ff. 140 v, 198 r) ēī (often) ej ej; eј̄: ej, (these four in ligature) eî
enim ╪╪
Ephesios effh̄e, efphēs, effēs, ephēs, efph̄
episcopus eps̄, epīs 'episcopis,' 'episcopi,' epm̄ 'episcopum,' epī 'episcopi,' ep̄os 'episcopos'
episcopm̄ 'episcopum'
epistula epīs 'epistula,' 'epistulae'
ep̄ 'epistula,' 'epistulae'
epistl̄ 'epistulae,' 'epistulam'
eple 'epistulae'
epistol̄
ep̄s 'epistularum'
ep̄i 'epistulae'
epīst
esse ęę̄, ēe, ēē

essem etc. ęęm; ę&, ęęt, ēet, eēt, 'esset'
est ē ÷ (see *hoc*)
et &
explicit expl̄, expl̄ic, expl̄i, exp̄(?), exp̄i
expositio exp̄, expōs
fratres fr̄s, ff̄, frās, ff̄s, fr̄t 'frater,' fr̄t͏e 'fratre,' ff̄s 'fratribus,' ff̄t 'frater'
Galatas gal̄a, gal̄
haec h̄ (h̄ec, f. 231 v)
Hebraeos hebr̄
hera (=section) hir̄, hr̄
Hieronymi HIER̄, IER̄, HIERON
hoc h· (f. 211 v)
hoc est h ÷ (5 times last, Caroline, scribe)
Iesus etc. ihs̄ etc., ihū 'Iesum' (f. 81 v), ihm̄ 'Iesu (*gen.*)' (ff. 155 v, 190 v)
incipit incip̄, incipt̄, incipī
Iohannes ioh̄
Israhel isrl̄, irl̄, isrl̄h̄, isrh̄l̄, israh̄l̄ (f. 239 v)
item it̄
loquitur loq̄r
Matheus math̄e
meus m̄s (for 'meos' f. 71 r)
mihi m̊
modo mō (f. 229 r)
nobis nob̄
uobis uob̄, ůb̄· (once)
nomine nom̄
non nō, n̄
noster[1] nr̄, nrā, nr̄m, nr̄i, nr̄ae, nr̄o, nrām, nrīs, nrōs, nrās (fully declined), nr̄m 'nostram' (f. 192 v)
nrā 'nostram' (f. 206 v)
nost̄
nā (n̄a[2]), n̄m̄, nī, nae (f. 87 r corr. al. man. nr̄e), (nē), nō, nām, nōs, nās, nīs
nos̄ra 'nostra'
n̄s 'nostris' (*ex* m̄s[3], f. 117 v)
ns̄t 'nostra,' nsm̄ 'nostram'
nt̄

[1] It is of very considerable interest to observe that *noster* is frequently unabbreviated in these phrases, dn̄i nostri ih̄u xp̄i, ihm̄ xp̄m dn̄m nostrum. This fact suggests that an ancestor of our MS had the early suspension n̄ for any case of *noster*.

[2] F. 130 v has nā gloria n̄a (=*nam gloria nostra*). Note the different positions of the abbreviation stroke. In this matter the MS is not consistent.

[3] Archetype must have had nīs.

uester ur̄, ur̄a, urm̄, ur̄i, ur̄ę, urām, urīs, ur̄s 'uestros'(f. 195 v.), urās, ur̄a 'uestram' (f. 171 r), ur̄ 'uestra' (f. 151 v), ur̄s 'uestris' (corr. m 2 ur̄is) (f. 254 v)
ūā, um̄, uāē, uam̄, uō, uās
uest̄ 'uester'
ūst 'uester,' 'uestra,' 'uestrum,' ūstrū, 'uestrum,' ūstrā 'uestram'
usrm̄ 'uestrum,' usram̄ 'uestram'

nunc n̄c, n̊
tunc t̊

omnipotens omn̄ips, om̄ps
omnis om̄s 'omnes,' 'omnis,' hom̄s (f. 108 v)
om̄a 'omnia'
om̄ 'omnes' (corr. al. man. f. 16 r), 'omnis,' 'omnem,' 'omne'
omn̄s (hom̄ns) 'omnes,' 'omnis': omn̄a 'omnia,' omn̄ 'omne' (f. 192 r)
passione pass̄
Pauli PAŪ, PAUL̄
per p̱, p̱, p· (Caroline scribe twice)
Philipenses phil̄, philip̄, philipen̄s, philipen;
populus p̄pls, p̄plū 'populum,' pplm̄ 'populum,' pplo̅ 'populo'
post p; p' (also in p'tulent 'postulent,' ap'tlo̅ 'apostolo,' p'tea 'postea')
potest p̊ (f. 235 v)
prae p̄ (p̱uaricator, f. 112 v, must be due to confusion of p· and p̄, because p̱ in this scribe means *per*)
presbyter pr̄bi 'presbyteri,' pr̄bm 'presbyterum'
presb̄i 'presbyteri'
prib̄i 'presbyteri'
prb̄ris 'presbyteris'
presbr̄χ 'presbyterum'
prima prī, prim̄, pⁱ
prī 'primae'
pro ꝓ
propter p̄pt̄ ppt̄, p̄pt̄, ppt̄, ppt̄, p̄pt, p̄pt̄, ppt̄
pp̄ (p̄p̄, first stroke erased, f. 133 r), p̄p, pp̄
ꝓt̄
p̄pter
prop̄
publicanus pul̄i· (f. 215 r)
-qu- qᵛ
qua q; (f. 140 v)[1]
quadraginta XLta
quae q; (sometimes corrected by another hand, as q; should be used for 'que' only) q̄; q:· ꝗ ꝗae ꝗ
quaeritur qr̄·
quam ꝗ q̊ ꝗ aliꝗuā (f. 220 r gives the 'uam' twice over, the second equivalent being an after-thought) ꝗ
quando qn̄o, qn̄
quare qrē
quasi q̄si (qs̄i)
que q; ꝗ ꝗ ꝗ ꝗ
qui q̄ qⁱ ꝗ
quia ꝗ qⁱa ꝗ q̊ q;
quid qt̄ 'quit' for 'quid' (three times)
qⁱd̄
quis q̄s
quod q̄d (qđ q̄d) ꝗ qůd qođ (once qod) quođ (once) ꝗ ꝗ(?)
ꝗ
quomodo qm̄o
quoniam qnm̄, qm̄ (most characteristic), qūm
quoque q̄q꜀
reliqua reliq· rēl; rel̄ rēlq: rl̄
respondit RP̄
Romanos rom̄
saecularis seclāria, scl̄aria, 'saecularia'
saeculum slō 'saeculo' (f. 60 r), secl̄i 'saeculi,' secl̄o 'saeculo, secl̄a 'saecula,' sēclorum 'saeculorum'
scl̄m, scl̄i, scl̄a
sanctificatio scīficationis 'sanctificationis'
sanctitas scītate 'sanctitate'
sanctus etc. s̄cs̄ etc., scs̄ 'sanctos' (f. 198 v *bis*), sīs (once) 'sanctis'

[1] A certain number of the *qu*-abbreviations appear to have been ignorantly employed.

secunda secūn̄, secund̄, secd̄, sec̄, secd̄a
secundum sec̄, secd̄ (sec̄d), secund̄, secd̄u (secdū)
semel seml̄ (f. 254 v)
sequitur seq̄r̄
sequuntur seqn̄r̄
sicut sic̄
spiritalis spītalis: spīritalia (f. 109 v)
spiritus etc. sp̄s, sp̄m, spū, spūi: spuū, spūum 'spirituum,' spūm 'spiritum'

Syllable Symbols:

con c̄ ɔ (f. 140 r)
e d̄ 'de'
en m̄ 'men,' 'membra' (f. 75 r), m̄bra 'membra' (the spelling *menbra* is frequent in MSS)
er t̄ 'ter,' b̄ 'ber'
is b̄ 'bis,' l̄ 'lis'
it p̄ c̄ x̄ ū b̄, incip̄t 'incipit,' credidt̄ 'credidit' (f. 253 v)
m suprascript stroke, generally of the collar-bone shape, slightly inclined from the vertical[1] (once at least beyond the letter in imitation of the ancient style, tu⁻)
n suprascript stroke, as for *m*
runt r̄
ur tr̆ t' tr̄ 'tur' (never t²)[2]

sunt s̄t̄ (st̄), s̄ (also poss̄t̄ 'possunt')
tamen tn̄
tantum tm̄
tempore temp̄r̄ (temp̄r)
tertia TER̄
Tesalonicenses tesol̄, thesal̄, tesalonoc̄, tesalon̄, tesal̄, tesalonocens̄
Timotheum timoth̄, tim̄o
uel ul̄ · ū · (ū)
uero ů, ūo
uersus uer̄
uicensima XXma

us b; b̄ 'bus,' d 'dus' (once, f. 85 v), l̄ l+ 'lus,' m; mʒ 'mus,' n; nʒ 'nus,' p; 'pus,' t̄ 'tus' (?)(f. 240 v), see *eius*[3]
ae ę
rum ꝝ rꝝ r̄ (r⁻, see under *m*) r. (f. 160 v)
nem n̆ (fairly frequent), beatitudin̆ 'beatitudinem,' multitudiN̄ 'multitudinem,' etc.
bun b̄ probab̄tur 'probabuntur' (corr. al. man. probabūtur), hab̄dauit 'habundauit,' diceb̄t 'dicebuntur' etc.
ssime s̄· plenis̄· 'plenissime' (f. 220 r) (suchlike earlier also)
centes c̄t̄ requiesc̄t̄ 'requiescentes' (?)
bin b̄ cherub̄ 'cherubin' (f. 251 r)

The extraordinary variety of abbreviation here would seem to indicate that various influences were converging on the centre where this manuscript was produced, and that no standard set of abbreviations had yet been evolved for that *scriptorium*. What may be regarded at once as certain, is that the immediate parent of this MS was in insular, in fact Irish, script. How otherwise could one explain the fact that insular abbreviations abound most in the part which is written in the Caroline script? The following symbols are insular: ħ, c̄, dt̄, dn̄t̄, dn̄r̄, h̄, m̊, p, q̄si, q, tn̄, tm̄, ɔ (=con), and the following are definitely Irish rather than Anglo-Saxon: ap̄, drē, h̄, qn̄, qn̄o, qr̄e, qm̄o. We need not therefore doubt that the im-

[1] What Prof. R. S. Conway calls the 'signum Floriacense': see his note on Livy v 43, 1; also the preface to his vol. II p. XXV.

[2] Dr Lowe tells me that t² first appears about A.D. 800, at Tours.

[3] From this point onwards the abbreviations do not figure in Prof. Lindsay's tables.

mediate ancestor was in Irish script. But this is by no means the only element. The following abbreviations are definitely non-insular: đ, ē, it̄, sic̄, ul̄, ·ū·, r̄ (= runt). Some of the symbols have a decidedly Spanish look: such symbols for *apostolus* as show the *stl*, *stls*, *sls*; episcopm̄; n̄s̄t̄, ns̄m̄, us̄t, us̄r̄m̄ etc.; omn̄s, homn̄s etc. An earlier stratum appears in the suspension abbreviations apos̄, epīs, n̄ (= noster, which we have postulated) etc.

The orthography is of the worst Merovingian type: *u* and *o* are constantly interchanged, as in *cognusco*, *subauditor*, *actos*; short *e* is substituted for short *i*, as in *crededi* etc.; the aspirate is often added, as in *himagines*; *t* is found for *c*, as in *mendatium*, and *c* for *t*, as in *noticia*; long *i* for long *e* as in *adimplicio* for *adimpletio*; short *i* for short *e*, as in *habit*; *y* for *i* as in *cybus*; internal aspiration is found, as in *typhus* for *typus*; *ae* for *e* as in *distruaerit*; *abstullit*, *necglegere*, *uellit*, *presura*, *abssens*, *alico*, *escandalizant*, *scilitit*, *stote* etc. Certain of the abbreviations of proper names given above also show how freakish the orthography is on occasion.

One or two notes with regard to the script may be here collected. Dr H. M. Bannister was struck by the forms of capital A R and Q. The R has the upper loop separate from the lower curve. As we find this also in certain Visigothic MSS, it has occurred to me that it may have been consciously imitated from the Visigothic ancestor already postulated. Bannister regarded the collar-bone suprascript stroke as indicative of an origin East of the Rhine, away from court influence, and he found many North German marks in the MS. The accents on monosyllables like *es*, *o*, *os*, *a*, *ae*, *his* are no doubt derived from the Irish parent. The letter *u* sometimes takes an extraordinary form after another *u*, the form being like a Greek minuscule stigma: uςlt (f. 123 v), uςltis (f. 173 v), paruςlus (f. 123 r), nouςm (ff. 125 r, 170 v). The MS also uses a form like C to represent V in numbers, thus Ϛ = VI (f. 238 v): the only parallels to this known to me are in MSS Gotha, membr. I n. 85 (from Murbach, saec. VIII—IX) and Vat. pal. 574 (from Lorsch, saec. IX)[1]. Dr Lowe was struck by the resemblance between my rotographs and the minuscule part of MS Épinal 68 (saec. VII—VIII) (formerly of Murbach). Prof. Lehmann, after inspecting the same rotographs, declared for the border of France and Germany as the place of

[1] *Das Decretum Gelasianum*...E. v. Dobschütz (Leipzig, 1912) p. 141.

origin of the MS. Dr Alfred Holder recognised the Reichenau *m*, but to my great regret I never obtained the results of a detailed examination from him[1]. Lehmann, Lindsay and Lowe have all suggested Murbach in Alsace as the place of origin of the MS, but with a query. In the *Notae Latinae*[2] the onus of this opinion is laid upon me: "according to Souter, the contents...suggest the possibility that it was written at Murbach." I will presently proceed to show how it is that the contents do suggest this, but first I ought to allude to two other MSS, which certainly belonged to Murbach, and which offer some analogies with M. They are Oxford, Bodl. Junius 25 (saec. VIII) and Manchester, John Rylands Library 15 (saec. VIII). Both these MSS were written by a large number of scribes: so was our M. Such manuscripts are on the whole exceptional, and it may have been a regular practice of the Murbach *scriptorium* at the end of the eighth century to apportion the task of copying among a large number. Again, a close study of the abbreviations in the Rylands MS shows many interesting points of contact with ours[3].

That there was a manuscript of Pelagius in the Murbach library at the middle of the ninth century, we learn from the catalogue of date about A.D. 840, published by H. Bloch[4], where the following entry occurs:

210. Exposicio Pelagii in epistolas Pauli.

The catalogue, moreover, contains another entry only less interesting: it is this:

39. Canones Ieronimi et Pellagii.

Now it happens that our MS comprises the contents of both cod. 210 and cod. 39, if the Canons in our MS may be identified with those in cod. 39, as surely they may be, seeing that internal evidence shows them to be of Pelagian origin[5]. But the Épinal MS which falls to be considered next, has the same contents, and it is possible that we ought to identify the Épinal MS with the Murbach

[1] My rotographs were in his possession from Sept. 1913 till his death in Jan. 1916.

[2] P. 471.

[3] See 'List of Abbreviations and Contractions, etc., in the John Rylands Latin Manuscript No. 15' by the present writer in *Bulletin of the John Rylands Library, Manchester*, vol. v (1918—1919) pp. 111—115.

[4] *Strassburger Festschrift zur* 46. *Philologen-Versammlung* (1901) pp. 271, 276.

[5] See below for references to De Bruyne and White.

MS. As a matter of fact, the Épinal MS was once in the Abbey of Moyenmoutier, but it may nevertheless have been earlier in Murbach, like Épinal 68 (saec. VII—VIII) and Épinal 78 (saec. IX), both of which were in Moyenmoutier in Montfaucon's time, but are nevertheless Murbach books. If we identified our Épinal MS with the Murbach Pelagius, then it would be tempting to identify the Paris MS (M) with the Lorsch Pelagius[1]. Yet even if M was once in Lorsch, it is not, Professor Lindsay tells me, a product of the Lorsch *scriptorium*. Murbach and Lorsch were as a matter of fact in close relations with one another[2], and we should expect their Pelagius MSS to be related with one another.

The MS '39. Canones Ieronimi et Pellagii,' which must have been a small MS, has probably perished. It is not impossible that it was an autograph, for the work is a pseudonymous production hardly likely to be earlier in origin than the seventh or eighth century. It is evidently based on the well known Canons so often found in Vulgate MSS of St Paul's Epistles[3]. But if it is lost, at least three copies which go back ultimately to the autograph, are still extant. The two copies discovered by me take precedence in age over the third copy, which is evidently that employed by Vezzosi for his supplement to Tommasi's works[4], and rediscovered and recollated by De Bruyne at Gotha in the Biblical MS membr. I 20 fol. 217 (saec. X), which is undoubtedly a Murbach book.

Murbach was in fact a very important centre. It was founded from Reichenau by Pirmin in 725, and both Charlemagne and Alcuin were in touch with it. The territory of the abbey extended as far as Lucerne in the ninth century. It was somewhat ravaged by the Swedes in the sixteenth century, but recovered its glory in the seventeenth century, when it passed to France. Abbot Bartholomew of Andlau had ordered a catalogue to be made in 1464, which catalogue exists both in Latin and in a French trans-

[1] See p. 28 above.

[2] Hauck, *Kirchengeschichte Deutschlands* Bd. II pp. 593 f.; Von Dobschütz, *Das Decretum Gelasianum* p. 143.

[3] 'Une Concordance Biblique d'Origine Pélagienne' in *Revue Biblique*, t. V (1908) pp. 75—83; Wordsworth and White, *Epistula ad Romanos* (Oxon. 1913) p. 12. I recollated the Canons myself at Gotha in 1913 and the Vezzosi text, a scarce book, later.

[4] *Thomasii...Opera Omnia*, tom. I (Romae 1747) pp. 489 ff.

lation[1]. In that catalogue the Canons MS still appears: 'n. 40 Canons de Saint Jérome et de Pélage[2],' but of the manuscript of the Pelagius commentary there is not a trace. About the seventeenth century the Murbach library was transported to Guebviller, and then by the Republic in 1791 to Colmar. There and earlier considerable leakages have taken place[3], and only fifty or sixty volumes are now known to exist, of which thirty-four are at Colmar[4]. One of these is a MS of the Pauline Epistles (saec. VIII), which does not contain our Canons, and does not seem to agree in Biblical text with my M or N[5]. The connexion of our M with Murbach is, therefore, not absolutely certain.

(8) *Épinal, No.* 6 (*saec.* IX *in.*) (N)

This manuscript belonged to the Abbey of Moyenmoutier[6] in the neighbourhood: fol. 1 r top reads 'Mediani Monasterii Catalogo inscriptus 1717.' Old shelf-marks are:

x 1 / No. 23 } Arm² No. 6 45 49 (these two are later than the others). All these are preserved on the cover, which is not older than the sixteenth century.

The MS now consists of 176 ff. (unnumbered). As the codex breaks off in the midst of a comment on section XXIIII of the Epistle

1 *Lettres et Pièces rares ou inédites publiées et accompagnées d'introductions et de notes* par M. Matter (Paris, 1846) pp. 40—76.

2 P. 46.

3 See the present writer in *Bulletin of the John Rylands Library, Manchester* vol. v (1918—1919) pp. 392 f.

4 P. Lehmann, *Iohannes Sichardus*...(München, 1911) pp. 164—175.

5 I have been favoured with select readings by Dr White, who now possesses a photograph. Literature on Murbach will be found in Lehmann, *loc. cit.* I have to thank Monsieur Léon Dorez and Dom Wilmart for references to A. Gatrio, *Die Abtei Murbach in Elsass*, 2 Bde (Strassb. 1895); F. W. E. Roth in *Strassburger Studien* Bd. III (1888) p. 339; Montfaucon (from Calmet), *Bibliotheca Bibliothecarum*...II (Paris, 1739) pp. 1175—1178; Mabillon and Ruinart, *Voyage Littéraire de deux religieux Bénédictins* (Paris, 1717) II p. 138.

6 On Moyenmoutier, Dom Wilmait kindly refers me to Montfaucon, *Biblioth. Biblioth.* II 1180, 1759 (cf. 1175); Calmet, *Histoire de Lorraine*, t. VII (2) (1757) pp. cli—clv; M. Jerôme, *Histoire de l'Abbaye de Moyenmoutier*, t. I (1902) (down to sixteenth century); Th. Gottlieb, *Ueber mittelalterliche Bibliotheken* (Leipzig, 1890).

to the Hebrews[1], the portion lost, assuming that it was identical with that in M, where it takes up six and a half pages, was not sufficient to fill a whole quaternion. The Canons at the beginning (occupying the first quaternion) are arranged in two columns to the page, but elsewhere there is one column only to the page. Each page contains 33 lines[2], and measures 335 mm. by 218 mm., while the written part measures 290 mm. by 172 mm. The MS appears to have been executed by at least three scribes. The first wrote quaternions 1—11 inclusive (= ff. 1 r—88 v): the second wrote quaternions 12—20 (= ff. 89 r—160 v) inclusive (except a small portion of fol. 117 v): the third wrote the first eleven and a half lines of fol. 117 v, and also quaternions 21 and 22 (= ff. 161 r to 176 v): a fourth seems to have written the last four lines of f. 136 r, perhaps most of f. 149 v, all of f. 150 r and the first three lines of f. 152 r: traces of other scribes are found here and there. The twenty-two quaternions which now compose the MS are all absolutely regular: .I. signed below the right-hand column of f. 8 v: | II | (below, middle of f. 16 v): so with | III | IIII | V | VI | VII | VIII: the ninth, tenth and eleventh bear no numbers; the 12th to the 21st inclusive (which, as we have seen, are by the second scribe) are lettered below the text, in the middle, on the respective pages, A B C · ∂ · ·ẹ· F· Ç · h · I · K · (for the most part in uncial letters). The twenty-second and last (surviving) quaternion is neither numbered nor lettered. The vellum is mainly thick and strong.

The contents are described above, but the commentary on Hebrews does not appear to agree closely with that in M, which suggests that while for the thirteen Epistles the two MSS are closely related, they derived their Hebrews expositions from separate sources.

At the foot of fol. 1 r the same hand (probably) which wrote the note of Moyenmoutier ownership, has written:

'*D. Hieronimi seu potius Pelagii heraesiarchae Commentarius in epistolas Pauli.*'

The scriptural lemmata are underlined with red ink down to

[1] At chap. vii 24: see Riggenbach, *Die ältesten lateinischen Kommentare zum Hebräerbrief* (= Zahn's *Forschungen* u.s.w. 8 Teil) (Leipzig, 1907) pp. 205 ff.

[2] But the first scribe has crushed 35 lines of small writing on to fol. 88 v in order to finish his portion there.

1 Cor. xiii 9 *et ex parte prophetamus* (f. 75 v). The characters are large and well-formed, and belong to the type associated with Murbach and related centres[1]: the second scribe in fact recalls the work of the first scribe of **A**, but he is hardly so elegant.

Quite early the MS was injured by damp and mice (?), as illegible words were supplied even before the rubricator began his work, that is, at earliest in the middle of the thirteenth century[2]. The damage affected the tops of the leaves, which are partly discoloured. The codex is too lavish with punctuation, by means of a dot placed after every two or three words. These points, the work of the original scribes, have been, for the most part, scraped out. This gives the MS a worse appearance than it would have had, if they had been suffered to remain. Portions of the margins of folia 78, 79, 92, 95, 98, 105, 107 and 127 have been clipped away, and a rent in fol. 91 has been most skilfully repaired by sewing. The first scribe gives no headings to the pages, but the second scribe, for example, heads f. 89 r (his first page) thus:

ADCORIN SECUNDA

The outer pages of folia are regularly the smooth side of the vellum, not the hair side. The following trifles occur at the points indicated:

mg. f. 102 v *Virtus* | *lampat* | *&* *sotiat* · | [*N*]*atiuitas* | *unde* (saec. XIII?).

mg. f. 103 v The alphabet is run up the margin, A being given in uncial and minuscule, while the other letters are in minuscule only (once each).

mg. f. 106 v *Virtus lampat & sociat Natiuitas unde nobis* (same hand as on f. 102 v).

mg. f. 146 v *k l m n o p q r s* (rest cut off by binder: a probatio pennae).

mg. f. 147 v *a b c d e f g* (rest cut off by binder: a probatio pennae).

As regards the forms of letters, etc. it may be remarked that open *a* is very common, that half-uncial F is sometimes found, and that the second scribe occasionally uses the capital R and S in the middle of writing otherwise minuscule. Accents are occasionally

[1] See p. 204. [2] Judging by the characters on f. 72 r.

found on the vowels of monosyllables, insular fashion: ó, éſ. The third scribe has a curious habit that I do not remember to have observed elsewhere, the use of a circumflex accent over the first consonant, where that consonant is doubled: thus *ac̑cione, ac̑cipere* (e.g. f. 167 v). The mark has doubtless something to do with pronunciation. Omission from homoeoteleuton, afterwards corrected, is quite frequent.

With regard to orthography it is enough at this stage to mention that aspirates are often wrongly present, or wrongly absent, that we also often find a consonant single, where it should be double, and that the second scribe spells *secondum, iracondus*.

The abbreviations in this manuscript are not nearly as numerous as those in M, but they are of considerable interest. It looks as if the scribes of N had received instructions to use as few abbreviations as possible, and it is therefore not improbable that most of those actually employed are taken over from the exemplar. I have added the letter M in brackets after each abbreviation of N which we have found also in M. The evidence will show, I think, that the two MSS belong to the same region, even if it does not prove that all abbreviations found in both belong to their common archetype.

apostolus apostl̄ (nom.) (M), apostl̄ (acc. sing.), apostl̄ (acc. pl.)
apost̄ (M)
apl̄ (M)
ap̄s (M)
apol̄s
apostol̄s
apostul̄
autem aū (first and second scribes) (M)
aūt̄ (first scribe rarely, third scribe always) (M)
aūm (m eras., f. 26 r)
capitulum cp̄ 'capitula,' cap̄ 'capitula' (M)
carissimus km̄s (M)
cetera c&̄r;
Christianus xp̄ianus (M)
Christus xp̄s etc. (M)
xpūm 'Christum' (f. 36 r)
Corinthii ch̄r̄s 'corinthios,' corint̄ 'corinthios' (M)
deus etc. ds̄ etc. (M)
dicit dit̄ (f. 64 v) (M)
dicitur dr̄ (M)
dominus etc. dn̄s etc. (M), dm̄n̄ (?) 'dominum' (once)
eius eīs (ff. 27 r, 33 r)
ei; (third scribe only, several times) (M)
enim ⊹ (M)
episcopus epōs 'episcopos' (M)
epistula epīs (M), ep̄ 'epistulae' (M), ep̄s 'epistulae,' 'epistularum' (cf. M)
esse ēē (M)
esset eēt (M)
est ÷ (M), ē (M)
euangelium ęuangl̄o 'euangelio' (f. 164 v)
expositio exp̄ (M)
fratres frās (f. 136 v) (M)
frt̄ 'frater' (ff. 46 r, 62 v) (M)
gratia grā
Hierusolyma hierusol̄ 'hierusolymis'
Iesus ihūs (f. 72 r)
incipit incp̄t, incip̄ (M)

Iohannes ioħ (M)
ioħs 'Iohannis' (f. 36 r)
Israhel isrħl (M)
meus m̄s (f. 58 v) (M)
mihi miħ (third scribe, thrice)[1]
m̄ (f. 168 v *bis*)
nobis nƀ, noƀ (M)
uobis uƀ
non n̄ (M), nō (M)
noster[2] nt̄ (M), nā (M), nm̄ (M), nī (M), nāē (M), nō (M), nām (M), nīs (M), nōs (M), nās (M)
nr̄ (M), nr̄o (M), nrām (M), nr̄m (M), nr̄a (M), nr̄i (M) (this type third scribe always)
nrt̄ (f. 141 r)
nost̄ (M)
uester ut̄, uā (M), um̄ (M), uāē (M), uīs
ur̄ (f. 135 r) (M)
ustā (corr. ūstū) 'uestrum' (once) (cf. M)
omnipotens omp̄s (M)
omnis om̄s 'omnes' (M)
om̄ (for various cases) (M)
omīa (first scribe), omā (second scribe) (M)
Paulus pauls
per p (M)
post p; (M)
prae p̄ (M)
presbyter prƀi 'presbyteri' (f. 161 r) (M), prƀim 'presbyterum' (f. 161 r)
pro ꝓ (M)
propter p̄p̄ter (M)
p̄pt̄ (M), (p̄pt̄ [M])
p̄p̄ (M)
prop̄ (corr. propt̄) (once) (M)
ꝓpte (e eras.) (once)
quae q:
quasi qs̄i (f. 172 r) (M)
que q (M), q; (M)
quia qꝛ (cf. M)
quid qt̄ (from 'quit') (M)
qđ
quod qđ (M)
quomodo quomođ (f. 16 v, end of line)
quomđ (third scribe, thrice)
quođo (once)[3]
quoniam[4] qūō (frequent)
qm̄ (sometimes) (M)
quōm (f. 24 r)
qn̄m (twice) (M)
reliqua reŀiq, rŀiq, reŀq (M), reŀi, reŀ (M), rŀq
Romanos rom̄ (M)
saeculum secŀi 'saeculi' (f. 162 v) (M), secŀrꝶ 'saeculorum' (f. 168 v) (cf. M)
scŀo 'saeculo' (f. 162 v) (cf. M)
sanctus etc. s̄c̄s etc. (M)
sicut sc̄ (f. 162 v)
sic̄ (twice at least, once where true text is *si cum*) (M)
spiritalis spītalis (M)
spiritus etc. s̄p̄s etc. (M)
spūm 'spiritum' (f. 55 v) (M)
sunt s̄ (M), s̄t (f. 160 r) (M)
Thesalonicenses thesaloncens̄s̄ (once)
uel ŀ, uŀ (M), ū (f. 144 r), (M)
uero uō (M)
uersus uēr (M)

SYLLABLE SYMBOLS:

con c̄ (M)
en m̄ 'men' (M)
er ƀ 'ber' (f. 171 r) (M), t̄ 'ter' (M)
is ƀ 'bis' (third scribe) (M), đ 'dis'
it c̄ 'cit' (M), p̄ 'pit' (M)
m suprascript stroke (M)
n suprascript stroke (M)
rum rꝶ (M)
runt r̄ (M)
us t̄s, tˢ 'tus'

[1] Lindsay, *Notae Latinae*, p. 125, explains this as a scribe's alteration of mħ of his original. This would suggest that the original was Veronese, but I know no other indication in N pointing to such ancestry.

[2] Written in full, ff. 27 v, 143 r.

[3] This and some other abbreviations were by oversight not communicated to Prof. Lindsay.

[4] Abbreviated apparently by the first scribe only.

There are some notable features in the abbreviations that N does *not* share with M: apoƚs occurs in a Fulda MS and in one now at Troyes; aūm clearly indicates a Spanish stage in the transmission[1]; eīs appears to be unknown elsewhere; miħ and m̄; nƀ and uƀ, doubtless copied straight from an insular copy; nr̄t appears to be not older than A.D. 800; traces of quomođ and quomđ are found at Flavigny (Autun) and Péronne respectively; all our abbreviations for *quoniam* might occur simultaneously in an insular original; sc̄ is very important, as it occurs in early specimens of insular, and is no doubt taken straight from the original[2]; the same may doubtless be said of ū, shared with M[3].

Here also then we seem to find clear proof that the immediate original of N was in insular script, and that there was behind this insular stage a Spanish stage in the transmission. And the arguments for a Spanish stage in the transmission of H_2 are not exclusively palaeographical[4]. In the cases both of M and N then we have arrived at this conclusion:

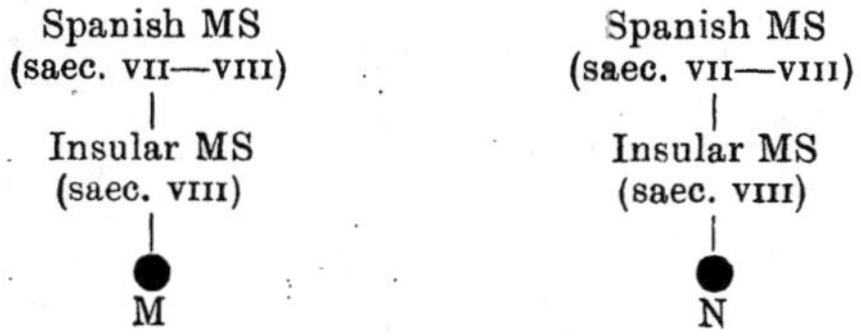

It is time to ask what is the precise relationship between M and N.

Before discussing whether the one MS is a copy of the other or not, it would be necessary to know for certain which was the older. M has altogether a more antique look, and probably most palaeographers would agree that it is rather older than N. The close relationship of the two MSS is not in fact a mere matter of sharing abbreviation symbols. They also share thousands of wrong readings, as well as the set of canons and other prefatory matter to which allusion has already been made, and the numerous interpolations which I hope to edit in a third volume. A few illustrations of wrong readings, where other MSS are right, may now be given.

[1] Lindsay, *Notae Latinae*, p. 25; C. U. Clark, *Collectanea Hispanica*, p. 84.

[2] Lindsay, *Notae Latinae*, pp. 286 f.

[3] Lindsay, *Notae Latinae*, pp. 311 f.

[4] See pp. 271 f. above.

			MN	True Text
In Rom.	v	9	custodiat	custodiet
		20	dicerint	dicerent
	vi	6	noster[1]	nostrum
	vii	13	(interp.) incipit	incipiat

M cannot have been copied from N, because at the famous lacuna in Rom. v N has no gap, while M has, as we have seen, a most precisely measured gap[2]. If M had been copied from N, it would have gone on without interruption, as N does. It is possible, if not probable, also, that if N had been copied from M, N also would have represented a gap, even if not so striking as that in M[3]. But there are hundreds, if not thousands, of differences between the readings of M and N which show that neither can be a copy of the other.

		M	N	True Text
In Rom.	ii 4	hominibus	homines	as M
	v 14	iusto	iniusto	iniustum
	vii 13	bonam legem	bonam legi	as M
	viii 3	(interp.) quoniam	quod[4]	as M
	viiii 26	plebs	ples	as M
	viiii 33	Petrus quoque—confundetur *om. homoeot.*	*habet*	as N (a most signal proof)
	xi 1	auxiliatur	consolatur (*ex*-or)	as N
1 *Cor.*	vi 15	id est—meretricis *habet*	*om. homoeot.*	as M (a most signal proof)

Such differences are in fact so very numerous and serious that it is inconceivable that M and N are both direct copies of the same MS. Between each of them and their common original there must have been at least one *codex* interposed. No doubt both these *codices* were insular, but I think M was copied direct from an Irish MS, and N direct from an Anglo-Saxon MS. Not one of the definitely Irish abbreviations which we have cited from M[5], occurs in N, and on the other hand N nearly everywhere employs quō, which is an Anglo-Saxon and not an Irish symbol. This Anglo-Saxon symbol

[1] Due no doubt to a wrongly expanded n̄, which does duty for every case.

[2] Cf. p. 271.

[3] Cf. the parallel case of **B** and the Merton MS, pp. 216 f., 225.

[4] The same corruption occurs near the beginning in another interpolated part, due to wrong expansion of *quō*.

[5] Above, p. 299.

never occurs in M, which habitually employs the Irish symbol qm̄. Furthermore, as will appear immediately, M often agrees with G (which we have seen was copied from an Irish exemplar), against N and the corrector of R. Now, we should expect an insular MS accessible to a Ratisbon scribe to be Anglo-Saxon rather than Irish. I should therefore sketch the connexion between M and N thus:

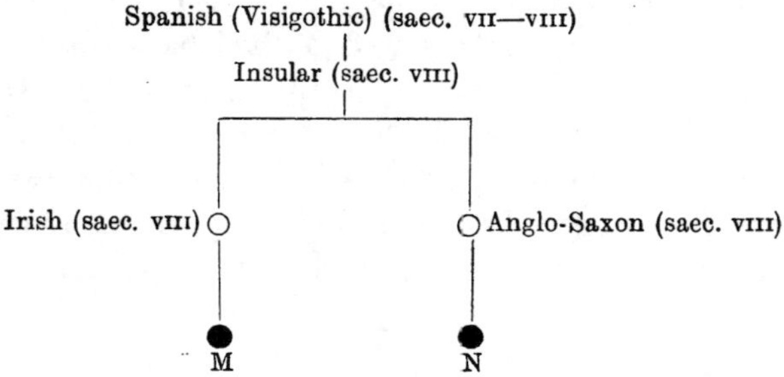

(9) *The lost MS used by the corrector of* R

One passage will serve to show what the connexion between the corrector of R and M—N really is. Let us take an interpolated passage, for which we have also the authority of G. It will be convenient to print the text of M and to record the variants of the other manuscripts in an apparatus. The passage comes after the word 'domini' (*in* 1 *Thess.* iiii 15) in MN, after 'inueniret' in R corr.

Hoc loquo hostendit ꝗ in die iudicii sub aduentu dn̄i quicumque sanctorum in ac uita inuenti fuerint non prius aduentante dn̄o obiam rapientur in nubibus caeli nisi sc̄i omnes qui superioribus retro temporibus in Christo dormierunt resurrexerint et tunc demum omnes simul hoccurrere dn̄o in aera in nubibus adsumentur nequis autem ambigat et extimet sc̄s in aduentum dn̄i gustaturos mortem nec post aliquem hominem natum non mortem desoluet hoc dr̄ adfirmante apostulo paulo q; in morte xp̄i baptizati sumus et consepulti cum ipso in baptismo in mortem.

1 loquo] loco NRG host.] ost. NRG ꝗ] quia NRG aduentū (¯*eras.*) N quiqumque N* 2 hac NRG aduenlente NG obuiam NRG 3 caeli] celi N *om.* RG sancti *om.* R homnes (h *eras.*) N qui] +in G superioribus *om.* NR temporibus] in tempore NR ∽ dormierunt in Christo NR 4 occurrere NR occurri G 5 et extimet] et exestimet G *om.* NR s̄c̄s (=sanctus)] s̄c̄o̅s NRG aduentu RG dn̄o N 6 post] potest NR posse G hominum G morte G desoluet] desolue N desoluere R desolui G dicitur (*in full*) G 7 apostolo RG paulo *om.* NRG q;] quia NRG babtizati R 8 illo G babtismo R baptisma G morte R.

The freakish (some of them Spanish) spellings of M are not shared by other MSS. There is a real relationship between N and R, which is not shared by M. M goes rather with G, though G is as elsewhere somewhat independent. Not infrequently M takes its own line against all other representatives of H_2.

The copy used by the corrector of R appears to have been a sister-MS of N or of the immediate predecessor of N. The relationship between N and R corr. will become clearer when the interpolations in H_2 are critically edited. It is impossible to suppose that R corr. had any surviving MS in front of him.

(10) *Troyes*, 486 (*saec. XII*[1]) (C)

Signs of former ownership and older shelfmarks are preserved as follows: (f. 183 v, foot): 'Liber Scē Marie clare uallis' (i.e. the great Cistercian Abbey of Clairvaux, immortalised through its connexion with St Bernard): (f. 184 r after the end of the MS) 'f. 43 (43 erased) 66,' and below this 'f. 66.' These are the shelf-marks in the Clairvaux library, as is confirmed, if confirmation were needed, by the evidence of the ancient catalogue of the fifteenth century[2], of which a copy made in 1645 exists at Paris[3]. The title of this copy is: 'Inventaire, et Declaration Des Volumes, et Livres de L'Esglise et Abbaye de Clerūaux De L'ordre de Císteaúx où Diòcese de L'Engres Fait ou Mois de May, L'An Mil Quatre Cens, Soixante et douze Par Nous Frere Pierre Nouuel Abbé dud. Lieu... Ledit Inuentaire Escript de Noueau, En Januier, L'An Mil six cens Quarente cinq A Dijon MS De la Bibliothèque de Mr le... Bouhier A. 52 MDCCXXI.'

On f. 39 the following entry occurs, referring to our MS:

'Item Un autre beau Volume conten. Explanation st Iēome. sur les xiiij Eprēs St pol. qui ē nōme. breuiariū. Sci Ieonīmi Com-

[1] M. Léon Dorez says not later than the middle of the century; Dr Bannister assigned it to the end of the century or to saec. XIII. (This latter date must be rejected in view of Dom Wilmart's discovery; see below.) I am deeply indebted to M. Dorez for much valuable help in connexion with this MS. He has made a special study of the MSS at Troyes. See also Dom Wilmart's exquisite tractate, *L'Ancienne Bibliothèque de Clairvaux* (Troyes, 1918 [dated 1917]) from *Mémoires de la Société Académique de l'Aube*, t. LXXXI [1917]).

[2] Troyes MS 521. [3] B. N. Fr. 22,364.

mencāt ou V Feuille q̄d p̄dixit ysaias. & Finissāt ou penult̄ entie. escript manentes ho. Sig' F. 66.

Dom Wilmart has discovered in a guard-leaf of Troyes MS 32 (of the end of the twelfth century) a portion of a still earlier Clairvaux catalogue, which belongs in fact to the twelfth century. Our MS fortunately appears in it under LIBRI SANCTI IERONIMI (88):

Breuiarium eiusdem super omnes epistolas pauli in uno uol.[1]

Wilmart rightly identifies that MS with the surviving F 66: Troyes 486.

The twelfth century is the Golden Age of the Clairvaux library. At that time, no doubt under the influence of Bernard himself, whose passion for learning seems to have equalled his holiness and his wonderful administrative ability, a large number of texts, some of them rare, were copied from manuscripts in every possible quarter. It is known, for example, that Spain and the Rhine country were laid under contribution. Dom Wilmart has recently discovered a Clairvaux MS at Troyes (no. 523, saec. XII), which contains the only known Latin rendering of a large number of discourses of Eusebius of Emesa, as well as five treatises of Tertullian and an opuscule of Pontius Maximus[2]. Nor are these texts merely careful copies of earlier MSS. They are corrected with a learning and intelligence unique in my experience[3]. Whether Bernard himself or some *notarius* of his was the corrector, I do not know.

The Pseudo-Jerome MS has had its edges clipped all round and 'marbled' by an eighteenth century binder. The pages now measure 325 mm. × 225 mm., each bearing two columns of writing measuring 240 mm. × 75 mm. The MS contains 184 folia. Some of the quaternion numbers have disappeared through the action of the binder, but it is possible to say that the manuscript consists

[1] Wilmart, *op. cit.* pp. 30, 32.

[2] Wilmart, *op. cit.* pp. 39, 43; *Journal of Theological Studies*, vol. XIX (1917—18) pp. 316 f.; *Analecta Bollandiana*, t. XXXVIII (1920) pp. 241—284; *Académie des Inscriptions et Belles-Lettres, Comptes Rendus des Séances de l'Année* 1920 pp. 380 ff.; *Revue de l'Orient Chrétien*, t. XXII (1920—21) pp. 72—94. I have to thank him for copies of these articles. See also A. Souter, *Tertullian Concerning the Resurrection of the Flesh* (London, 1922) pp. 162—196. I have collated all the five treatises of Tertullian. There is the same careful correction in this MS that we have found in our C.

[3] I infer that the hundreds of other MSS are like the two I have studied.

of twenty-three quaternions. The guard-leaf (fol. 1) is separate, and the signatures now traceable are found thus: I (f. 9 v), III (f. 25 v), IIII (f. 33 v), V (f. 41 v)...IX[1] (f. 73 v)...(wanting f. 105 v) ...XIX (f. 153 v)...XX (f. 177 v). The last is thus constituted:

It is possible that the MS is not now absolutely complete. The Canons which we have found in M and N, would have filled a quaternion, and it is conceivable that they once formed a part of the MS, though not quaternionised. On the other hand Bernard may have objected to them as heretical in origin, and ordered them to be suppressed. There is of course the further possibility that they were not in the archetype of the Troyes MS at all. The rest of the prefatory matter appears exactly in the same order as in the older members of the family, not only at the beginning of the codex, but at the commencement of each Epistle. It contains the same Hebrews commentary as that found in N[2]. We have already seen that M differs somewhat from N in that exposition.

The following notes indicate the learning and care bestowed upon the text:

(fol. 28 va mg.): 'Nota lector quod fere ubique textus et expositio transposita sint et sibi inuicem confuse mixta, ita ut praecedat expositio et sequatur textus, quod nisi diligenter aduerteris, totum sensum confundet.'

(fol. 30 b) after a sign: 'Quos autem p(rae)d(estinauit) requiritur ad praemissum signum uerso folio. Hoc secundum signa post paginam ab (sign) usque sacerdos.' On fol. 30 va we find the same sign (like a capital L, somewhat ornamented in its transverse stroke).

(fol. 91 a mg.): 'capitulum alterius loci secundum notulam superpositam' (section viii of 2 Cor.). At end of section ix above 'quod' has a sign with '$\overline{\text{xpc}}$,' and in the margin opposite the same sign with 'capitulum alterius loci iuxta indicem superpositum.'

Similar marginal notes occur ff. 94 vb, 106 b, 119 b.

The corrector altered defective texts of scripture from a copy in his hands. The sign of this is crushed writing *in rasura*.

[1] Note IX, not VIIII. Whether anyone has discussed the age of the symbol IX in MSS, I do not know.

[2] Riggenbach, *Die ältesten lat. Komm. zum Hebräerbrief*, p. 206.

After the colophon (f. 183 v *red*) 'Explicit sc̄i ieronimi expositio in xiiii^{cim} ep̄tis pauli ap̄ti' follow:

'Versus á ieronimo editi ad damasum papam. I(*red*)am dudum saulus...(f. 184 ra) monstrare triumphos. (*red*) Expliciunt.' F. 184 is blank. There are many lovely coloured initials in the book, some of which recalled to Dr Bannister the work of Limoges and Toulouse. Some rare colours are employed on occasion.

The most interesting feature of this MS from a textual point of view is the treatment of the lacunae in Romans v. We saw that there were two blank spaces there in M, while in N the text runs on in both cases almost without warning that anything is wrong. In C however[1] an attempt has been made to fill up the gap, and it is of great interest to observe that it was not Ambrosiaster that was used for this purpose, but the Cassiodorian (Pseudo-Primasius) commentary, and the procedure followed was openly avowed. After 'praeceptum' (fol. 20 a = Rom. v 14) there is a gap of about nine or ten letters in length: then a new line begins with 'Item mors' etc., but before this, in the gap, a sign occurs, and there is another on fol. 20 b mg. (after 'grauia'). Opposite the first sign in the margin occur these words: 'Quantum signis distiguitur in exemplari non inueni.' The words he did not find in the 'exemplar' are these:

Item: Mors ex originali malo ueniens usque ad legem sola regnauit. Ideo dixit regnauit quia totum mundum generaliter occupauerat. Alia uero peccata nequaquam regnare uidebantur quia non per uniuersos dominabantur. Naturalis enim iustitia uigebat in plurimos (*corr.* is) et cętera delicta non hereditaria sed uoluntaria erant. Ergo obligatio primi hominis sola usque ad moysen per se mortem operata regnauit. A legis autem tempore genus aliud delictorum in reatum neglectae legis accessit, quod ante eius promulgationem non poterat inputari. Ac sic introeuntibus nouis praeceptis iniquitas multiplicata est. Lex enim non ut tolleret peccatum, sed ut demonstraret uel uendicaret aduenit, et ideo hic abundantiam gratiae apostoli doctrina commendat, quia non tantum adę debitum quod solum usque ad legem uelud tyrannica dominatione regnauerat sed etiam innumeras offensas praeuaricationis et reprobę conuersationis bonitas redemptoris credentibus redonauit. Propterea dixit iudicium quidem ex uno id est delicto in condempnationem, gratia autem ex multis delictis in iustificationem. Ac sic prima obligatio ueteris offensę usque ad legem sola dominata est, alia uero delicta usque ad interdictum legis non uidebantur, uel non intellegebantur esse tam grauia.

[1] And in its descendant F; cf. also p. 317.

Except for the last sentence, this is taken with slight modifications from Cassiodorus (Pseudo-Primasius, Migne, *P. L.* LXVIII p. 440 D—p. 441 B).

At fol. 21 r a (= Rom. v 20) *Sicut ait saluator · cui plus dimit | titur* the sign is placed after *dimit.*, and in the margin opposite we have the words: 'Nec hoc in ęxemplari habetur.' After *gratiae magnitudo et* the MS proceeds thus:

per indulgentiam remissionis, cresceret debitum caritatis. Manifestantur beneficia, cum e contrario indignorum meritis conparantur. Mors enim per Adam regnauit, uita per Christum. Regnauit inquit mors ab adam, usque ad moysen. Quod etiam sic intelligendum est, usque ad moysen, id est usque ad finem legis et initium gratiae debitum naturale regnauit. Sed cursum fenoris sui perdidit, post quam Christi sanguis cyrografum originale deleuit. Sed dicit aliquis. Ecce per cathecuminos et gentiles diuersasque nationes originis malum regnat. Quibus respondendum est. Tunc uere pestis late diffusa regnauit, quando medicus deerat, quando mortalitas generalis omnes ad inferna mittebat. Ubi uero portam paradisi redemptio de caelis missa patefecit, ubi mundo attulit uitae auctor salutem, mors perdidit potestatem, quae oblatis a saluatore remediis, non perdit nisi uolentes. Ac sic iam non regnat quia regnum eius gratia regnante destructum est.

This is for the most part taken from Cassiodorus (Pseudo-Primasius, Migne *P. L.* LXVIII p. 441 B—C), but there has been rather more editing here.

The companion mark is after 'destructum est' (f. 21 a). After 'caritatis' (near the beginning) there is a gap of a line and a half. After 'destructum est' two and a half lines are blank.

As to the relationship of this MS to the others of the H_2 family, it has already been pointed out that it is closer to N than to M. If we take the passages selected above to show the relationship between M and N[1], we observe the value of C without much difficulty. Riggenbach noted that in the Hebrews exposition it is a better MS than N. *In Rom.* v 9 it has *custodiet* rightly (MN *custodiat*); v 20 *dicerent* rightly (MN *dicerint*); vi 6 *nostrum* rightly (MN *noster*); vii 13 *incipiat* rightly (MN *incipit*). Again, in the other list, we observe the following readings: *in Rom.* ii 4 *hominibus* rightly (N *homines*); v 14 *iniustum* rightly (M *iusto*, N *iniusto*); vii 13 *bonam legem* rightly (N *bonam legi*); viii 3 (interpol.) *quoniam* rightly (N *quod*); viiii 26 *plebs* rightly (N *ples*); viiii 33 has (with

[1] See pp. 308 ff.

N) the passage wrongly omitted by M; xi 1 *consolatur* rightly (M *auxiliatur*); *in* 1 *Cor.* vi 15 has (with M) the passage wrongly omitted by N. This character is borne by the MS throughout.

The MS, however, is not faultless. There is a case of omission by homoeoteleuton, for example, at *in Rom.* viii 3 (interpol.), where it omits 'Dicens in similitudinem carnis peccati,' which M and N preserve.

It can be proved that C also harks back to an insular exemplar. At Rom. xi 4 where MN have rightly $\overline{\text{ds}}$, C* has *dicitur* which could only have come from $\overline{\text{dr}}$, the insular symbol for *dicitur*, which owing to the similarity between *r* and *s* in that script, may be confused with the other symbol. Again, at 1 Thess. v 23 (interpol.) *quia* was written, and afterwards corrected to *quam*, because the scribe at first mistook ꝙ for ꝗ. This confusion was possible in insular script alone. MS C will be descended either directly, or with one remove, from the insular MS (saec. VIII) which we saw reason to suppose lies behind the parents of M and N. If it had come direct from one of these parents, it could not have been so free from error. Its immediate parent need not however have been in insular script, though it doubtless retained insular symptoms. In endeavouring to guess the locale of this parent, the analogous case of another Troyes (Clairvaux) MS may help us. Koetzschau in his edition of Origen-Rufinus *De Principiis* (Leipzig, 1913)[1] appears to prove that the Troyes (Clairvaux) MS of that work (saec. XII, double columns, like ours) is a copy of the still preserved Metz (S. Arnulphus) MS (saec. X) of that work. The parent of our MS was probably found somewhere in the Rhine country, not too far from M and N; perhaps at Lorsch[2].

(11) *Florence, R. Biblioteca Mediceo-Laurenziana, Plut.* XV *Dext. Cod.* I *(saec.* XII—XIII*)* (F)

This manuscript, formerly of Santa Croce, though it is the best of all the Pseudo-Jerome MSS, need not detain us long, as it is undoubtedly descended direct from C, with one codex only intervening. In proof of this, it is enough to mention the identity of

[1] Pp. xxxvii f. [2] Cf. pp. 28, 302.

contents, and the fact that the corrections of C find their place in the text of this MS. That F is not a direct copy, however, of C, is proved by the fact that in a certain number of places it bears signs of an intervening exemplar, into which some further corrections had been entered: for example

In Rom. xv 25 ut ueniam deinceps F: deinceps ut ueniam C* cet.[1]; ut deinceps ueniam C corr.

In 1 *Cor.* i 2 deus ipse F: ipse C cet.

It would be easy to fill pages with evidence of the character of F, which I collated with the same fulness as the MSS already discussed, in order to be quite certain about its place in the genealogical scheme. The MS is at points fairly heavily annotated in the margin in a fifteenth century hand by some reader who was intensely interested in the subject-matter. These notes have, however, no value for the restoration of the Pseudo-Jerome text, and I have ignored them. Another sign of the care with which the MS was studied may be seen in the marginal *r*(*equiras*), where text or teaching was of doubtful character.

(12) *Cambridge, University Library, Ff.* 4. 31 (*saec.* XV)

This manuscript, which was written by one W. More, connected with Oxford[2], is of the same branch of the H_2 family as C and F. It is headed: '*Incipiunt breues annotaciones beati ieronimi presbiteri super ep*(*isto*)*lam ad romanos.*' W. More was a scholarly man, as we see from his insertion of the passage from the 8th chapter of Cassiodorus (f. 40 v b), and, later, a short biography of St Jerome. He mentions that he finished the MS of the Romans part on 6th May (f. 80 v b). It is without the Canons of M and N, but appears to have all the other prefatory material. At Rom. v it gives the Cassiodorian insertions at the same places as C and F, but without the indication provided by these that the passages were not in the 'exemplar.' I have refrained from collating this MS in full, as the specimens taken prove it to be secondary in character, and quite unlikely to contain anything of value not present in C or F. Yet

[1] Many of the alterations are changes of order of words like this, showing evidence of interest in style.

[2] See the Catalogue.

a good scholar, with no other MS to aid him than this, could improve the published Pseudo-Jerome considerably[1].

Here ends our examination of the Pseudo-Jerome MSS. Though it has been long, it is yet in a sense merely provisional. The problem of the relation between the two recensions has hitherto baffled me. It is almost impossible to study it until all the interpolations are before one in print, and it may for ever defy complete solution.

CASSIODORUS (PSEUDO-PRIMASIUS): REVISION OF PELAGIUS

In the first chapter[2] attention was called to a very important passage in the *Institutiones*[3] of Cassiodorus, where he describes a copy of a commentary on thirteen Epistles of St Paul in his library, which was in wide use and was falsely attributed to Pope Gelasius[4]. Finding Pelagian poison in it, he cleansed the Epistle to the Romans with what care he could, and left the expositions of the other epistles in a 'chartaceus codex' (i.e. a papyrus *book* of the modern shape), for his monks to correct in the same way. The annotations thus attributed to Gelasius were undoubtedly the expositions of Pelagius.

After he has enumerated complete commentaries on St Paul's Epistles he proceeds to mention commentaries on single epistles. It will be instructive to set down here, in the same pure text as before, the exact words he uses about commentaries on the Epistle to the Romans in his possession:

§ 13. Sancti Pauli prima omnium et ammirabilior destinata cognoscitur ad Romanos, quam Origenes uiginti libris Greco sermone declarauit, quos tamen supra dictus Rufinus in decem libris redigens adhuc copiose transtulit in Latinum.

§ 14. Sanctus uero **Augustinus** ipsam epistulam inchoauerat exponendam, in cuius tantum salutatione unum librum se profudisse commemorat, et—ut eius uerbis utar—operis ipsius magnitudine ac labore deterritus, in alia faciliora deflexus est.

[1] The Dean of Wells turned it to profit in the paper mentioned on p. 41 n. 4.

[2] P. 15.

[3] Written between 551 and 562 (P. Lehmann, in *Philologus*, Bd. LXXI [1912] p. 295).

[4] The names 'Gelasius' and 'Pelagius' were sometimes confused: e.g. in the MSS of the Decretum Gratiani (composed between 1139 and 1142) 'Gelasius' appears as 'Pelagius,' cf. Von Dobschütz, *Decr. Gelas.* pp. 120, 192.

§ 15. Qui etiam **scribens ad Simplicianum episcopum Mediolanensem sublimes et exquisitas de eadem epistula tractauit aliquas quaestiones, quas nos predicto codici iudicauimus inserendas, ne, dum expositio diuisa queritur, legentis intentio noxie differatur.**

A reference in his *De Orthographia*[1] to works he had composed in monastic retirement is also important:

post expositionem epistolae quae scribitur ad Romanos, unde Pelagianae haereseos prauitates amoui, quod etiam in reliquo commentario facere sequentes ammonui.

The meaning of section 15, which no one prior to myself appears to have read with any care—else Cassiodorus's revision might have been identified about four centuries ago—, is that he had inserted in his depelagianised Romans some of the *De Diversis Quaestionibus ad Simplicianum* of Augustine. Clearly, then, if one is in search of Cassiodorus's revision, one must look for an exposition of the thirteen Epistles, which has extracts from Aug. *De Div. Quaest. ad Simplicianum* in the Romans commentary. Yet no one appears to have done so.

Instead, we have Garnier suggesting that the printed Pseudo-Jerome is Cassiodorus's revision of Pelagius, and in spite of obvious difficulties this view held the field for over two centuries. The strong commonsense of Zimmer destroyed it, but his own view that the Pseudo-Primasius is the Gelasio-Pelagian commentary as it reached the hands of Cassiodorus, is also impossible. Dr C. H. Turner, as we have said, first guessed the true situation, that Pseudo-Primasius is Cassiodorus's revision, and it was left for me to prove this view the right one, by producing the passage in section 15. There is only one commentary on the Pauline Epistles which has long extracts from the *Div. Quaest. ad Simpl.* incorporated in it, and that is the commentary published at Lyons in 1537 under the title 'Primasii | Vticensis in Afri|ca Episcopi, in omnes | D. Pauli epistolas commentarij perbre|ues ac docti, ante annos mille | ab autore editi. | Nunc uerò primùm Ioannis Gagneij Theologi, ac | Doctoris regij opera in lucem emissi. | Apud Seb. Gryphium | Lugduni. | 1537. | Cum Priuilegio regio ad Sexennium.'

But, if this be so, how came Gagney to call it by the name of

[1] Praef. (Keil, *Grammatici Latini*, vol. VII p. 144).

Primasius? This error can, I think, be explained. In the year 1536, the year preceding the publication of 'Primasius,' there appeared at Strassburg the first edition of Zmaragdus's *Expositio Libri Comitis*. Amongst the authors Zmaragdus professes to have excerpted are Pelagius and Primasius. In his margins he generally employed $\overline{\text{P}}$ for Pelagius, $\overline{\text{PR}}$ and PRI for Primasius. Now the latter symbols never occur in Zmaragdus's MSS except in reference to extracts from the genuine commentary of Primasius on the Apocalypse, while the former symbol occurs only in passages from the Pauline Epistles. It is clear, therefore, to us that Zmaragdus knew no Primasius on the Epistles; but the first editor carelessly expanded $\overline{\text{P}}$ everywhere into 'Ex Primasio.' Gagney found a number of these extracts in the (anonymous) commentary he had discovered. He therefore not unnaturally assumed that 'Primasius' must be its author, and put his name on the title page.

Gagney found his commentary, he tells us, in a manuscript of the 'coenobium diui Theuderici, apud oppidum...quod uulgo Sanctum caput appellant. Colonia est Viennensis archiepī, non procul Lugduno in Delphinatu.' This means 'the religious house of St Thierry at St Chef in Dauphiné, subject to the Abp of Vienne, and not far from Lyons.' There can be little doubt that the St Chef MS, if it still existed, would be in the Grenoble library. But it is not there, and for its text we must now depend on the *editio princeps*[1].

But there is an (anonymous) MS of the commentary at Grenoble, which was formerly in the Grande Chartreuse, and this, strange to say, appears to be the only surviving manuscript of it. The fact is strange, because there were several other copies in existence in the ninth century. The following commentators certainly possessed copies, for they made use of the Cassiodorian compilation; Zmaragdus of St Mihiel (between 819 and 830), under the symbol $\overline{\text{P}}$; Claudius of Turin (between 815 and 820), under the symbol ANT̄[2] (apparently = ANON[3]); Sedulius Scottus of Liége and the

[1] Reprinted at Cologne in 1538, at Paris in 1543: later reprints precede that in Migne (*P. L.* LXVIII), which is much less accurate than the *editio princeps*.

[2] In a MS of his comm. on Tit. Philem. Hebr. (Paris 10,878 [saec. IX]).

[3] Hatto of Vercelli's commentary on these epistles appears to be identical with

Rhine country (between 848 and 859) as ISID; Haymo of Auxerre[1] (about 850?).

The mention of this Haymo is of especial interest, because the commentary on Hebrews which forms part of the published Pseudo-Primasius, has nothing to do with Cassiodorus, and is in fact the production of Haymo, monk of Auxerre[2]. Cassiodorus distinctly says that the Pelagian commentary he had in his hands concerned *13* epistles. The fact is that when a commentary on Hebrews was required to complete the set of Epistles, [Haymo[3]] was attached to [Cassiodorus], in the same way that [Alcuin] was attached to [Ambrosiaster], and a commentary was added to [Pelagius] in the longer Pseudo-Jerome form.

That Pseudo-Primasius is not really the work of Primasius of Hadrumetum, was suspected by some readers at an early date. In the Hort copy of Pseudo-Primasius, *editio princeps*, since his death the property of the Dean of Wells, we find two MS notes contemporary with the book to the following effect: 'Commentarios hos non esse Primasii duplici patet argumento. Tum quod trithemius huius operis non meminit Tum etiam quia Cassiodorum citat folio 526[4] Qui iuxta consentientem Historiographorum sententiam Primasio recentior est.' Further, the words (*in Phil.* i) *sed etiam corda tetigisset quamuis in Actibus legamus, fidem uoluntariam esse: tamen* are underlined, and we find in the margin: 'Vide scolia titulo diui Hieronymi que uidentur hoc loco pelagium authorem habere non hieronymum, nisi hieronymum faciamus pelagianum.' We have seen also that Thomas Gataker, that miracle of learning, doubted Primasian authorship[5].

The St Chef and Grande Chartreuse copies both contain the Haymo on Hebrews, without any indication of difference of author.

Claudius of Turin (see Riggenbach, *Die ältest. latein. Komm.* pp. 25—33, as regards Hebrews).

[1] See Riggenbach, *op. cit.* pp. 185 ff.

[2] Riggenbach, pp. 41 ff.

[3] I think I have seen all the old MSS of Haymo, and in none of these is there an author's name by the first hand. The copy of Haymo *in Hebr.* used to complete Cassiodorus was defective, having a lacuna at the end of c. iii. As the lacuna is indicated at the wrong place in the printed editions, instead of after *Dominus* or *fide* (p. 709 l. 1), I was misled in my attempts to trace the MS of Haymo used.

[4] On a passage of Hebrews.

[5] *Adv. Misc.* II 20 (*Opera Critica*, Utrecht 1698 fol.) p. 389 c.

They therefore come from a common original not older than the middle of the ninth century. Copies prior to that date, such as those in the hands of Zmaragdus, Claudius, Sedulius and Haymo himself, must have been without a commentary on Hebrews.

The recovery of the original form of Pelagius and the identification of 'Primasius' as Cassiodorus have made it possible to study Cassiodorus's methods to perfection. The first thing to do is to underline in Cassiodorus all that has come direct from Pelagius. It has long been recognised that Pelagius is abundantly represented in 'Primasius.' When once the Pelagian material has been set aside, one can study the remainder more easily. There is real Cassiodorus in the commentary on Romans, which has been carefully rewritten, but in the other epistles, the work of his pupils—perhaps not more than three in number—there is very little that is original. But most of the non-Pelagian part throughout is borrowed from other authors. The list of these authors and their works already identified, will add substantially to the catalogue of the Cassiodorian library, compiled by A. Franz fifty years ago[1]. The following identifications are my own, with two exceptions:

Augustine, *De Diversis Quaestionibus LXXXIII.*
„ *De Diversis Quaestionibus Ad Simplicianum*, pp. 448—454, 477—487.
„ *De Genesi ad Litteram.*
„ *Contra Academicos.*
„ *Epistulae* 140; 147.
„ *Contra Duas Epistulas Pelagianorum.*
„ *De Natura et Gratia.*
„ *De Peccatorum Meritis et Remissione.*
„ *De Spiritu et Littera.*
„ *De Praedestinatione Sanctorum.*
„ *De Perfectione Iustitiae Hominis.*

*Claudianus Mamertus, *De Statu Animae.*

A Gallican (saec. V) commentator on the Psalms, p. 427 (*Faustus Reiensis[2]).

[1] *M. Aurelius Cassiodorus Senator, ein Beitrag zur Gesch. der theol. Litt.* (Bresl. 1872). I have asterisked *authors* not in Franz's list (pp. 80—87).

[2] Suggestion of Dom Morin.

Eucherius, *Instructiones*[1].
Jerome, *Comm. in Galatas*.
„ *Apologia ad Pammachium* (= epist. 48 [49]).
„ *Comm. in Esaiam*.
*Prudentius, *Apotheosis* 918—919, p. 442, ll. 4—5[2].
Tyconius, *Rules*[3].

The value of Cassiodorus's revision for the restoration of the Pelagius text is very considerable, as we seem to possess it in a state of remarkable purity. In other epistles than Romans its text has real weight in deciding the text of Pelagius. In Romans Pelagius is of course handled with much more freedom, and is often rewritten in the interests of Augustinian teaching. Occasionally Cassiodorus modifies the Pelagian language rather than the Pelagian thought.

In view of the well-known connexion of Cassiodorus with *codex Amiatinus* of the Vulgate, it is a matter of some interest to see what Cassiodorus has done with the Pelagian Biblical text[4]. This becomes perfectly clear, so far as Romans is concerned, by collating the Cassiodorian text with the Vulgate of Wordsworth and White. There is not the least doubt that Cassiodorus substituted the Vulgate for the Pelagian text. This Vulgate text was very close to Clm 4577 (saec. VIII—IX[5]), a manuscript sometimes cited by W.-W. In fact I am tempted to think that this Munich MS contains a text extracted from a copy of the Cassiodorian commentary in the same way as MS 1163 (saec. XII) of the Vienna library contains a text of Ephesians extracted from the genuine commentary of Jerome on that Epistle[6]. Cassiodorus has, as might be expected, done his work very carefully, but here and there he has by oversight allowed a reading of Pelagius (D type) to remain.

[1] See *J.T.S.* XIV (1912—1913) pp. 69—72; cf. also Porson's *Letters to Travis* (Lond. 1790) p. 351.

[2] Identified by Prof. W. B. Anderson, University of Manchester, after I had in vain consulted other scholars.

[3] See *J.T.S.* XI (1909—1910) pp. 562 f.

[4] Cf. Dom Chapman in *Revue Bénédictine* t. XXVIII (1911) pp. 286 ff., who has made a considerable study of the subject.

[5] E.g. at Rom. i 31 *absque honore* is read by Clm 4577 and Cassiodorus, but by no other authority known to W.-W.

[6] De Bruyne's discovery, *Revue Biblique*, t. XII (1915) pp. 361 f.

Nearly always the Grenoble MS gives a better biblical text than Gagney, where the two differ. Incidentally, this investigation is an excellent confirmation of the judgment of the Oxford editors of the Vulgate, who have made no use of Pseudo-Primasius in constituting their text.

Something must be said with regard to the other Epistles also. The evidence is the same, so far as examined. I have taken at random 1 Cor. x, 2 Cor. iiii, Gal. v, Eph. iiii, Phil. ii. The differences from the Vulgate are few, and in almost all cases trifling. There can be no reasonable doubt, therefore, that Cassiodorus's pupils, like Cassiodorus himself, intended to substitute the Vulgate text throughout.

To pass to the comments, which are our main concern. What sort of text of Pelagius did Cassiodorus possess? In the first place, it was absolutely without the Pseudo-Jerome interpolations. Did it then belong to the **A** family, or the **B** family, or to some otherwise unknown family? The answer appears to be, rather to the **B** than to the **A** family. One or two examples will make this clear.

In Rom. i 30 'elatus' est qui effertur supra mensuras suas Cassiod., **B**: mensuram suam **A**.

In Rom. ii 1 omnes qui huiusmodi iudicabant (iudicant *cod.*) Cassiod., **B** (*om.* qui): omnes quidem iudicabant **A**.

In Rom. ii 5 ad maiora abuteris uulnera Cassiod.: ad uulnera maiora uteris **ABH**. Here altered by Cassiod.

In Rom. iii 1 reddit rationem quod lex inanis non fuerit, sed Cassiod.: reddit rationem quod lex contempta non prosit, et **BH**: reddita ratione quod lex contempta non prosit et **A**.

In Rom. iiii 24 non ut sciremus tantum qualis fuerit, sed ut nobis in omnibus exemplo sit, ut filiis pater Cassiod.: non ut eius solum fidem sciremus, sed et eius quasi patris imitemur exemplum **H**: non ut eius fidem solum sciremus (sciamus **A**), sed et ut eius quasi patris imitemur exemplum **AB**.

Further instances of the character of the Cassiodorus text have already been given in other connexions[1]: and the printed text is good enough to render the use made of it by Zimmer, Riggenbach and Hellmann as profitable now as at the time of the publication

[1] Pp. 230 f., 243 etc.

of their works. The agreement of Cassiodorus with any of our other witnesses gives us a sixth century reading which can never be safely neglected. If Cassiodorus stand alone, we may well be in presence of some deliberate alteration made in his *scriptorium*.

The only fear that one sometimes has is that the authors of the Cassiodorian compilation occasionally consulted the Pseudo-Jerome in their hands. Yet it is more probable that they confined their attention to the Pelagius, and made no use of the Pseudo-Jerome they had.

The Grenoble (Grande Chartreuse) MS 270 is of the end[1] of the twelfth century. It is a very large MS, and the portion with which we are concerned consists of ten perfect quaternions (namely XX—XXVIIII), the folia of which are misnumbered, because four leaves have been overlooked. Fol. 76v is therefore really fol. 80v[2]. All the preceding part of the MS has been lost, and is not at Grenoble. The MS never had any prefatory matter to Romans. It begins 'INCIPIT epistola beati pauli ap(osto)li ad romanos' with no name of author. The pages have each two columns. Cassiodorus in my view found no name on his Pelagius, and added no name to his revised Pelagius.

A comparison of the *editio princeps*[3] with the Grande Chartreuse MS shows that the St Chef MS was a sister of the Grande Chartreuse MS. There can be no question of one of the two being a copy of the other[4]. Probably the Cassiodorian autograph, or an early copy of it, reached Lyons[5], where in the ninth century a copy of it was made, and the Haymo commentary on Hebrews was

[1] The catalogue 'saec. XII': Dr Holder, to whom I showed the MS, dated it more precisely as above. I have to thank the Paris authorities for enabling me to study the MS there, as also Monsieur Omont for permission to get the photograph of part of a page published in *Proc. Brit. Acad.* vol. VII, opposite p. 291.

[2] Folia neglected between 7 and 8, 44 and 45, 60 and 61, 67 and 68.

[3] Dr H. A. Gibbons, Prof. W. B. Anderson, and above all my brother, John B. Souter, rendered me most valuable help in the collation of the *editio princeps* with Migne.

[4] The proof of this and many other points connected with Cassiodorus is properly reserved for my Vienna edition of Cassiodorus.

[5] There is reason to believe that some of the Cassiodorian books came to Lyons. I believe Grenoble MS 197 (saec. XII) is descended from Cassiodorus's copy of Augustine *Contra Duas Epistulas Pelagianorum* (cf. *J.T.S.* XVI (1914—15) pp. 156 f.).

added. The St Chef and Grande Chartreuse MSS are independent copies of this ninth century MS. What Gagney sent to press was a copy of the St Chef MS. he had caused to be made. An excellent edition of the Cassiodorian text can be made by the joint study of our two authorities, neither of which can be said absolutely to surpass the other. Hundreds of errors have crept into the text in the course of reprinting: the *editio princeps* is a good deal better than Migne.

WUERZBURG (WB) AND OTHER GLOSSES

The MS which bears the signature Mp. th. f. 12 in the University Library in Würzburg, is a copy of the Epistles of St Paul in Latin, written at the beginning of the eighth century in Irish minuscule. Its Irish glosses are among the most prized documents of the Celtic scholar[1]. But it also contains far more Latin glosses. These have been copied and studied by Zimmer[2]. As 'the glosses are, most of them, patently much later than the text[3],' they are not likely to have as much value as they had twenty years ago, when the text of the original Pelagius was still undiscovered. Yet they are not without value. Zimmer has shown that they are taken from Pelagius in one form or another, Origen-Rufinus *in Rom.*, Jerome *in Gal. Eph. Tit. Philem.*, Augustine, Gregory, Isidore, and Hilarius (= Ambrosiaster) *in Rom.* Most of them are labelled, but some are anonymous. By far the majority are called 'Pl.' (i.e. Pelagius). An analysis of the notes on Rom. i 9—31 will give some idea of the character of the compilation. In all there are 49 notes[4] on this passage. Of these 49, 27½ are rightly labelled 'Pl.,' as they are to be found in the uninterpolated Pelagius, but 10½ are wrongly labelled 'Pl.,' not being discoverable in the uninterpolated Pelagius. On the other hand there are 7½ anonymous notes, which are as a matter of fact to be found in the uninter-

[1] Cf. H. Zimmer, *Glossae Hibernicae* (Berol. 1881) pp. 1—198; W. Stokes and J. Strachan, *Thesaurus Palaeohibernicus*, vol. I (Cambr. 1901) pp. xxiii ff., 499—712; R. Thurneysen, *Handbuch des Alt-Irischen*, 2 Teil (Heidelberg, 1909) pp. 2—14 (selections), etc.

[2] *Pelagius in Irland*, pp. 39—112, and passim; pp. 25 ff. above.

[3] Lindsay, *Notae Latinae*, p. 493.

[4] I have not counted here five notes labelled 'Pl,' which should have been called 'Hl' (Ambrosiaster), as Zimmer has shown (pp. 127 f.).

polated Pelagius, while 3½ anonymous notes are not found there. There are relics of a very good text of Pelagius in these glosses, e.g. *in Rom.* i 17 et ideo 'ex' et 'in' posuerit ut tautologiae uitium declinaret; i 21 a naturali sapore; *ibid.* recedens; i 24 cauteria et combustiones. These are the correct readings, corrupted in many of our authorities.

But in the first note, i 9 'Pl.,' the words 'plena ueritate' come from Cassiodorus, and it is clear that we cannot rely on the presence or absence of a symbol as any indication of authorship[1]. The glossator also took the words or clauses that suited his purpose, and omitted those for which he had no use or no room. Further, he abridged even the matter he used, in the interests of space. It is therefore remarkable that there should be as much in the way of good readings as there is.

It is perfectly clear that the compiler had both the original form of Pelagius and the Cassiodorus revision in his possession, because there are places where both notes are given, though the one is ultimately derived from the other, for example:

In Rom. i 21 per insitam sibi rationem uel ex mundi factione (= Cassiod.).
In Rom. i 20 per naturam uel per facture rationem (= Pelag.)[2].

There is one matter of relationship to which reference must be made. There are real points of contact with Sedulius Scottus, where all our other authorities differ, for example:

In 1 *Cor.* vi 20 Wb **qui non est sui**(?) **non suam** faciat **uoluntatem sed illius a quo emptus est.** Pl. **sanguine Christi:** sangui (*sic*) egrorum aliis nocet sanguis Christi mundum **redemit.**

Ibid. Sedul. **qui non est suus, non** debet sibi uiuere, **sed** illi cuius sanguine **emptus est....non auro,** non **argento, sed sanguine Christi.** sanguis aegrorum aliis nocet, sanguis uero Christi mundum **redemit**[3].

In these two authorities, and apparently in these alone, these two notes are juxtaposed; the thick type represents Pelagian material. The last part is un-Pelagian. The MSS of Sedulius

[1] For instance, *in Rom.* i 18, a real Pelagian extract is labelled 'Aug.' (Zimmer, p. 130). Similar instances on the same page and on p. 132.

[2] Cf. Zimmer, p. 124.

[3] The parallel is alluded to by Zimmer, p. 72 n.

give $\overline{GG}$ (= Gregory) as a source in this neighbourhood, but Wb and Sd can hardly be independent of one another. I am quite ready to believe that the glossator used Sedulius Scottus, if the palaeographers will consent to date the glosses as late as his time[1].

In 1 *Tim.* iiii 1 Wb, spiritus qui doceat eum per se, id est, per Paulum semet ipsum, ut **antiqui dicebant: haec dicit spiritus sanctus;** post quam de misterio intimauit, indicat quod illud heriticorum nutibus (*sic*) obscuratur[2].

Ibid. Sd, per ipsum scilicet Paulum **prophetalem inducit affectum quo modo antiqui dicebant: haec dicit spiritus sanctus**....postquam de sacramento intimauit, nunc indicat quod illud sacramentum hereticorum nubibus obscuratur.

It is hard to believe that Wb is not secondary to Sd here. Again the only Pelagian portions are given in thick type. Other instances of the same kind may be seen at Eph. iii 19[3] and Philem. 16[4], etc. Hellmann, who recognises the relationship between Wb and Sd, would make Wb the uncle and Sd a nephew[5].

Whatever be the truth of their relationship, the value of Wb is merely that of an occasional makeweight, where there is some doubt as to the value of our main authorities.

Zimmer also introduced us to the Vienna glosses (Wn). These are contained in MS 1247 (formerly Theol. CCLXXXVII, olim 49), which was written by Marianus Scottus, the founder of the Irish monastery in Ratisbon, between the middle of March and 17 May 1079[6]. This is also a MS of the Pauline Epistles. Here Pelagian glosses are introduced by 'P' or 'Pel,' or are anonymous. The total number of glosses is much smaller than in Wb, but there are in proportion more glosses of considerable length, and their text is purer and more accurate than those of Wb. I have chosen *in Col.* ii 6—iii 12 as likely to afford the best test of the quality of the glosses. In this section there are 32 notes. Of these about 9 are not really by Pelagius, though 6½ of these have 'P' attached.

[1] They appear to be of various dates.

[2] The differences here from the text in Zimmer (p. 107) and Hellmann (pp. 165 f.) are due to study of Stern's photograph, *Epistolae Beati Pauli*... (Halle a. S., 1910).

[3] Hellmann, pp. 168 f. [4] Hellmann, p. 166. [5] Hellmann, p. 170.

[6] Facsimile of a page in Chroust, *Monumenta Palaeographica* I Ser. X Lief. 1 Taf.

Of the anonymous glosses 2 are by Pelagius, and 2 are not. In this MS also there are interesting points of contact with Sedulius:

In Col. ii 11 Wn, 'P' quia peccata sepeliuntur in babtismo: tres unde babtismi tres dies in sepulchro significant.

Ibid. Sd, quia peccata sepeliuntur in baptismo[1].

None of this is Pelagius. Augustine is the authority last named in the Sedulian margin.

In Col. ii 15 Wn, sine timore...non latenter.

Ibid. Sd, sine timore...non latenter.

Neither of these two notes is Pelagian[2].

Zimmer estimates that only 21 'Pelagius' glosses are shared by Wb and Wn, while 15, anonymous in one, are called 'Pelagius' in the other[3]: so that Wn must be regarded as a witness independent of Wb.

The number of manuscripts containing glosses ultimately or directly derived from Pelagius, must be very large. It is quite natural that not many have been discovered where Pelagius is used by name. Yet there are one or two in addition to Wb and Wn. Anonymous Pelagius glosses occur, for example, in Clm 9545 (saec. X) (formerly of Altaich[4]). In Berlin Codex Phillippicus 1650 (saec. X ex.—glosses XI ex.), (formerly of St Vincent of Metz), a manuscript of the Pauline Epistles, glosses occur with the title 'Pelg.' or 'Pelagius'[5]. But the vast majority of them are anonymous, and Sedulius is also cited (by name). Even Lanfranc's name is attached to Pelagian material; there seems no end to the complication in which these studies are involved. Clm 18530 (saec. XI—XII) (formerly of Tegernsee) is related to the Berlin MS, and enumerates at the beginning the commentators used: Lanfranc, Augustine, Ambrose, Origen, Pelagius, Sedatius (=Sedulius)[6]. Hellmann surmises, on the basis of information communicated to him by E. Steinmeyer, that as the Berlin and later Munich MSS

[1] Zimmer, p. 147 n., who points out that the second part of Wn is represented *in Irish* in Wb.

[2] See also Eph. iii 19, Col. i 18, ii 19 in Hellmann, pp. 168 f.

[3] Zimmer, p. 155.

[4] Hellmann, pp. 152, 186 ff.

[5] Riggenbach, *Unbeachtet geblieb. Fragm.* p. 22; Hellmann, p. 183.

[6] Hellmann, p. xv.

along with Berlin theol. fol. 481, Einsiedeln 16, Karlsruhe Aug. LXXXIII, contain Old-High-German glosses, these manuscripts may be related in other respects also; in other words, they may contain Pelagian material in their Latin glosses[1]. I have not pursued the matter.

CLAUDIUS OF TURIN

This section must be more of the nature of an appeal than a statement of facts. Commentaries on all the Epistles of St Paul, with the exception of First and Second Thessalonians, and First and Second Timothy[2], have come down to us under the name of Claudius, Bishop of Turin, a native of Spain. He produced Galatians about A.D. 815, Ephesians and Philippians about A.D. 816, Romans about A.D. 816—820, and First and Second Corinthians about A.D. 820[3], but of these the commentaries on Galatians and Philemon alone are published[4], with one or two prefaces to others. Yet there are a good many MSS, and some of them at least are of superlative quality. I believe the following list is more complete than any other published[5], and I have made a personal examination of all those at Paris and Rome:

Monte Cassino 48 (saec. XI in.[6]) (Rom. 1, 2 Thess. 1, 2 Tim. Tit. Philem. Hebr.).

Orléans (Fleury) 88 (85) (saec. IX) (all).

Paris, B.N. 2392 (saec. IX in.) (ff. 147) (Rom. 1 Cor. 2 Cor. [down to xi 23])[7].

„ „ 2393 (saec. XI) (Rom., Hebr.).

„ „ 2394 (saec. X[8]) ([five quaternions lost at the beginning] Eph. Phil. Col. Tit. Philem. Hebr.).

„ „ 2394 A (saec. X) (Gal. Eph. Phil. Col. Tit. Philem. Hebr. 1 Thess. 2 Thess. 1 Tim. [stops abruptly at iiii 10], 2 Tim.)[9].

[1] Hellmann, p. xv.

[2] The commentaries on 1, 2 Thess., and 1, 2 Tim. in Claudius MSS appear to be unaltered Ambrosiaster.

[3] The dates in *Monumenta Germaniae Historica: Epist.* tom. IV (=*Karolini aevi* II) (Berol. 1895) pp. 596 ff.; Manitius, *Gesch. d. lat. Lit. des MA*. I pp. 394 f.

[4] Migne, *P. L.* CIV pp. 841—912, 911—918, after Mai.

[5] Cf. Manitius, p. 395.

[6] The date from Lowe, *Beneventan Script*, p. 342.

[7] Possibly author's autograph.

[8] See note 1 on next page.

[9] Add this MS to those in Delisle, *Cat. des MSS* t. II pp. 405 f.

Paris, B.N. 2395 (saec. X[1]) (Hebr. [latter part], 1 Cor. 2 Cor.).
„ „ 10878 (saec. IX) (Tit. Philem. Hebr.).
„ „ 12289 (Fleury) (saec. IX) (Rom., 1 Cor. [quaternion lost between ff. 96 and 97], 2 Cor.).
„ „ 12290 (Fleury) (saec. IX) (certainly Eph. Phil. Col. Tit. Philem. Hebr.).
Rome, Vat. 5775 (Bobbio, written at Tortona) (A.D. 862) (1 Cor. 2 Cor.)[2].
„ „ Reg. 98 (Fleury) (saec. XII) (Rom. 1 Cor. 2 Cor.[3] Eph. Phil. Col. Tit. Philem.).

(Vat. lat. 9530 and 9546 are merely the copies which Mai made.)

Certain facts which have come to my knowledge, must be here very briefly mentioned.

(1) *Romans*. He uses Aug. and Orig.-Ruf. On Rom. viii he has the same part of Aug. as Cassiod. has (Migne, *P.L.* LXVIII pp. 460 D, 461 A). On Rom. ii there is Pelagian material: on Rom. xii he is identical with Cassiod. (p. 496 C), and there is a parallel also on Rom. xvi 16 'non ficto—saluatorem' (p. 505 D). I copied the entire text of Claudius's exposition of Rom. v from what appeared to be the best MS, Paris B.N. 2392. Cassiodorus alternates with some other source or sources. The following extracts occur from him: Migne *P.L.* LXVIII p. 437 ll. 35—45; p. 437 l. 55—438 l. 30; p. 438 ll. 32—35; ll. 47—56; p. 438 l. 57—439 l. 15; p. 439 ll. 28—31; ll. 52—55; p. 440 ll. 46—47; ll. 50—54; p. 440 l. 57—441 l. 39; p. 441 ll. 50—51; p. 442 ll. 54—56. The Cassiodorian notes on this chapter fill 327 lines of Migne, and of these 327 lines 135, or about five twelfths, have been taken over by Claudius. This chapter was selected by me merely because

[1] The date of these MSS must be saec. X, because Elisha the Archdeacon of Auxerre mentioned in them as owner, is recorded in the obituary of Auxerre (Paris MS B.N. lat. 5253 (lat. 894) [saec. X—XI, Lebeuf dates MS about A.D. 1007]); 'XIII Kal. Ian. [=20 Dec.] ob. Eliseus archidiaconus, qui dedit fratribus suis res proprietatis sue, in uilla quae dicitur Gratiacus' [=Grisy] (*Recueil des Historiens de la France: Obituaires* t. III (Paris, 1909) p. 246); cf. Lebeuf, *Histoire d'Auxerre* t. I (Paris, 1743) p. 748; Max Quantin, *Dictionnaire Topographique du Département de L'Yonne* (Paris, 1862) p. 63. I am deeply indebted to Monsieur Léon Dorez for these facts and references.

[2] A photograph of one page in Ehrle-Liebaert, *Specimina* no. 31.

[3] Catalogue errs in giving 'Gal.' also.

of its interest in connexion with the incriminating passage of Pelagius.

(2) *First Corinthians.* The preface consists of the Ambrosiaster preface interwoven with the preface that we have found in the second class of Pseudo-Jerome MSS. Claudius, however, may have taken the latter from a biblical MS.

(3) *Second Corinthians.* The preface consists of genuine Ambst. + [Pelagius] prologue + genuine Ambst.[1], thus combining the whole of both. First part of commentary is genuine Ambst., as is also the conclusion.

(4) *Ephesians.* He gives the Cassiodorian prologue, but adds a piece to it. There is evidence of use of the Cassiodorian commentary also (e.g. p. 625 ll. 14—18 (which = Pelagius); ll. 31—35).

(5) *Philippians* has exactly the Ambrosiaster prologue.

(6) *Colossians* has the Ambrosiaster prologue followed by another.

(7) *Titus* has the Cassiodorus prologue. Paris MS 10,878 is the only one known to me that has the authorities indicated in the margin. It specifies $\overline{\text{IH}}$, $\overline{\text{AN}}$, $\overline{\text{AG}}$ (= Jerome, Anon., Augustine, respectively). It has $\overline{\text{AN}}$ seventeen times, and every time the passage so marked is from the Cassiodorian commentary.

(8) *Philemon* has the Cassiodorus prologue.

(9) *Hebrews* seems to have the usual biblical prologue.

It is fairly clear even from this slight examination that Claudius exploited the Cassiodorian commentary, but there is no evidence known to me that he had either Pelagius or Pseudo-Jerome in his hands. That he was hostile to Pelagius is quite clear from the introductory letter to the Ephesians commentary[2].

With the commentaries of Claudius are closely connected those by Hatto of Vercelli, edited by C. Burontius del Signore from the autograph of Hatto (which still exists[3]) in two delightful folios, at Vercelli itself in 1768. Riggenbach has shown that Hatto took over

[1] Cf. *J.T.S.* IV (1902—03) p. 90.

[2] (Best edited in) (M.G.H.) *Epistolae Karolini Aevi* t. II (Berol. 1895) p. 598 ll. 22—23.

[3] Vercelli, Bibl. Capit. 40 (XXXIX) (saec. X) a page photographed in *Monumenta Palaeographica Sacra* (Torino: Bocca, 1899) no. xvii; the only other MS is Karlsruhe, Aug. CL (saec. X—XI), as Dr Holder informed me. But 1, 2 Cor. also in Bamberg, B. II 20 (saec. XI). The commentaries are reprinted in Migne, *P.L.* CXXXIV.

the commentaries of Claudius on Philemon and Hebrews practically unaltered[1]. I can testify that the same is true with regard to that on Titus. It would appear that Hatto is more independent of Claudius in the longer epistles, but that he used him throughout. Of Hatto, as of Claudius, it may be said that 1 and 2 Thess. and 1 and 2 Tim. are Ambrosiaster. Hatto once[2], however, uses Pelagius by name:

In 1 *Cor.* xv 31: Pelagius dicit quia 'per' non semper pro iuramento accipitur: nam cum dicimus: 'per puerum misi' et similia, non iuramenti est.' This is a paraphrastic reference to the commentary, which we remember was known at Verona in the Middle Ages[3]. Hellmann[4] cites three passages where Cassiodorus is used by him, but he naturally had no occasion to ask whether these passages come direct from Cassiodorus or through the mediation of Claudius.

ZMARAGDUS OF ST MIHIEL

Zmaragdus[5] in his own preface (of date between 819 and 830) declares that he used 'Pelagius' in his compilation. There is no evidence that he did so anywhere else than in the Pauline Epistles. It is of some importance, therefore, to enumerate the passages of the Epistles in the Lectionary for the understanding of which his exposition was compiled. They are these, with the column of Migne[6] added, where the exposition of each section begins:

		col.			col.			col.
Rom.	i 1—6	15	1 Cor.	viiii 24–x 4	100	Gal.	v 25—	
	vi 3—11	399		x 6—13	414		vi 10	455
	19—23	405		xii 2—11	419	Eph.	i 3—8	41
	viii 12—17	411		xiii 1—13	112		iii 13—21	461
	18—23	362		xv 1—10	433		iiii 1—6	466
	28—39	526	2 Cor.	i 3—7	531		23—28	480
	x 10—18	507		iii 4—9	439		v 1—9	133
	xii 1—5	75		vi 1—10	118		15—21	485
	6—16	80		viiii 6—10	436		vi 10—17	491
	16—21	91		xi 19—		Phil.	i 6—11	496
	xiii 8—10	96		xii 9	103		ii 5—11	199
	11—14	512	Gal.	i 11—20	392		iii 17—21	501
	xv 4—13	515		iii 16—22	442	Col.	i 9—11	505
1 Cor.	i 4—8	471		iiii 1—7	62		iii 1—4	221
	iiii 1—5	519		22—31	148	1 Thess.	iiii 1—7	129
	v 7—8	224		v 16—24	448	Tit.	ii 11—15	55[7]

[1] *Die ältesten lat. Kommentare* pp. 25 ff. [2] Riggenbach, p. 30 n.

[3] See p. 23. [4] P. 182, n. 7. [5] See pp. 31 f. [6] *P.L.* CII.

[7] For Hebrews passages see Riggenbach, *Die ältesten lat. Komm.* p. 39.

Zmaragdus's compilation is preserved in whole or in part in the following MSS[1]. Those marked with an asterisk I have myself collated for symbols, and in some cases also for the Pelagian readings.

Angers, 233 (saec. IX), second part only (from St Aubin).

*Berlin, Lat. 695 theol. fol. 344 (saec. X) (from Werden).

Boulogne-sur-mer, 25 (saec. X) (from St Omer) (see Pitra in Migne, *P.L.* CII p. 1112 ff.).

Córdoba, Mosque (Cathedral) Library 1 (olim 72) (saec. X) (about A.D. 960).

*Einsiedeln, 39 (saec. IX) (from Reichenau?) (imperfect).

*London, Brit. Mus., Additional MSS 21914 (saec. X) (imperfect).

*Luxemburg, 135 (29) (saec. X) (from Orval).

Madrid, Archivo Histórico Nacional I (saec. XII).

*Munich, Clm 6210 (saec. IX) (from Freising)[2].

*Munich, Clm 6214 (saec. X) (from Freising).

*Oxford, Bodleian, Barlow 4 (saec. IX—X).

*Paris, B.N. 2341 (saec. IX) (from Reichenau?).

*Paris, B.N. 12045 (saec. IX), defective at beginning and end (from St Maur-des-Fossés).

*St Gall, Stiftsbibliothek 424 (saec. IX).

*St Gall, Stiftsbibliothek 435 (saec. X).

*St Omer, 257 (saec. X), second part only.

*Zürich, Kantonsbibliothek XII (saec. X) (from Rheinau).

*Zürich, Kantonsbibliothek XXXII (saec. X) imperfect (from Rheinau).

For a detailed account of the symbols used throughout the work in the MSS, the reader is referred to my two articles[3]. Here it is enough to say that P was employed by Zmaragdus to indicate 'Pelagius,' whether, as in the vast majority of cases, it be the original

[1] This list is, I think, fuller than any other published: I owe two items to the kindness of Dom Wilmart.

[2] The collation of this MS I owe to the courtesy of the ever lamented A. H. Kyd, B.A., of Wadham Coll. Oxon. and the University of Manchester.

[3] *Journ. Theol. Stud.* vol. IX (1907—1908) pp. 584—597; vol. XXIII (1921—1922) pp. 73—76. The *Essai Critique sur la vie et les œuvres de Smaragde, thèse soutenue par* Louis Barbeau 29 *janvier* 1906 *et jours suivants*, has not, I believe, been published. I have to thank Dom Morin and M. Henri Omont for information about it. I have not seen J. Schmidt in *Der Katholik*, Bd. LXXXVI (1906) pp. 241—257.

form of Pelagius, or, as in a very few cases, the passages quoted are taken from the Cassiodorian revision of Pelagius[1]. As already mentioned[2], the erroneous 'ex Primas.' of the editions everywhere represents a P̅ (= ex Pelagio) of the MSS. It is not too much to say that Zmaragdus relied most of all on 'Pelagius' for notes on the Pauline Epistles, all the more perhaps because he was not in possession of Ambrosiaster[3]. In addition to Pelagius and Cassiodorus, he employed for the Epistles of St Paul, Origen-Rufinus on Romans, Jerome on Galatians and Ephesians, Chrysostom latinised, Cassiodorus (apart from the revision of Pelagius), Isidore[4], Cyril on Philippians latinised, Victor of Capua, Gregory, Augustine *De Diuersis Quaestionibus* LXXXIII, Pseudo-Augustine *Quaestiones Veteris et Novi Testamenti* CXXVII[5].

Zmaragdus's method may be illustrated after Riggenbach[6]: the Pelagian portions preserved by Cassiodorus are in thick type. The text is naturally that of Zmaragdus[7].

(*In Rom.* vi 19 = Zm. 406 C) P̅. Hoc est, maiora quidem exigere a uobis pro diuinae seruitutis retributione deberem, sed condescendens et temperans **infirmitati uestrae** humana et possibilia praedico atque suadeo, ut sicut prompti fuistis ad sectanda noxia atque contraria, ita alacres sitis ad ea quae utilia et saluti amica sunt peragenda.

Hoc] Id 2 *codd. Zm.* suadeo] persuadeo *Cassiod.*

Clearly Cassiodorus only, and not Pelagius, was before Zmaragdus's eyes here. Pelagius differs very seriously from both.

(*In Rom.* vi 11 = Zm. 403 A—B) P̅. id est: sicut caput uestrum **semel** est mortuum, sic et uos **membra** illius effecti, uitae eius **exempla** sectamini, ut nihil morti ulterius **debe**atis, hoc est, ut in uobis locum mors secunda non habeat. ille autem **uiuit deo**, qui Christi uestigia humilitate, sanctificatione, pietate sectatur.

This is exactly Cassiodorus: of it Pelagius has hardly a word[8].

It is clear, however, that in most places Zmaragdus used Pelagius rather than Cassiodorus. Let us take an instance where the two differ rather seriously:

[1] Riggenbach, *Unbeachtet gebliebene Fragmente* pp. 6 ff. [2] P. 320.

[3] The MS of Ambst. on Romans now at St Mihiel (16) is dated 'saec. x,' and is therefore later than Zmaragdus's time.

[4] In at least one case (p. 415) Isid. = Ps.-Ambr. *De XLII Mans.* 13.

[5] See my edition p. xxvi. [6] Pp. 8 f.

[7] All three texts are, however, critically edited according to the MSS.

[8] Cf. also *in Gal.* v 18 (Zm. 449 D, Cassiod. 601 A) (Hellmann, p. 157).

In Rom. viii 12

(ZM. 411 B—C = PELAG.)	CASSIOD. (459 A)
Hoc totum agit ut ostendat eis legem non esse necessariam, quae carnalibus data est.	Hoc totum agit ut ostendat legem ueterem fidelibus non necessariam, quae carnalibus et peccatoribus data est.

Hardly ever do we find any evidence of use of Pseudo-Jerome, but citations in the section *in* 2 *Cor.* vi 1—10 (Zm. pp. 118 f.) are several times made from $\overline{\text{H}}$, side by side with $\overline{\text{P}}$. It is possible that the references to $\overline{\text{H}}$ refer to small portions of genuine Jerome sandwiched here and there between other borrowings: certain portions of this section have not yet been traced to their real author or authors.

The MSS of Pelagius and Cassiodorus in Zmaragdus's possession were good. It is not often that Zmaragdus's theological prepossessions lead him to contradict Pelagius, but they do on one occasion at least, *in Rom.* viii 29, where Pelagius says: 'praedestinare idem est quod praescire,' but Zmaragdus deliberately inserts the negative 'non' before 'idem.' Hellmann groups Zmaragdus as a textual authority with Sedulius and the Vienna glosses[1]. All are of good quality, but my own opinion is that Sedulius is, alike in extent and textual purity, the most important of the three.

SEDULIUS SCOTTUS

Nothing is known of this scholarly Irishman before his appearance in Liége about A.D. 848. There he laid the foundations of an extended influence. After 850 he is found at Cologne, and he is known to have been in touch with Fulda, Metz and other places[2]. One of his strongest interests was the study of the Bible, on various parts of which he made collections. The 'Collectaneum in Epistolas Pauli' was edited by Johannes Sichardus as early as 1528

[1] *Sedulius Scottus* pp. 150 ff., 170.

[2] Cf. Manitius, *Geschichte* pp. 315 ff.: on his works see also M. Esposito in *Proceedings Royal Irish Acad.* vol. XXVIII (1910) section C pp. 62—95; *Hermathena* vol. XVI (1911) pp. 58—72, 329; Hellmann, *Sedulius Scottus* (München, 1906); Von Dobschütz (*Jahresbericht der Schles. Gesellschaft für Vaterl. Cultur* 1913), 'Ein Bücherkleinod' pp. 5 ff.

at Basle, but the book is by no means rare[1]. His text was based on an old Fulda manuscript, and has since been reprinted several times[2]. Sedulius or his school is now associated with certain Graeco-Latin Biblical MSS; the Bibliothèque de l'Arsenal Psalter, the St Gall Gospels (Δ), and the Boernerianus (Gg) of the Epistles of St Paul.

Though his influence was strong, his works have not been preserved in many copies. Traube, and after him Hellmann[3], could enumerate only five surviving MSS of the Pauline compilation; that from which the *editio princeps* was printed has perished, like most of the great Fulda collection. These MSS are:—Clm 9545 (saec. X) (from Oberaltaich), Clm 6238 (saec. X ex.) (from Freising), Zürich, Kantonsbibliothek, codex LXXII (saec. X) (from Rheinau), Fulda (saec. XI—XII) (= Weingarten 27), Bamberg B v 24 = Bible MSS 127 (saec. XI ex.[4]). In the opinion of Hellmann, the best MSS are those of Zürich and Bamberg. I have therefore fully collated the Pelagian extracts in these, as also in the *editio princeps*. I have further collected the symbols indicating authorities used, in the two Munich MSS: the Fulda MS I have not seen.

Even a careless reader of the first printed edition would see that Pelagius was one of the authorities employed by Sedulius, for near the beginning of the commentary there occur in the text (not in the margin) the words: 'Aliter secundum Pil(agium)[5].' But, as the first editor ignored the marginal symbols, which reveal that the work is only what it claims to be, a 'collectaneum,' even Zimmer declared that it quotes sources only here and there[6]. Hellmann's *Sedulius Scottus* revealed the real situation, and on the basis of a collation of the four MSS named I was allowed to publish 'The Sources of Sedulius Scottus' *Collectaneum* on the Epistles of St Paul[7].'

[1] Best account of its genesis in P. Lehmann, *Iohannes Sichardus* u.s.w. (München, 1911) pp. 54 f., 120.

[2] Lastly Migne, *P.L.* CIII. The orthography of the *editio princeps* is better than that of Migne, and a certain number of variations in reading have crept in since 1528.

[3] Pp. 190 ff.

[4] Hellmann, 'saec. XII.'

[5] The Irish spelling of Pelagius. The archetype had many Irish 'symptoms,' as a palaeographical study of the MSS reveals.

[6] 'Die (d. h. Pseudo-Primasius u. Sedulius) selbst überhaupt nur ganz vereinzelt Quellen citieren,' p. 112.

[7] *Journ. Theol. Stud.* vol. XVIII (1916—1917) pp. 184—228.

This investigation proved extensive use of Pelagius, as the leading authority, under the symbols PELAG, PELA, PEL, PILAG, PILG, PIL. It proved also that he had used the following: Albinus (Alcuin) *in Hebr.*; Ambrosiaster on Rom. 1 Cor.; Theodore of Mopsuestia (in Latin) on Galatians; Augustine (various works); Pseudo-Augustine (Ambrosiaster) *Quaestiones* (the earlier edition); at least one Pseudo-Augustinian sermon; Basil; Bede; Cassian; Cassiodorus *De Actibus ac Disciplinis, In Psalterium*; Eusebius-Rufinus *Hist.-Eccl.*; Faustus Reiensis; Gennadius; Gregory; Jerome *in Gal. Eph. Tit.*[1], and a number of other works; John (i.e. Chrysostom); Isidore, which means nearly always the Cassiodorus (Pseudo-Primasius) commentary (occasionally the *Etymologiae*); Origen-Rufinus *in Rom.*; Junilius[2]; Sedulius (about a column of original matter).

To judge by the Pelagian extracts, Sedulius copied his sources most carefully. He has no knowledge of the Pseudo-Jerome, and so far as the Pelagian comments are concerned, he comes perhaps nearer to **A** (the Reichenau MS) than any other authority of which I have knowledge[3]. Unfortunately I did not make the same critical study of Sedulius's biblical text as I have devoted to the notes, but from a study of such hints of it as are obtainable from the printed text and my collations, I have the impression that Sedulius must have taken over for his lemmata the **BD** (*Book of Armagh*) type of text from his copy of Pelagius[4]. In other words, his procedure was to take Pelagius, text and commentary, as the basis of his *Collectaneum*, omit from the notes what was unorthodox or useless for his purpose, and fill out its meagre, glossarial character from the contents of his library. I suggest therefore that a collation of the biblical text in the best MSS would be decidedly worth while, as a control over the **B** readings. It is quite clear that Sedulius did not use on this occasion the *g* text, as Traube at one time imagined.

Study of Sedulius's Pelagian extracts has been rendered easy

[1] *Never* Ps.-Jerome on the Epistles of St Paul.

[2] Junilius occurs in an unpublished part of Sedulius I found in the Rheinau MS, but overlooked in writing the article just mentioned.

[3] Cf. *in* 2 *Cor.* x 1 uindicandum ASdWb; delicti **GH**: *in Eph.* vi 23 nam caritas AGSd; caritas **H**: *in* 1 *Tim.* iiii 8 aeuo **ABSd**; eo H_1; aeternum GH_2.

[4] See W.-W.'s apparatus to *Romans* passim.

by the most convenient fact that Hellmann restored their text critically from the MSS before publishing such as he used. He has had no difficulty in showing that it is a good text, much superior to Pseudo-Jerome and G, wherever it is available. Parallels between Wb and Sd have been already alluded to. They have un-Pelagian notes in common, e.g. at 1 Cor. vii 19 on *circumcisio nihil est* and at 2 Tim. iiii 3 on *prurientes auribus*[1]. The contact with Wn is even more striking. Hellmann enumerates nine passages shared by Wn and Sd, not one of which is genuine Pelagius. One passage (*in Col.* i 2) shared by Wb and Wn, is also un-Pelagian. Facts like these suggest that some at least of the glosses in these MSS come from Sedulius. In Hellmann's scheme[2], Zm, Sd and Wn are represented as coming from one common root, and Wb is, so to speak, the uncle of all three.

Of the Hebrews commentary in Sedulius the reader may be referred to Riggenbach's account[3].

HAYMO OF AUXERRE

Exegetical material, attributed in print sometimes to Haymo Bp of Halberstadt, sometimes to Remigius of Auxerre, has now been successfully vindicated for Haymo, a monk of Auxerre[4]. The oldest MSS, of the Pauline commentary at any rate, are anonymous. It appears to have been composed about the middle of the ninth century, and was first printed in 1519 at Strassburg[5]. The following MSS have come to my knowledge, though I should say I have made no effort to record any later than the eleventh century:

Paris, B.N. 2409 (saec. IX) (Rom. 1, 2 Cor. 1, 2 Thess.).
„ „ 13409 (saec. IX) (1 Tim. [part only], 2 Tim. Phil. Eph. Hebr.) (first of St Peter's, Corbie, then of St Germain-des-Prés).
„ „ 2412 (saec. X) (Hebr.) (under name of Ambrose).

[1] See Hellmann, p. 159; but his other two examples are real Pelagius.

[2] P. 170.

[3] *Die ältesten lat. Komm.* pp. 212 ff.

[4] Riggenbach, *op. cit.* pp. 178—201.

[5] '*Haymo Sax. episc. Halberstatt. in diui Pauli epistolas cum breuis tum perlucida expositio*: Excusum Argentinae per Renatum Beck Anno MDXIX.' Copies appear to be very rare.

Paris, B.N. 12303 (ancient no. 821) (saec. X) (2 Cor. 1, 2 Thess. 1, 2 Tim. Phil. [also by a different scribe, Phil. 1 Thess.] Eph.). This MS and 2412 are two parts of the same MS, once together in St Germain-des-Prés[1].

„ „ 2452 (saec. X).

„ „ 17290 (saec. X) (Romans wanting; partly arranged as a lectionary).

London, B.M. Harl. 3102 (saec. IX) (Rom. 1 Cor. down to XV 27—28, rest lost) (a French MS).

St Gall 333 (saec. X).

Avranches 115 (saec. XI).

Douai 343 (saec. XI): 344 (saec. XI) (Hebr.).

Le Mans 229 (saec. XI) (Rom. 1, 2 Cor. Hebr.).

Angers 67 (saec. XI): 1902 (saec. XI) (title and one leaf).

Milan, Ambros. A 138 sup. (saec. IX—X) (Rom. Hebr. 1, 2 Cor.) (Bobbio).

Rome, Vat. lat. 615 + Vallicell. A. 8 (saec. XI—XII) (Rom. 1 Cor.)[2] (formerly of S. Euticio in Nursia ?).

„ Bibl. Capitol. C. 102 (saec. XI) (lacks Tit. Philem. ?).

„ „ „ 103 (Gal. Eph. Phil. Col. Hebr.).

Naples, Bibl. Nazionale, vi B 3 (saec. XII) (written in S. Lorenzo in Carminiano near Troja, between 1145 and 1165)[3].

„ Bibl. Nazionale, vi B 11 (saec. XI—XII) (formerly of Troja).

Monte Cassino ff. 209 (pp. 420) 25 × 34 cm. (saec. XI in.).

Having copied various portions of the British Museum MS, which is perhaps the very oldest of all the MSS, and compared it with the printed text, I can testify that Haymo is exceedingly well represented in print. But he is not of much use for constituting the text of Pelagius. He fished in most waters, and was an independent thinker besides. In Romans we can see use made of Ambrosiaster, Origen-Rufinus and Cassiodorus (Ps.-Primasius)[4].

[1] See 'Dismembered Manuscripts' by the present writer in *Revue Bénédictine*, t. XXIX (1912) pp. 367 f.

[2] See the article cited in the last note.

[3] This superb MS like the other Naples and Monte Cassino MSS was kindly indicated to me by Dr Lowe (see now his *Beneventan Script* p. 322 etc.).

[4] He has the tell-tale *animositas* at *in Rom.* i 29 (Pelag. *intentio*).

I did not discover any evidence of direct use of Pelagius. But in any case he used his sources with considerable freedom, and much of his work seems to be original, at least in this sense that it is not derived from other professed commentators on the Epistles. He appears on occasion to have used Zmaragdus (e.g. *in* 2 *Cor.* vi 5 is taken from Ps.-Aug. *Quaest. V. et N. T.* 120 through Zmaragdus).

ISIDORE

Isidore of Seville was the arch-compiler of the Middle Ages, and it can be shown that he extracted material from Pelagius among many other authors.

Etym. vii 9, 9 '"electus," sicut in Actibus Apostolorum spiritus sanctus dicit (xiii 2): "Segregate mihi Barnaban et Paulum ad opus quod **elegi** eos,"' is from Pelag. *in Rom.* i 1 'sicut in Actibus Apostolorum spiritus sanctus dicit: "Segregate mihi Barnaban et Saulum ad opus quod **elegi** eos[1]."'

Etym. x 46, '"contentiosus" ab intentione uocatus, qui non ratione aliquid, sed sola pertinacia uindicat,' is from Pelag. *in Rom.* i 29 'contentio est, ubi non ratione aliquid, sed animi pertinacia defenditur[2].'

Etym. xi 2, 20 'dicitur igitur "mulier" secundum femineum sexum, non secundum corruptionem integritatis: et hoc ex lingua sacrae scripturae. nam Eua statim facta de latere uiri sui, nondum contacta a uiro, mulier appellata est, etc.' is from Pelag. *in Gal.* iiii 4 'hic mulieris nomen non corruptionem, sed sexum significat, sicut et Eua statim ut facta est, mulier appellatur.'

De Ecclesiasticis Officiis II 18[3] 'et si non uis esse maior, esto uel minor, quia liberae uoluntatis es. nuptiae enim peccatum non sunt, sed per sollicitudinem mundi qui nubunt legem dei

[1] Mr M. Esposito informs me that Isidore habitually uses the Vulgate (vg. here has *adsumsi*).

[2] Hellmann, p. 184, who gives other parallels also from the 10th book.

[3] This parallel I owe to Hellmann, but I have collated three MSS of Isidore; Karlsruhe Augiensis CCLIV (saec. VIII—IX) f. 135, copied from a Visigothic original, St Gall 222 (saec. x) copied from an insular original, 240 (saec. IX): this last MS has lost some leaves (perhaps a whole quaternion) between pp. 280—281, words from *uictitantes aut pane solo* (Migne, *P.L.* LXXXIII 795 A)—*in nouo autem testamento* (807 C). Neither the first nor the second MS seems particularly good, nor can one be said to be really better than the other, to judge by this passage.

seruare uix possunt. Aliter. Illos dicit non peccare si nubant, qui nondum uouerint deo castitatem. ceterum uel qui in corde suo promisit, si aliud fecerit, habet damnationem, quia primam fidem, sicut ait apostolus, irritam fecit. quod enim erat per naturam licitum, per uotum sibi fecit inlicitum, sicut Annanias et Saphyra, quibus de pretio possessionis suae retinere nihil licuit, ob quam causam et subita morte prostrati sunt.' This is from Pelag. *in* 1 *Cor.* vii 28: Isidore adds *dei* to *legem*, *per naturam* before *licitum*, and touches up the order of words once or twice, but otherwise the correspondence is exact.

Quaest. de Vet. et Nov. Test. 32 §§ 37, 38 (ed. Arevalo, tom. v, p. 255): 'Dic mihi: *dilectio* uel *caritas* in quot modis consistit[1]? In iiii. Hoc est, primum in dei timore uel dilectione; secundum, sicut nosmet ipsos sic deum amemus; tertium, proximos; quartum, etiam inimicos. deum ergo plus quam nos diligere debemus, proximum sicut nos, inimicum ut proximum; et nisi deum primum dilexerimus, nosmet ipsos minime diligere poterimus.' This is from Pelag. *in Gal.* v 14 '*dilectio* uel *caritas* quattuor modis constat: hoc est, in dei dilectione, quae prima est; secunda, si nosmet ipsos secundum deum amemus; tertia proximos; quarta, etiam inimicos. deum ergo plus quam nos diligere debemus; proximum sicut nos; inimicum ut proximum...nisi deum primo dilexerimus, nos minime possumus non peccando diligere....'

Like Isidore, Luculentius had borrowed from Pelagius without acknowledgement. Passages are *in Rom.* xii 6, 8[2]; there are perhaps others.

Note on Prologues or Arguments

It is notable that while the *Primum quaeritur* prologue is found in nearly all Vulgate MSS, a complete set of Pelagian prologues has not yet been produced from a biblical MS. Dom de Bruyne, the leading authority on Latin biblical prologues, has, however, discovered a few traces of them[3]. They are these:

arg. Phil. Paris, B.N. 9380 (saec. VIII—IX) (formerly of Orléans), 15180 (saec. XII) (formerly of Foigny); Ste-Geneviève 10; Puy; Brussels 2.

arg. 1 Thess. Paris, B.N. 9380; 15180; Ste-Geneviève 10; Puy; Basle BIC; Brussels 67; 68; Engelberg, 245.

[1] *Arev.* consistunt.

[2] Migne, *P.L.* LXXII pp. 815 ff.

[3] *Revue Bénédictine* t. XXIV (1907) p. 263, where add *non* before *sit* in the note.

arg. Col.	Paris, B.N. 9380; 15180; Puy; Basle BIC; Brussels 42.
arg. 1 Tim.	Paris, B.N. 9380; 15180; Ste-Genev. 10; 18; Puy; Basle BIC; Brussels 2; 68.
arg. 2 Tim.	Paris, B.N. 9380; Ste-Genev. 10; 18; Puy; Brussels 68.
arg. Tit.	Paris, B.N. 9380, 15180; Puy; Engelberg, 245.
arg. Philem.	Paris, B.N. 9380 (partly).

It is understood that Dom de Bruyne will edit all known Latin biblical prologues in the *Collectanea Biblica Latina*. It has not been possible for me to collate any of these MSS except Paris 15180; the great Theodulfian Bible was not accessible to readers during the war. In view of what has been written above, the fact that the oldest biblical *testis* for the prologues has Spanish connexions is interesting.

Summary

(a) *Textual Authorities*

The leading authorities are **A** and **B**, **A** especially for the extent of the commentary, **B** particularly for the biblical text. G, V and **H** come next in importance, so far as the commentary is concerned, for they contain practically the whole of it. The Cassiodorian revision is of almost equal value, subject to the qualifications that the language and the thought are modified, especially in Romans, in the interests of Augustinian theology, and a considerable portion of Pelagius is unused, while a Vulgate text is substituted in the lemmata. Sedulius Scottus used apparently the **B** type of Biblical text, and is a most exact quoter of the large portions of the commentary present in him. Other authorities, such as Zmaragdus, and the Würzburg and Vienna glosses, are on occasion useful as makeweights. In using all the post-Cassiodorian authorities, caution is required in distinguishing between the original Pelagius and the Cassiodorian revision, for both appear to have been accessible to them.

(b) *Citations of Pelagius by Name*

The investigation in this and the second chapters has tended to show that the name 'Pelagius' might be attached to any form of the Pelagian commentary. Yet it is not without interest to tabulate here, chronologically and locally, such references to the

Pelagian commentary *by name* as have been discovered, mainly by other scholars.

Authority	Date	Place
Augustine	A.D. 412 and later	North Africa
Marius Mercator	A.D. 429—431	Constantinople, etc.
Arnobius Iunior	about A.D. 450	Rome (?)
Anon. comm. in epp. canon. (cod. Aug. CCXXXIII, saec. IX).	about A.D. 650	Ireland
Irish Canons	about A.D. 700	Ireland
Book of Armagh	A.D. 808	Ireland
Würzburg, MS theol. F. 12	saec. VIII in. (glosses by various scribes, of uncertain date)	Würzburg
Zmaragdus	A.D. 809—830	St Mihiel
St Riquier catalogue	A.D. 831	St Riquier (Picardy)
Murbach catalogue	about A.D. 840	Murbach (Alsace)
Sedulius Scottus	A.D. 848—858	Liége and Rhine country
St Gall catalogue	about A.D. 850	St Gall
Lorsch catalogue	about A.D. 900	Lorsch (s. of Darmstadt)
Hatto, Bp of Vercelli	about A.D. 960	Vercelli
Lucca plut. I 1[1]	saec. XI	Italy
Vienna MS 1247	A.D. 1079	Ratisbon
Berlin, cod. Phill. 1650	about A.D. 1100	Metz
Cod. Bodl. Laud. Misc. 350	about A.D. 1100	Eberbach (Bavaria)
Clm 18530	about A.D. 1100	Tegernsee (Bavaria)
Paris, B.N. 11929[1]	saec. XII	Udine, Italy
Cambridge, Corpus Christi Coll. 48, E. 3 (saec. XII late) Eton MS 26 Bk. 3. 2 (saec. XII—XIII) Cambridge, St John's Coll. 183 (G. 15) (saec. XII—XIII) Dublin, Trin. Coll. A. 2. 2 (51 Abbott) (saec. XII—XIII) (belonged saec. XV to West Dereham in Norfolk)	about A.D. 1200	St Albans, England[2]
Berne MS A 73	saec. XIII	France (?)
John of Verona	saec. XIII	Verona
Milan, Bibl. Brera AE XIV 9[1]	saec. XIII	Italy

[1] De Bruyne, *Revue Biblique* t. XII (1915) p. 383.

[2] About this group I have learned from Dr James' Catalogues. I have collated the C.C.C. MS, and Professor John Fraser kindly copied the Dublin MS for me.

SUPPLEMENTARY NOTE ON THE SHORTER FORM OF PSEUDO-JEROME (pp. 268 f.; 276)

The connexion between the *Martyrologium* of Pseudo-Jerome and the Pauline commentary of Pseudo-Jerome (H_1, the shorter form) may be rather early and close. To the former are prefixed two supposititious letters, one from Chromatius and Heliodorus to Jerome, and the other from Jerome to Chromatius and Heliodorus[1]. The reader will recall that the supposititious letter preceding the shorter form of the Pseudo-Jerome commentary is also addressed to Heliodorus. The view occurs to one that both these supposititious books, therefore, come from the same workshop. This idea is confirmed by the occurrence of the rather rare word *lassescere* in both the letters attributed to Jerome himself. If this hypothesis be correct, then the shorter form of Pseudo-Jerome is probably an Italian product, and it certainly antedates Cassiodorus, a view that we have seen to be probable from other considerations (p. 265): for Cassiodorus actually refers to the letter of Jerome prefixed to the *Martyrologium*[2].

[1] *Martyrologium Hieronymianum*...ediderunt Ioh. Bapt. de Rossi et Ludov. Duchesne (Ex Act. SS., Novembris t. II) (Bruxelles, n.d.) p. lxxxii.

[2] *Inst.* c. 32, quoted by De Rossi and Duchesne, p. xlvii.

INDEXES[1]

1. NAMES AND MATTERS

[1] The more important references are indicated in thick type.

2. SCRIPTURE REFERENCES (TEXT OR EXPOSITION)

3. LATIN WORDS

4. MANUSCRIPTS CITED

5. MODERN AUTHORITIES[1]

[1] Published work is not included here.